CONTEMPLATION AND INCARNATION
THE THEOLOGY OF
MARIE-DOMINIQUE CHENU

Marie-Dominique Chenu was a key figure in the re-vitalization of theology and renewal of the Church that culminated in the Second Vatican Council. He successfully combined a return to the medieval sources of theological reflection with a new sensitivity to the contemporary circumstances of the Church while grounding the theological enterprise in the contemplative experience.

Relying on both Chenu's previously unpublished materials and his many publications, Christophe Potworowski examines the role of faith and contemplation in the Dominican life and in theology as well as considering the historical and social dimensions of the human situation in terms of individual and ecclesial existence. He discusses the prophetic role of the theologian and some of the problems this involves.

Potworowski raises the question of how incarnation as an overall structure is related to the particularities of Christology and provides insights into the development of Catholic theology in the crucial period leading to Vatican II. The accompanying bibliography of Chenu's complete writings, unavailable elsewhere, is a valuable instrument of theological research.

CHRISTOPHE F. POTWOROWSKI is president of Newman Theological College, Edmonton, Alberta.

McGill-Queen's Studies in the History of Ideas

1 Problems of Cartesianism
*Edited by Thomas
M. Lennon, John M. Nicholas,
and John W. Davis*

2 The Development of the Idea
of History in Antiquity
Gerald A. Press

3 Claude Buffier and Thomas
Reid
Two Common-Sense
Philosophers
Louise Marcil-Lacoste

4 Schiller, Hegel, and Marx
State, Society, and the
Aesthetic Ideal of Ancient
Greece
Philip J. Kain

5 John Case and Aristotelianism
in Renaissance England
Charles B. Schmitt

6 Beyond Liberty and Property
The Process of Self-
Recognition in Eighteenth-
Century Political Thought
J.A.W. Gunn

7 John Toland: His Methods,
Manners, and Mind
Stephen H. Daniel

8 Coleridge and the Inspired
Word
Anthony John Harding

9 The Jena System, 1804–5:
Logic and Metaphysics
G.W.F. Hegel
*Translation edited by
John W. Burbidge and
George di Giovanni
Introduction and notes by H.S.
Harris*

10 Consent, Coercion, and Limit
The Medieval Origins of
Parliamentary Democracy
Arthur P. Monahan

11 Scottish Common Sense in
Germany, 1768–1800
A Contribution to the History
of Critical Philosophy
Manfred Kuehn

12 Paine and Cobbett
The Transatlantic Connection
David A. Wilson

13 Descartes and the
Enlightenment
Peter A. Schouls

14 Greek Scepticism
Anti-Realist Trends in Ancient
Thought
Leo Groarke

15 The Irony of Theology and
the Nature of Religious
Thought
Donald Wiebe

16 Form and Transformation
A Study in the Philosophy of
Plotinus
Frederic M. Schroeder

17 From Personal Duties
towards Personal Rights
Late Medieval and Early
Modern Political Thought,
1300–1600
Arthur P. Monahan

18 The Main Philosophical
Writings and the Novel *Allwill*
Friedrich Heinrich Jacobi
Translated and edited by
George di Giovanni

19 Kierkegaard as Humanist
Discovering My Self
Arnold B. Come

20 Durkheim, Morals, and
Modernity
W. Watts Miller

21 The Career of Toleration
John Locke, Jonas Proast, and
After
Richard Vernon

22 Dialectic of Love
Platonism in Schiller's
Aesthetics
David Pugh

23 History and Memory in
Ancient Greece
Gordon Shrimpton

24 Kierkegaard as Theologian
Recovering My Self
Arnold B. Come

25 An Enlightenment Tory in
Victorian Scotland
The Career of Sir Archibald
Alison
Michael Michie

26 The Road to Egdon Heath
The Aesthetics of the Great in
Nature
Richard Bevis

27 Jena Romanticism and Its
Appropriation of Jakob
Böhme
Theosophy – Hagiography –
Literature
Paolo Mayer

28 Enlightenment and
Community
Lessing, Abbt, Herder, and
the Quest for a German
Public
Benjamin W. Redekop

29 Jacob Burckhardt and
the Crisis of Modernity
John R. Hinde

30 The Distant Relation
Time and Identity in Spanish
American Fiction
Eoin S. Thomson

31 Mr Simson's Knotty Case
Divinity, Politics, and
Due Process in Early
Eighteenth-Century
Scotland
Anne Skoczylas

32 Orthodoxy and
Enlightenment
George Campbell in the
Eighteenth Century
Jeffrey M. Suderman

33 Contemplation and
Incarnation
The Theology of
Marie-Dominique Chenu
Christophe F. Potworowski

CONTEMPLATION AND INCARNATION

The Theology of Marie-Dominique Chenu

Christophe Potworowski

McGill-Queen's University Press
Montreal & Kingston · London · Ithaca

© McGill-Queen's University Press 2001
ISBN 0-7735-2255-7

Legal deposit fourth quarter 2001
Bibliothèque nationale du Québec

Printed in Canada on acid-free paper

This book has been published with the help of a grant
from the Humanities and Social Sciences Federation of
Canada, using funds provided by the Social Sciences
and Humanities Research Council of Canada.
Funding from Newman Theological College
is also gratefully acknowledged.

McGill-Queen's University Press acknowledges the
financial support of the Government of Canada
through the Book Publishing Industry Development
Program (BPIDP) for its activities. It also acknowledges
the support of the Canada Council for the Arts
for its publishing program.

**National Library of Canada Cataloguing
in Publication Data**

Potworowski, Christophe F., 1953–
Contemplation and incarnation: the theology of
Marie-Dominique Chenu
(McGill-Queen's studies in the history of ideas: 33)
Includes bibliographical references and index.
ISBN 0-7735-2255-7
1. Chenu, Marie-Dominique, 1895–1990. I. Title.
BX4705.C46358P68 2001 230'.2'092
C2001-900878-3

This book was typeset by Dynagram inc.
in 10/12 Baskerville.

Contents

Acknowledgments   ix

Preface   xi

1 Contemplation and the Dominican Vocation   3

2 Faith and Theology   41

3 Christianity and History   83

4 Church, Society, and Mission   116

5 Word as Sign   155

6 Incarnation and Christology   196

Conclusion   226

Abbreviations   233

Bibliography of Marie-Dominique Chenu   237

Bibliography   322

Index   329

Acknowledgments

AT ONE POINT in his lengthy 1975 interview with Jacques Duquesne, Marie-Dominique Chenu recalled what first struck him during a visit as a young man at the Dominican house of Le Saulchoir in Belgium: a particular mixture of liturgy, prayer life, and intellectual activity in research and study. It seduced him and soon after he entered the order. That mixture is visible to this day in Le Saulchoir. I have, on several occasions, been privileged to be a guest of the community for many weeks. During my stays, the brothers of the community have allowed me to share their life of research and prayer. It is through this more than anything else that I have become able to understand Chenu.

This book is a small token of my gratitude to the Dominican religious community of Le Saulchoir in Paris. In a special way I am indebted to Fr. André Duval, the archivist, Fr. Vincent Cosmao, the superior at the time, and Fr. Michel Albaric, the librarian at the time. Lengthy conversations with Fr. Duval, as well as with Fr. Régis Morellon and others, have shown me a Chenu barely visible in the writings.

I would like to thank Joseph Komonchak, from Catholic University in Washington, who initially encouraged me many years ago to pursue archival research on Marie-Dominique Chenu. Several conversations with him since then have also proven extremely beneficial to this project.

The bibliography would not have been possible without the efforts of those who have preceded me in this path. In the first place, there is André Duval OP, without whose patience and resolve very little of this research would have seen the light of day. In those archives which he generously opened to me, I found much advanced bibliographical research on Chenu by Ms. Marina Boni Sani, from whose work I also benefited.

Several of my graduate students and assistants have contributed to this publication as well. In particular I thank Peter Huish, Mary Ellen Malolepszy, and Richard Bernier. The governments of Canada and Quebec have helped through generous SSHRC and FCAR grants. Finally, none of this work would have come about without the support, the cajoling, and the challenges of my friends and family. Friendship is the only true context for theology.

Preface

IT WOULD BE VERY DIFFICULT to write an accurate history of twentieth-century Catholicism without granting a pivotal role to the contributions of French theologian Marie-Dominique Chenu (1895–1990). As part of the Dominican team at Le Saulchoir, his views on the historical status of Christianity and on the centrality of incarnation for theology were at the core of the renewal efforts in the Church culminating with Vatican II. His significance for Catholic theology, however, is related not only to the renewal of medieval studies and the clarification of theological method but also to the increasing awareness of the pastoral dimensions of theology. In reaction to the theological rationalism dominant in the neo-scholasticism of his day, and in answer to the positive aspirations of the modernists, Chenu successfully combined a return to the medieval sources of theological reflection with a new sensitivity to the contemporary circumstances of the Church and, at the same time, grounded the theological enterprise in the contemplative experience.

In seeing the advent of modern times as a source of major concern for the Church, Chenu belongs to a long tradition of Catholic theologians ranging from the beginnings of the Tübingen school in the nineteenth century, through some of the radical interpretations of the modernists, to the pastoral constitution *Gaudium et Spes* of Vatican II. In fact, Chenu borrowed much of his vocabulary from the nineteenth-century theologians from Tübingen, Johann Adam Möhler and Johann Sebastian Drey, thoroughly supported the introduction of historical methods in theology, and participated in the redaction of *Gaudium et Spes*. What is perhaps unique to Chenu is the optimism with which he viewed recent historical events. Modernity, for him, was the witness of a development by which new dimensions of humanity came to consciousness and to which the Church is called to respond in new ways. The Church must be present to its time and to the progressive humanization occurring therein.

Chenu's understanding of the encounter between the Church and modernity was guided by the model of incarnation. The modernity, which serves as the general context for the theological use of incarnation, refers not only to the particular problem of the introduction of his-torical-critical methods in theology but also to the wider pastoral issues raised by the dechristianization of large segments of the population. The idea of incarnation was used by Chenu to clarify both these areas and indeed is central to his whole theology. My purpose in this book is to provide an evaluation of the meaning and function of incarnation in Chenu's theology.

When asked in an interview about the single most important contri-bution of this idea, Chenu replied: "I felt very strongly the exigencies of the Incarnation. If Christianity is about God incarnate in matter, the di-vinisation of man implies that it include matter … Humanisation is al-ready a capacity for divinisation."[1] In another interview, Chenu pointed to the unifying principle underlying the variety of his writings: "All that I have done: work, studies, practical and theoretical reflection, all this has grown within me around the pivot of the Incarnation."[2] The centrality of incarnation not only is a matter of doctrine but is reflected in Chenu's method, as attested by the subtitles of his two-volume collection of essays, *La Parole de Dieu: La foi dans l'intelligence* and *L'Évangile dans le temps*. Chenu alludes to the inner unity manifested by the two titles, "whose parallelism is grounded in the law of incarnation of the Word of God, in the human mind as well as in the unfolding of history."[3] The parallelism continues with the later and shorter volume of essays *Peuple de Dieu dans le monde*.

Chenu's sensitivity to the exigencies of incarnation is partially ex-plained by the historical context in which he was writing. The 1930s and 1940s, when Chenu was formulating the main ideas of his theology, were years of intense ferment in the Church of France. A great amount of energy was directed at finding adequate means of dealing with dechristianization. Under the banner of Action catholique, movements such as Jeunesse ouvrière catholique (JOC) sought new ways of effec-tively proclaiming the gospel message in a secularized world, particu-larly among the working classes. The pastoral enthusiasm of the 1930s

1 "Le théologien et la vie" (1965), 30.
2 "Une théologie pour le monde" (1967), 17.
3 "Présentation" (1964), in *Parole* 1, 8.

was matched only by the rude awakening of the war experience, which brought with it the painful realization that these attempts were only partially successful. The barrier separating the Church from modern society continued to exist. It was in view of this separation that more radical attempts, such as the Mission de France and the Mission de Paris, were brought to the fore, giving birth to the worker-priest movement. The Dominicans of Le Saulchoir, both in Belgium and later in Paris, were very close to these developments.

Such pastoral ferment placed specific demands on theologians. It carried an implicit critique of existing neo-scholasticism for being too closely allied to an obsolete social order and for being ill prepared to meet the modern secular world. The pastoral experience called for a renewal of traditional Catholic teaching with a new sensitivity to the existing social, cultural, political, and economic situation. On the other hand, certain tendencies in theological reflection proved to be particularly fruitful on the pastoral level and in fact contributed to the success of the various pastoral experiments. Such was the case with the ecclesiological reflections on the mystical body of Christ and the popularization of the doctrine of incarnation. Thus, one JOC chaplain wrote in 1945: "The mystery of the Incarnation was truly the favourite mystery of the young JOC."[4] Reciprocally, it was in the *praxis* of the JOC and the missionary movements that Chenu saw the basis for a renewal of the teaching on incarnation.

For Chenu, the doctrine of incarnation provided a theological model with which he viewed the advent of modernity, a framework within which the various movements of Action catholique acquired their theological significance. Even more important, it provided a framework for a theology informed by developments in human history. This theological framework involved extending the traditional teaching on incarnation to include the social, historical, and economic dimensions of humanity. The doctrine of incarnation is, in fact, about a process of continued incarnation. The incarnation of God did not occur once and for all in a corner of Judaea, but continues throughout history.[5] The idea of con-

---

4 J. Ball, "Pour une spiritualité eschatologique (Lettre d'un ancien aumônier jociste)," *Masses ouvrières*, 7 (1945), 29; quoted in B. Besret *Incarnation ou eschatologie?* (Paris: Éditions du Cerf, 1964), 41.

5 Cf. "Dimension nouvelle" (1937), in *Parole* 2, 89: "*Car l'Incarnation de Dieu, dont elle [la nouvelle chrétienté] est le signe et le mystère à la fois, ne s'est pas faite une fois pour toutes dans un coin de Judée; elle dure toujours, elle vaut toujours, elle vaut partout, et tout ce qui échapperait à son emprise dans l'homme, dans ce monde distendu et magnifique, retomberait à sa misère: la rédemption du monde serait pour autant manquée.*"

tinued incarnation for the purposes of clarifying the Church-world relationship is not original to Chenu. Möhler, for example, developed it in
conjunction with the notion of living tradition. Chenu applied it with
particular vigour in the context of a secularized world. The law of the
two natures in Christ, as formulated by the Council of Chalcedon, becomes the model for a theological understanding of history. The law of
incarnation states that all aspects of humanity, as they are progressively
discovered in the course of history, are to be assumed and divinized.
What is not assumed is not redeemed.[6]

There are several constitutive elements in this theological perspective.
For Chenu, Christianity was primarily the economy of God's action in
history. In recognizing the true dimensions of humanity in the course of
its history, we are able to discover the true dimensions of God's action.
The law of nature becomes the law of grace. This inductive method is a
hallmark of Chenu's theology. In this sense the Christian economy is
both mystery and history: in the words of Chenu, "mystery in history
and history in the mystery of Christ."[7]

Another important element concerns the Church's mode of existence in the world. In the perspective of incarnation, the Church is always already situated within a particular society and civilization; in other
words, it is located in a historical context. Chenu's favourite example for
illustrating Christianity's historicity was the twelfth and thirteenth centuries, during which the Church witnessed the radical social, cultural, and
economic shift from the feudal regime to that of the communes. Under
the prophetic prodding of the mendicant orders, the Church was called
to a new way of being present to the world. A social mutation heralded a
new incarnation. The "sign of the times" characteristic of modern times,
in turn, is the socialization of human life. This new dimension of humanity, most visible in the phenomenon of work, becomes the matter
for a new incarnation on the part of the Church.

What is involved with the law of incarnation is more than a question
of efficiency or adaptability in matters of pastoral management and relations. Against a docetic separation of the temporal and spiritual realms,
Chenu argued that socialization is constitutive of the human condition

6 Cf. ibid., 92: "*Si telle est la loi de l'Incarnation dans le Christ, telle est aussi la loi d'incarnation
de la vie divine, au cours des siècles, dans l'Église du Christ. C'est tout l'homme, selon toutes ses ressources et avec toutes ses œuvres, qui est assumé par la grâce.*" The analogical use of the term "incarnation" is signified by the shift from capital "I" to lowercase "i" and by the use of the
definite article. The precise meaning of the analogy, however, remains to be defined.

7 "Les sacrements dans l'économie chrétienne" (1952), in *Parole* 1, 325.

and hence is something that must be integrated into the Church. It represents the new exigency in the process of continued incarnation.

Although Chenu's vocabulary is prone to some fluidity and is partially dependent on whatever theological debate was current, the theme of incarnation seems on the whole to remain constant as a unifying perspective. However, Chenu never clarified it or developed it into a system. Rather, he called upon it as a hermeneutical principle of discernment with regard to specific historical situations, such as the role of the Church in a dechristianized world or in relation to the poor and the oppressed in the struggle for liberation. A major task of this book is to provide some measure of clarity and precision for the different uses and meanings of the term incarnation. Chenu's position is not without difficulties and is open to various criticisms based particularly in a theology of the cross. Thus the present study also raises the critical question of the problem of evil. Chenu's incarnation perspective is examined in relation to its ability to cope with the discernment of deviations from progressive humanization.

The proximity to historical events is crucial to any understanding of Chenu since, without it, his theology is open to the very charge of abstraction and extrinsicism that he levelled against much of contemporary neo-scholasticism. Chenu's commitment to the concreteness of history – or, better, to the historicity of human knowing – is most clearly expressed in his view of theology as a reading of the signs of the times. An adequate account of this relation to history, for the purposes of a critical reflection on Chenu's theology, presents one of the delicate methodological problems of this book.

This problem cannot be resolved by reproducing *wie es eigentlich gewesen ist* the historical fabric that served as the context for most of Chenu's writings. My work primarily belongs not in the historical, but in the systematic, field. History is obviously important to the present analysis, but in terms more of its place in Chenu's thought than of a faithful and complete reproduction of the original context. My topic is not historicity but incarnation. The primary aim is to understand the precise meaning and function of the term incarnation in the theology of Chenu, keeping in mind the historical character of this theology. The term provides a unifying perspective in a variety of theological areas ranging from a discussion of the nature of theology and a proper understanding of anthropology, through historicity and socialization, to the place of the Church in a modern and secularized world. These areas cannot all be examined at once, yet separating them runs the risk of losing the proximity to history.

It is precisely a concern for the historical context that led me to begin this work with a consideration of Chenu's Dominican vocation. This area has been the object of little study, yet it provides a foundation for much of Chenu's theology. The archives of the French Dominicans contain much valuable material wherein Chenu reflects on the significance of the Dominican vocation for our times. What emerges very clearly from this material is the centrality of contemplation in the Dominican life. Coupled with the recent publication of large excerpts of Chenu's doctoral dissertation on contemplation, along with many articles on the relation of contemplation to theology, this centrality may no longer be ignored. Incarnation is not a mere structure but the object of Chenu's lifelong contemplation. Likewise, and in light of this centrality, discernment of the signs of the times and listening to the God who speaks today are far from being academic exercises.

The strategy of the present study is to approach an understanding of incarnation gradually, moving progressively towards the point where theological reflection is closely bound to the historical situation. After an initial encounter with incarnation as the architecture of the Dominican mixed life, the structural elements of incarnation appear more clearly in the discussion on the nature of faith and theology. For this reason, the writings on the nature and method of theology offer a natural continuity to the reflection on the Dominican life and the role of contemplation. In moving from the relatively simple to the more complex, the examination of theology understood as a reading of the signs of the times comes only after a detour through a discussion of the role of incarnation in theological method and in bringing anthropology in line with the situation of the modern world.

The order of the following chapters may thus be seen as a gradual approach to the concreteness of the involvement of theology with historical events when it is understood as a reading of the signs of the times.[8] The first two chapters, on the role of faith and contemplation in the Dominican life and in theology, are followed by two chapters on the historical and social dimensions of the human situation in terms of both individual and ecclesial existence. The fifth chapter deals with the task

---

8 Although I am not committed to a chronological analysis of Chenu's writings, the order of the chapters *does* follow a roughly historical order. While his early writings were devoted mostly to the history and nature of theology, they were not insensitive to contemporary pastoral issues. Likewise his later writings on social issues were always related to questions of theological method. Though his ideas developed in many ways, Chenu remained a Dominican all his life.

of reading the signs of the times in the context of the modern world and with some of the problems involved in this process of discernment. The final chapter raises the question of the relation of incarnation as overall structure to christology. Each step on the way is meant to shed additional light on the meaning and function of incarnation, not to provide an exhaustive analysis of Chenu's position on the nature of theology, history, socialization, or the role of the Church in the modern world. These areas are treated only to the extent that they help to elucidate the meaning and function of incarnation.

Despite Chenu's significance in the history of twentieth-century Catholic theology, the secondary literature on him is generally very scarce, and practically non-existent in the English language. I hope this small contribution will help to rectify the situation and encourage more study in this important area. The complete bibliography of Chenu's writings, unavailable elsewhere, is another step in this rectification.

In citing the writings of Chenu, only a shortened version of the title and the original date of publication are given. Except in ambiguous situations, Chenu's name is usually omitted from the reference. A key to abbreviations is given at the beginning of the bibliography, which is arranged chronologically. Unless otherwise noted, if an article is reproduced in a later collection of essays, the later edition is used in this book, although the original date of publication is included in the footnote references for historical purposes. All translations are my own.

CONTEMPLATION AND INCARNATION

1

Contemplation and the
Dominican Vocation

A THEOLOGY IS BORN NOT in a vacuum but as a result of an encounter. This encounter then reveals a vocation. In looking for the traces of such an encounter, in looking for the origin of vocation, and hence for the roots of a theology, there are always the dangers of psychologism, of reducing the objective quality of a body of work to a subjective and perhaps even sentimental experience. Yet it is the very objectivity of a work that points to its living source. These roots would remain secret and hidden were it not for these pointers.

In the little book *St. Thomas et la théologie*, written in 1959, which he considered one of his favourites, Chenu begins the presentation of St. Thomas by recalling the historical origins and the cultural impact of the mendicant orders and by underlining the significance of his vocation to join the Dominican order: "The evangelical vocation of brother Thomas is at the origin of his theology."[1] The fact of evangelism, as a religious, cultural, and historical factor, then becomes the hermeneutical key for the understanding of the writings of St. Thomas. But Chenu goes even further. In the context of describing the Thomistic position on contemplation, which he calls the principle and the end of his life, he says the following: "In defining the structure and the laws of this contemplative life, St. Thomas has given us, under the guise of the impersonal objectivism of doctrine, the secret of his personality just as if he were sharing a confidence in 'confessions' after the manner of Augustine."[2] A similar remark can be made in relation to Chenu's own

---

1 *St. Thomas et la théologie*, 17: "*La vocation évangélique du frère Thomas est à l'origine de sa théologie.*"
2 Ibid., 52.

religious vocation and its significance for the development of his theology in the context of his account of the Dominican life.

The contention of this book is that the Dominican vocation of Chenu is crucial to an understanding of his theology. The Dominican order is the soil from which his theology grew. A genetic approach to his writings must not only consider the development between the earlier and the later writings but must also raise questions about the sources of his thought. Of course these sources include the ambient culture and the intellectual influences of his day. But, more important, they lie in the structured life provided by the Dominican order to which he belonged. It is therefore important to look at the Dominican order and especially at Chenu's own reflections on this life and the unity it provided. What emerges is a life whose unity is founded on contemplation. The inevitable implication, to be verified, is that Chenu's theology is inseparable from the Dominican spirituality in which it grew. Such a separation would introduce a dualism between his theology and the living source from which he drew his insights. It would be tantamount to giving a disincarnate reading of one who spent his life fighting dualisms and promoting the implications of the incarnation.

A RELIGIOUS VOCATION

There is little information on the origin of Chenu's vocation. In the 1975 book-length interview with Jacques Duquesne, he noted that his vocation was not primarily a priestly vocation but a religious one; he was attracted by the Dominican life. Chenu also told Duquesne of an encounter, probably in 1913, that was to be decisive for his life. A friend from school named Lavergne invited Chenu to Le Saulchoir for his ordination. The Dominican convent and house of study was located at the time in Belgium because of the expulsions of religious orders from France in 1905. Chenu accepted the invitation: "And so I went. And there, I experienced a vivid sense of what the Dominican life was … I stayed barely two days, and I was smitten. It is difficult to explain now … What struck me was a very beautiful liturgy which meshed with a life of studies and community discipline."[3] What was it that he perceived and that attracted him so? What was it that seduced him? The starting-point chosen for this inquiry into the theology of Marie-Dominique Chenu is thus the charism of the Dominican life as it presented itself to the young Chenu.

3 *Duquesne* (1975), 27.

Anticipating a little, we can say he was attracted by a unity of life. We may never attain a clear and explicit understanding of this religious experience. It belongs to the secret area of personal life ("it is difficult to explain") and is not open to public scrutiny.[4] Still, we do have some access to this foundational experience through Chenu's own writings and statements. The point is not to attempt some psychologizing interpretation of his theological writings but simply to take seriously a starting-point given to us by Chenu. Fortunately, we have another important clue in the form of a remark made by Chenu in a late article on the unity of his life-long commitments. Commenting on his choice of the role of contemplation in St. Thomas as a topic for a doctoral thesis, he writes: "Without being fully aware of it, I sought to formulate 'scientifically' the intense experience undergone during a stay at the house of studies of Le Saulchoir (near Tournai). This was a Dominican community where the religious state, the fullness of liturgical life, and assiduous study (animated by a team of young professors equally committed to research and to teaching), combined in a heady atmosphere supported by individual fervour. From this moment on I invested the word 'contemplation' with its full meaning."[5] There are several other instances, as we will see below, where Chenu stated that he entered the Dominican order through the contemplative door. These passages further confirm the importance of contemplation in that initial encounter and thereafter. There are also many comments and reflections by Chenu about the role and place of contemplation in the Dominican life. We begin, however, with the "scientific" account of contemplation that Chenu has left us.

"DE CONTEMPLATIONE": THE DISSERTATION OF 1920

Shortly after his ordination, Chenu went to Rome to pursue his studies at the Angelicum. There he wrote a doctoral dissertation on the psychological and theological aspects of contemplation under the direction of Reginald Garrigou-Lagrange. Although it had long been known that Chenu's thesis was on contemplation, the manuscript itself was only

4 Chenu himself made several remarks about the private nature of this interior life. In an interview published in *Ecclesia* 122 (May 1959), 112, when asked about the origin of his vocation, he answered: "*Ce sont des choses dont on ne peut guère parler.*"

5 "De la contemplation à l'engagement" (1988), 100–1.

rediscovered recently.[6] The text anticipates many of Chenu's later positions and theological options, particularly with regard to the rejection of dualisms that destroy the integral character of the human person.[7]

Although spirituality has regained a good deal of prominence in contemporary theological circles for a variety of reasons, there remains a certain unease when the modern reader is faced with the language and conceptual distinctions of neo-scholasticism. From the outset then, some basic questions arise: In concrete terms, what did Chenu mean by contemplation, given the stated relationship between the 1913 religious experience in Le Saulchoir and the thesis? What is the significance of such a choice for a dissertation topic in the first decades of this century? What question was Chenu asking when he turned to the topic of contemplation? Given that contemplation is so central in all of his theology (as I hope to show), notwithstanding the various changes and developments that the idea underwent (from "aristocratic" to more evangelical), there should be a clear and concrete understanding of it at the outset of the presentation.[8]

Although not all these questions can be answered fully, a brief look at the historical context can be helpful. One element of the answers is found in theological discussion at the turn of the last century concerning the relationship between knowledge and mysticism.[9] The challenge of Kant's *Critique of Pure Reason* made the subjective conditions for knowing an inescapable question in philosophy. In theology, the turn to the subject, as it became generally known, meant a greater concern for the subjective dimensions of the act of faith. All aspects of religious experience and mysticism came under scrutiny. This perspective sometimes came about as a countermeasure to a perceived extrinsicism where revelation

6 A partial edition with some commentary was provided by Carmelo Guiseppe Conticello, "*De contemplatione* (*Angelicum*, 1920). La thèse inédite de doctorat du P. M.-D. Chenu," *RSPT* 75 (1991), 363–422. The complete manuscript is located in the Dominican archives in Paris.

7 See ibid., 365, for Conticello's general assessment of the thesis: "*Manifeste de son option théologique et surtout étude de grande envergure, le* De Contemplatione *demeure un acquis fondateur de sa pensée. Le P.Chenu y est entièrement, dans sa perspective comme dans ses choix. La suite, l'éventail de ses activités, les recherches comme les engagements, en constitueront pour ainsi dire le cheminement naturel et l'aboutissement.*" This statement must be nuanced by the shift towards evangelism brought about by the encounter with the JOC.

8 See Chenu's interview in *Ecclesia* 122 (1959), 113, where he describes the thesis and its significance for him: " ... *c'était un sujet neuf à l'époque. Du capital spirituel et théologique alors acquis, j'espère n'avoir rien perdu; en tout cas, ce me fut toujours une sauvegarde contre la tentation de l'activisme en vie dominicaine où la contemplation est la terre nutritive de la théologie comme de l'apostolat.*"

9 Conticello refers to some of this discussion. See also Émile Poulat's *Critique et mystique. Autour de Loisy ou la conscience catholique et l'esprit moderne* (Paris: Éditions du Centurion, 1984), 254–306; Étienne Fouilloux, "Les premiers pas de *La vie spirituelle*" in his *Au cœur du XXᵉ siècle religieux* (Paris: Les éditions ouvrières, 1993), 219–30.

occurred and was received without any consideration for the receiving subject (i.e., the believer). Chenu thus often opposed the faith of obedience (e.g., Billot). Sometimes, as was the case with some modernists, the subjective viewpoint was expressed with what came to be known as the way of immanence, soon to be called "immanentism" by the authors of the encyclicals *Pascendi* and *Lamentabili*.[10]

Yet it is not enough to point to an existing debate in philosophical and theological circles about "*la question mystique*" in order to justify its importance and significance, or even to gain a grasp of the subject. Contemplation is central to the issue of revelation, Christian faith, and the nature of theology. What seems decisive in this case, at least as a starting point in the present reflection, is Chenu's personal desire to understand his own lived experience of 1913 in Le Saulchoir, even if that desire was unconscious. We are dealing, then, with a lived experience.

What, in concrete terms, is contemplation? What are we studying when we study contemplation? What is the object of study of Chenu's dissertation? Chenu describes contemplation at the outset of the thesis: "It is the supreme act of the human intellect in which man draws closest (*maxime appropinquat*) to the nature of angels and God himself."[11] Further, he says: "Contemplation, inasmuch as it is the perfect act of the intellect, is the supreme human act assimilating us to God."[12] Chenu defines the area of study in those introductory paragraphs. Within this most human act, the act by means of which we fulfill the deepest human desires and aspirations, by means of which we are brought closest to God, the various operations of the intellect are conjugated with the light of God, providing an assimilation to God's knowledge of himself. The question arises as to the precise relation and conditions between the infusion of divine light, out of God's goodness, and the human capacity for such an extension of the human desire to know (*capacitas obedientalis*). The discourse of the mystics on the nature of this relationship is far from being intellectually satisfying. Hence, the object of Chenu's thesis is the nature of contemplation, both

---

10 See Chapter 2 for a discussion of faith as obedience, and the roles of Billot and Gardeil in Chenu's background. See also Roger Aubert, *Le problème de l'acte de foi. Données traditionnelles et résultats des controverses récentes*, 4th ed. (Louvain: Éditions Nauwelaerts, 1969).

11 "*Contemplatio enim est actus supremus intellectus humani in quo maxime appropinquat homo ad naturam angeli et ipsius Dei; – est actus maxime vitalis et immanens, ab intimis at profundioribus mentis humanae procedens, praeter multiplicitatem et mobilitatem operationum inferiorum – et ideo, licet quoad se sit magis intelligibilis, quoad nos tamen abscondibus est et mysteriosus: si quaecumque cognitio jam est quoddam mysterium naturale, quid dicemus de cognitione intellectuali contemplativa, qua est assimilatio et possessio veri in quiete apprehensionis perfectae?*" *De contemplatione*, 1.

12 "*Contemplatio, utpote perfectus actus intellectus, est supremus actus humanus maxime assimilans ad Deum*," (ibid., 3; cf. Conticello, 383).

in genere, where the focus is the nature of human contemplative knowing, according to the basic psychological resources of the basic human structure, and *in specie*, where the focus is the nature of supernatural mystical contemplation. The concern for the integrity of a human phenomenon is already manifest in Chenu's interest in the psychological structure, in his effort to lay down the basic human dimensions of the problem prior to tackling the issue of supernatural contemplation.

Many matters clearly fall under consideration here: the relationship of nature and grace, the operations and capacity of human knowing, the distinction between reason and intellect, the nature of divine mission and especially the mission of the Spirit, the active and passive dimensions of human knowing, the role and function of experience. All are considered at least synthetically by Chenu in light of the various positions offered by contemporary scholars.

According to Chenu's own account later in life, the dissertation is built on two doctrinal positions of St. Thomas, one psychological and the other theological. The first holds that a distinction is to be made between human intellect and reason. With the former, we can have simple perceptions or intuitions. With the latter, we are equipped for analysis, conceptual development, and demonstrations. Both belong to the basic psychological human resources, yet their functions are significantly different. Upon the foundations of this basic human structure, a theological perspective introduces the activity of the Holy Spirit with the twofold category of gift and virtue. The influence of Ambroise Gardeil is decisive here. The ultimate word on contemplation is thus given in the context of theological life according to the virtues of faith, hope, and charity.[13]

A fundamental objective of the thesis, stated at the outset, concerns the idea of the intellect in St. Thomas: to locate the doctrine of contemplation, which represents the principle and rule of religious and spiritual life, in the "intellectualism" of St. Thomas.[14] All seem to agree that contemplation, as our communion with God, represents the end of human

13 See Chenu's comments in "De la contemplation à l'engagement," (1988), 100. The reference to these doctrinal positions of St. Thomas was meant to fulfill two intentions: to gain an understanding of the experience of the visit to Le Saulchoir (*"Pour en avoir l'intelligence"*), and to meet the academic standards of a doctoral dissertation.

14 Cf. ibid., 2, and Conticello, 383: *"Finis autem operantis, ut scholastice dicam, haec est: invenire in 'intellectualismo' Sancti Thomae doctrinam de contemplatione, quae sit principium efficax et regula firma vitae spiritualis et religiosae, imo et mysticae."* Note that contemplation is described as *"principium efficax et regula firma vitae spiritualis et religiosae, imo et mysticae."* This foreshadows the central unifying role it will play in the architecture of the Dominican life as portrayed by Chenu.

life for which we were created. Human happiness is found in the act of wisdom, the summit of all virtues. Christians would agree that the gift of wisdom perfects the knowledge of faith. However, there is a disagreement over how we conceive this wisdom and this contemplation. On this subject, Chenu refers to the unfortunate opposition between intellectualism and mysticism, an opposition which he firmly and characteristically rejects. The other opposition, between asceticism and mysticism and equally rejected, holds that contemplation is reserved for few while moral asceticism and the pursuit of perfection are the lot of the many.

Rejection of these notions is but the underside of one of Chenu's basic positions, namely, the unity of theology and, more profoundly, the unity of human reality in its relation to God. In fact, his position on the unity of life is a foundation for what he says about the Dominican "mixed" state of life advocated by St. Thomas.[15] Here, he wishes to draw attention to the psychological and affective components of knowing, as well as to the intellectual underpinning of mysticism. In one passage of the mainly Latin text, he writes: "One must manifest the contemplative and 'mystical' value of understanding (*intellectus ut intellectus*), and maintain its preponderance even in the mysterious depths of mystical union where, as everywhere else, it is a force of order and light. No false and empty opposition therefore. It is enough merely to understand correctly the thomistic *intellectus* and not to reduce it to the reasoning and anti-mystical faculty of Descartes and Leibniz. Mysticism for St. Thomas, it has been said, is integral intellectualism."[16]

This confidence in reason, and hence in the reasonability of faith, is a trait that remained throughout Chenu's writings, most notably in works dealing with theology as science. At stake, once again, is a question affecting not only the discipline of theology but the unity of the human being: "*intellectualisme intégral.*"

One way to understand the "integral" character of this position is to contrast it with the other positions rejected by St. Thomas and Chenu.

---

15 See below.

16 Ibid., 3, original text in French. Cf. Conticello, 383. The last sentence, as Conticello points out, is a reference to Pierre Rousselot's *L'Intellectualisme de saint Thomas* (Paris: Alcan, 1908): "*S. Thomas n'est donc pas religieux quoique intellectualiste; il croit plutôt devoir être intellectualiste parce que religieux*" (xxv) and "*il faut sentir intimement que l'intellectualisme fut pour lui vie intense, et le mysticisme, intellectualisme intégral*" (235). See also 3, n. 1 of the thesis, where Chenu offers the following comment on his use of the word mysticism: "*Je prends – un peu hardiment – ce mot, précisément aux adversaires de l'intellectualisme thomiste. Il est extrêmement confus; je l'emploie cependant, puisque ce travail déterminera le sens que je lui donne, redressant quelque peu son acception courante, pour lui donner une valeur et une précision théologiques – ce qui est le seul moyen de l'éclaircir.*" On the importance of Rousselot see Roger Aubert, *Le Problème de l'acte de foi*, 451–511.

The intended opponents here were Augustine and the variety of Augustinians dominant in the twelfth century. They drew a firm distinction between the speculative and scientific function of the intellect, qualified for the knowledge of earthly realities, and the faculty of wisdom, aided by love, and qualified for the knowledge of divine and eternal realities. In this view, contemplation is clearly not a function of the intellect, which is limited to earthly realities. Rather, there is a kind of "*ratio superior*" that is specially devoted to this higher activity, independently of the abstractions of the intellect and the use of sensible images (*conversio ad phantasma*). Contemplation proceeds by divine illumination.[17] Implicit in this position is that we can contemplate on condition of leaving behind what is human and intrinsic to us. The unity of the human person is thus fragmented.

St. Thomas rejected this dualistic position. For him, the unity of human intellect, that is, its integral character, is a value that must be preserved. Contemplation is an act of the human intellect. It is a natural act. The human soul does not have "two faces," an inferior one drawn to material things and a superior one contemplating immaterial things. Its structure is one and simple rather than complex.[18] The analytic and discursive reason also belongs to the same intellect, representing a different function rather than a separate faculty.

Rousselot gave the modern interpretation of the Thomistic position in his *L'intellectualisme de saint Thomas*, from which Chenu drew copiously.[19] According to this position, it is not necessary to posit a superior faculty

17 Cf. ibid., 50; Conticello 403, where Chenu comments: "*comme si, dans l'âme, l'esprit pur émergeait, attiré, hors de ses opérations connaturelles, à une opération purement spirituelle, dans sa contemplation.*"

18 Cf. 40; Conticello 400: "*S. Thomas e contra, cum suo magistro Alberto Magno, eidem facultati secundum eumdem modum cognitivum, – per abstractionem scilicet, – operanti, tribuit et cognitionem scientiae et cognitionem contemplativam sapientiae: idem omnino est in nobis principium secundum quod anima discurrit ad res temporales cognoscendas, et secundum quod capax est cognitionis veritatum aeternum, imo et visionis Dei. C'est là le point de divergence, non seulement de deux théories* peri psyches, *mais de deux mentalités, de deux spiritualités, de deux mystiques. Et in hoc consistit 'intellectualismus' S. Thomae, prout opponitur doctrinae de illuminatione divina seu mysticismo psychologico, ut aiunt, cujus proprium est agnoscere in homine aliquam potentiam supra-rationalem, (imo et super-intellectualem) quae connexionem immediatam habeat cum intelligibilibus et sit quidam sensus perceptivus divinorum.*"

19 A marginal note on 40, reproduced in Conticello 401, gives the following text from Rousselot: "*Le point capital est que, pour S. Thomas, la faculté qui nous fait capables de cette action transcendante (vision, contemplation de Dieu), est identiquement celle qui, selon un autre mode d'agir, forme nos concepts et combine nos déductions … Par de semblables paroles, qui ne sont pas une affirmation jetée en passant, mais l'âme même de sa pensée, S. Thomas, … s'oppose aux Augustiniens, plus près d'Augustin que ces Augustiniens-mêmes, et maintient, avec la tradition grecque, que nous trouvons dans l'intellect comme tel tout ce qu'il y a de meilleur, simpliciter.*" Cf. Rousselot, *L'intellectualisme*, 38–40. On 56 of the thesis, Chenu picks up once again this text of Rousselot in note 1.

ordered to contemplation, which is then dependent on some kind of voluntarism in its ascent, rather than a common principle in order to assure the unity of the subject.

Of the many aspects involved in the contemplative act as treated by St. Thomas in the *Summa Theologiae II-IIae, q. 180,* Chenu chose to focus on the two most important, affectivity and intuition.[20] Following St. Thomas, Chenu defines contemplation as a "simple intuition of truth" (*simplex intuitus veritatis*), and thus distinguishes it from other acts of the intellect.[21]

He begins by considering the activity of human knowing (*cognitio intellectualis*) whereby the human subject relates to the reality around him. There are three levels to this knowing. Chenu does not develop to any great length the relationships among the three; he is more concerned with situating contemplation within the various dimensions of human intellectual activity. On the first level is verbal knowing, whereby a student reproduces formulas learned from a master and accepted superficially without penetrating their fuller meaning. Speculative and abstractive knowing is the second, more sophisticated, level. Here, the various tools of human reason are put to use: distinction, deduction, abstraction, conceptualization, syllogism, and so forth. What is not involved here are the affective and appetitive dimensions, whereby the object of knowing is related to the human desire for the true, the good, and the beautiful. In other words, the affective and appetitive dimensions are not taken into account. Only on the third experiential level of human knowing, knowledge by connaturality, do these become explicit.[22] This kind of knowledge

20 Cf. ibid. 14 and Conticello, 392: "intuitivas, *scilicet, quae unitatem et simplicitatem vitae intellectuali confert, secundum nostrum desiderium 'intus-legendi',* – affectivitas, *quae vivificat assimilationem cognitivam, purificando et coaptando totas vires appetitivas subjecti in ordine ad connaturalitatem cum objecto obtinendam. Tales sunt proprietates 'sapientae'* (analogice applicandae ad sapientiam in ordine naturale et in ordine supernaturali) *ut est* perfecta *cognitio supremi Intelligibilis.*" Unfortunately, the sections on affectivity (26–34, 55–65) were not included in Conticello's partial edition.

21 Ibid., 15; cf. Conticello 393. See also Lemonnyer's *La vie humaine, ses formes, ses états,* 501–2, for a commentary on *IIa-IIae, q. 180, art. 3,* where this definition occurs in St. Thomas. Chenu goes on: "*In sua simplicitate, intuitus contemplativus, triplici modo importat perfectionem in cognitione:* primo, *prout obtinetur in termino progressus vitae intellectualis,* secundo, *prout supponit apprehensionem unam et syntheticam objecti cognoscendi,* tertio, *prout excellenter efficit assimiliationem vitalem subjecti ad objectum, in qua stat ratio formalis omnis cognitionis*" (ibid., 16; cf. Conticello 393–4).

22 Cf. ibid., 8–9: "*Denique, alia est cognitio* experimentalis, *qua objectum, in sua unitate profunda, ut est simul verum et bonum, per quemdam contactum immediatum intellectus attingitur, ita ut per affinitatem et coaptationem anima ipsa connaturalis fiat objecto, et sic, delectabiliter illud apprehedens, eo fruatur, admiratione repleta.*" See 8, n. 1, for further clarification of the threefold distinction.

represents that towards which our intellectual life strives: "Such, however, is the end of our intellectual life: that we might thus apprehend the supremely intelligible object in a wise, profound, and as it were 'experiential' assimilation – this is the formal principle of knowledge." From this follows the basic definition of contemplation: "Such is contemplation – whether this expression be taken in the strict sense of the contemplation of God, the supremely intelligible, or in the broad sense of the contemplation of any intelligible object; for by this name of 'contemplation' everyone means a cognition that is affective and, in some way at least, immediate."[23]

One of Chenu's examples of affective knowing concerns John the evangelist, whose immediate knowledge of Jesus Christ is distinguished from the rationalizations of scholastic metaphysical theology on the two natures. John had a religious intuition (*religiosa apprehensio*) born of daily contact, familiar instinct, and friendly conversation. Such knowledge is based on an "*adhesio*" to the other person; it "is the total adherence of the beloved disciple's soul to the Word, who is revealed and contemplated in the flesh." Chenu calls this type of unitive knowing "*lumen vitae*" and points to the function of contemplation in unifying the different dimensions of human life.[24]

This unifying function becomes apparent when we consider contemplation in relation to affectivity. It is not a question of suggesting a merely functionalist understanding of contemplation. Rather, the relation of contemplation to affectivity brings out more clearly than other aspects the integral intellectualism that Chenu, following Rousselot, found in St. Thomas. Furthermore, contemplation is the highest act of this integral intellectual life. It represents the fulfillment of our intellectual activity.

Affectivity (*affectivitas*) is involved in contemplation in three different ways: it supplies the proper disposition (*causa disponens*), provides the motivation (*causa movens*), and defines the proper end of the contemplative act. In the consideration of intuition, the integral character of the intellect is affirmed in terms of its unity and the homogeneity of its intellectual activity (there is "inferior" and "superior" intellect). Now, in

23 Ibid., 9; cf. Conticello, 387.
24 Ibid., 13; cf. Conticello, 390. It should be noted that Chenu is not advocating by means of this distinction the very dualism between mysticism and speculation that he so opposes. On the contrary, as he will say in *Une école de théologie*, it is spirituality (read "contemplation") that gives rise to a theology. What he opposes is theological speculation that has been cut off from its roots in the life of faith, that is, from its roots in theological contemplation.

the consideration of affectivity in relation to the doctrines of the true and the good, the focus is on the unity of intellect and will in the supreme act of the spiritual life.[25]

First, then, for all types of experiential knowing, that is, knowing through experience, an initial condition is required: "If therefore knowledge comes about by a connatural inclination to the object, it presupposes a certain harmony between them, proceeding from love and producing connaturality."[26]

Second, affection is a principle of movement which incites us towards contemplation of the object encountered in love. Now, this motion is not merely a factor that remains extrinsic to the act of contemplation (i.e., *per modum applicationis ab extra imperatur*); there is a much more intimate relationship between love and apprehension. Thomas speaks of a reciprocal inhabitation in *Ia-IIae q. 28 a.2, ad 1*: "The beloved is contained within the lover, in the sense that the latter's affection for the former causes the beloved to be etched into the feelings of the lover ... the lover is contained within the beloved, in the sense that the lover strives in some way after what is most profound in the beloved." Chenu comments: "From this affective harmony and communion there springs a sort of continuous movement towards a friendly and pleasant apprehension, such that in this way the understanding is totally possessed and seized by this reciprocal attachment."[27]

Third, affection brings to an end and completes the act of contemplation in a delectation. The end of contemplation is not only when the divine truth is seen, but when it is loved.[28]

The close relationship of affection and intellect brings out the unitive function of contemplation. In the act of contemplation, according to St. Thomas, truth takes on the value of a good which is desirable, loved,

---

25 Cf. ibid., 27.

26 Ibid., 28. Chenu refers to Thomas' argument in *III Sent. d. 35 q. 1 a. 2 q. 1*. In the *IIa-IIae, q. 180, a. 2, ad 2*, the purifying role, so necessary in the contemplative life, is attributed to the moral virtues. Cf. ibid., 29: "*Unde, sicut ad intuitum contemplativum requiritur, ut vidimus, unificatio seu 'uniformitas' progressiva mentis, ita ad affectivam cognitionem requiritur coordinatio et unificatio progressiva omnium motuum appetitus: unitas et simplicitas totius vitae interioris est, non solum mystica sed et psychologice loquendo, conditio et fundamentum contemplationis.*" In a note, Chenu refers to the intellectual and mystical doctrine of Denys, an important source for Thomas here, whose entire emphasis lies in the movement from multiplicity to unity.

27 Ibid., 30. Cf. also St. Thomas, *Contra Gentiles* IV, c. 19, *versus finem*, on the same theme.

28 Cf. ibid., 31.

and delectable.[29] Often, we reach truth through the intellect, and the will for its part attains the good; the two are separate and distinct operations. The result is lack of unity. Truth remains true, but loses its attraction or its compelling character. In the act of contemplation, being is at once known in its truth and loved in its goodness.[30] Only in God are knowledge and love, intellect and will, identified, in the act of pure intellect and eternal love. Yet through contemplation, human nature, which is composite and suffering from imperfect multiplicity, may attain the unity wherein lies perfection. In this sense, contemplation provides our lives with unity: "And thus, in proportion as intellectual unity (Dionysius would say 'uniformity') is greater, our contemplation brings about *the unity of our entire moral and spiritual life*, freeing us from division, freeing us from opposition, freeing us from the scattering of our acts and faculties and aspirations."[31] Underlying this view, of course, is the idea that being and goodness are identical. Truth is good, otherwise it would not be desirable. And the good is true, otherwise it would not be intelligible.[32] Such is the root of objective wisdom, which Chenu calls the habit of contemplation and whose proper quality is to apprehend truth in its identity with the good and with perfection. Herein lies the distinction between science and wisdom. Under the coordination of love, says Chenu, speculative knowledge becomes the *lumen vitae*, and science is transformed into wisdom: "Since, moreover, the esteem and love which the one loving has for his idea of the beloved brings about a harmony between the subject and the object, it follows that wisdom not only judges according to the perfect use of reason-apprehending-truth, but also according to a connaturality and sympathy with the object as its good."[33]

Up to now, contemplation has been considered in a generic sense, that is, regardless of whether its object is natural or supernatural. Now, in the examination of contemplation in the properly mystical sense, there is the added factor of the theological virtues and the gifts of the Holy Spirit.[34] Here the relationship of nature and grace is seen in its most concrete dimension, namely, within the context of a theological life.

29 Cf. *IIa-IIae* q. *180, a. 1, ad 1:* "*Ex hoc ipso quod veritas est finis contemplationis, habet rationem boni appetibilis et amabilis et delectantis.*"

30 Cf. ibid., 32: "*in actu contemplativo, e contra, ens* et *cognoscitur in sua veritate* et *amatur in sua bonitate, quasi unico actu sympathico et vivido; et non solum idealiter, sed effective objectum possidetur.*"

31 Ibid., 32, Chenu's emphasis.

32 Cf. *Ia* q. *79, a. 11, ad 2*, and *de Ver. q. 3, a. 3, ad 9.*

33 Ibid., 33.

34 On the gifts of the Holy Spirit, Chenu owes a great deal to the work of Ambroise Gardeil; see for example his article "Dons du saint Esprit" in *DTC* 4.2 (1911), cc. 1728–81.

Once again, the purpose is not to summarize Chenu's thesis but to bring out certain highlights of his approach that will illuminate later developments. Having characterized the dominant interpretations of his day concerning "*la question mystique*" in terms of maximalist and minimalist approaches,[35] Chenu's own approach emphasizes the unity of the human person and its intellectual processes. Following St. Thomas, Chenu at once stressed the homogeneity and unity of the intellect's ascent to the primary truth, and developed an elaborate theology of the gifts of the Holy Spirit. The living context for this view of things is the interaction of the theological virtues (faith, hope, and charity) and the human psychological and intellectual structure they presuppose and perfect. The theological life is where the real interaction occurs. It is the living theatre where the divine and human levels cooperate to make up Christian existence.

What emerges at the heart of this integrally conceived ascent of the human intellect is passivity. Something takes place that is not the result of some voluntarism or intellectual construction. On the contrary, the acting role of the intellect is relinquished in favour of the light of faith, whose origin does not lie in the human person. Yet – and herein lies the genius of the Thomistic position followed by Chenu – the integral character of the human person is not thereby violated. The preservation of this integrity has already been "prepared" through the twofold characterization of generic contemplation as intuitive and affective that remains in the presence of the light of faith. For Chenu, while mystical contemplation is the normal end of the grace given in baptism, assuring the unity of Christian experience, the human intellect cannot by itself reach the vision of God. In addition to the theological virtues of faith and charity, there are special gifts of the Holy Spirit that perfect the *habitus* of faith. In this mystical contemplation, then, passivity of the intellect is the primary characteristic.[36]

---

35 Both positions err by breaking the unity of the intellect's operations, one through an excessive and one through a defficient view of contemplation. The minimalist view sees mystical contemplation as part of the initial baptismal grace with only a difference of intensity, while the maximalist view sees mystical contemplation as an extraordinary grace with no continuity in the act of faith.

36 Conticello has underlined the importance of the Dionysian *pati divina* in Chenu. See also Paul Agaësse "Mystique," *Dictionnaire de spiritualité* 10 (1980), cc. 1939–78, especially section III, cc. 1955–78, on criteria of mystical experience, *pati divina*, passive purification, and theopathic union. For a recapitulation of previous articles mentioning the topic of passivity in the *DS*, see Aimé Solignac "Passivité," 12.1 (1984), cc. 357–60.

CONTEMPLATION IN OTHER WRITINGS

Chenu's dissertation on contemplation was ultimately just that, a dissertation. It clearly showed strong indications of positions that would become characteristic of theology. Yet its tone is necessarily academic, and therefore somewhat abstract, closely tied to the scholastic methodology in which it was written. The tone is very different in a 1932 series of conferences Chenu gave to the Dominican sisters of the Monastère de la Croix,[37] in which the significance of contemplation acquires a more concrete sense in the context of the Dominican religious life.

First, the starting-point is notably different and stands out. Here is a reflection on a contemplative life lived in the context of a religious order, an experience not only common to the audience and the speaker but central to their way of life.

Second, the unity of intellect and affectivity acquires a more concrete dimension. Contemplation is situated at the intersection of two fundamental movements in our being: the spontaneity and freedom of love, and the desire for clarity, order, and reflection. As such, it is an intuition of the intellect motivated and fulfilled in love, and located at the summit of all our actions. This intuition is translated into the contemplative life of the religious order: "In our Dominican life, there is an affirmation of the absolute primacy of the contemplative act."[38] It is in light of contemplation that all the rest is ordered.

Third, the meaning of passivity in contemplation is clarified.[39] There is a clear shift in emphasis from the artist's or the poet's initial drive to conquer in natural contemplation. Yet even in that form, passivity was shown to be an integral part of human intellectual life. Now, it is no

37 There is a thirty-eight-page typed, single-spaced *reportatio* in the Dominican archives in Paris.

38 Ibid., 6: "*Dans notre vie dominicaine, il y a affirmation de la primauté absolue de l'acte contemplatif.*" See also 31, where knowledge and love are situated in contemplation and where charity is declared "*principe intérieur de la contemplation*": "*Dans l'acte de la contemplation, le regard de la foi sera imprégné de charité: il sera le regard de celui qui aime, qui ne contemple que parce qu'il aime. Acte de connaissance et d'amour totalement unifié, où la connaissance reste première, mais où elle ne peut se concevoir sans un amour qui la provoque, la conduit, se trouve inclus en elle.*"

39 Cf. ibid., 2: "*Nous sommes passifs, certes, dans le regard de la contemplation; mais dans cette passivité, il y a un maximum d'activité. Il ne faut pas subir, mais posséder la vérité, comme une matière à vivre; il faut que dans notre vie elle soit une chose assimilée, maîtrisée, qui devienne notre chair et notre sang; il faut que ce soit une acquisition. C'est donc une attitude fausse en mystique que cette sorte d'annihilation intérieure sous prétexte de recevoir. Au contraire, c'est une emprise de nous sur la vérité qui doit devenir nôtre. Dieu accepte d'être la nourriture de notre esprit, mais à condition que sa vérité devienne vraiment la vie de notre esprit.*" Note the allusion to an incarnate structure.

longer we as individuals who adhere to the spirit being contemplated; it is the object that invades our interior and seizes us from within. The entry into the zone where God's own life takes command is ruled by the gifts of the Holy Spirit, which build on the basis of the theological virtues of faith, hope, and charity. Yet this extraordinary communion with the divine life does not violate our human nature. Just as in the dissertation, so too in these talks Chenu was careful to lay out the wide-ranging human resources which make contemplation possible: "The supernatural life, and the contemplative life which it contains, is not something outside our human constitution, as though superimposed upon it. Supernatural life is inserted into the organism of our soul, and grace adapts itself within us to our personal temperament; the act of contemplation is itself linked to our temperament."[40] This is in line with the realism of the Thomistic doctrine which Chenu followed and is thus distinct from the quietist position, which verges on self-annihilation. It also anticipates the theme of incarnation so important in Chenu's theology.

Finally, the role of the theological life is further explored: the divine life within us, the home of faith which lives in cooperation with our reason and intellect. The gifts of the Holy Spirit, which perfect faith's drive to vision, do not represent a superior faculty devoted to mystical contemplation. They do not require that we leave the domain of faith; they are not superimposed on faith but rather inserted into the very imperfection of faith in order to bring it into communion with God: "Even at this summit of contemplative life, we remain within human psychology, both psychologically and theologically, this is how the contemplative act must be explained: not as a venturing outside our mind (*esprit*), but as a normal activity. It is a normal activity of our mind from the natural viewpoint, and of faith from the supernatural viewpoint."[41] The theological life is the human relationship with God – not with the anonymous creator but with the personal God who seeks out our love and becomes an object for our intellect and our love. Such a relationship is naturally impossible and beyond our natural abilities. Yet, as transcendent to us as it is, it is so intimate to our human structure that it becomes our own: "God has such a capacity to communicate himself to us that we will possess him just as we possess our intelligence and our will; so much so that we shall find ourselves with the full array of our faculties in the supernatural world, invested with the value of divine

---

40 Ibid., 16. There is a reference here to the work of Gardeil and his effort to preserve "*les bases solides de l'expérience.*"
41 Ibid., 27–8.

life."[42] The distinction between moral virtues and theological virtues refers to a difference of order. The theological life has God for its object, whereas the moral life concerns our self-government. There is no such difference of order between the theological life and the mystical life where the latter is the blossoming and perfection of the former through the action of the Holy Spirit. It is the existence of such a sphere as the theological life that prevents the destructive dualism between asceticism and mysticism.

THE STRUCTURE OF DOMINICAN LIFE ACCORDING TO CHENU

A full grasp of the role and place of contemplation requires us to set it in the context of the Dominican life. The preceeding section represented a first step in this direction. Yet the unitive function of contemplation becomes manifest only in relation to concrete elements of a life such as work, study, prayer, and so forth. In becomes manifest in action, that is, in a life so united.

The Dominican religious life is an example of such a unity. Several texts by Chenu from the early 1930s on religious life are quite important for an appreciation of the role of contemplation and, by extension, for an overall understanding of his theology. To a large extent they have so far been unavailable to the scholar, or else have been ignored.[43]

Although, because of the specific audience, the 1932 talks give a much more concrete sense of the role of contemplation in religious life, the texture of Chenu's life as a Dominican still remains to be explored. A major source for Chenu's understanding of the structure of Dominican life is the unpublished text of a retreat preached to the same Dominican sisters of the Monastère de la Croix in 1934.[44] The theme of

---

42 Ibid., 33.

43 The article by Emilio Garcia Alvarez is a notable exception. He writes a great deal about the role of contemplation in the Dominican life, yet the study is far from adequate to the subject.

44 The manuscript of 113 pages, typewritten and single-spaced, contains sixteen lessons on the topic of the structure of the Dominican life. It is accompanied by seventy pages of typewritten notes that served as the basis for the retreat. Both manuscript and notes are to be found in the Dominican archives of the French province in Paris. The retreat was preached between November 30 and December 7, 1934. The text is a *reportatio* made by members of the audience. The faithfulness of their recording is attested to by the typewritten notes specifically written by Chenu for the occasion. That this text represents an important, rather than a peripheral, source is suggested by the existence of two other texts reproducing the first four and the first five lessons almost verbatim, but clearly for a different – male – Dominican audience.

the retreat text is the structure of Dominican life; thus, the living context for contemplation is far more evident. This carefully structured text, though not scholarly in the technical sense, is clearly the product of a mature mind. It came fourteen years after the Roman dissertation *De contemplatione*, shortly before the important 1935 article "La position de la théologie," and less than a year and a half before the famous panegyric "Veritas liberavit vos," which served as the basis for *Une École de théologie. Le Saulchoir* and which echoes many of the themes found in the retreat text.

The sixteen lessons, given at a rhythm of two a day, are organized along two main lines. In the morning series Chenu addressed the theme of the Christian life, with lessons on the theological virtues of faith, hope, and charity, life in Christ, the sacraments, the eucharist, and the Virgin Mary. The evening sessions focused on the religious life, with lessons on contemplation, the moral virtues, the life of evangelical counsels, study, the common life, and the apostolic life. The last lesson is on the theological optimism of the Dominicans.

The relationship and intersection of these two elements, forming the architecture of the Dominican life, is the general theme of the retreat. Rather than speaking on one or another aspect of the Christian or the religious life, Chenu considers "the order of these elements in relation to one another."[45] He explains his approach as follows: "[The retreat] will be *the presentation of a framework, of a spiritual architecture* where you will be able to control, adjust, by means of your personal experience, each one of the elements. This will enable you to pursue this life as it should be, not by constantly renewed artificial means, but by something more solid, by a constant reflection, and thus arrive at a well-balanced construction. In this spiritual edifice, what will be the master-beams, the two essential braces which must be watched more carefully than the details and around which everything is organized? ... The two main beams are on the one hand *our Christian life* and on the other *our religious life.*"[46]

Several things may be noted from the outset. First, the metaphor of architecture is fundamental and returns throughout the sixteen lessons, acquiring a particular importance in the lesson on contemplation. Next, the emphasis on order and organization is typical of a Thomistic viewpoint, to which Chenu returns in several places and which is a common theme in his writings on theological method, especially *Une École de théologie.* Also to be noted is Chenu's use of the first person plural in

---

45 Retreat (1934), 2.
46 Ibid., 4. Unless otherwise noted, the emphasis is in the original document.

addressing the question of the Dominican life. To the extent that his reflections touch on the Dominican life and the Dominican charism, they
are eminently illustrations of Chenu's own self-understanding. Finally,
there is the matter of the "construction" to be achieved. This topic requires some clarification, as it touches the heart of the reflective effort
of self-appropriation and relates that effort to the original experience
where the call to religious life first became evident.

There are days when we have seen clearly, when we have understood what it is
to know something, to pray, to be called by God, and our soul has been definitively marked by this – when we have understood the pressure brought to bear
on us, understood that God has called us to this intimacy with him, to religious
life. One must not place these riches aside; it is by these that we live. At that
time, we received a light from which we still live and to which we must continually return because we have there the maximum of spontaneity under the impe-
tus of God. However, an intuition cannot feed on itself. Now, the intuition must
be fed; this life, glimpsed from afar, must now be constructed. We are not like
angels who see their whole life in a simple intuition, in a single glance. We live
our lives day by day, in little portions dispersed among our hours and our faculties. Therefore, there is an urgent need for us to unify our life, even if it already
seems so simple. Indeed, the more our life is simple, the more it requires to be
strongly constructed, lest we fall into some sort of interior nothingness ... Our
spiritual life must be built the way our body is constructed, or a house. In a ca-
thedral, there is a keystone, columns, naves ... etc. ... and yet there is a magnificent unity; our soul must also have this unity, we must be the architects of our
lives. We can be excellent religious by following the rule, but that is not all, we
must live in spiritual beauty.[47]

The object of the construction is thus the unity of our life in relation
to the original intuition where the call of God left its definitive mark.
The task of unity will leave no aspect outside its periphery. All human
and psychological resources require balanced integration "that everything be according to the light, the brightness, the clarity of God's
work."[48]
    The text clearly points to the foundational value of the original intu-
ition: "*c'est de cela que nous vivons.*" The constant return to this intuition,
in its value of reference point, further justifies our own starting point in

47 Ibid., 2–3.
48 Ibid., 3.

this study with Chenu's initial visit to Le Saulchoir, where he perceived the unity of a life and was attracted by it.

As mentioned earlier, the two elements to be constructed and unified are the religious life and the the Christian life: in this case, the Dominican life and the Christian life. From the outset, Chenu delineates the basic position: the religious life is for the sake of the Christian life, which has an absolute superiority. The Christian life is a theological life, composed of faith, hope, and charity, while the religious life with its associated counsels belongs to the moral life. The theological life is a participation by grace in the very life of God, and is for that reason called *theo*logical: "The object proper to this life, its nourishment, is God himself, in the most secret and intimate aspect of his being. The beatitude of God is handed over to us as our own good."[49] The religious life is situated much more on the human plane. It concerns our effort at organizing our resources towards moral perfection. In this sense, the call to Christian life, which is entered into through baptism, is more eminent than the recognition of a vocation to the religious life.

From this established hierarchy between the Christian and the religious life follows the further distinction between, on the one hand, the life of grace and the infused or theological virtues and, on the other hand, the life of the evangelical counsels and the acquired virtues. Everything belonging to the religious state – the whole system of precepts and monastic regulations and their observation – all is ordained to the perfection of charity and the primacy of the theological life of grace. The religious life is a means ordered to an end, which is the Christian life.[50]

Having laid out the essential relationship between the call to the Christian life and the religious vocation, the remainder of the retreat text is concerned with the problem of the architecture of human life, the problem of the unity of life. As noted earlier, the morning sessions considered the components of the Christian life, the theological virtues of faith, hope, and charity, and the marks of a life in Christ. The evening sessions considered the Dominican religious life in its relation to the theological life, the issue of moral perfection under the evangelical consels and the moral virtues. Moral perfection, here, docs not refer to

49 Ibid., 5.

50 Cf. ibid., 11: "*Notre vie religieuse dominicaine si éminente soit-elle n'a pour but immédiat que la perfection morale, l'équilibre parfait devant Dieu afin d'être ensuite en perpétuelle disponibilité pour l'amour dans le Christ.*"

some exaltation of one part of our life; it is rather the equilibrium of the whole "as a frame which supports the building."[51]

CONTEMPLATION AND THE END
OF DOMINICAN LIFE

Within this structure, a pivotal role is given to contemplation. First of all, on the level of the theological life, there is faith. Faith is our participation, as minimal as it may seem, in God's self-knowledge. It is seeing with the eye of God. Now, the expression of this virtue of faith, on the level of Dominican religious life, is contemplation. In this sense, contemplation is at the very crossroad (*carrefour*) between the theological and the religious life. "We are now at the keystone of our spiritual edifice; here the two forces of our lives are supported like two flying buttresses. We are truly at the heart of the problem. Here alone do we reach the summit. Our whole theological life and our whole Dominican life meet and find their equilibrium: this is where the two arches of the theological life and the religious life must be established. This is the point where they will have to intersect. And if we have grasped this, we will should reach this culminating point, this summit, both as an ideal and as an element of unity."[52]

In trying to locate the place of contemplation within the elements of the religious life, Chenu borrows from Lemonnyer a schema on the ends of the Dominican life.[53] There is first of all the end that is both general and individual, that is common to all forms of religious life and to be fulfilled personally by all: the perfection of charity. In other words, all the elements of the religious life are ordered to the perfection of the

---

51 Ibid., 19.

52 Ibid., 27. It is here that the architectural imagery finds its most pointed application.

53 Cf. ibid., 28. Chenu refers to a commentary by Lemonnyer on the Dominican Constitutions. I have been unable to locate any explicit commentary on the constitutions, either published or unpublished. The reference, which occurs several times in his retreat texts, is most likely to Lemonnyer's commentary on the treatise on religious life by St. Thomas in the *Revue des Jeunes* edition, where Lemonnyer writes about the primary and secondary ends of religious life. Lemonnyer, however, does not use the adjective "absolute." See 557 on the hierarchy of ends: "*En premier lieu vient la charité elle-même, de laquelle procèdent les oeuvres de charité, qui leur confère leur caractère d'oeuvres de charité et qui fait leur valeur et mérite. En second lieu, vient l'oeuvre propre de la charité pour Dieu, qui est la contemplation, la charité elle-même étant d'abord un amour de Dieu. En troisième lieu, viennent les oeuvres de charité ou de miséricorde pour le prochain, l'amour du prochain, d'où elles procèdent, venant après l'amour de Dieu, dont il représente une extension d'ailleurs nécessaire et homogène.*"

divine life in us, and this perfection is charity. Then there is the special and individual end, the specifically Dominican characteristic to be fulfilled by all members of the order: contemplation.[54] Finally, there is a special end common to all the order without being compulsory for each individual member of the order: the apostolate through preaching and teaching. Such is the structure of the Dominican religious life.

Contemplation is thus not situated as a means towards an end, but as an end in itself, despite the earlier affirmation that all the religious life is a means towards the theological life. It is not the case that we contemplate in order to be more effective in the pastoral field. Pastoral action will come later, but it does not emanate from contemplation.[55] The case of contemplative Dominican nuns confirms this: they are integrally Dominicans without apostolate; their vocation is purely contemplative. A Dominican involved in pastoral activities without contemplation would not be a true Dominican: "A Dominican defines himself by this. This is the pivot, the heart which will pump the blood throughout the entire organism. Everything is tied together here, it is truly the keystone. If it were to shift, everything would collapse and fall down. A Dominican who has lost the sense of the contemplative life is nothing. If we lack contemplation, our lives will be like bodies without blood, emptied of their blood and heart."[56] Contemplation inserts an element of divine life into religious life. As an exercise of the virtue of faith, it is a work properly belonging to the theological life (*oeuvre théologale*). As such, it is not ordered as a means to moral perfection. In this, Chenu is far from the purely ascetic views of contemplation, which would insist that the contemplative act must result in personal conversion or in some moral resolution.

Chenu rejects the dualism between acquired and infused contemplation. He insists on the unity of contemplation, whose only principle is the virtue of faith in its normal development, attaining God in his – that is, God's – very life. Within this one act are the gifts of the Holy Spirit, so inserted into the act of faith that they become our own: "But these divine powers, these virtues are placed entirely at our disposal. Divine life becomes so much a part of our own nature that these are our own

---

54 Cf. ibid., 28: "*L'Ordre dominicain est organisé comme une immense machine où chacun doit tendre à la contemplation.*"

55 Cf. ibid., 29, where Chenu says: "*Je ne vais pas regarder Dieu pour m'occuper des hommes. Du moment où je regarde Dieu, il n'y a rien au dessus à quoi la contemplation peut servir.*"

56 Ibid., 29.

acts. Faith is such a part of us because God has so entered into us that when we make an act of faith, we see with the eyes of God."[57]

Since our human capacity is limited, the gifts of the Holy Spirit are necessary to fill the gap, so to speak, to give us a more immediate perception of divine life. Within this domain of intimacy with God, the gift of wisdom reigns supreme. The characterization of this gift of wisdom in terms of intuition provides us with a glimpse of Chenu's own theological creativity. It is well known that Chenu did not write a theological system but rather developed key theological intuitions. The reflection on contemplation and the gift of wisdom provides the genetic locus for these intuitions. From the original intuition leading to the religious vocation, to the intuition of the contemplative act, the Dominican life develops.

At the outset, the act of contemplation is an intuition. The prayer of a contemplative religious must be the prayer of a theologian, but prior to any speculation, it is an intuition. This is why it is not necessary to be a great theologian in order to be a contemplative. The primary intuition which has initially directed us towards the religious life was a first contemplative act. This intuitive character, which gradually commits one more and more to a project of meditation, of reasoning, of studies, will grow and develop in order to end up with an even more higher intuition. Our life must be lived in the contemplation between these two intuitions and, without losing any of the freshness of the beginning which must perdure, all kinds of elements must be added, until it reaches the perfect fulfilment.[58]

We see here the significance of Chenu's original encounter in Le Saulchoir in 1913. The prompting of an intuition directed him to pursue the contemplative life in the Dominican order. The passage suggests that his whole life was situated between the original intuition of a vocation and the striving towards an even greater intuition of contemplation. The striving was expressed in the work of meditation, study, teaching, in the labour of reason.

Contemplation, then, is the characteristic of the Dominican order, the keystone unifying love, thought, and action. In this the Dominicans differ from both the Benedictines and the Franciscans, for whom life is centred around the liturgy and the choral office. For Dominicans, the

57 Ibid., 31. It is no coincidence that the echo of Thomistic epistemology is so evident here.

58 Ibid., 32–3.

office belongs properly to the religious life, while contemplation is a divine act.

Although present already in the early writings on the Dominican life, the reflection on evangelism became much more prominent after the initial encounter between Chenu and the JOC. My purpose here is not to give an exhaustive account of the importance of evangelism in the theology of Chenu, as this would take us too far, but to note its role in the shifting concept of contemplation.

There are two separate but related aspects to the idea of evangelism in the Dominican charism. The first is the primitive fact of evangelism, that is, its presence as a constitutive factor in the foundation of the order. The second is the particular face of this evangelism in the present world. This latter aspect will clearly vary according to the circumstances; it has, for instance, a different accent in 1936, during the Front Populaire government and the Action catholique period, from that at the height of the war.

A 1945 letter from Chenu to H. M. Féret shows well Chenu's dissatisfaction with the traditional schema of contemplation-action for understanding Dominican life, and articulates the reasons and causes of this dissatisfaction. At issue is a more total and more realistic view, one that would be true to both the human reality and the evangelism constitutive of the Dominican life. The letter is revealing in terms of Chenu's inability to resolve the tension fully:

An aggressive encounter (quite a summary one) with Marxism, and, at a deeper level, a certain apostolic involvement at strategic points, bring me to a more comprehensive conception of the relations between contemplative life and active life – where both human realism and Gospel realism are better implemented. It is true, as you say, that a certain contemplative snobbery (*aristocratisme*) – more Greek than Christian – unconsciously denigrates active labour and the role of man in creation. The mediaevals gathered together the whole economy of human existence under two headings: creation and re-creation (= redemption); while we, in a purely profane (that is, 'naturalist') philosophy, reject this first division, always being carried out by man himself. Even Augustine did not give in to this dualism because his recovery from Manichaeanism safeguarded him against it. Nonetheless I will grant that our evangelism is a dynamite difficult to handle! And I am far from possessing all the links which organize it into Thomistic 'wisdom': I try to grasp the two ends of the chain firmly; in other words, St. Dominic (and St. Francis) and St. Thomas. The path leading from the one to the other has moreover never been travelled without a hitch ... But we are at a juncture *(conjoncture)* where it is St. Dominic who renews St. Thomas – and prevents him from being no more than a ... superstructure (as Marx would say).[59]

The last remark is especially significant for the objective of this chapter. In the contemporary context, that is, towards the end of the 1940s, the renewal of Thomism was by way of St. Dominic. It is well known that the renewal of French theology was due in great part to the aposotolic *engagement* of many, but here the inspiration for the engagement is seen from within Dominican life.

The question that arises is what Chenu meant by "*aristocratisme*" in speaking of the traditional division between contemplation and action. In a 1978 conference to a group of Dominican provincial sisters, Chenu spoke of socialization and the need to think of salvation beyond individualistic terms. The dangers of individualism can also appear in our conception of the contemplative life and make it "aristocratic."

There is a sort of snobbery (*aristocratisme*) here, in contemplative life as well. And I, who (when I entered the Order) had experienced so strongly the contemplative life and its absoluteness – I thank God that I did not lose my bearings when I was in the vortex. Nonetheless the contemplation-action duo still seems to me to be insufficient to account for the reality. It is not part of the Gospel vocabulary. One never finds the distinction between contemplation and action

---

59 Letter of Chenu to H.M. Féret, 26 August 1945 (Archives OP France): "*Une rencontre offensive (bien sommaire) avec la philosophie marxiste, et, à un plan plus profond, un certain engagement apostolique aux points stratégiques, me mènent à une conception plus totale des rapports de la vie contemplative et de la vie active, où sont mieux ménagés le réalisme humain et le réalisme évangélique à la fois. Il est vrai, comme vous le dites, qu'un certain aristocratisme contemplatif, plus grec que chrétien, méprise inconsciemment le labeur actif et le rôle de l'homme dans la création. Les médiévaux rassemblaient toute l'économie humaine sous deux chefs: création et ré-création (= rédemption), – tandis que nous rejetons dans une philosophie purement profane, voire 'naturaliste', la première tranche, toujours en cours par l'homme précisément. Même Augustin n'avait pas cédé à ce dualisme car sa cure de Manichéisme l'avait garanti. J'accorderais cependant que notre évangélisme est une dynamite difficile à manier! Et je suis loin d'avoir tous les chainons qui l'organisent en 'sagesse' thomiste: j'essaie de tenir ferme les deux bouts; autrement dit: S. Dominique (+ S. François) et S. Thomas. Le chemin qui va de l'un à l'autre ne fut d'ailleurs jamais parcouru sans accrochage ... Mais nous sommes dans une conjoncture où c'est S.Dominique qui renouvelle S.Thomas – et l'empêchera de n'être plus qu'une ... superstructure (comme dirait Marx)."*

in the Gospel. The distinction is applied to the episode of Martha and Mary; but this is a dislocation of the episode. In other words, I give priority to this immersion in the world; without casting oneself into it so as to lose one's identity as a Christian. We see many laity and priests who become secularized; whatever judgment we may have to make later, this judgment is secondary.[60]

Evangelism is here associated with "*cette immersion dans le monde.*" Yet the text ought not to suggest that such immersion displaces the primacy of contemplation. What is displaced is the structure "contemplation-action" in favour of something more realistic. Later texts from Chenu show to what extent the primacy of contemplation remains constant.

The fact is that there is a displacement, of which Chenu is well aware. This was made apparent in a 1957 retreat preached to the Dominicans of Poitiers: "The way I construct my discourse now is not the way I would have done it twenty years ago: I would have begun with contemplation-action, ends and means. I have changed a great deal on this point. I would not wish to be untrue to what I was; what I have said to you over these four days is the new Chenu, since 1936. The old Chenu, the one who entered the Order, was not like this at all. The Lord has had me live a striking upheaval. I entered to be a contemplative! He certainly showed me."[61] The reference to 1936 situates the shift in its historical context. The situation of the French Church, the situation of the Dominican order, and Chenu's own place within these contexts, all called for a different kind of reflection. The very survival of the order required a different approach.

The objective is still the same, namely, to reflect on the nature of the Dominican vocation, to grasp the unity of a life. What in 1934 was the original experience of one's call is here replaced by a reflection on the sources of the Dominican charism. Inherent in this charism is the initial encounter with the world. This is the Dominican claim to evangelism: "This initial shock and the living milieu which conditioned it, this primitive fact on this side of the contemplation-action axis, we Dominicans have this always in our blood."[62] Chenu explains that the term *évangélisme* became current in the 1936–1940 period, at the height of

60 *Conférence aux Provinciales à Monteils*, 1978 (Archives OP de France), 15. Note the personal attestation to the importance of contemplation in Chenu's reference to his personal difficulties.

61 *Retraite à Poitiers*, 1957 (Archives OP de France), 30.

62 *Retraite à Poitiers*, 3: "*Ce choc initial et le milieu vital qui l'a conditionné, ce fait primitif en-deçà même de l'axe contemplation-action, nous, les dominicains, nous l'avons toujours dans la peau.*"

the Action catholique movements. Prior to that, it was associated with Protestantism and was suspect in Catholic circles. There were also different kinds of evangelism in the thirteenth century, some suspect in the eyes of the Church (e.g., Pierre de Vaux), others like that of St. Francis. Dominican evangelism must still be differentiated from these, at least, from the Benedictine charism, and the monastic tradition with its emphasis on the life of the counsels and on observances. Jordan of Saxony called St. Dominic *vir evangelicus* and this characterization is still retained in the Dominican constitutions.

Evangelism means, first of all, that the gospel is primary, not as moral teaching but as the good news, "*l'Évangile à l'état pur.*" Much of its prophetic power comes from an almost literalist reading of the gospel. This literalism is seen as a return to the gospel, but in terms of something actual: "God speaks today and we come back by it to the Church ... for the Spirit is present, the Spirit speaks today, by an act of presence in the Church."[63] Evangelism is thus actual: "Because of this actuality, today I am 'the man of men' (*l'homme des hommes*) (Liégé) in Christ who was made man, for his mystery is of today and he speaks today: this is the assurance that I am really on the ball, that I am able to be in touch with human experiences now in progress."[64] In this sense, the prophetic element is inherent in evangelism. Still, it is not possible to live evangelism by oneself, only within community. "But if I had to start over, I would start over, and even better! Ten, fifteen years ago, I would have spoken to you according to the received categories which were still valid. I would have said that the Order of St. Dominic is built around two poles: contemplation-action, a strong axis which will respond to the needs of today. Very well, we will come back to this; but we will begin instead with the primitive fact of the Order."[65]

Two things are important here. First, Chenu is talking about the situation of the Order in 1957, answering the question of what it meant to be a Dominican at the time. Because of changed circumstances in the Church and in society, this question has become inseparable from a reflection on socialization. The reference to the contemporary is crucial for an understanding of his Dominican vocation. Second, there is Chenu's changed approach, the different starting point, as compared to ten or fifteen years earlier. Yet the text from a 1941 retreat at Le

63 *Retraite à Poitiers*, 3.
64 Ibid.
65 *Retraite à Poitiers*, 2.

Saulchoir also begins with the "*fait primitif,*" and is especially attentive to the historical context of 1941 in terms of evangelism. We need to go back to the 1934 retreat text for the starting-point based exclusively on the contemplation-action axis. Yet even in 1957 Chenu does not reject the foundational role of contemplation, as the later sections of this retreat text show. There are many passages about contemplation that are taken *verbatim* from the earlier retreat texts.

Chenu again describes contemplation in absolute terms, dependent on nothing else. It is properly situated on the level of the theological life. This is different, according to Chenu, from the approach of the Benedictines, who are much more cultic than contemplative: "We must realize that is a gratuitous knowledge, pure, disinterested, a spiritual operation *par excellence,* with no useful purpose! It is gratuitous ... So much so that a Dominican faces the temptation of exclusive contemplation, to enter the Carthusians for example."[66] Chenu's so-called temptation is documented elsewhere. It testifies to the centrality of contemplation in his life.[67] "Building the community life, balancing the forces at work in a convent, this is contemplation. Without it, we either fall into the established institution or else everything falls away piecemeal. The unity of the *vita communis* will not be present ... Contemplative life structures a Dominican house: contemplation is the locus of unity, both in the house and in the apostolate. A community of brethren in the faith; this is contemplative life."[68] Contemplation is further described as "an extraordinary power of invention in order to discern new apostolic forms"; it is inventive in the discernment of apostolic reality.[69] Why are such dignity and primacy attributed to contemplation? "Because contemplation will reach even the theological virtue, for it is a unique act which gathers together the whole power of faith, of the love of Christ in himself and in his brothers, a kind of passionate hope: the Kingdom, I will build it."[70]

There follows a personal witness on the role and function of contemplation: "And even I, in twenty five years, have never missed what is called meditative prayer (*oraison*), it seems to me a vital reflex; if I don't

66 *Retraite à Poitiers,* 1957, 30–1.

67 See on this the letter of Chenu recently published by A. Duval in *Vie spirituelle.* See also *Saint Thomas et la théologie,* 62.

68 *Retraite à Poitiers,* 31.

69 Ibid., 31: "*une puissance d'invention extraordinaire pour inventer les nouvelles formes apostoliques*"; cf. also 33.

70 Ibid., 32.

do it, I become anemic. I do more than the required half-hour, I must have moments of absolute gratuitousness … It is likely that if I did not have this fidelity, there are times in these last fifteen years where I would have gone off the rails."[71] Also: "This interiorization concentrates my strength and gathers my energies. When there is a goal to be reached, everything becomes focused. Nothing makes you quite as free. People ask themselves, How can you live with all these chains, in all this mess? First of all, part of it is habit, yes, but also, beyond that, there is this kind of freedom."[72] Still, it is not only a personal affair: if one fails in contemplation, the whole community suffers. "If contemplation were to lack, the whole Dominican reality would be diminished. Contemplation is necessary for the Order to remain faithful to the inspiration of St. Dominic, that is, to be an evangelical order."[73] For Chenu, there is always an ecclesial reality involved in the most personal contemplation.

The apostolate is also an absolute end. Contemplation does not exist to result in apostolic action, through some kind of emanation. That would make contemplation the sole end: "This would be the same as seeing only one end: contemplation. In the past (*autrefois*), I used to think this way. This is a mistake for the apostolate is a value in itself, it is autonomous and one can speak of an apostolic wholeness."[74] Why confer such dignity on it? Because apostolic action is a gesture of love, an act of the theological virtue of charity. In this context, contemplation is related to redemption: "In the end, my contemplation is linked to the economy of redemption, and if the preacher sometimes is silent, his silence is not that of the desert, of the monastic city, but it is a silence before the world."[75] The world plays a crucial function. Hence, there is a complete break with a certain view of the Greek idea of contemplation, according to which the world is only an appearance to be overcome in favour of immaterial reality.

A further piece of evidence for the centrality of contemplation, even in the context of evangelism, is found in the text from the 1941 retreat given at Le Saulchoir. Prior to his consideration of the ends of the Dominican life, Chenu begins a reflection on the Dominican charism with the primitive fact of evangelism. It is "primitive" because it belongs

71 Ibid., 32.
72 Ibid., 29.
73 Ibid., 32.
74 Ibid., 33. It is not clear when the "*autrefois*" refers to, perhaps to the early thirties when he said that a given retreat could end with the talk on contemplation.
75 Ibid., 34.

to the constitutive experience of Dominican life. A return to the sources, to the origins of the Order's inspiration, is thus a part of any endeavour of self-reflection. The necessity of "recovering one's milieu" is further dictated by the situation of the Church. It is this situation that has changed since Chenu first entered the order. There now exists the phenomenon of socialization, which calls for a re-examination of an individual's reasons for being a Dominican, or simply a Christian. "Since the 16th century, when Luther harnessed all the evangelical forces, we have been afraid of this strong wine, and we leave the world to its misery and ignorance. It is now others who have stepped in (e.g., K. Marx)."[76]

What, then, is the form of evangelism in the contemporary context? What is the task of the "*témoin évangélique*" in September 1941? "As a first step, we must absolutely enter, each and every one of us, into the distress of the world, the suffering of souls and bodies, even those of our momentary conquerors, in this darkness, in this social, economic, and political breakdown on a global scale, *massa peccati*. Original sin is reaching maturity. I cannot remove myself from this and live in a pseudo-fervour, in a pseudo-detachment: the Order was born from the observation of an identical distress, it can only live in this way; never will it have so many reasons to live."[77] Chenu makes clear the link between the evangelism of the thirteenth century and the present situation. It is even more dramatic because of the circumstances in occupied Paris. The reflection is not an abstract theorizing about the sinful condition of the world, since the reality of the war penetrates even the walls of Le Saulchoir: "What can be done in this unfinished convent, with our 25 prisoners, this bleeding wound through which I feel a part of our strength is seeping away every day – I think of this or that Father whom we would need so much for our present work – in an occupied France, liberated tomorrow, what can be done?"[78]

Whatever the particular context, the work of Le Saulchoir remains clear. The scholarly efforts during the war period attest to the Dominican freedom. "I have shared with you that I entered the Order by the door of contemplation, which normally would have led me to the Carthusians. But now I am stuck; the call of St. Dominic seized me with great sorrow – cosmic, human, Christian sorrow – before a great distress, at the time when my German brothers and my Russian brothers

---

76 *Retraite au Saulchoir*, 1941 (Archives OP de France), 8.
77 *Retraite au Saulchoir*, 34.
78 *Retraite au Saulchoir*, 34.

were killing each other with an insatiable hatred, when the most dreadful famine was sure to arrive on the morrow ... Nonetheless, sharing in this sorrow (even in our feelings), we do not wallow in it, we do not cease to be masters of our own work, we do not on its account skip over even the smallest footnote on a page."[79] Despite the clarity of the task to be continued, the concrete conditions for the work are far from clear. The old Christendom is gone, but no-one knows what will replace it. The awareness of the dawn of a new world yields uncertainty and darkness rather than euphoria. How will the order of St. Dominic be present in these circumstances? What are the concrete conditions for this presence? Chenu answers:

In darkness. For a year now, when people have come to see me, I have had to reply that I see nothing. I am in darkness ... Let us not be surprised at this, it is the law of the species. When he started in 1205, St. Dominic didn't know where he was going and he didn't see clearly ... One must work in the dark. What is needed is spirit, whole, without plans and without recompense, in the twofold night of matter's opacity and man's freedom ... One, and only one, point of reference: the power of truth ... There is a work to be undertaken: work with a broad vision, this is the standard today for dealing adequately with men and events. What is needed in the Church today is not so much each one of us, as teams equal to the task – and we are by rights such a team. Any problem posed today other than in global terms is badly posed. What will give me this? Contemplation, that disinterested knowledge (cleared of so-called practical solutions); and therefore not activism under the pretext of going as fast as possible. One must always rise in this way above one's surroundings, like a swimmer who always keeps his head above water. It is contemplation which gives one this power of vision and this independence.[80]

Far from displacing it, the dramatic circumstances only serve to heighten the witness to the primacy of contemplation in the Dominican life.

STUDY

The unifying role of contemplation was developed by Chenu in relation to all facets of religious life. We will have occasion to return to some of them. One, however, deserves to be treated here: the place of study in

---

79 Ibid., 34–35.
80 *Retraite au Saulchoir*, 34.

the Dominican life. The relationship between study and the theological act of contemplation is of special interest; the more technical relationship between faith and theology is left to the following chapter.

Study is an immediate means of the contemplative life.[81] As a Dominican, one must constantly be in quest of greater light; one must keep the mind open to the life of Church: "Inwardly one must always seek light, always keep one's soul open to light; not only to high points of doctrine, but to the activity of the Order, to the Missions, to the life of Christendom. Here we will find many questions; one must keep one's eyes open to this. The cloister furnishes us with means of contemplation, but our contemplation remains apostolic; one must defend oneself against a certain narrowness of horizon, one must have some basic vista. St. Thérèse was as it were haunted by the battle being waged in the Church. She knew the struggles of the Church against Luther, the councils, the battles ... one ought to know that presently, such and such a problem exists, and have the sense of certain contemporary pains of Christendom. It is a contemplative exercise."[82]

This passage reminds us of Chenu's list of "signs of the times" given just a few years later in *Une École de théologie*. For Chenu, the relation between intellectual appetite – the quest for light – and the contemplative act is undeniable. It is a characteristic of the Dominican order. He makes this clear in the last words in the conference on study: "May your contemplation be nourished by this study, so that you may live in the spirit of the Order and in this way you may be not merely religious but truly Dominican religious."[83]

The role of study in the Dominican life is spelled out in the Dominican constitution. In the 1968 reform of the constitution, there was a shift in favour of a greater role for study, which moved the Order closer to the original intentions of the founder.[84] Chenu's role in that reform was inspirational. The role of study is obviously crucial in a theological centre such as Le Saulchoir. Chenu spelled out the role of

81 Cf. *Retraite au Monastère de la Croix*, 1934, 75: "*L'étude, la lecture spirituelle, ce n'est pas un exercice entre plusieurs d'autres; c'est une pièce maîtresse organisée, ordonnée à notre vie contemplative ... c'est un moyen immédiat de vie contemplative.*"

82 Ibid., 75. The mention of the cloister (*clôture*), of course, comes because of the nature of the public of this retreat. Yet the link between study, intellectual curiosity, and contemplation is valid for all members of the Dominican order.

83 Ibid., 76.

84 Emilio Garcia Alvarez, "La teología en el carisma Dominicano," *CT* 76 (1985), 277–96.

contemplation in the general development of theological research and formation.

In March 1936, as regent of studies at Le Saulchoir, Chenu gave the traditional panegyric on the feast of St. Thomas. It was an important talk, the basis of what was to become the following year the booklet *Une école de théologie. Le Saulchoir.* It was a reflection on the spirit of Le Saulchoir, as well as on the constitutive components of the Dominican life in relation to its intellectual vocation.[85]

Specifically, the objective of the panegyric was to give an account of spiritual freedom as the principal characteristic of the Dominican order: clarity and intellectual independence manifested in the various expressions of Dominican scholarly work. The technical labour, the monthly or weekly periodicals, all point to a cult of truth. The conference takes as its theme the liberating function of truth, its sources, guaranties, and conditions, looking first at the life and works of St. Thomas as a point of reference, then at life in Le Saulchoir.

Since we will later be discussing St. Thomas in detail, a mention of his freedom in relation to Aristotle and Averroes and of the claims of "natural" reason in the face of revelation, will suffice here. The sources and guarantee of this freedom lie in the distinctions made on the epistemological level between formal objects of knowledge. More profoundly, such freedom is grounded in the pure contemplation of truth.[86]

The conditions for the exercise of such freedom are the same in the twentieth as in the thirteenth century. The foundation of the modern Le Saulchoir took place in the midst of the modernist crisis, while the very term "modernism" was coming into existence. The first condition of Le Saulchoir's spiritual and intellectual freedom lies in its permanent openness and state of invention. Its working method concentrates on texts, on primary sources, with an orientation to original problems and questions rather than ready-made answers. In this context, Le Saulchoir has strived to distance itself from the "commentary" genre or any identification with a "Thomist school."[87] The second condition lies in episte-

---

85 "Veritas liberabit vos. 'La vérité vous rendra libre' (Jn 8, 32)" (1990), 97–106.

86 Ibid., 101; cf. also 98–9.

87 Ibid., 101–3. This argument and the arguments for the second and third conditions are renewed and developed extensively in *Une École de théologie.* We will be returning to this subject in a later chapter.

mology, in the proper management of the scientific approach to various levels of knowledge.[88]

The third condition concerns the theme of this chapter more directly. When we juggle texts, various levels of knowledge, and different formal objects, we quickly move beyond the indispensable intellectual and religious unity. For this unity a permanent source of recapitulation is needed, otherwise "we would perhaps have a freedom to work, but we would lose the inner freedom through the scattering of our mind."[89] In this context, the third and supreme condition of Dominican freedom is contemplation. "As for me, I do not think that we can maintain (either psychologically or religiously) our unity of spirit and work outside of a contemplative life. This is, moreover, the authentic statute of the Order, both as a religious institution (contemplation is its end) and as a 'theological corporation'. This, at any rate, was the essential rule of St. Thomas and the key of his spiritual freedom – throughout an intellectual undertaking which, at certain times, was dramatic inside and out. So it must be for us, individually and collectively."[90]

As in other texts, here Chenu once again affirms contemplation as the end of the order and its "authentic status." The function of contemplation is to provide the unity of life and, now, to guarantee Dominican freedom. Far from being an occasional exercise fulfilled out of obligation and lying "outside" or "beyond" the daily order of things, contemplation is the "*spiritual milieu where we will hold the fervour of invention and the methodical order in which knowledge is organized.*"[91] It is thus the necessary ground for the first two conditions of freedom, determining the very structure of theology, which will be both "a delightful adherence to the given (*donné*) of revelation, then a trust in the working of reason with all its instruments in the midst of this faith."[92]

88 Ibid., 102–3.

89 Ibid., 104: "*Nous aurions peut-être une liberté de travail, mais nous perdrions la liberté intérieure par la dispersion de notre esprit.*" Chenu continues: "*Au dessus de la science et des sciences, il nous faut une 'sagesse'.*"

90 Ibid., 104.

91 Ibid., 104, Chenu's emphasis. He continues: "*[La contemplation] n'est que connaissance pure, désintéressée, où la vérité n'est pas traitée comme une chose 'utile', même apostoliquement parlant, mais comme un objet de contemplation. De là notre conception de la théologie. Notre théologie est contemplative non pas seulement en principe, en gros, mais dans sa structure même.*" From here, he moves to the argument in favour of the primacy of the *donné* received in faith and its fruitfulness in terms of theological progress.

92 Ibid., 105.

We shall return to this theme when considering the function and tasks of theology.

THEOLOGICAL OPTIMISM AND
THE GROUNDS FOR HOPE

The last conference of the 1934 retreat is also of interest to anyone beginning a study of Chenu's theology. Bearing on Dominican life itself, its theme is the theological optimism of the order. During the crisis of the worker-priests in the early 1950s, and during and after the Council of Vatican II, Chenu was often accused of excessive optimism. It is a charge that was never satisfactorily explained, somewhat resembling an aftertaste that can never quite be pinned down. In this text from 1934, Chenu reflects on optimism as related to the very charism of the Dominican order: "If I seek at the end of these conferences to rewrite the drama of our life, if I attempt to grasp the appearance of its architecture – well, the artist who contemplates his work sees not only its parts, but beyond these something more subtle, something very spiritual which animates it all. If I want to set down in one word this impression, to grasp the spirit which animates our Dominican institution, it seems to me that I do not end up with this or that resolution ... it seems to me that I end in an interior fulfilment, a security, a simplicity of soul. We have added one element to another, and yet all of this is very simple; we reconquer, and we renew in ourselves that which makes, at the core of our soul, for Dominican optimism. It is surely with this word that I would wish to end."[93]

Such optimism is first of all grounded in a state of health, achieved though a perfect exercise of life's virtues, "*une vitalité en perfection*," a hygiene of the soul. The Dominican life involves all of life's functions, organised in a regime of counsels and precepts. However, this life is not seen in terms of an individual project, a result of our own construction, or as a formalism: "It is something entirely natural which flows from the source."[94] There is an element of passivity, a reliance on trust in the Holy Spirit. Such is the equilibrium of the Dominican life.

Yet it is all still on the moral plane. It would remain an unattainable ideal, an abstract ideal, were it not incarnate. The beautiful and complex architecture that the Dominican life represents is to be inhabited by God, who is person rather than ideal. The second ground for Domin-

93 Retreat (1934), 108.
94 Ibid., 108.

ican optimism is thus the theological life, God's life in us. If Dominican life were only on the human level, there would be grounds for fear. As it is, the life of God is so incarnate in the human virtues that there is a state of hope, a state of security. The presence of God is not proportional to human efforts and discipline: "Religious and Dominican life is a life of greatness. Because all our strength is in God, we are at once humble and great."[95]

Here, Chenu takes another crucial step. Theological optimism is grounded in Christ and finds there its point of reference. "But all this divine strength is grounded in Christ; and therefore this health, this theological optimism, this is still very human. God is our model. Such a virtue cannot be seen in the abstract; we must experience it in God. But this divine behaviour, where can we see them? We can see them only in Christ because in him we find behaviour at once divine and human, with all the realism this entails. Such is the balance of our Dominican life. We Dominicans, more than others, have this sense of the Incarnation, the sense of this fullness of divine life given to man."[96]

The step becomes more concrete – and this bears specifically on the charge of excessive optimism – when Chenu considers the question of sin, present despite the grandeur of the architecture. Once again, the problem of human weakness, of human sinfulness, is not resolved through an effort which would be nothing more than moralism, but through a reference to Christ. The solution is from above: "Let us have the courage of our faults, not in ourselves, but in the suffering and dying Christ, and thereby we will escape the lukewarmness and mediocrity awaiting us in our spiritual life; we will thereby master our sins and we will escape, not directly, but upwards in Christ. And that which was the cause of our fall will become an occasion for growth. Sin itself is thus an occasion of growth in the divine life. '*Felix culpa.*'"[97] This christological reference is not unique in the 1934 retreat text. There are long sections on the sacraments and the life in Christ, to be considered more particularly in the chapter on the place of Christ in the theology of Chenu.

The final ground of Dominican optimism lies in contemplation, the gaze of faith animated by love. The health of an ordered and full life, its equilibrium, all find their summit in the contemplative act. The unfolding (*épanouissement*) of the intimacy of the life in God occurs of its own

95 Ibid., 110.
96 Ibid., 110.
97 Ibid., 110.

accord. Here lies the origin of Dominican freedom. Far from leading to a life of compulsory exercises, contemplation yields a liberation. It does so primarily through providing the unity of life – of the exterior and the interior life – a unity which manifests itself as joy, participation in the joy of Christ.[98]

THE MIXED LIFE

Although Chenu at times exaggerated his rejection of his former "aristocratic" view of the "contemplation-action duo," it is clear that contemplation remains paramount within a renewed understanding of evangelism. Herein lies the significance of calling the Dominican order a "mixed" order. This appellation does not imply a mixture of action and contemplation, nor contemplation with a view to action, in a sort of emanatism, "but a contemplation which is sought and cultivated for itself, as a supreme good, a definitive value, whose fullness will be such, however, that it will overflow in a radiance of religious light, in a teaching or a preaching."[99] The much vaunted freedom of the Dominicans is at least partially grounded in the status of a mixed order. "The more contemplation is regarded as a supreme value, then the more it will be pursued as an end and established as a keystone (not only in the progress of an individual, but in the structure of the institution), and the more it will be *free*, the more it will be *pure*, even unto its most compromising contacts. None of its incarnations so embodies its light and power that contemplation finds itself fastened and weighed down by that incarnation. A formidable dignity. But our daily failures do not give us the right to neglect this fine point. The whole history and the whole spirit of St. Dominic's Order is here, in this fierce and candid independence with respect to every compromise – whether economic, social, political, even 'clerical' (*sit venia verbo!*)."[100] The mixed state underlines the primacy of contemplation and therefore the ever-new gaze on reality, seeking the world in com-

---

98 Cf. 112–13.

99 "Une religion contemplative," *VS* 43 (1935), 86. The text is from Chenu's favourable review of M.-M. Davy's *Les Dominicaines*.

100 Ibid., 88–9. In an interview with *La Croix* (15–16 November 1981), Chenu gives a more popular definition of the Dominican mixed status; see 11: "*Un être entièrement polarisé par la parole de Dieu. Et sur la parole de Dieu. Un dominicain c'est celui qui sait tenir les deux à la fois. L'ordre des Frères prêcheurs est un ordre de prêtres mais moi ce n'est pas le sacerdoce qui m'y a attiré, c'est la parole. L'écoute de la parole* [i.e., contemplation] *déclenche en moi une vie contemplative. Et presque aussitôt, dans un second temps, se déclenche l'envie de dire la parole.*"

munion with "the generosity, the impatience, and the curiosity of generations in the course of time."[101]

Although the mixed life represents the fullest context in which to understand the relationship between contemplation and action in the Dominican life, we might object that this view is limited to the early Chenu. Can it not be said that the primacy of contemplation is superseded by concern with the social question and rivalled by the primacy of evangelism resulting from Chenu's encounter with the JOC?

We have already seen that, in the text preached at the 1957 retreat at Poitiers, Chenu maintained the primacy of contemplation and at the same time stressed the need to begin with the primitive fact of evangelism. Chenu's *St Thomas et la théologie* provides a mature view of contemplation in the doctrine of St. Thomas. It is a very compact presentation of the theology and spirituality of St. Thomas, but it is also a highly personal interpretation. In it, St. Thomas is fully appropriated, presented very much as a living theologian whose thought is highly relevant to the twentieth century. Chenu devotes an entire chapter to Thomas the contemplator.[102] In the life of St. Thomas Chenu finds the elements of evangelism fully integrated with the pure act of contemplation. Both are clearly situated within the theological life.

Contemplation is simply an act of the theological life, of the divine life that is in us in participated form. As such, it is immediately beyond the scope of all acts belonging to the merely religious life. The contemplative person no longer lives for God, but of God. Hence love is primary: "Thus charity inspires and sets the standard. Who better than the contemplator of God to gauge his acts in terms of charity? At the heart of his love, all of the lofty sentiments which make up the 'religious' soul grow deaf, in an acute sense of the Father's transcendence and the uttermost sense of his mercy; but at the same time the great apostolic vocations are born, vocations which, in the Gospel witness, set in motion sensitivity to the wretchedness and hope of men."[103]

Contemplation is both theological and evangelical. For Chenu, there is no contradiction: "Thomas Aquinas expresses the primitive Gospel in doctrine and accomplishes it in his life. *There is no greater sign of love than to go and contemplate.*"[104] The all-encompassing unity of contemplation,

101 Ibid., 89.
102 Cf. "Le contemplatif," in *St Thomas et la théologie,* 51–84.
103 Ibid., 56.
104 Ibid., 58, Chenu's emphasis.

as architectural keystone for life, overcomes the dangers of any aristocratic or moralistic tendency by providing a unity of life (the mixed
state) greater than a life of pure contemplation. The unity of action and
contemplation stems from a passion for the gospel, an evangelical passion where the active love of others is the very love of Christ in others:
"No humanism can reach this unified wholeness where the preoccupation with the salvation of the world flows from the living knowledge of
the incarnate God. These are the two faces of the same mystery, in the
humanity of God."[105]

A reflection that began with the significance of an encounter has led
from a consideration of contemplation as the highest act of our intellectual and spiritual life, to the role of contemplation in the Dominican life
as provider of unity, and finally to the incarnation as the ultimate reason
for the mixed state of life.

---

105 Ibid., 63.

2

Faith and Theology

IN THE PREVIOUS CHAPTER, the concept of incarnation emerges as the ground for the mixed life whose primary objective is contemplation. From the intimate and personal matters of the life of faith and the organization of that life in a religious order, we move to the more public writings of Marie-Dominique Chenu.

The first step in our gradual approach to an understanding of incarnation takes us into the midst of a neoscholastic discussion of the role of faith in theology and the nature of theology as a science. The discussion is important for this study because Chenu's contribution to it clearly manifests the basic elements of the function of incarnation: to preserve the transcendent character of faith and at the same time to respect the integrity of human knowing in all its manifestations. Chenu's contribution establishes a pattern that will be repeated in the later chapters. Its aim in this case is to overcome the alienating dualism between faith and reason by stressing its theandric nature, that is, its supernatural character and the integrity of its human condition.

After a brief examination of theological contexts and available options of the time, Chenu's doctrine of faith is presented here in light of its use of incarnation language and motifs. An analysis of Chenu's position on the relationship of faith and reason and the development of theological science follows. Finally, theological reflection is described in terms of mystical perception, rational construction, and the centrality of contemplation, all of which Chenu brings to bear in striving to overcome an alienating dualism between mysticism and theology by means of incarnation.

BACKGROUND AND FORERUNNERS

Much of Roman Catholic theology in the early 1900s was characterized by an anti-Protestant tendency. This post-Tridentine theology was a reaction against a perceived threat of reductionism to the religious sentimentality of subjective experience. Chenu's theological effort would be in reaction to this anti-Lutheran theology, which proclaimed the faith of authority in opposition to any emphasis on subjectivity or mysticism in the experience of faith. In the view of Chenu and his colleagues at Le Saulchoir, the fear of mysticism made some throw the baby out with the bathwater.

The anti-Lutheran theology proclaiming the "faith of authority" is an explicit allusion to Louis Billot (1846–1931), who was the best-known representative of mainstream scholastic theology at the turn of the last century.[1] Chenu acknowledged the importance of the Gregorian university professor; he even compared Billot's role in Roman theology to that of Cardinal Merry del Val in Roman politics. Billot was concerned with countering the rationalistic tendencies of nineteenth-century Roman Catholic theology and its view of faith as a syllogistic argument. He distinguished scientific faith, which is arrived at by means of rational argumentation, and a "*foi d'autorité*" or a "*foi d'hommage*" given on the basis of the credibility and authority of the witness. In this case, the witness is God. Faith is thus the intellectual assent to the authority of the witness of God, the initial assent independent of the rational work that follows.

Billot successfully untangled faith from a rationalizing burden imposed on it by the scholastic inheritors of the Enlightenment, allowing it to transcend its assimilation in a syllogism. This was a major achievement, and Billot's position was recognized and generally accepted as the new consensus. Still, there were problems with his position, not least among them the danger of fideism. Billot's radical separation of faith and reason resulted in a gulf between belief and the actual motives for the Christian act of faith. Any rational effort at understanding the reasons for belief was suspect of promoting "scientific faith," and the so-called motives of credibility remained without any real connection to the act of faith. The two poles of faith and reason found themselves

---

1 For background on Louis Billot, his theology of faith, as well as some of the criticisms it encountered, see R. Aubert, *Le problème*, 241–55. Billot was also known as a ferocious opponent of modernism.

locked in an almost dualistic tension. Ultimately, both reason and grace were shortchanged.

Chenu lamented Billot's one-sided emphasis on the intellectual dimension of faith and the consequent displacement of the mysterious and the personal in the experience of faith. "Billot, whose works I studied much at that time [i.e., 1910s], was a first class theologian, but he was enclosed in one sector of theology arrogantly ignoring all the others. Confined to one sector, he became sectarian, in the etymological sense of the word. He was highly intelligent but his intellectualism made him insensitive to the irrational paths of the mystery of faith. He expressed the mystery in a purely intellectual way, beyond all personal experience."[2]

Billot's suspicion of anything subjective in the area of faith and theology is attested by an unconditional commitment to his version of cognitive clarity. It can also be confirmed by his reaction to the modernist crisis and his involvement in the opposition to it. At one time, it was even suggested that Billot was responsible for the redaction of the encyclical *Pascendi domini grecis*, which officially condemned modernism, although it is more likely that he only participated in its preparation. Be that as it may, he remained always contemptuous of any appeal to subjective experience, spiritual or affective. For Chenu, the ultimate implication of Billot's position was "a theology of faith entirely defined by conceptual and juridical authority, without any methodological influence of the mystery which is, for all that, its very object."[3] The danger in such an authoritarian position was that theology might turn into ideology, that is, become an instrument of power.

As a first step towards restoring the coherence between faith and reason, it was necessary to give faith a real role in the epistemological foundation of theology. It was precisely to overcome the dualism inherent in Billot's position that Ambroise Gardeil, followed by Chenu, emphasized the supernatural character of faith. In Chenu's words, Gardeil opposed

---

2 *Duquesne* (1975), 30. Chenu notes that Billot was closed to any historical approach; he was "*tout à fait étranger aux résultats de l'histoire.*" See also Jean Galot's notice in the *NCE* 2, 558: "Billot is justly praised for possessing a remarkable ability to speculate dogmatically and for his concern in giving a vigorous structure to theology. On the other hand, it must be admitted that he showed almost no interest at all in positive theology, and that at times he even mistrusted it."

3 *Duquesne* (1975), 31, cf. "Foi et théologie" (1956), in *Parole* 1, 272. See also "Vérité et liberté" (1959), in *Parole* 1, 340: "*un intellectualisme autoritaire peu sensible aux voies du mystère de la foi comme aux réalités de l'histoire*".

to Billot's "faith of simple authority," the accredited theology of the time, "a mysterious faith in which grace would obtain a shadowy view of the testimony warranted by God."[4]

Along with the likes of P. Battifol, L. de Grandmaison, and M.-J. Lagrange, Gardeil has been historically located as a "*progressiste*," occupying a third-party position between the extremes of the modernists on the left and the anti-modernist integralists on the right.[5] Gardeil is a transitional figure between the "older" theology of the nineteenth century and the "new" theology that foreshadowed the second Vatican Council. He represents a reorientation within the tradition of neoscholasticism, a tendency that attempted a dialogue with recent developments in modern thought on the basis of a rediscovery of medieval sources. More specifically, Gardeil is credited with the rediscovery of the Thomistic teaching on the *lumen fidei* and the supernatural character of faith. Faith is not empty obedience, as Billot and his school suggested, but "an active understanding of the mystery, a progressive outline of the definitive vision." Chenu offers the following evaluation of Gardeil's work: "It is in effect the point of impact of P. Gardeil's Thomistic theology: against the most widespread opinions ... P. Gardeil restores the substantial supernaturality of the faith, in its theological reality and its systematic definition."[6]

Gardeil was concerned with the reform of theological studies in the face of acute criticisms regarding the extrinsicist character of theological reflection. He emphasized the nature and dignity of theological reasoning, intending to show its validity in terms of both revelation and Christian experience. Hence, he focused on the continuity ("*homogénéité*") between revelation and the theological conclusion: "No antinomy therefore between the religious knowledge of the believer and the speculation of the theologian, but a deep homogeneity." Likewise, Gardeil saw no discontinuity among the transcendent revela-

---

4 "Foi et théologie" (1956), in *Parole* 1, 272. On Ambroise Gardeil (1859–1931), see H.-D. Gardeil, *L'Oeuvre Théologique du Père A. Gardeil* (Paris: Vrin, 1956); "Notes et communications," *BT*, 8 (31), 69*–90*. On the importance of Gardeil's *Le donné révélé et la théologie*, see Chenu's Preface to the second edition (Paris: Éditions du Cerf, 1932), also published in *Parole* 1, 277–82.

5 This classification was made by Étienne Fouilloux, "Le Saulchoir en procès (1937–1942)," in M.-D. Chenu, *Une école de théologie: Le Saulchoir* (Paris: Éditions du Cerf, 1985), 43; this is a reissue of the 1937 *pro manuscripto* edition. Cf. also Émile Poulat, *Le catholicisme sous l'observation* (Paris: Le Centurion, 1983), 177, 180.

6 "Foi et théologie" (1956), in *Parole* 1, 270, 273.

tion, personal appropriation, and theological speculation. The focal point where this continuity is played out is precisely the *lumen fidei*: "It is faith which from one end to the other spreads its light ... an interior illumination of the Holy Spirit, even to the point of using reason's minor premises."[7]

Gardeil's basic rediscovery concerns the Thomistic teaching on the light of faith, the inward illumination of the Spirit that presents the truths of revelation in terms of values perceived by the religious subject. The act of faith is given moorings in human reality without at the same time having its non-human or divine origin denied. A bridge is thereby erected between the data of revelation and the believing subject.

This attention to the subject reveals the wider context of the discussion, namely, scholasticism's answer to the Blondellian challenge and that of the modernists. Gardeil was writing at the very dawn of the renaissance of Thomism, when scholasticism was still mired in Cartesian and Wolffian rationalism. The religious and intellectual crisis that Christianity was undergoing at the time centred on a radical critique of intellectualist understanding, extrinsicism, and juridicism. In the view of Chenu, Gardeil was able to steer a middle course between the extremes of the modernist left and the reaction of the right. Without falling victim to a "certain Thomist overbidding" of established scholasticism, Gardeil offered a reflection determined by "scientific detachment." His work thus remained outside the immediate fray and beyond the heat of the battle: "It was doubtless the way to escape the fever, dangerous in the realm of science as elsewhere, of those who live under a state of siege." Gardeil probably offered the most lucid and comprehensive theological answer to the problems triggered by the modernist controversy.[8]

Such is the background to Chenu's theological *corpus*. His contribution to theology is oriented in terms of the positions delineated above.

7 "Préface" (1932) to the second edition of Gardeil's *Le donné révélé et la théologie*, in *Parole* 1, 280, 279.

8 *Une école de théologie* (1937), 39. The "state of siege" mentality is described more fully on 44. Established by the Thomists of the sixteenth and seventeenth centuries, it was a reaction against the humanism of Erasmus, the religious revolution of Luther, the scientific revolution of Galileo, and the philosophical revolution of Descartes. See also G. Angelini, "La vicenda della teologia cattolica nel secolo XX," *Dizionario Teologico Interdisciplinare* (Torino: Marietti, 1977), 3, 614: "*La riposta teologica probabilmente più lucida e comprensiva alla problematica suscitata dalla controversia modernista ...* " Schoof, *Survey*, 68, refers to the work of Gardeil and Rousselot as "[t]he only signs of theological life that were to be found in the Church after the defeat of modernism."

We would not be far from the truth in describing his work as a development of the fundamental intuitions of Gardeil and a rejection of the extrinsicism typified by Billot.

CHENU'S TREATISE ON FAITH

It is in his treatise on the doctrine of faith that Chenu introduces the language of incarnation. As in the matter of the mixed character of the Dominican life, here too the incarnation serves to hold together two elements that would otherwise collapse reductively or else fall into dualism.

Essentially, Chenu follows the Dominican position on the doctrine of faith and its supernatural character, as represented by the writings of Gardeil, although he frees the latter from a certain emphasis on the theoretical and the abstract. He is less bound to neoscholastic terminology and more open to the context of life in the contemporary Church. One author has described Chenu's effort as belonging to "a tendency to vivify what the work of the masters [i.e., Gardeil and Garrigou-Lagrange] retains of its somewhat abstract and rigid content, by means of a more conscious reference to the concrete data of religious psychology."[9] Chenu himself acknowledged the decisive contribution of Gardeil and his role during the crisis years (1904–05), noting that Gardeil's *Le donné révélé* represented "the breviary of theological method" in Le Saulchoir and adding that Mandonnet and Lemonnyer made Gardeil's theory less heavy and abstract.[10]

In many ways Chenu was fighting the same surviving elements of baroque scholasticism that were challenged by the modernists. In each case the enemy was excessive extrinsicism and juridicism. Far from buckling under, this type of theology felt itself vindicated by the Roman condemnation in *Pascendi*.[11] Chenu was still denouncing all attempts at

---

9 Cf. René Aubert, *Le problème*, 588. A little further (589, n. 4), commenting on Chenu's *Une école de théologie*, Aubert notes in parentheses that "*il semble que parmis les motifs possibles de la récente mise à l'index de cet ouvrage, il ne faille pas compter sa doctrine sur la foi qui est dans la pure tradition thomiste.*" In *Survey*, 194, Mark Schoof writes: " ... Gardeil's rather barren vision was ultimately transformed by Chenu's emphasis on the contemporary context, his realistic approach to history and his consistent elaboration of the full humanity of the scientific study of theology."

10 Cf. *Une école de théologie* (1937), 40.

11 Cf. M. Schoof, *Survey*, 68. See also *Transcendence and Immanence*, 220, where G. Daly correctly points out that this vindication applied to "mainline theology." This remark undercuts the claim according to which this Roman theology was the only kind available until Vatican II.

glorifying the divine and the supernatural at the expense of the human reality. In his assessment of the modernist crisis, he protested against the excesses of the conservatives, who were victorious with *Pascendi* and who concentrated all their efforts on eradicating the modernist heresy instead of answering its challenge. Chenu's description of the sixteenth-century Roman theologians defending Catholic truth against Luther and the humanism of Erasmus might equally be applied to the *Pascendi* theologians. A state of siege mentality involving a defense of the truth and dignity of faith saw the transformation of a process of conservation into an instance of petrification, of a spirit of invention into a spirit of possession: "A state of siege, in which the grandeur of their faith and the resistance of their knowledge were worthily manifested, but in which they happened by a strange psychological inversion to treat the truth as a possession, creating rights, proprietary rights, upon which one rests as upon a definitive claim." After further denouncing the "cheating" of manual theology and the decadence of school theology, Chenu describes the spirit of contemporary theology as following the same path as in the sixteenth and seventeenth centuries, rather than that of the medieval Summas. A theology based on a defense against enemies, for Chenu it should instead build and develop on the basis of its own principles: "A theology is not built with an *anti-*, but according to its own principles and the internal hierarchy of its objects."[12]

Chenu's effort to restore the supernatural character of faith by emphasizing the realism of the "supernatural illumination" and the "interior mystery of divine knowledge" was grounded in a return to the original texts of St. Thomas. At the same time, it was expressly conceived as an answer to the challenges and aspirations of the modernists. Unlike them, Chenu took as his starting point the traditional base of scholasticism, though vivified and transformed through a return to the original sources. However, his concern was similar to that of the modernists, namely, to make room for the subjective aspects of the act of faith, to combat the elements of juridicism and extrinsicism, elements that made the Catholic faith so foreign to anyone committed to the modern world and the values of subjectivity.

Chenu addresses the concerns of subjectivity in the scholastic language of homogeneity, which refers to the continuity between the divine truth assented to and its reception in the subject. These concerns are even more evident in Chenu's dedication to preserving the integrity

12 *Une école de théologie* (1937), 44, 52.

of all that is human (e.g., faith is always human faith) against any encroachment by false notions of the transcendent. However, it is Chenu's uncompromising commitment to the supernatural character of faith that allows for such a freedom with respect to the various powers of human reason. It is in relation to this twofold aspect of faith – its supernatural character and its human condition – that Chenu introduces the language of incarnation.

The Supernatural Character of Faith

For Chenu, faith is a paradox, both *substantia rerum sperandarum* and *ex auditu*. It is a paradox wherein the divine and the human elements are analogous to the two natures of Christ. To this extent, we can speak of the "theandric mystery" of faith.[13]

First, the act of faith is the substance of things hoped for, *substantia rerum sperandarum*. Chenu calls it "the realist perception of the mysterious divine reality." This "realism of faith" is in fact based on a particular section of the Thomistic treatise on faith to which Chenu devoted a number of historical and theological studies.[14]

Chenu's position on faith, the role of reason, and the nature of theology, is grounded in a theological and historical study of St. Thomas. Specifically, he focused on two articles in the treatise of faith of the *Summa Theologica* (*IIa-IIae, q. 1, a. 1–2*) and on a third article about the scientific nature of theology (*Ia Pars, q. 1, a. 2*). In one of his portraits of Chenu, Yves Congar has underlined the structural value of the three articles for the development of Chenu's thought, particularly with respect to the two natures of faith (i.e., its supernatural character and its human integrity) and the significance of this pairing for theological reflection. "These three articles, which are of a structuring value, gave P. Chenu not only the two fundamental elements of his synthesis, but their organization: the absolutely supernatural quality of faith; and the form it takes in a human subject whose conditions it espouses and in which one may say that it is incarnated. P. Chenu would not tire of living, applying and explaining this unity-without-confusion-or-division,

---

13 Ibid., 61.

14 Ibid., 59. See especially the 1923 article "Contribution à l'histoire du traité de la foi. Commentaire historique de *IIa-IIae, q. 1, a. 2*," in *Parole* 1, 31–50. It is the position developed in these early articles that culminates in the programmatic essay *Une école de théologie* of 1937. Cf. G. Alberigo, "Christianisme en tant qu'histoire et 'théologie confessante'," in *Une école de théologie: Le Saulchoir* (Paris: Éditions du Cerf, 1985), 20.

this sort of Chalcedonian statute of theology. He would not cease to affirm the divine character of the faith by refusing and denouncing anything that would be a divinism without a full and consequent humanity."[15] Chenu's emphasis on the supernatural character of faith was not really a novel position; it belongs to the tradition of Dominican Thomism. What was more innovative, at least in terms of twentieth-century scholasticism, was his emphasis on the integrity of the human condition. The initial influence of Rousselot on the latter was decisive.[16]

Chenu calls faith a "realist perception" of the divine mystery, making reference to the "realism of faith" and the "divine realism." Such "realism" is explained in terms of a technical detail in the treatise of faith, concerning the intentionality of the act of faith, whose object is not the dogmatic proposition but the divine reality itself. It is not a concept, a formula, a system of truths, but the One who fulfills the human quest for happiness and all the deepest desires of the soul. Chenu writes: "The act of the believer does not terminate in the dogmatic proposition, but in the divine reality itself which it expresses in a human way. Thus, not a concept, formulas, or a system of thought, but the One in whom I recognize the whole of my life, the loveable object of my happinness."[17]

Chenu explains this intentionality in terms of the light of faith, that is, the presence within us of God's own self-witness: "This realism of faith … finds its psychological cause in the strictly supernatural quality of the interior light, of the 'word of God' in me."[18] As a result of this divine presence, there occurs a dialogue between God and the soul, encompassing God, the believing subject, and the world. "It consists of a dialogue between my soul and God, concerning the very life of God; in this light, my vision touches and discovers with astonishment the vision God has of himself, of the life of the world, of my life; myself in the mysterious destiny of the world, with my own destiny, also mysterious, before the Triune

15 Yves Congar, "Le Père M.-D. Chenu," in R. van der Gucht and H. Vorgrimler (eds), *Bilan de la théologie du XXᵉ siècle* (Paris: Casterman, 1970), II, 776. Congar also wrote: "*Rarement une oeuvre s'est autant développée à partir d'une perception perpétuellement reprise.*"

16 See the references to Rousselot in Chapter 1. For the supernatural character of faith, see R. Garrigou-Lagrange, "La surnaturalité de la foi," *Revue thomiste*, 22 (1914), 17–38.

17 "Position" (1935), in *Parole* 1, 117. Cf. also "L'unité" (1937), in *Parole* 1, 15: "*Connaissance réaliste, c'est-à-dire qui touche la chose divine.*" The reference in St. Thomas is *Summa Theologica IIa IIae, q. 1, a. 2: "actus credentis non terminatur ad enuntiabile, sed ad rem."*

18 *Une école de théologie* (1937), 59. Cf. also L.A. Gallo, *La concepción de la salvación y sus presupuestos en M.-D. Chenu* (Rome: Libreria Ateneo Salesiano, 1977), 91: "*En el fondo, sobrenaturalidad de la fe significa que ella tiene una densidad homogénea con lo divino y que, por lo tanto, ella misma es 'divina'.*"

God." In this sense, faith is the assimilation to God's self-knowledge: "Faith ... is assimilation to the knowledge that God has of himself, man's vision touches God's."[19] Faith is supernatural because its light is not produced by the efforts of human reason or understanding, but rather results from God's self-revelation to us. "Knowledge of God within me, the word of God is wholly grace, personal grace, placing me in dialogue and in direct exchange with Him, mysterious presence to which the 'new man' has access, not because his reason has introduced him, but because God reveals himself, *sibi ipsi testis* [witness to his own self]. '*Qui credit in Filium Dei, habet testimonium Dei in se* [The one who believes in the Son of God has the testimony of God in him.]' (1 Jn 5:10)"[20]

Chenu continues by saying that faith is thus wholly transcendent and interior, dependent on neither word nor manifestation, and not bound by time ("*elle n'est pas engagée dans le temps*"). It results from a divine initiative. The supernatural character of faith originates in its relationship to the beatific vision, which implies some sort of connaturality with God. What is given is a foretaste, a preview of the beatific vision; "a vital knowing, the beginnings of a later breakthrough to vision, to objective evidence." And what is given in faith, in faith's witness, is not any concept or formula, but the divine reality itself. "Now note that this object, passed on in a confidential exchange which calls forth trust, is not just any intelligible matter, but is the very reality of my beatitude: it is God, substantial truth, the saturating end of all my desires, which gives itself through hope: *substantia rerum sperandarum*."[21]

Chenu's emphasis on the existential, as distinguished from the rational, is a reaction against the one-sided intellectualism opposing the

19 "L'unité" (1937), in *Parole* 1, 14–15, 17.

20 *Une école de théologie* (1937), 59. On faith as witness, see "Position" (1935), in *Parole* 1, 117: "*Il s'agit bien d'un témoignage, mais il est de Dieu sur lui-même: le témoignage n'est ici que le véhicule d'une connaissance* réelle, *nous livrant, fût-ce dans le mystère, en objet de perception et d'amour, une réalité divine.*" On the supernatural character of faith, see also "Sociologie de la connaissance" (1958), in *Parole* 1, 66, where Chenu writes of "*la transcendance de la lumière de foi ... par rapport à la nature et à l'histoire de l'homme*" and states that "*la foi, comme dit l'École, est substantiellement surnaturelle.*"

21 "Position" (1935), in *Parole* 1, 117. Cf. *La théologie est-elle une science?* (1957), 31: "*La foi est vraiment alors l'amorce de la vision béatifique, la prélibation de la contemplation future.*" Cf. also *St Thomas d'Aquin et la théologie* (1959), 36–7: "*Mais ces formules ne sont pas l'objet terminal de la foi: au-delà d'elles la foi est toute tendue vers la réalité mystérieuse de Dieu tel qu'il est en lui-même. Cette 'intention' de la foi les anime, et a travers elles ouvre l'âme à Dieu. Ainsi est-elle une lumière, homogène à la divine réalité.*" See L.A. Gallo, *La concepción*, 90: "*La sobrenaturalidad de la fe radica en su relación con la visión beatífica. El 'ver a Dios cara a cara', implica una connaturalidad con Dios mismo y una 'elevación' al orden divino que capacite a dicha visión.*"

modernists. Chenu lamented this "false theology of faith, which renounced its substantial supernaturality for fear of not being able to ✓ offer the rational apologetic of a mystical assent." Because of the perceived threat of Protestantism and subjectivism, the ecclesial and authoritarian dimension of faith's assent was emphasized at the cost of faith's realism.[22]

The Human Integrity of Faith

As noted earlier, in arguing for the "*surnaturalité substantielle*" of faith, Chenu did not contribute any radically new elements to the treatise of faith. It was an accepted though sometimes forgotten part of the heritage, particularly in the Thomist tradition. His contribution was more original with regard to both the conditions assumed by faith in the human subject and the denunciation of the erroneous exaltations of the transcendent that short-change the integrity of human reality and disregard the laws inherent in the human condition.[23]

On this subject, Chenu begins by affirming the paradoxical structure of the act of faith, which is wholly supernatural yet whose object is available only in a particular teaching or a dogmatic formula: "Paradox of faith which, *substantia rerum sperandarum*, yet does not find its object except *in* a received teaching: *fides ex auditu* [faith comes from hearing]. The word of God is given to us in human words, and supernatural faith ✓ becomes an assent to determinate propositions." In this context, an immediate application of this paradoxical structure is the dogmatic formula no longer seen merely as a juridical statement extrinsic to the revelation it presents; rather, "it is the incarnation, in concepts, of the ✓ word of God."[24]

The act of faith, then, involves the presence of the word of God in a human subject. That presence is described by Chenu in terms of an "economy" of the word and thus suggests a dynamic and progressive ✓

22 *Une école de théologie* (1937), 62. It should be noted that this theology not only opposed the modernists but was opposed by them in the first place. It represented, in fact, one of the causes of the modernist reaction. Cf. "Les yeux de la foi" (1932), in *Parole* 1, 23–4, where Chenu offers a critique of the development of faith as mere obedience and orthodoxy in reaction to the Protestant emphases. He also presents a short historical account of the "obedience and authority" mentality.

23 Here again, the texts in *Une école de théologie* (1937) will serve as our guide, particularly one passage on 60–1 where Chenu's position on faith and its place in the human subject in presented in a nutshell.

24 Ibid., 60. See also "Sentiment" (1935), in *Parole* 1, 223–7, and "Les yeux" (1932), in *Parole* 1, 21–7.

relationship. "Such is the economy of this word: it speaks humanly; it is
clothed in the forms of the human mind and produces itself in the human mind according to all the conditions required by the mechanism of
a psychology bound to the slow and heavy complexity of notions and
judgments, bound to the categories of time and space, as the philosophers say, bound up with a history." This brings Chenu to cite the Thomistic principle according to which anything, if it be known by a human
subject, must be known according to the human laws of knowledge: *cognita sunt in cognoscente ad modum cognoscentis.* To exclude God and divine
revelation from these laws is to succumb to a spiritual confusion of false
transcendence and mysticism: "If indeed man knows God, he will know
him humanly."[25]

It is in this context that Chenu introduces the language of incarnation
in order to express the integrity of the human dimension in the act of
faith while at the same time maintaining its divine realism. The light of
faith is to reason what grace is to nature. One *lives* within the other: "No
more than grace is with respect to nature, faith is not a light laid upon
the surface of reason: faith lives in reason."[26] Faith is not superimposed
on the human subject; rather, it is incarnate in the human subject.

Chenu then makes the explicit connection to the two natures in the
person of Christ and speaks of a single theandric mystery. Faith is no
more contaminated by such an intimate relationship to human understanding than the divine nature is diminished by its incarnation. "Double theandric mystery, or better yet, unique mystery, which is the very
mystery of Christ, in whom the divine and the human are one: unique
Person, in whom faith places me, eternal Son of God come into history.
The Christ of faith in the Christ of history."[27] Just as the word of God became truly human in the assumption of a human nature, so too the
structure of human language may not be violated by the coming of the
word if it is to be an intelligible revelation. Yet Chenu seems to be sug-

25 *Une école de théologie* (1937), 60–1. For the Thomistic principle, see *Summa Theologica*
IIa-IIae, q. 1, a. 2. Cf. also "Position" (1935), in *Parole* 1, 119, where Chenu writes of the "*dé-
sordre spirituel d'une fausse mysticité.*" Chenu's concept of "economy," which is central to his
theology, is treated more extensively in Chapter 3 of this book.

26 *Une école de théologie* (1937), 61. L.A. Gallo, *La concepción* (58, n. 72; 92), has pointed
out the importance for Chenu of words such as "*posée*" or "*superposée*" in describing false
relationships from the perspective of incarnation.

27 *Une étole de théologie* (1937), 61. On the relationship between divine economy and the
birth of theology, cf. *La théologie est-elle une science?* (1957), 30: "*Par le Fils, Dieu homme né
d'une femme, nous avons accès au Père. C'est à l'intérieur de cette économie que ma foi trouve son objet,
Dieu même, Vérité première. C'est là aussi que s'engendre en moi la théologie.*"

gesting more than a mere parallelism along the lines of "just as, so too". The relation of faith to human reason is somehow based analogically in the christological mystery: "Double theandric mystery, or better yet, unique mystery, which is the very mystery of Christ ... "

Clearly, the language of incarnation is used by Chenu to suggest the compatibility of intellectual reasoning and the experience of faith. Faith does not abolish the laws of human reason but lives in them and uses them for its own expression. "The gift of God is gift to the point that it becomes human property: faith is a *habitus*. It is not an extraordinary charism, whose transcendence would keep it distant from our human way of thinking; it is an incarnation of the divine truth in the very fabric of our mind."[28] This compatibility, of course, will have serious implications for the role of faith in the nature and development of theology. Even with all its critical apparatus, theology will not be something foreign to faith but rather its product, "by the incarnation of this faith in a human mind." Chenu goes on: "The marvel of the divine light which takes possession of the mind to this point. Not the tightening of a dialectical scaffolding, but an interior framework which faith itself creates for itself in its all-human and all-divine intellectual health: it dares, in its communion with the knowledge of God, to seek the "reason" behind the works of God, and so to obtain understanding of his mystery. *Fides quaerens intellectum.*"[29] In 1937, the same year that *Une école de théologie: Le Saulchoir* was published, Chenu wrote a short article entitled "L'unité de la foi: réalisme et formalisme." As the title indicates, Chenu pursues the theme of the paradoxical nature of faith, wherein a mystical perception is accompanied by an assent to propositions; he also pursues the resolution of the paradox in terms of a christological analogy. His problem is to coordinate the two exigencies of faith: the formalism of adherence to a teaching and the realism of a communication between a divine and a human person. To coordinate them requires "not that one juxtapose them by way of compromise, camouflaging their importance, but that one discern their reciprocal inclusion."[30]

28 *Une école de théologie* (1937), 70. Note the implied critique of escapism in the name of transcendence. Cf. also "Position théologique de la sociologie religieuse" (1950), in *Parole* 1, 60: "*La foi ... n'est pas un acte qui, sous un impératif extérieur, se poserait en queleque sorte sur la surface de notre esprit ... La foi se plante dedans l'esprit, s'enracine dans ses tissus les plus profonds, s'énonce selon ses lois ... *"

29 *Une école de théologie*, (1937), 72, 73.

30 "L'unité" (1937), in *Parole* 1, 14. Again, note the rejection of dualism intended by "*juxtaposer.*"

Here again, while defining faith as the assimilation into God's self-knowledge, Chenu emphasizes the inevitability and integrity of the human condition. Although faith is described as absolutely transcendent, it cannot be absolutely alien to the human condition or it would be meaningless.

Such is this human condition, at least in terms of human understanding, that it follows certain laws: "My intelligence is obliged to compose, to divide the real." The reasoning and conceptualizing apparatus may be tiresome; it is, however, inevitable: "*il faut en passer par là.*" The dialogue of the soul with God, Chenu reminds us, needs words. Briefly, faith is realistic in that it truly knows God; yet its realism is human: "Realism of faith, yes, but human realism!" And he adds: "Let us never forget that the very guarantee of the realism of faith is that *our faith be always HUMAN.*"[31]

The very understanding of the supernatural is at stake. In this context, Chenu warns against the "false mystical evanescence of the spirit." A theological perspective is erroneous if it situates the supernatural outside ("*hors*") the laws and the psychology of the human condition. It is in error because it defeats the very purpose of the supernatural. "All that is supernatural is an 'incarnation' of the divine; otherwise the matter is botched. If man must eliminate the normal and sound content of his life to enter into the supernatural, it is a failure, for it is precisely all this human content that must be raised to the supernatural and thenceforth blossom on that plane."[32] Here the allusion to christology becomes explicit. Christ assumed all there is in human nature in order that all may be saved and divinized. Such is the law of incarnation. Its denial becomes a form of false idealism which is a form of docetism. "If Christ became incarnate, it was to take on all that there is in man, for it is the whole man that is redeemed and divinized in him. The Word was made flesh; he is utterly man, even to being tempted. Avoid that false idealism which would tend to see in Christ human appearances alone (Docetism)."[33]

The law of incarnation applies to faith and its relationship to reason. Faith originates and develops according to the laws and procedures of

31 Ibid., 18; Chenu's emphasis. Cf. L.A. Gallo's comment on this passage in *La concepción*, 91: "*El principio esta claramente enunciado: si de verdad el hombre conoce a Dios, tiene que conocerlo humanamente. Un conocer a Dios que es divino y que, empero, se lleva a cabo segun la realidad del hombre, porque constituye una real encarnación.*"

32 "L'unité," 18. Such statements may lead to ambiguity and need to be clarified. Chenu seems to maintain the "economic" perspective as the only viable and legitimate view in theology.

33 Ibid., 19. For one treatment of the patristic background to the phrase, "What is not assumed is not redeemed," see Maurice Wiles, *Religious Studies* 4 (1968), 47–56.

the human condition. "The work of a loving knowledge of God, it is born, grows, expresses itself according to the laws and processes of human knowledge – formulas and all the rest. Otherwise the matter is botched, and, under the appearance of mystical exaltation, the whole human zone of the life of the spirit remains in its misery, in an inhuman (and thus vain) participation in a superior understanding and light."[34] Just as the actions of Christ are called "theandric," so too our understanding, our concepts, and our dogmatic formulas in faith are theandric. It is important to note the soteriological corollary of this incarnation model. In the passage just cited, Chenu describes as crucial the expression of faith by means of the whole register of human understanding; "otherwise the matter is botched." In other words, it is essential for the success of the divine initiative towards humanity; without it, our participation in divine life is inhuman and hence in vain. The particulars of the development of faith in relation to reason are discussed in the next section, on the origins of theological reflection.

FAITH AND THE ORIGINS OF THEOLOGY

Now we must treat of the dynamism of faith as well as of the origin and development of theological reflection in the human subject. It is helpful for this discussion to recall that Chenu was fighting the intellectualism in the theological circles of his day, reacting against the break between intellectual knowledge and religious sentiment. He was opposed to a view of faith as mere assent, with no cognitive value of its own. In this context, he pursued the realist dimension of faith, its radical dissatisfaction in relation to a possible fulfillment with the beatific vision, its curiosity and, finally, its dynamism. In terms of the law of incarnation, Chenu saw the human integrity of faith as extended to include the mind's quest for evidence and clarity. The incarnation perspective states that the propensity to theologize is inherent in faith.

Credere, assensus, *and* cogitatio

As we saw earlier, Chenu was critical of the modern authors who denied any cognitive value to faith and who limited faith to a juridical concept of legal obedience. They were forced to speak of an "*esprit de foi*" over

---

34 Ibid., 19. Chenu adds, "*il y a une véritable incarnation de lumière divine* dans mon *esprit.*" He is, however, careful to include the qualifier "*toutes proportions gardées.*" Such qualifiers are the bane of interpreters, because one never knows the extent of the qualification.

and above the assent of faith in order to account for its life-giving dimension. He, on the contrary, maintained: "Faith, taken alone, is assimilation with the knowledge of God: it bestows theological life, and it is an error to seek beyond it for a 'spirit' that would bring it alive. Faith has nothing above it that could vivify it: by its whole being and by all its strength, it reaches directly the life-giving God." However, in this very knowledge and this very possession of the divine reality, faith sets in motion an insatiable curiosity. Even in indefectible obedience, the believer remains dissatisfied. From the glass through which one sees darkly, drawn by the very object of life, the believer strives towards a fuller and clearer vision. "For even in his unfailing obedience, the believer remains unsatisfied; far from being complacent in his social servitude of faith, and enclosing his mind in a too narrow security, he is taken by his mysterious object and, as much as he can, he seeks to have some understanding of the mystery of the divine life. It is the work of theological science. It is the work above all of contemplation." The experience of the presence of faith within human reason includes a certain dynamism, a striving towards fuller vision and fuller understanding. The striving, the thirst are progressively fulfilled as faith becomes more and more incarnate in reason and its quest for the certitude of knowledge.[35]

Such is the "economy" of faith. It will find expression even in the most arcane constructions of reason in the scientific conclusion. Chenu's position is that the development of faith into theological reflection and theological science is not only legitimate but necessary. It flows from the very logic of faith. The development of such knowledge is inherent within the structure of faith. To stress the continuity between the experience of faith and the development of theological science, Chenu refers to theology as "*la foi* in statu scientiae" or "faith seeking theological understanding."[36]

The possibility and the importance of this development are dictated by the law of incarnation. Any disregard for this law, such as the wish to keep the matter of faith beyond the grasp of reason out of respect for its transcendence, represents a lack of realism. Revelation presupposes the validity of the human laws of understanding, "for if God consents to give himself to human reason, it is – after making it capable – in accepting

---

35 "Les yeux" (1932), in *Parole* 1, 26. See "Position" (1935), in *Parole* 1, 117: "*C'est dans l'appétit même de bonheur, au plus profond de la nature, que vient s'enraciner la grâce de la foi. C'est de là même que tend son dynamisme, dans l'impatience de la vision.*"

36 "Position" (1935), in *Parole* 1, 116: "*la foi en oeuvre d'intelligence théologale.*"

the native law of this reason." And so, faith gives rise to knowledge: "Faith, by these rational promotions, of itself begets a 'knowledge', a miserable mime of the future vision, and yet a human refraction of the knowledge of the blessed."[37]

Chenu locates the origin of theological reflection in the very definition of believing *(credere)* as opposed to knowing *(scire)* or doubting *(dubitare)*. The realism of faith, by which faith is the assimilation to God's self-knowledge, is by definition imperfect. Faith is a foretaste of vision; it is not vision itself. Faith's dynamism is really nothing more, and nothing less, than the impatience for vision. "For in the end all of this is but hoped for, and this provisional knowledge, in darkness as it were, is radically imperfect. The eminent dignity of its object does not rehabilitate it except in principle, without reducing that total non-obviousness which is the sign of a very feeble knowledge, obtained by an act of the will." The origin of theological reasoning, then, lies in the disproportion between the massive desire and the lack of evidence. Certainly, the witness of God lends some authority to the object of faith, but it fails to satisfy the mind's desire for clarity. "Disproportion painful to the mind: the witness of God obtains for it an unfailing certainty; but in such a way as is needed to steady the mind, not in the least to satisfy it ... *Credere Deo* [to believe God], certainly, to believe testimony; but in order to tend, in this testimony, to clear sight: *credere in Deum* [to believe in God]." In this context, Chenu uses the Thomistic formula, itself borrowed from Augustine, "*credere est cum assensione cogitare* [to believe is to think with assent]" and locates the theological enterprise in the *cogitatio* which lives side by side with the *assensus*. The *cogitatio* is not an optional activity of the mind that may or may not be exercised, but a trait intrinsic to the definition of faith: "The *cogitatio*, that quest, that always renewed inquiry of the unsatisfied believer, is not an optional feature of faith; it is an intrinsic element, of which the coexistence with a categorical *assensus* properly constitutes the *credere*, as much by opposition to the *scire* as to the *dubitare*." Chenu underlines

---

37 Ibid., 116. Chenu goes on to define these "*promotions rationnelles*": "*fermentation, dilatation, fructification, exploitation de ce 'donné', dans l'intelligibilité appâtée par ce nouvel objet ... du surnaturel incarné dans une raison en travail, travail d'assimilation ou travail de construction ...*" Cf. *St Thomas d'Aquin et la théologie* (1959), 35: "*Ma foi ne sera pas un transport mystique hors de ma condition, mais une communion à mon niveau psychologique, réalisée dans des mots humains habilités, selon leur loi et leur comportement, à énoncer Dieu dans mes formulations terrestres.*" See also *La théologie est-elle une science?* (1957), 33: "*Ainsi, la foi est, de nature, et par promotion spontanée de sa grâce, grosse d'une théologie.*"

this structural necessity by calling theology "the fruit of the justified dissatisfaction which, in the believer, sets his faith to work: *Fides quaerens intellectum.*"[38]

In *Une école de théologie*, Chenu describes this dissatisfaction as the weakness ("*débilité*") of faith which gives rise to theology. Yet theology is also born of the power ("*puissance*") of faith which perceives in the finite proposition the infinite power of God. "Theology emanates from faith; it is born from faith and by faith. It is born of faith's weakness, of the radical weakness (for the mind) that is assent to propositions it neither sees nor measures. But theology is born also of faith's power, of that power which stores up in a soul striving after possession the realist perception of the mysterious divine reality, *substantia rerum sperandarum.*"[39] In other words, the very structure of faith gives rise to rational elaboration.

The motivation for this elaboration must now further be clarified. The believer knows the dissatisfaction is temporary. But far from glorifying an attitude of mere social obedience and orthodoxy, the lack of evidence triggers a curiosity and a quest. In an important article on the psychology of faith, Chenu writes on this theme: "The appetite for happiness which determines reason's assent, far from enclosing it in a too narrow security, ceaselessly provokes its search: '*Motus ejus nondum est quietatus, sed habet cogitationem et inquisitionem de his quae credit*' [His mental activity is not yet quieted, but he has thoughts and questions from those things he believes.]"[40] It is here that St. Thomas, followed by Chenu, introduced Augustine's formula in the definition of faith's assent: "*credere est cum assensione cogitare.*"

For Albert the Great, the *cogitatio* comes either before or after the *assensus*. In either case it remains extrinsic to the act of faith. *Credere*, for Albert, is essentially defined as *assensus*; the *cogitatio* belongs to it only *per*

---

38 Ibid., 117–19. Cf. *La théologie est-elle une science?* (1957), 34: "*Se développe donc, dans cette fécondité de la foi, une activité de l'esprit selon les diverses ressources de sa nature, puisque la lumière divine de la foi est comme incarnée dans cet esprit … L'assentiment ne se ferme pas sur une obéissance objective, mais déclenche une curiosité où nature et grâce, nature de mon intelligence et grâce de la foi, sont en travail.*"

39 *Une école de théologie* (1937), 58–9. Cf. *St. Thomas d'Aquin et la théologie* (1959), 35: "*C'est là que va naître la théologie, au-dedans de cette foi. Car, ainsi implantée dans mon être, la foi n'est évidemment pas comme un corps étranger dans l'organisme comme un lot de propositions inertes dans mon esprit … Elle est en moi une puissance, dont les ressources vitales d'intelligence sont prises dans une espèce d'appétit biologique vers sa plénitude, disons vers la vision béatifiante de Dieu, dont elle est l'amorce terrestre.*"

40 "Psychologie" (1932), in *Parole* 1, 96, quoting St. Thomas, *De Ver.*, q. 14, a. 1 corp. in fine. Cf. Pascal's "*inquiétude*" and Augustine's *cor inquietum*.

accidens. For Thomas, on the contrary, the *cogitatio* is an intrinsic element of faith. Even more, it is that property by which faith differs from any other kind of assent. Thomas saw faith as characterized by the coexistence of *assensus* and *cogitatio* in the unity of one act: " ... in faith, by a sort of interior discord, assent and cogitiation, rest and movement, go together as pairs."[41] It should be noted, however, that the principal motive is a matter of love and desire. The *assensus* is caused by a movement of the will, not by the efforts of reason or intelligence. In other words, we are dealing with the desire of the soul in the face of its appetite for beatitude.

Chenu comments on the subtlety of Thomas' coordination of Augustinian restlessness and Aristotelian epistemology, noting that, far from representing a "*concordisme de surface,*" it represents the expression of a religious intuition and a mentality that is conscious of its aim. He describes this mentality thus: "Mentality is the effect of that conviction according to which infused faith neither enters nor develops in our mind apart from the laws of this mind; and consequently, the transcendence of its object is translated into a raising up of our faculties, and not into a disordering of our psychological organism."[42] Chenu emulates the same mentality and protests against any docetic tendencies in theology. It is the mentality of the incarnation model.

The end of the article on the psychology of faith mentions the task of constructing a theological "science" of the act of faith (i.e., theology as science). Chenu notes that some, such as Hugh of St. Victor, did not venture into this task. He goes on to list the requirements of such a theological science (*épistéme*): "It is that, in order to have 'scientific' knowledge of a supernatural reality, the light of faith must involve reason itself even unto the intimacy of its own work – a reason armed with its own resources, in short a philosophy." What Chenu calls the "engagement" of the light of faith in relation to reason is nothing more than the fulfillment of the law of incarnation as it applies to the origin of theological reflection and science. The law requires that the human be assumed and respected in all its integrity. Chenu is careful to point out that such a theological elaboration is not in conflict with the transcendence of faith and that it is not developed on the basis of a previously granted extrinsicism. "This is neither to belittle faith nor to threaten its supernaturality,

---

41 Ibid., 98. See also R. Bellemare, "Credere: Notes sur la définition thomiste," *Rev. de l'U. d'Ottawa, sect. spéc.*, 30 (1960), 37–47.

42 Ibid., 98.

but on the contrary it is to proclaim its primary and most profound claim on man. Neither is it at all to repair, by a tardy conjunction, an extrinsicism (in harmony at first) of nature and grace, for theological reason is born and operates within the faith which imbues it with its light."[43] Yet it must be remembered that this involvement of reason is not a case of rampant intellectualism. Chenu goes to great lengths to point out that the assent and the appetite for beatitude are a matter of love (*affectus*). The assent of the believer is given by a movement of the will, *determinatio voluntatis*: "His adherence as such is a work of love, of appetite for God who bestows beatitude."[44]

The Origins of Theology

For Chenu, faithful to the Thomistic tradition, the quest of reason for intelligibility within the assent to faith develops into a body of knowledge. In this context, Chenu characterizes theology as faith *in statu scientiae*. We must now point out the significance of incarnation within the nature and development of this body of knowledge. In terms of the preceeding discussion on *credere*, *assensus*, and *cogitatio*, there are questions concerning how the appetite for fulfillment will be exercized, and how the *cogitatio* will in fact develop. A further question has to do with how the law of incarnation will be manifest in this body of knowledge. The guiding theme here is the law of incarnation, which Chenu invokes in order to describe the paradoxical structure of faith. Theological reflection and theological science are really only the logical development of the same principle: "Faith, in begetting theology, is within the very logic of its perfection."[45] Chenu is here alluding to the dynamism of faith in its pursuit of vision and the the fulfillment of its innermost desire.

Inasmuch as faith is the "incarnation of the divine truth in the very fabric of our mind," it follows that it will somehow find expression in the very laws and procedures of this mind. Faith is not some extraordinary charism in the sense that its transcendence would keep it outside the range of the human mind and its ways of thinking.

With the necessary discernments and discretions, all the tools and techniques of human reason are placed within and at the disposal of the believer's mystical perception. Chenu's list of techniques and proce-

---

43 Ibid., 99.
44 "L'amour dans la foi" (1932), in *Parole* 1, 111.
45 *Une école de théologie* (1937), 70. Chenu adds: "*La logique suivra donc son cours.*"

dures, in *Une école de théologie,* includes the various forms of conceptualization, the multiplicity of analyses and judgments, definitions and
distinctions, explanatory measures, and finally deductions, insofar as deduction is the most characteristic operation of scientific reason, where
the process of rationalization is most efficient.

Chenu's list betrays the date of the redaction of *Une école de théologie*
with its concern for the proliferation and the validity of "theological conclusions." Yet the principle of incarnation must be held. If deduction
and the ability to produce conclusions represent the epitome of human
reasoning, then faith and theology must accept them as simply a further
instance of the kind of knowing implied by incarnation. Such is the basis
for confidence in the coherence of faith and reason. "The same law
which, a moment ago, had us calling for an incarnation of the word of
God in human words over the course of history, urges us now to accept
utterly the regime of knowledge which this incarnation implies: theology
is in solidarity with the theandric mystery of the word of God, Word
made flesh. There alone can theology find such a daring confidence in
the coherence of faith and reason."[46] This, then, is the task and the challenge of developing a theology: "to accept utterly the regime of knowledge which this incarnation implies." For Chenu, doing so meant, in the
first place, establishing the scientific character of theology.

THEOLOGY AS SCIENCE

Chenu developed his own understanding of the nature and function of
theology primarily through historical studies on the Thomistic view of
theology as a science. The process of appropriation involved here is remarkable. At the same time, it makes it difficult for us to distinguish
clearly what belongs to St. Thomas and what belongs to Chenu. Yet, as
Chenu teaches us, true fidelity can be creative only if it is to remain a
living thought.

In focusing on the problem of theology as science, Chenu points
to the one moment in the history of theology – the middle of the
thirteenth century – when its methodological self-reflection underwent a revolution of major proportions. The prize in this struggle was

46 See ibid., 70. Cf. *St. Thomas d'Aquin et la théologie* (1959), 46: "*Le triomphe de la foi est
précisément de conserver à la raison l'efficacité propre de ses lois, sans tricher apologétiquement, sans
ajouter non plus à la lumière divine. C'est bien le mystère théandrique de la Parole de Dieu, Verbe fait
chair. Il faut être saint pour le réaliser en théologie.*"

the legitimacy of reason and its scientific procedures in the sphere of faith: "the installation of the 'ratio' with all its apparatus on faith's territory."[47]

The thrust of Chenu's contribution is to articulate the centrality of the role of faith while maintaining for theology its subjective and religious basis in experience, as well as its objective and rational development in scientific form. The pivotal point of this contribution is the theory of subalternation. The value of Chenu's work lies in illuminating a structural characteristic of theological knowing whose significance outlives the technical discussions of the thirteenth century and their revival in the twentieth. The aim of his work lies in a new relationship between the experience of faith based on mystical perception and rational elaboration in the form of scientific method.

The fact that St. Thomas argued for the scientific character of theology is not in dispute. The relation of this argument to modernist claims and aspirations on the one hand, and to neo-scholastic views on theology on the other, is another matter, one which we will now examine. Chenu first dealt with the subject in a 1927 article, "La théologie comme science au XIIIe siècle." It was reprinted in book form in 1943 with significant changes in the underlying perspective. A 1957 edition contains only minor changes. Our discussion therefore begins with the 1927 articles, referred to as the first edition.[48]

The First Edition

The basic conclusion of Chenu's 1927 article "La théologie comme science au XIIIe siècle" is essentially maintained in both later editions of the work ("but not without noticeable nuances") and is, in fact, quoted in their preface: "St. Thomas was the first who knew – and dared – to posit plainly the principle of an integral application of the mechanism

47 "La théologie comme science au XIIIe siècle" (1927), 33–4. Chenu writes of "*le principe d'une intégrale application du mécanisme et des procédés de la science au donné révélé.*"

48 The 1927 article on theology as science was followed by two later versions published in book form: *La théologie comme science au XIIIe siècle, Deuxième édition, pro manuscripto* (1943); *Troisième édition, revue et augmentée* (1957). From here on, unless otherwise noted, references to the three editions will be given by date only: (1927), (1943), and (1957). Parallel references are given for all three editions, unless there is no duplication. Henry Donneaud has written an excellent study on the differences of perspective in the first two editions and the reasons for that development; see "Histoire d'une histoire. M.-D. Chenu et 'La théologie comme science au XIIIe siècle'" in *Mémoire dominicaine. Histoire-documents-vie dominicaine* 4 (1994), 139–75.

faith as principle not as matter to be mastered.

and processes of science to revealed data. Thus was constituted an organic discipline in which Scripture, the article of faith, is no longer the material itself – the subject of the report and research (as in the *sacra doctrina* of the twelfth century) – but the *principle,* known in advance, from which one works according to all the exigencies and laws of the Aristotelian *demonstratio.*[49] The significant point is not a matter of definition, but rather that an autonomous reason is working on the datum of revelation according to the laws of Aristotelian science. At issue is the legitimate autonomy of reason within the sacred science.

Prior to St. Thomas, it was generally agreed that the role of reason (i.e., philosophy) in theology was very much accidental and ancillary. Not permitted within the elaboration of faith, reason was admissible only as an exterior aid in the defense of faith against the attack of unbelievers. At least, such was the role of reason stated theoretically; the actual practice of theology carried a different witness.

The noted English theologian and commentator of Lombard's *Sentences,* Robert Kilwardby (d. 1279), for example, manifested a wide divergence between the theoretical account of the meaning and function of reason in the domain of transcendent faith and in actual theological practice. Chenu demonstrated an implicit repugnance to admit the intervention of reason – or even the principle of such an intervention – within the domain of revelation.[50] Kilwardby's motive, of course, was the protection of the transcendence of faith, which could be threatened with the formal introduction of reason and the autonomous work of rational and scientific methods.

The discrepancy between the theory and the practice of theological reflection was blatant. The difficulty lay in the explicit inclusion of philosophical reason on the level of methodological reflection of principles. "This was a spontaneous reserve, a sort of timidity, before the revealed truth and the divine reality: even as they were swept along to a hardy speculative investigation of this supernatural object, they held, in their principles, to the pure adoration of faith, apart from the exploits of dialectical argumentation."[51] Chenu writes of an "intellectual modesty" on the part of theological minds imbued with the spirit of Augustine and Augustinian *sapientia* which, for them,

49 (1927), 33; (1943), 9–10; (1957), 11.
50 Cf. (1927), 46: "*Il y a une implicite répugnance à admettre dans le domaine de ce donné révélé l'intervention, ou mieux le principe même de l'intervention propre de la raison.*"
51 (1927), 56–7.

excluded the inconvenient exigencies of science and its rational techniques.

The exclusion of something from the realm of faith for fear of contaminating the sacred and the transcendent alternates with the inclusion of something by reason of both the integrity of the human reality and the law of incarnation. This alternation recurs repeatedly in the history of theological method. It is the grid through which Chenu reads the methodological debates of the thirteenth-century theologians. In this context, St. Thomas' breakthrough occurred against a "false notion of the supernatural."

In actual fact, the breakthrough occured with a shift in the location of the scientific apparatus. The articles of faith were no longer the object to which the scientific method was applied, but the *principles* on the basis of which a science could be elaborated; that is, "they are the principles from which the arguments will be developed and the conclusions deduced."[52] The functions of reason are to develop the virtualities of revelation and to extend the light of faith towards questions not explicitly resolved in that revelation.[53]

The transposition of the Aristotelian concept of science was more than a mere sleight of hand. The application of the meaning and function of a principle *per se notum* to the article of faith was still problematic and was resolved only when Thomas utilized, in the Aristotelian doctrine of science, the theory of the subalternation of the sciences. Until then, it was precisely the case that the articles of faith were *not* self-evident, or at least not in the same way that the principles of a science are evident to the light of the intellect. Thomas introduced the theory of subalternation in order to account for the apparently abnormal character of a science whose principles are not self-evident. It was insufficient to say that the articles of faith were principles self-evident to the believer, as he had suggested in the *Commentary on the Sentences*. They were precisely not self-evident, but evident only in faith.

The 1927 article located the decisive step in the application of the theory of subalternation to theology and the obscure status of the articles of faith. Thomas acknowledged the obscurity of the articles and invoked the category of a science whose principles are not self-evident but are received from a science of a higher order. The principles in this case are borrowed, and the light of their evidence is borrowed from a differ-

---

52 Ibid., 58.
53 This is generally how the *revelabilia* of *Ia Pars, q. 1, a. 3* are interpreted.

ent science. One science "believes" the principles of the higher science. Thus, for example, the physician is dependent in his understanding of the elements on the science of physics, and the musician proceeds on the basis of principles provided in the science of arithmetic. In the same way, *sacra doctrina* receives its principles by means of faith from the science of God, *scientia Dei et beatorum.*

The immediate consequence is that the argumentation of reason no longer exists for the purpose of proving the principles of sacred doctrine, since these principles receive their evidence from elsewhere (i.e., the science of God). Rather, the role or function of reason is to proceed from these principles towards the manifestation of other truths, "*sed ex eis procedit ad aliquid aliud ostendendum* [but from these proceeds to various other things to be shown]." It is this function that becomes the focus of debate in the contentious issue of theological conclusions.

The theological function *par excellence* is defined as the argumentation proceeding from the articles of faith towards other truths. The emphasis given to it in the original 1927 article becomes a point of retraction in the edition of 1943. However, Chenu insists on showing that it is in following Aristotle's theory of science that the nature and method of theology were renewed by Thomas: "In reality, by pushing to its limit the application of the concept of science to the sacred teaching, St. Thomas renewed the entire concept and economy of theological work."[54]

The theory of subalternation is the heart of Chenu's presentation, the place of integration between revelation and science, faith and reason, the light of faith and the speculation of reason. "This theory of the subalternation of the sciences which, legitimizing on the one hand the establishment of dialectic on the territory of revelation, attaches on the other this whole dialectic to the very knowledge of God, *scientia Dei et beatorum* – this theory, I say, is a fine testimony to a synthesis, very perfectly one, between the mysticism of the believer and the science of the theologian." Because of the crucial methodological and structural role of faith, the curiosity of the human intellect does not become a false and awkward intellectualism but a religious act: "The immense curiosity of the human understanding becomes a religious act, better yet an exercise of faith."[55]

54 (1927), 67. Cf. (1943), 64–6.

55 (1927), 70, 71. Here Chenu alludes to Jacques Maritain's best-seller, *Distinguer pour unir,* and describes the achievement of St. Thomas in clarifying the relationship of faith and reason: "*Parce qu'il a pleinement distingué la foi et la raison, conservant à la foi sa transcendance et à la raison son autonomie, saint Thomas a pu ensuite les unir, au sens le plus fort du mot, dans une sagesse active et indéfiniment féconde. Gratia non tollit naturam, sed perficit.*"

In Chenu's own later opinion, the 1927 article contained a one-sided emphasis on the deductive function of scientific reason, and furnished a generally abrupt presentation of what is really a much more subtle thought. Its focus was the integration of the Aristotelian theory of science in the traditional understanding of *sacra doctrina*, and the point of insertion of this theory, so to speak, was the teaching on the subalternated sciences.

The role of the theory of science – and its significance for the contemporary debates – is to assure continuity and homogeneity among divine revelation, faith, and the rational elaboration of theology. Even in the 1927 article, the axis of this continuity is the article of faith in its capacity of principle in a science. "The article of faith finds its 'locus' ['*lieu*'] in the immense genesis of truth which goes from God, Primary-Truth, to the modest theological conclusion: the theory of knowledge which seemed bound forever to consecrate the heterogeneity of the divine light of faith with the laborious and human speculation of the theologian, emphasises on the contrary (with the necessary distinctions) its fertile continuity."[56]

The Later Editions

In the preface of the 1943 edition, Chenu writes something of a retraction with regard to the tendencies, but not the substance, of the 1927 article. He remarks on the rigidity with which the deductive function in theology assumed a central role: "Formerly we gave in to a rather too heavy interpretation of the deductive function in theological reason, and delineated its role in blunt formulas, bending in this direction the thought of St. Thomas (which was more supple in reality), as much for the transposition of the concept of science into sacred teaching as for the variety of functions of reason; deduction has, to be sure, a scientific quality in theology, [but] it is neither the principal nor the noblest operation in *intellectus fidei*."[57] In a 1968 preface to a new edition of the French translation of the first question of the *Summa*, Chenu reminisces

56 (1927), 63; (1943), 79; (1957), 74. Note the use of the helpful yet ambiguous qualifier "*sous les distinctions nécessaires.*"

57 (1943), 9; (1957), 11. In the same context, namely, the critique of the hard position on the deductive function of theological reason, Chenu cites Y. Congar, *BT*, 15 (1938), 500: "*La qualité scientifique de la théologie ne se prend pas de la déduction de vérités nouvelles, mais de la construction rationnelle de l'enseignement chrétien par un rattachement de vérités-conclusions à des vérités-principes.*"

in a similar vein about half a century of theological reflections: "[F]or my part, I arrived at a better balance of the function and dignity of theological knowledge in the economy of salvation, and shifted some emphases in my remarks from before 1930." In a comment on the Thomistic synthesis of faith and theological reason, Chenu continues: "Let us acknowledge that his operation did not succeed: St. Thomas was not followed, and even, at the delicate point of the operation, was condemned – as we know, as we forget, forgetting at the same time (beneath the honours with which we cover him) the risks that he ran, risks inherent in any operation of this type. It is time to undertake once again the operation."[58] Chenu's call to renew the "operation" carried out by St. Thomas is in fact the characterization of his own effort at theological reflection. It is ultimately at the root of his work on the nature of theology as science. In this context, Chenu is aware of the historical contribution of his work to the debate on the nature of theology: his work offers "a precious light for the solution of the recent controversies, in France and in German-speaking countries, on the nature of theology."[59]

In general, the later editions of *La théologie comme science au XIIIe siècle* are much more sensitive to the centrality of faith in theology. It is noteworthy that the character of *sacra doctrina* as *quasi*-subalternated and hence as an imperfect science is brought out and acquires a special significance. The third edition (1957) is also particularly sensitive to the importance of scripture in theology. Again, it is the theory of subalternation that resolves the antinomies found by previous generations of theologians. Subalternation represents "the technical piece of an epistemological elaboration apt to rationalize the 'scientific' use of understanding in theology, in that very place where this theological science has no possible existence save in the mystery of the Word of God."[60]

The language of incarnation is not present in this work, at least not in the sense of an explicit reference to the analogy with the theandric mystery. However, insofar as the main characteristic of the law of incarnation concerns the maintenance of both the transcendence of grace and the integrity of the immanent reality, the theme of incarnation is very much present. For example, in the context of the dependence of

---

58 "Préface," in *Saint Thomas d'Aquin. Somme théologique: La théologie* (1968), 8, 9. Cf. 93–167 of the same edition for some helpful material by H.-D. Gardeil on the scientific character of theology in St. Thomas and in the more recent controversies.

59 (1957), 13. The text includes a footnote (n. 2) with references to the *Verkündigungstheologie* and the *nouvelle théologie*.

60 Ibid., 13–14.

theology on texts where the word of God is expressed, Chenu manifests the concern of the incarnation theme. "Since the word of God has expressed itself in human language, flowing in the words, the phrases, the images, the structures, the literary genres of the human word, this divine 'scripture' will find its paths of intelligibility in the very paths of the interpretation of words, of phrases, of figures, of the literary genres of human language."[61] In any given period of its development, theology was thus dependent on the ways and means of textual production and interpretation provided by the contemporary culture. The light of faith, says Chenu, remains free from this dependency on cultural resources, but "its human condition binds it nonetheless, for the construction of theology, to these modest comportments of the spirit."[62] The reason for this is precisely the law of incarnation. There were some medieval theologians who, motivated by a respect for the transcendence of faith and its objects, turned away from the use of grammar in the understanding of the *pagina sacra*. For Chenu, their attitude represented a theological error; they misunderstood the economy of revelation, which occurs by means of expression and incarnation in a human language, analogously to the incarnation of Christ."They did not realize that this precisely is the economy of revelation, to be expressed and incarnated in the language of man, whether it be that of Moses, Paul or Donatus, just as it is fulfilled in the authentically human incarnation of the Son of God."[63] The same motif of incarnation is present when it is no longer grammar but philosophy and science knocking at the door of theology. With the "third entry" of Aristotle, the stakes were higher than in the adoption of grammar and dialectics as a tools in theological understanding. The introduction of theology into the scientific domain presupposed the transfer of philosophical concepts into "holy ground," the right for reason to be installed within the light of faith and to work there with all its concepts and techniques, according to its own laws.[64]

---

61 (1943), 14; (1957), 16.

62 (1943), 15; (1957), 17.

63 (1943), 17; (1957), 19. See (1957), 43, where Chenu writes of the "*principe d'accommodation de la parole de Dieu à la nature rationnelle de l'homme à qui est addressée cette parole.*" The theological error of misunderstanding the incarnation recalls a similar judgment in the name of the economy of revelation against the denial of historical criticism by the "*conservatisme négatif*" of the anti-modernists; cf. *Une école de théologie* (1937), 37.

64 Cf. (1943), 26; (1957), 27. On the "third entry" of Aristotle, cf. Y. Congar, *A History of Theology* (Garden City, NY: Doubleday, 1968), 60, 85–91.

In *La théologie comme science au XIIIe siècle*, Chenu has an entire section on the "resistance" of some theologians to the encroachments of philosophical reason into the domain of *sacra doctrina*.[65] The notion of the danger of crossing the proper boundary and introducing reason into the heart of faith, and thus stripping faith of its true merit, is repeatedly and vehemently denounced.[66] In many ways, the second and third editions of *La théologie comme science au XIIIe siècle* reflect Chenu's own experience with the "resistance" he met on account of his own writings on the thirteenth century and on contemporary methodological debates. The audacious, in both the thirteenth and the twentieth centuries, have to contend with "*conservatismes maladroits.*"[67]

The pivotal chapter is the fifth, in which Chenu introduces the "*pièce technique*" of the matter, namely, the theory of the subalternation of the sciences.[68] He recalls the fundamental principle underlying all Thomistic teaching on the problem of knowledge of God. If humans are to know and to think of God, they will do so humanly, that is, according to the discursive process of reasoning which is human: "Had he to think of God, man would think of him humanly, that is according to the discursive process that is his own, in that very place where God, in his supreme simplicity, enjoys a perfect intuition."[69] The theologian will use all the resources of the human mind, including the state of the art in scientific method – which in this case was the *ratio scientiae* of Aristotle – as long as reason remains at the service of faith and under the light of faith. "He must observe all necessary discretion; but, this done, his reason, under the light of faith and at its service, enjoys all its rights, of its native rights as of its expert methods – definitions, divisions, analogies, comparisons, inferences, deductions – from the moment they are true. For faith does not overturn the nature of the mind in which God infuses it; on the contrary, it adopts the mind's modes, of which rational discourse is typical." In a footnote to this passage, Chenu refers to the *locus classicus* of *IIa-IIae, q. 1, a. 2*: "*Cognita sunt in cognoscente secundum modum cognoscentis* [Things known are in the knower according to the manner of knowing.]" The main textual support, however, comes from

---

65 Cf. (1943), 25–32; (1957), 26–32: "Les résistances."

66 Cf. (1943), 31; (1957), 31.

67 (1943), 32; (1957), 32. This is partly confirmed by Chenu's somewhat cyclical view of the history of Christianity and its periodic renewals. Cf. Chapter 3 in this book.

68 (1943), 71–101; (1957), 67–92. See also the preface to the third edition (1957), 13–14.

69 (1943), 74; (1957), 69.

Thomas' commentary on the *De Trinitate* of Boethius, where Thomas defines the *ratio scientiae* as the movement of the mind, which goes from the known to the unknown by means of discursive reasoning: " ... *cum ratio scientiae consistat in hoc quod ex aliquibus notis alia ignotiora cognoscantur ... scilicet discurrendo de principiis ad conclusiones* [... as the *ratio scientiae* consists in this, that things of which we know less are known from things of which we know more ... namely, in reasoning from principles to conclusions.]"[70]

The *ratio scientiae* represents the type of human reasoning and knowing, as well as that which will be adopted by faith as its human mode of expression. The expression of faith within a *ratio scientiae* is where Chenu sees the articulation of a concern with the theme of incarnation.

The stumbling blocks were many: Will the integrity of the light of faith be preserved when it is planted in the soil of rationality? "How one may pass from the divine mode, from that thought of God from which faith must emanate, to that scientific work which sets faith to work?"[71] The issue is continuity and homogeneity, both spiritual and epistemological. The role of the theory of subalternation is to assure this continuity. The concern for continuity is in fact the concern for incarnation, in the sense of maintaining the transcendence of faith and the immanence of rationality – the two are held together without confusion and without division or separation.

Until St. Thomas, the main obstacle to applying *scientia* to theology was the lack of self-evident principles, *per se nota*. His innovative contribution was to make this very obstacle the cornerstone of his theory of science. The theory of subalternation, as pointed out earlier, accounts for a field of science whose principles are not self-evident to itself but to a higher science. The lower subalternated science does not possess the evidence of its own principles but "believes" them, receiving the evidence from a higher subalternating science. Thus, physics does not possess the evidence of its own principles, which come from mathematics, but "believes" them.

70 (1943), 74; (1957), 69–70. The phrase "*du moment qu'elles sont vraies*" only highlights the difficulty. Also, Chenu is more aware of the limits of the rational method in his later writings. See, for example, (1957), 45, n. 1, where, on the basis of a fruitful conversation with H.-I. Marrou on the theology of the Greek fathers, Chenu acknowledges the limits of Aristotelian *episteme*. See also the numerous references to the *lumen orientale* in *Théologie XIIe* (1957) and in *La théologie est-elle une science?* (1957), which point to the importance of the symbolic dimensions in knowledge. The Latin citation is from *In Boetium de Trin.*, q. 2, a. 2 in corp.

71 (1943), 75; (1957), 70.

Theology, likewise, does not possess the evidence of its own principles. By faith, the theologian believes the principles that are self-evident
to the science of God and to those who "see" God. In this sense, theology is only a particular case of a more general condition in the sciences.
"The 'docility' of the theologian who 'believes' his principles without
their being evident is thus no more than a particular case of the normal
regime of the sciences. The *faith* which obtains for him his light, his spiritual atmosphere, is the analogue of the spiritual coordinates which
make up for the expert his place of work." Aristotle's theory of subalternation has transformed the key objection to the scientific character of
theology (i.e., lack of evidence) into that which affirms this scientific
character: "That which seemed bound to rupture all contact, on the
contrary assured the normal cohesion."[72]

One of the immediate consequences concerns the role of faith in the
definition and development of theology. Faith is that by which theology
possesses the evidence of its principles. It is faith that makes subalternation possible. The label of "science" is to be applied to theology only on
account of faith. Conversely, it is the technical requirement of science,
as well as the sense of the religious, which asks that theology work out of
faith, since it is faith that assures the continuity between the "science of
God" (subalternating) and theological science (subalternated).

It seems ironic that the scientific structure of theology requires such a
prominent role for faith. Thus, this recovery of the Thomistic teaching
on the scientific character of theology becomes part of Chenu's attack
on the rationalistic and extrinsicist theology that calls for an intellectual
"obedience" to God along with an adherence to propositions accepted
on the basis of authority, but without any cognitive role for faith. This
attack situates the topicality of Chenu's contribution on theology as
science.

Likewise, the scientific structure of theology satisfies the mystical exigency to reject as inauthentic all religious knowledge that is "a rational
dialectic derived from a non-believing adherence to the articles of
faith." The traits of continuity and subalternation satisfy both the ratio-
nal-scientific and the religious-mystical requirements. "The very thing
which makes theology is a science is that which makes it mystical. The
theory of subalternation is no more than the technical formula of this
structural requirement of theological knowledge."[73]

72 (1943), 76–7; (1957), 71–2.
73 (1943), 79; (1957), 74.

The close correlation of the scientific and the religious contributes to the unique epistemological status of theology: "By right, theology is pious, it is worthy of being called *impressio divinae scientiae* [an impression of divine knowledge]." The key is the permanent presence of faith, which assures the "*continuité*" with the science of God and thus becomes the law of all theological endeavour.[74]

Chenu writes of the "perfect communion of religious value and scientific quality" as one of the fruits of the application of the theory of science to theology. The scientific structure of theology – more specifically, its relation to the science of God – dictates that the end of theological reflection is not the multiplication of conclusions, but the knowledge of God as God is revealed to us. This idea is also reflected in the fact that theology represents a subalternation of principles, not a subalternation of object. The object of theologians is no different than that of the science of God. Hence, in the case of theology, it is more proper to speak of a quasi-subalternation and an imperfect science. Yet the real subalternation of principles will prevent theology from reflecting "a certain extrinsicism" in relation to faith.[75]

It should be clear that the incarnation perspective does not make theology a particular case within the larger rule of human rationality. The fact that *sacra doctrina* is an imperfect science because it involves only a quasi-subalternation already signals a very special instance of human reasoning and knowing, and a transformation of the ordinary categories of principles and science. The continuity and the law of subalternation, in other words, impose on the subalternated science a certain critique composed of purification, transformation, and illumination.[76]

The proponents of a "pure" scripture theology unadulterated by philosophical concepts and reasons protested against the attempts to introduce scientific reason into sacred doctrine and thereby to dilute

74 (1943), 83; (1957), 77. The Latin phrase is from *Ia Pars, q. 1, a. 3, ad* 2. See also (1943), 108; (1957), 98.

75 Cf. (1943), 83–4; (1957), 77–8: "*La fin du labeur théologique, ce ne sont pas les 'conclusions,' c'est de connaître Dieu tel qu'il se révèle à nous.*" See also (1957), 84, n. 1, and the reference to Gagnebet's distinction between the subject and the object of theology: the subject is God and the object is the theological conclusion. On quasi-subalternation, see (1943), 86–92; (1957), 80–5.

76 This transformation of the subalternated science by the subalternating one is the basis of the answer to the charge of humanistic rationalism and horizontalism that may be levelled against the work of Chenu. It becomes particularly important in the development of the incarnation perspective in the historical and the social realms (cf. Chapters 3 and 4 in this book).

the strong wine of divine wisdom by mixing water: "*Vituperabiles sunt doctores sacrae scripturae philosophica documenta miscentes* [Those doctors of sacred scripture are blameworthy who mix in philosophical examples.]" The answer of St. Thomas was that the scientific enterprise in theology meant not the dilution of wine by means of water but the transformation of water into wine.[77]

Chenu shared this vision of the introduction of scientific reasoning into sacred doctrine. Human philosophical concepts, used as middle terms by theologians, are transformed. "So it is expressly in the act proper to science where, in reasoning, the theologian has recourse to a middle term to elaborate the revealed datum. This rational middle term must be controlled and as it were transposed from within, to be accredited in the sacred knowledge, beyond its original milieu." This use of human reason represents, in a certain sense, the limits to the incarnation perspective: the integrity of the human, yes, but the human is transformed. The rule in such cases is the analogy of faith. In this way, the unique character of theology is preserved and affirmed: "One even observes that, in the construction of theological reasoning, the revealed datum does not present itself as a particular case of a general rule, such that it is the minor premise of a syllogism of which the rational major premise is a universal principle; but it must be treated as a case that is eminent, original, specific – a case of which reduction to the common module cannot be done except under the safeguard of analogy. This must be in an impregnation and strict regulation of faith, such that the reasoning does not appear as the application of philosophical notions to a heterogeneous datum."[78]

However, the incarnation is real enough. The transfiguration of human concepts and reasoning does not involve a betrayal of human nature in the sense of making theology unnatural. Theological reason remains reason: *Gratia non tollit naturam sed perficit* (Grace does not remove nature but perfects it.) "Nonetheless this transfiguration does not overturn the rational structures at work in these concepts and reasonings: there is no denaturing. Theological reason, *ratio fide illustrata*, remains reason." Such a relationship between faith and reason, for Chenu, implies a real confidence in the ability of reason to serve and not to destroy the experience of faith: "It involves a *true* confidence, thanks to which

---

77 *In Boetium de Trin.*, q. 2, a. 3, obj. 5, ad 5; in (1943), 94; (1957), 86.

78 (1943), 95; (1957), 87. In this lies the origin of the freedom and the "divine right" of the theologian vis-à-vis the rational instruments of the other sciences.

reason enters *into* sacred doctrine, and exercises there a true causality, well beyond a mere occasionalism."[79]

Finally, the role of science and scientific method in theology is one of propaedeutic and comforter, as dictated by our human condition and by the mystery of incarnation. "A comfort, for – apart from its vanities, and granted its contemplative incompetence – science brings to faith the means of information (in one's reason) and of strengthening (in one's conduct) required both by our terrestrial condition and also by the terrestrial mystery of the Word made flesh."[80] The "contemplative incompetence" of reason and the scientific method naturally leads us to a consideration of the role of contemplation in the genesis and development of theological reflection. It will be set in the context of a more radical consideration of the relationship between the *donné* and the *construit* in theology.

THEOLOGICAL REFLECTION

How does the theological act of reflection actually work? To find the answer, we begin by considering the relationship of the *donné* and the *construit*, one of the most dynamic actualizations of the incarnation perspective. We also see that the central reference to contemplation in any theological construction points to the ongoing role of incarnation and to the importance of its permanent and living source. Finally, we examine the christological categories of the incarnation perspective used by Chenu to overcome the unproductive dualisms in theology.

Donné *and* construit

In many ways, the discussion about the role of the *donné* in relation to the constructive work of theological speculation parallels that about the role of faith in relation to reason, and is usually its extension within the more specific language of neoscholastic theological method.

In Chenu's understanding and practice of theology, the primacy lies with the "*donné révélé.*" This is more than a logical primacy; it is one of dignity and fecundity as well. The "*donné,*" a notion inherited from Gardeil, is the first principle of the object of faith. "The first principle of the

79 (1943), 96; (1957), 88.
80 (1943), 105; (1957), 96.

object of faith, the basis for its status, that which properly and inviolably
constitutes it as object of faith, is that it is 'given'. It is a teaching on a
reality which, of itself and by nature, by the nature of things and by
nature of man's mind, is beyond man's grasp; man receives it from without." The *donné* thus belongs to the heart of humanity's relationship to
God in the context of knowledge and understanding. It defines the area
within which the work of reason will take place in its quest for understanding, as well as the limits which may not be transgressed by the
believer's constructions. "The believer has thus to do with a 'given', and
any subsequent construction which would allow itself to slide however
slightly away from the 'given' would be for all that without real content."[81] This principle dictating the limits of speculation will become
particularly effective in relation to the domain of historical reality and
its claims on the *donné*.

The truth of the primacy of the given, along with the limits to the
speculation dependent on that given, is applicable not only to theology
but to any scientific enterprise. The *donné* in other sciences is secured
and taken for granted, as opposed to being revealed. In both cases, however, it retains a position of primacy. "The 'given' [*datum*] in the sciences is acquired; in theology, it is revealed; but in both cases, it is the
workplace, the field which yields not only elements and materials, but –
let us say it without any metaphor – the very sap which gives life:
[namely] the experienced or experienceable data, and the principles
making up the light under which these experiences are perceived, rea-
soned out, coordinated."[82] In this view of theology, speculative elaboration and construction – "the rational application" – are valid and
legitimate, but the primacy always lies with the *donné*. The constructs of
theology remain dependent on the given. Speculation is seen as an incarnation of the light of faith into rational structures. "The speculative
construction is not a conceptual edifice superimposed on a prior, and
once-for-all acquired, perception. It is a living embodiment in rational
structures, as in admirable works of the mind, of the light of faith." In
Une école de théologie, the *donné* is defined as a *présence*, hence there is
a special kind of primacy, "not only the sole dialectical primacy of
a proposition; but a *presence*, with the inexhaustible realism and silent

81 "Position" (1935), in *Parole* 1, 123. See also *Une école de théologie* (1937), 60: "*Le donné
révélé, le donné théologique n'est pas 'scientifique': il est révélé.*"
82 Ibid., 123–4.

insistence that this word implies – for the glance which has consented."
The *donné* is not something once and for all acquired, "not only a catalogue of propositions recorded in some kind of Denzinger, but a living,
copious material, always in action in the Church acting as depository,
pregnant with divine intelligibility."[83]

The description of the *donné* as a "*présence*" also affects the task of rational elaboration and speculation by shifting the emphasis from construction to allowing the given to manifest itself. "It is a permanent
presence, like that of the sap in a tree. An enveloping presence, for it is
not the 'constructed' that surrounds the 'given' with its subtle framework: it is the 'given' which, as a spiritual milieu overflowing on all
sides, builds itself up from within and under its own pressure." Such an
incarnational relationship between the *donné* and the *construit* will lead
Chenu to one of his fundamental theses, one that brought charges of
modernism from his Roman censors. In emphasizing the primacy of
the data of revelation as a living source for theology, Chenu assigns to
the faith perception acquired in contemplation a key function in the
genesis of theological reflection. Hence, Chenu can say: "It is contemplation which draws forth a theology, not theology which leads to contemplation."[84]

Chenu does not deny the rightful existence of the speculative function in theology; he even sees it as necessary. However, he does deny
that speculation will ever be wholly adequate to the religious perception of the given and to the spiritual experience of faith. In this context, he is happy to quote the maxim from the Tübingen theologian
Johannes Kuhn, "no theology without a new birth."[85] For Chenu, the
theologian must be a believer: "The theologian is a believer; he is a believer par excellence, and his task is formally accomplished in that mystery into which his faith has brought him, and not in the projection
into human words of the word of God ... This precisely is the dramatic
effort of the theologian to maintain in radical fragility of propositions
in which he embodies the realist perception of the mysterious reality
of God: a dialectic where his strength triumphs over his weakness – in

83   *Une école de théologie* (1937), 54, 69, 55. This clarifies the definition of the *donné* as an
enseignement given in "Position" (1935), in *Parole* 1, 123. In *Une école de théologie*, 69, writing
of this presence, Chenu adds: "*C'est en elle qu'on peut maintenant construire.*"

84   *Une école de théologie* (1937), 54. For the difficulties encountered by this statement,
see the next section of this chapter on the relationship between spirituality and theology.

85   "Position" (1935), in *Parole* 1, 115, 122; *Une école de théologie* (1937), 60.

faith." The theologian's task, according to this text from *Une école de théologie*, is to incarnate the *donné* – which is both "light of faith and revealed truths"[86] – into the "radical fragility" of concepts and propositions.

Further on in *Une école de théologie*, Chenu returns to the definition of the theologian and the theological task. The definition is centred on an incarnation of faith in reason. "[T]he theologian is he who dares to speak humanly the Word of God. Having heard this Word, he possesses it, or more exactly: it possesses him, to such a point that he thinks by it and in it, to such a point that he thinks the Word. The gift of God is a gift to such a point that it becomes human property: faith is a *habitus*. It is not an extraordinary charism, of which the transcendence would keep it apart from our human ways of thinking; it is the incarnation of the divine truth in the very fabric of our mind ... Faith dwells *in* reason, thus made competent to *theologein*." By pursuing the intelligibility of revelation by means of the various scientific tools, the theologian is true to faith's own logic: "Faith, by begetting theology, is within the very logic of its own perfection." The process of scientific rationalization and all other forms of intellectual construction in theology are only consequences and implications of the "regime of incarnation." "The same law which, a moment ago, had us calling for an incarnation of the word of God in human words over the course of history, urges us now to accept utterly the regime of knowledge which this incarnation implies: theology is in solidarity with the theandric mystery of the word of God, Word made flesh. There alone can theology find such a daring confidence in the coherence of faith and reason."[87] In this key passage, Chenu affirms the centrality of incarnation for the understanding of the proper relationships of faith and reason in the origins and developments of theological reflection.

---

86 *Une école de théologie* (1937), 59–60, 54. Similarly, the dogmatic statement is seen in an incarnation perspective on 60: "*La formule dogmatique n'est pas un énoncé juridique extérieur à la révélation qu'elle présente: elle est incarnation dans des concepts de la parole de Dieu.*" On theology without faith, see Chenu's sarcastic comment, ibid., 53–4: "*Désormais, l'assentiment purement formel à la formule dogmatique suffit, et le non-croyant peut bâtir sur elle un bon argument, si son syllogisme respecte la loi des trois termes. La théologie ne serait plus pieuse, elle resterait vraie. Nous, nous disons qu'elle serait morte, et, à la lettre, sans âme, jeu rationnel à la surface d'un donné. Théologie dérisoire: theo-logia, la 'parole de Dieu' ne parle plus en elle.*" Cf. *La théologie est-elle une science?* (1957), 42: "*Une théologie qui pourrait être vraie sans être pieuse, serait en quelque sorte monstrueuse.*"

87 *Une école de théologie* (1937), 69–70.

Just as faith is incarnate in human reason, so too is faith incarnate in scientific reason.

The Centrality of Contemplation

The incarnational structure set out by Chenu precludes the separation of the *construit* from the *donné*, the rational and scientific elaboration from the "mystical perception" and the *lumen fidei*. It is the ground for his dictum on the centrality of contemplation: "It is contemplation which draws forth a theology, not theology which leads to contemplation."[88]

It is also the ground for his writing, "all the techniques of reason are set to work within, and for the benefit of, the mystical perception of the believer." Chenu is adamant in keeping the unity of the theological (*"théologal"*) order. Accordingly, he rebukes those Thomists of the seventeenth century who sought to write a mystical theology by removing all speculative elements. The same Thomists advocated the radical separation of positive and speculative theology, a separation rejected by Chenu. According to him, they lost the "religious sense" of theological reflection; they abandoned to positive theology the return to the *donné*, which is the only way to renew this religious sense. "Theology, faith seeking theological understanding, is truly and properly a factor in the spiritual life. We do not do theology by adding *corollaria pietatis* [pious afterthoughts] to abstract theses cut from their objective and subjective datum, but in maintaining oneself in the profound unity of the theological order."[89]

The relationship between the mystical perception of the *donné* and the rational construction of theology is so intimate that Chenu makes theological construction an expression of this spiritual perception. Thus the grandeur and the truth of Bonaventurian or Scotist Augustinianism lie entirely in the spiritual experience of St. Francis. Similarly, the grandeur and the truth of Molinism lie in the *Spiritual Exercises* of St. Ignatius. A particular spirituality carries its own regime of intelligibility, which becomes the key to a particular set of theological reasonings and theological systems: "A theology worthy of the name is a spirituality which has found instruments adequate to its own religious experience."

88 Ibid., 54.
89 Ibid., 70–2; cf. also "Position" (1935), in *Parole* 1, 134.

Chenu continues: "It is that, categorically, theological systems are but the expression of spiritualities."[90]

This relationship between theology and spirituality is also the ground for progress, creativity, and invention in theology. Such progress, for Chenu, is not measured by the exploitation of a system or the proliferation of new conclusions; it originates with the permanent fecundity of the *donné*, from which arises the insatiable appetite of faith. This appetite strives for nothing less than the beatific vision. "The normal realm of discovery [*invention*], always at work beneath secular constructions, is thus (scientifically and religiously) this contemplative perception, from which a ceaseless return to the given obtains an always fresh perspective, and which arduously subtends the hope of vision." Contemplation, then, becomes the normal environment for the theologian. It is not an option to be exercised at will or when the need is felt. "Thus for the theologian, contemplation is not a summit, reached here and there by a burst of fervour, beyond his study, as it were by escaping from his object and his method. It is [rather] his normal, constitutive milieu, where alone scientific organization and new discovery can remain together in a unique fruitfulness."[91] So does Chenu reiterate the unique character of theological science, as well as the unique requirements on the practitioner of that science.

False Categories and Christological Errors

Theology is often produced without allusion to the role of faith and the faith experience. The inevitable result of any separation of theology

90 Ibid., 75. Congar has commented on this in "Le Père M.-D. Chenu," *Bilan* II, 779: "*On a voulu subodorer du modernisme dans cette idée. Il n'y en a pas. Il est exact qu'il faudrait apporter de nouvelles explications pour en préciser et en fonder pleinement la vérité.*" See also the fourth proposition of the 1938 condemnation reproduced in the reissue of *Une école de théologie* (Paris: Éditions du Cerf, 1985), 35: "*Sacra Theologia non est quaedam spiritualitas quae invenit instrumenta suae experimentiae religiosae adaequata; sed est vera scientia, Deo benedicente, studio acquisita, cuius principia sunt articuli Fidei et etiam omnes veritates revelatae quibus theologus fide divina, sattem informi, adhaeret.*"

91 Ibid., 76. Cf. also 52–3, where Chenu writes of the structural exigency of "religious perception." On the necessity of prayer, see *La théologie est-elle une science?* (1957), 41: "*La théologie ne peut se développer sainement, religieusement, et, à la limite, sans erreurs ... que si elle consent cordialement, 'fidèlement', à l'atmosphère sacrale et sacrée du mystère. Elle travaille là dans la curiosité de sa foi, mais dans une discrétion qui est à la fois l'effet de l'esprit de finesse et le signe de l'Esprit. Pauvre théologien, celui chez qui ... le mystère s'est détendu ... C'est dans la prière, dans l'adoration, dans la dévotion, au sens profond du mot, que naît et vit la théologie, l'intelligence de la Parole de Dieu.*"

from its *donné,* both as light and as content, is that theological reasoning and affirmations become groundless. Such separation usually takes the form of fideism or extrinsicism. Its error, as Chenu points out, is the denial of the incarnational structure of theology: "Always the same error, according to which theology is seen to be exterior to faith by its conceptualism, that is it is seen as conceptualizing without faith instead of being its product; the product of faith by the incarnation of this faith in a human mind."[92] Significantly for the law of incarnation, Chenu criticizes such errors in terms of christological heresies. A brief analysis of his references will contribute to an understanding of the incarnational position.

When Chenu criticizes the excesses of the *"conservatisme négatif"* of the anti-modernist reaction, particularly in the matter of historical research, he refers not only to a denial of legitimate research methodology but also to a theological error concerning the economy of revelation and its law of incarnation: "This was not only misunderstanding of a legitimate order of research, historically, but a theological error, if it is true that it is the very law of the economy of revelation that God manifests himself by and in history, that the eternal is incarnate in time where only the mind of man can reach it." Specifically, Chenu alludes to the problems encountered by the exegete M.-J. Lagrange in applying the historical method to scriptural studies. For Chenu, Lagrange represented an incarnational position. In his doctrine of inspiration, Chenu holds that "the incarnation of the word of God takes place even unto the very letters of words ... and the very letter, with all its grammatical, literary, historical force, is properly the path of access to the understanding of faith." The incarnational position on this matter could be stated as follows: "The word of God is *in* the human word: the strength of God is revealed in this weakness." Correlatively, Chenu characterizes the position of those who deny this incarnational view as "scriptural docetism": "Scriptural Docetism is but the false modesty of a fearful faith in a badly-placed theology."[93]

Chenu repeatedly reacts against an exaggerated emphasis on the supernatural and the spiritual, with its consequent depreciation of the natural and the material. The temptation in all relations with the divine is to skip the mediating structures and seek the encounter face to face.

92 *Une école de théologie* (1937), 72.
93 Ibid., 37, 62–3. On Lagrange, see also "Vérité et liberté dans la foi du croyant" (1959), in *Parole* 1, 338–59, esp. 340.

"The temptation of the believer is to reject what is human, all that is human – to separate himself from what upholds his activity in other domains, but seems to fetter him here: could we not skip steps and provoke already from down here the revelations of a forever-purified dialogue?" The mystical tendency, which minimizes all formal aspects of faith, sees dogma only as a dry and arbitrary formulation serving more as an obstacle than a mediating structure. Chenu, following the principles of Thomistic epistemology, calls dogma "the incarnation of the light in human words." In his doctrine of faith, Chenu warns against "false mystical evanescence of the spirit," which wants to leave behind all that is human: "It is a false exaltation of the supernatural to situate it outside the law and psychology of our nature." If we must eliminate all that is human prior to entering the supernatural, then, in Chenu's words, "the matter is botched": "If man must eliminate the normal and sound content of his life to enter into the supernatural, it is a failure, for it is precisely all this human content that must be raised to the supernatural and thenceforth blossom on that plane."[94] We must avoid the "false idealism" of docetism, which sees in Christ only the appearance of a human nature.

Chenu is aware of the almost instinctual care to "protect" the supernatural character of the perception of faith and the consequent denial of the human dimension. "Now, it sometimes happens that, out of concern and as it were eagerness to express the supernatural quality of the perception of faith, we neglect as though of slight importance its firm seat in the mind of the believer." The work of faith, and thus the work of theology, is such that it seems to escape the ordinary way of human acting and thinking. The subsequent tendency is to equate supernatural and super-human, as if the supernatural knowing of faith were super-rational. Chenu sees this tendency as an unfortunate reductionism, which eliminates the "human equilibrium of grace" and violates the law of incarnation: "Troublesome telescoping which, in the end ruins the human equilibrium of grace, or truer still, ruins the insertion, the incarnation of the divine life in the very organism of our action."[95] Faith would no longer be human faith, and the life thereby engendered would no longer be human life.

94 "L'unité" (1937), in *Parole* 1, 17, 18, cf. *Une école de théologie* (1937), 60, 70. See also L.A. Gallo, *La concepción*, 92, who refers to an "implicitly docetic" tendency.

95 "Position" (1935), in *Parole* 1, 131, 132. Chenu continues: "*La foi ne se produit pas en nous par une série de charismes, ordinaires ou extraordinaires; mais elle se fixe par un enracinement dans le tissu même de notre esprit.*"

Chenu's doctrine of faith, in which he follows Gardeil in the rediscovery of the *lumen fidei*, is the first area where the law of incarnation is manifest. In an effort to overcome the destructive dualism created by rationalism in theology, Chenu invokes the law of incarnation to stress the twofold nature of faith, namely, its supernatural character and the integrity of its human condition. Faith is incarnate in reason and is thus related to the theandric mystery of the two natures in Christ. Neither is contaminated by this relationship of incarnation.

Echoing Augustine's *cor inquietum*, faith, for Chenu, includes a quest for intelligibility within the assent given by the believer. This inner curiosity, like an insatiable thirst, gives rise to a theology which is thus called *fides in statu scientiae*. The theory of subalternation, by which theology is said to be a science, is in fact a technical application of the law of incarnation preserving the supernatural character of faith as well as its expression in the scientific apparatus of reason. It is significant that this expression involves the transformation of human reasoning and concepts. By definition, the theologian must be a believer. In this context, contemplation is a structural necessity, the normal environment for the theologian.

The law of incarnation functions to maintain the necessity of faith in theology, to preserve the proper balance in the relationship of *donné* and *construit*, and to overcome any docetic tendencies in theological reflection on nature and grace. As such, its intention is not only methodological but substantive.

3

Christianity and History

WHAT WAS TRUE OF THE ECONOMY OF THE WORD in relation to the human condition of understanding (i.e., what is known is known according to the knowing of the knower), is equally true of the concrete human condition to the extent that this condition is not accidental but enters the very definition of human existence. In the Christian economy of revelation, it is the human condition that decides the basic configuration of the *donné*. Christianity is an economy because we are historical beings. The principle of divine communication reaches its highest manifestation in the mystery of the incarnation. In Chenu's terms, "humanization is the path of divinization." The discovery of the true dimensions of human existence thus leads to a better appreciation of the true proportions of the divine economy. The law of nature becomes a law of grace.[1]

The previous chapter outlined the model of incarnation as a basic two-in-one structure of supernatural and natural, divine and human. The field of description, however, was limited to the rational dimension of human existence, bracketing out, so to speak, the historical, social,

---

1 "Théologie et recherche" (1970), 68. The full passage is as follows: "*Ce n'est pas là seulement un fait à enregistrer, comme à regret; c'est le principe même de la communication du Dieu révélateur. Principe dont le jeu est consommé par l'incarnation même de cette Parole: opération, si l'on peut dire, qui est le tout du christianisme. L'humanisation est la voie de la divinisation.*" Cf. "Dimension nouvelle" (1937), in *Parole* 2, 92, with regard to the social dimensions of human existence: "*Loi de nature qui devient loi de grâce.*" See also "*Révolution communautaire*" (1944), in *Parole* 2, 366: "*[C]e ne sont pas seulement les lois de la nature humaine en général, les lois éternelles et métaphysiques, qui vont rendre raison du comportement de la grâce et en manifester les voies; ce sont les états concrets de cette nature, ses conduites présentes dans l'évolution des sociétés et la variété des civilisations.*"

and practical dimensions, and thus calling for a broader treatment of incarnation in relation to a more comprehensive view of human existence.

Continuing the gradual approach set out earlier, the present chapter extends the scope of incarnation by including the historical dimension of the human situation and the corresponding self-understanding of Christianity as economy. Although this extension turns towards the concrete and the historical, it still remains heavily abstract. The turn to the concrete will be completed in the next chapter, with the consideration of the pastoral situation of the French Church in the face of growing dechristianization and the challenge of secular modernity. In this sense, the present chapter removes only one set of brackets. To anticipate, however, we can point to a survey of *La vie intellectuelle* in 1933–35 on the reasons for contemporary unbelief. In particular, we draw attention to its concluding theological evaluation by Congar, in which the separation of faith and life, or "disincarnate faith," is described as the most basic element in the process of dechristianization and, therefore, as calling for a strategy of presence and incarnation that would reassimilate the human element in its concreteness. Christianity had to regain those aspects of human existence that it had lost in the privatization of faith. "What is not assumed is not redeemed."[2]

In Chenu's writings, a first sketch of the meaning and function of incarnation is now amplified by his confrontation with the problem of historicity and his effort to integrate the claims of historical consciousness within theology. We begin with Chenu's understanding of the challenge of history in terms of a shift from an abstract, spiritualist view of the human situation to a concrete, existential view. We then move to his explicit attempt to integrate the recovery of time in theology. The writings under consideration are primarily, though not exclusively, from the mid-1930s to the mid-1950s. Although systematic in the organization of its theme, our approach is mainly expository and interpretive. As the earlier chapter focused on the incarnation of faith in human understanding, so the present one focuses on tempo-

---

2 Cf. Y. Congar, "Une conclusion théologique à l'enquête sur les raisons actuelles de l'incroyance," in *VI* 37 (1935): 241–2, 248: " ... *partout où il y a de l'homme, de l'humanité, il doit y avoir Corps mystique, extension de l'Incarnation rédemptrice ... Il faut que la foi redevienne humainement présente, comme le Christ.*"

rality as a fundamental *locus* for the incarnation of faith. The theme is therefore the incarnation of the eternal in time, or *L'Évangile dans le temps.*[3]

THE HUMAN SITUATION

If the revelation of the divine economy proceeds according to the conditions of the recipient of divine grace, it follows that a study of anthropology would figure prominently in any theology, and that it would include a position on the concrete human situation. Chenu rejects any form of dualism, and his view of the human person as incarnate spirit here becomes explicit. Christian existence, as based on incarnation, implies more than a disembodied "reason" or "spirit"; it also involves a material situation conditioned by space and time. We therefore begin with a short description of the dualism inherent in what may be called the "spiritualist" position. Then we sketch the characteristics of Chenu's view of the human situation in terms of a threefold recovery of lost elements: the material, the historical, and the social. Incarnation remains the focus of interest throughout, and the overcoming of destructive dualisms continues to be its principal function.[4]

Dualism or the Augustinian Option

Chenu clearly states that his anthropology is based on the choice of one particular position, as distinguished from other options available in the history of Christianity. Specifically, he follows the unified conception of

---

3 The reference is to the title of the second volume of Chenu's collected essays, which parallels the title of the first, *La foi dans l'intelligence.* Cf. "Présentation" (1964), in *Parole* 1, 8: "*le parallélisme se fonde sur la loi d'incarnation de la Parole de Dieu, tant dans l'esprit de l'homme que dans le déroulement de l'histoire.*"

4 Cf. "Pour une anthropologie" (1974), 98: "*L'homme doit être considéré dans toute sa réalité concrète, selon le mot biblique, purgé de ce qu'il peut y avoir de dualisme dans les oppositions entre âme et corps, esprit et matière – et j'ajouterais, en téléscopant les analyses, entre histoire et cosmos, et même entre grâce et nature.*" See also "Homélie" (1970), 44–5, where Chenu gives an extensive definition of the term "*situation*": "*La 'situation' inclut la totalité de la conscience créatrice que l'homme a de lui-même à un moment déterminé, la somme des formes scientifiques, sociales ou morales, dans lesquelles la conscience d'une génération trouve, avec son expression, la satisfaction de ses espérances.*"

human existence offered by the Thomistic option, as opposed to the dualistic one found in the tradition of Augustinianism.[5]

From the outset, Christianity has involved two irreducible elements joined together in the mystery of the incarnation. Some form of tension is inevitable. The transcendent and the immanent always represent a two-in-one relationship and thus a danger of a potential one-sided reduction. The Christian faith does not impose a particular anthropological position, as long as the doctrine of the soul's immortality is respected and the body is not seen as being a consequence of an evil principle. There remains, therefore, a wide range of possible and legitimate opinions as to the meaning of the human person and the relative value of the material body.

In the unfolding of the history of Christianity, however, the practice was quite different. More often than not, there was a tendency to interpret the particular relationship between material and spiritual realities in the human being as regrettable. As a result of the pervasive influence of Platonism, the body was described as, at best, a temporary dwelling and, at worst, a prison, while the world was seen as no more than the preparatory ground for the celestial city.[6] In Chenu's reading of this history, the inclination long persisted to emphasize the values represented by the eternal, the spiritual, the ahistorical, and the abstract, and correspondingly, to neglect the values represented by the temporal, the material, the historical, and the concrete.

Dualism, most visible in the relationship between the material and the spiritual, was a dominant position in Christian history. Indeed, an entire tradition of thought conceived this relationship on the basis of a dualism that no amount of sophisticated coordination could dissolve. "The inmost history of Christianity reveals, beneath the clearest dogmatic forms against all Manichaenism, the permanent attraction and presence of a certain dualism which transposes into psychological structures the conflict between nature and grace ... [I]t pushes to the margin of contemplation, at least, if not of salvation, all that matter grasps within its determinism." Plato, or at least Platonism, was seen as the

5 See "Devenir social" (1947), in *Travail,* 109–10: "*Je reconnais qu'en m'avançant ainsi, j'opte pour une certaine conception de l'homme: la conception qu'a proposée saint Thomas d'Aquin ... j'opte expressément ... pour la philosophie qui considère la personne humaine, corps et âme, comme un tout.*" Chenu acknowledges, however, the legitimacy and orthodoxy of other philosophical options. Even his position on St. Augustine is more nuanced than appears; cf. "Pour lire saint Augustin" (1930).

6 Cf. "Présentation" (1967), in *Matière,* 8.

master of this mentality. Augustine was its representative in Christianity. Chenu refers equally to Platonism, Augustinianism, and Cartesianism as proponents of "a certain duality of the human composite." In this sense, Augustinianism is far from being the only source of modern dualism. According to Chenu, most of the spiritual writers from the nineteenth century held a dualist position that was diffusely inherited not only from Augustinianism but also from Cartesianism and its related by-products.[7]

Christianity was also been haunted by the temptation of dualism when it emphasized the higher region of the soul as the locus of communion with God, the secret place that escapes the chains of corporality. In this sense, the Christian religion represented an escape from the trappings of temporality. Carried into christology, such a bias becomes monophysitism and docetism, categories that Chenu is fond of applying to all manifestations of dualism: "intemporal Christianity, in a more or less Monophysite Christology." This kind of "psychological dualism" leads not only to a depreciation of the material order and to a general indifference to the human presence in the world but also to an overall insensitivity to history. With another reference to christological categories, Chenu describes the need for a reflection "[a]gainst an unconscious Docetism, which has for too long fed an abstract, intemporal and acosmic 'spirituality' ... "[8] Similarly, he writes of the docetic and monophysite dispositions which kept "the incarnate Word away from its human nature, away from the reality of the world, and which today would keep it away from history, in an intemporal contemplation."[9]

---

7 "Réflexions chrétiennes" (1948), in *Parole* 2, 447. cf. "Pour une théologie" (1952), in *Travail*, 35. See "Condition nouvelle" (1960), in *Parole* 2, 470, where the hidden dualism of spirit and matter is seen as the root of the rejection of technology by much of modern Christianity. Chenu is careful to make a distinction between Augustine and Augustinianism; for example, on the view of the body as the result of an evil principle, see "Présentation" (1967), in *Matière*, 8: "*Le génie d'Augustin surmontait le grave déséquilibre de pareille conception; mais la vulgarisation de cette philosophie 'spiritualiste' pesa pendant plus d'un millénaire sur le comportement chrétien ... On succombait ainsi à la tare de la philosophie grecque et de son aristocratisme antiévangélique.*" See also "Spiritualité" (1962), in *Parole* 2, 457, n. 2. Chenu adds: "*Sans parler d'une certaine philosophie laïque, dans l'honorable bourgeoisie de ce temps. Aujourd'hui, psychologues, sociologues, phénoménologues ont réagi vigoureusement; ne les incriminons point de matérialisme!*"

8 "Histoire" (1968), 31–2: "*Conception intemporelle de l'homme, qui, chez le chrétien, atrophiait le sens de l'économie du salut et la visée eschatologique de sa foi.*" This is related to the dualism of *ratio inferior* and *ratio superior,* cf. "Ratio inferior et superior. Un cas de philosophie chrétienne" (1940). Note the use of christological categories to describe tendencies of Christian thought in general, setting the stage for an advocacy of the incarnation model. Cf. "Un'antropologia" (1975), 297.

9 "Présentation" (1967), in *Matière*, 11.

Elsewhere, Chenu interprets the liturgical and biblical renewals as attempts to root out docetic tendencies in the name of an incarnation perspective that holds temporality as a positive characteristic to be valued. "The biblical movement and the liturgical movement ... reject emphatically this 'spiritualism', this 'eternalism', this pseudo-scholastic idealism. The Christian is not in eternity. In short, an unconscious Docetism, to the extent that it blurs an incarnation of which the temporality is one of the signs of human reality, whether it be the Word in sacred history, or whether it be Christ himself."[10] As this passage clearly shows, temporality will be included in the renewed perspective in the name of incarnation and also in the name of human realism.

The spiritualist position, however, is guilty not so much of ignoring history and the temporal predicaments of human existence as of viewing them as no more than *accidentally* important, as extrinsic to the essential human destiny. They become no more than the amorphous and meaningless receptacle of actions and decisions whose norm is extrinsic and spiritual, located in "an immobile eternity."[11]

To a philosophy of essences that emphasizes the eternal values, time always appears as something unintelligible, irreducible to the mystery of being, which must remain beyond the realm of the temporal. Time must thus be expurgated as something unclean. The instability of the present, in terms of the succession of moments and in relation to its disappearance from the future and into the past, points to the radical deficiency of the temporal as compared to the eternal. From the viewpoint of essences, only being is immutable and therefore identical to itself. Becoming involves changing and thus non-being. Human existence receives its meaning from participation in the immutability of the creator. In this view, temporality may even become the impediment to this participation rather than its expression. Human existence in the world is then only a temporary pilgrimage. In this obscure drama, the world is not a dwelling-place.[12]

10 "Histoire sainte" (1961), in *Parole* 1, 286.
11 "Matérialisme" (1948), in *Parole* 2, 463. Chenu adds: "*Tous les fixismes sociologiques ont là leur justification métaphysique.*"
12 See "Situation" (1960), in *Parole* 2, 422–3: "*Pour une philosophie des essences, le temps apparaît toujours comme quelque chose d'inintelligible, d'irréductible à la définition d'un être, laquelle ne peut qu'être indépendante du temps. Il le faut donc expurger, comme une souillure. L'instabilité de l'instant, des instants qui composent le temps, est l'indice de sa débilité radicale, dans l'affaissement continu du présent entre le passé et l'avenir. L'être est immuable, se définissant par l'identité à lui-même; changer, c'est ne plus être; le devenir est du non-être.*"

Serious consequences arise when the notion of time as uncleanliness and stain is related not only to being but also to truth. Truth is also immutable and does not change with time. Therefore, to the extent that it follows the precepts of truth, human existence may escape the vagaries of temporality. Conversely, eternal truth has no room for historicity.

The Recovery of Matter: The Unity of Body and Soul

Chenu begins his description of the human situation with a consideration of the basic relationship between matter and spirit. It is in this relationship that the weakness of the dualist position is most glaring. The issue of the adequacy and validity of the spiritualist and dualist position is resolved not in relation to cosmic principles or eternal truths but in relation to its understanding of concrete human existence. Anthropology is thus the point of contention in the battle arena between dualism and an alternative vision.[13]

Starting with the irreducible duality of the two elements, Chenu asserts that the transcendence of the spiritual does not involve a rejection of the material, but rather an acceptance of matter in terms of the different levels of the human composition. The transcendence of the spirit operates in and through the material. The human being is thus in solidarity with the cosmos; human perfection does not consist in transcending the relationship to the world, as something to be left behind, but in seeking fulfillment within worldly existence. Only in the world will the human being find moral and ontological balance. "Man is not an alien come down from another world; he does not understand himself except to the extent that, recapitulating the cosmos, he possesses it in a way by slowly and laboriously penetrating it with his mind; in rendering it rational, as he virtuously makes rational his own body, of which the world then is seen to be the extension." When there is a dualism in our view of human existence, when there is no solidarity with the cosmos, there follows a rejection of any *earthly* development, commitment, or value. The only recognized value is the one that transcends *and leaves behind* the here and now. It is in this context that the argument for the consubstantial unity of body and soul really becomes effective. According to this view, human immanence

13 Chenu's preference for the concrete as opposed to the abstract is reflected in his understanding of Christianity as a historical economy concerned with concrete events. On the understanding of human existence as the point of contention, see "Pour une théologie" (1952), in *Travail*, 34–7, where it is called "*le point de rupture*" between Aristotelianism and Augustinianism. Chenu also refers to this as "*le plus âpre champ de controverse*" ("Spiritualité" [1962], in *Parole* 2, 457). The body-soul issue was "*le point chaud*" of the controversy ("Saint Thomas innovateur" [1975], 43).

in the world does not dissolve the transcendence of the human spirit, whereas spiritualist dualism implies the denial of any earthly commitments and values. The point is not to dissolve the connection to the world through the body, but to realize its essential function in the quest for human and religious fulfillment: "Immanence to the world, which destroys nothing of the transcendence of his spirit."[14]

In this view, human immanence in the world does not impede or destroy the spirit. For Chenu and the Aristotelian-Thomistic tradition, the transcendence of the spirit is not denied by the values of the material realm, since its own reality remains preserved: "The transcendence of the spirit is in no way clouded by this immanence to the world, for in the consubstantiality of soul and body, the subsistence itself of the spirit remains intact." In fact, not only is human transcendence not subverted by its situation in the world, but its fulfillment is tied to that of the world: "It fulfils itself in fulfilling the world ... The universe is not a provisional scaffolding in the construction of humanity."[15] This approach will clearly bear serious implications for any theology of pastoral action.

Chenu does not create such claims without any basis. His thought in this area is firmly grounded in the recovery of Thomistic teaching on the dignity of matter. Characteristically, Chenu returns to the thirteenth century to seek the inspiration needed in the twentieth. When it was first articulated, the teaching of St. Thomas on the consubstantial unity of body and soul was the cause of much controversy. Nor did it fare well after Thomas, since it was almost forgotten by the Church and its theologians. Only with certain developments of modernity, as witnessed by the progress of psychology, have the conditions been created for a fruitful recovery of Thomistic anthropology.[16]

---

14 "Situation" (1960), in *Parole* 2, 432; "Condition nouvelle" (1960), in *Parole* 2, 471.

15 "Situation" (1960), in *Parole* 2, 432. Chenu here refers with approval to Hans Urs von Balthasar's treatment of the human "situation" in relation to the cosmos in *Dieu et l'homme d'aujourd'hui* (Paris: Éditions du Cerf, 1958), 67–9.

16 Cf. ibid., 428, where Chenu points to the conflict between Aristotelianism and Augustinianism as centring on the relationship of body and soul: " ... *il n'est pas exagéré de considérer ce conflit comme le pivot sur lequel, même en théologie, les problèmes trouvèrent position et les mentalités leurs clivages.*" Cf. "Présentation" (1967), in *Matière*, 9: "*De fait, malgré la fidélité, purement scolastique d'ailleurs, de ses disciples, l'anthropologie de saint Thomas ne pénétra guère dans la mentalité des docteurs ni dans le comportement des maîtres spirituels chrétiens. Aujourd'hui seulement, avec le progrès de la psychologie, avec une vision du monde qui engage dans l'histoire humaine la domination de la nature, le crédit officiel de saint Thomas dans l'Église devient efficace.*" Cf. also "Réflexions" (1948), in *Parole* 2, 449, where Chenu speaks of each age in history as having the vocation of highlighting one or another of the poles of opposites in the basic relations between the two elements. The emphasis in our age is on the "*vérité humaine de la matière.*"

In his work, St. Thomas was rejecting not only summary forms of dualism between matter and spirit but also the multiple forms of anthropological dualism which, in one way or another, denied the full consubstantiality of body and soul. For Chenu, following St. Thomas' teaching, the soul is immaterial, yet it is the form of the body. It is thus substantially united to the body by the nature of its own essence. Chenu offers the following formulation: "It is in the soul itself that one must seek the body's reason for being: inapt to subsist in a separated state, though its spiritual nature guarantees its survival once it exists, the soul calls for substantial conjunction with a body – ontologically, so as to exist, and psychologically, so as to act." The implication for an understanding of matter is clear. In such a unity, matter is *good* and a source of good; it is not the result of some ontological fault: "It is even more than a mere condition for the conquest of spirit by itself."[17]

In this way, matter is rehabilitated, so to speak, and acquires a vital rôle in the very life of the spirit: "Thus reintegrated with human nature, unto the very person of man, matter is clothed with a dignity which we have dared to call a 'spirituality'." Following the Thomistic maxim that matter is the principle of individuation, Chenu shows that the human being becomes a human *person* through the material body. While the material body provides individuation to the spiritual soul, it is the soul that provides organization, life, and existence. Though immaterial, the soul includes a reference to matter in its access to existence. Separated from the body, the soul is not a person: "[T]he personhood of man does not consist in the exclusive emergence of spirit."[18]

One of the first implications of such a unity between body and soul appears on the level of understanding. It is not the mind that knows and carries on the different activities of the intellectual life, but the human person as a whole *by means of the mind*. Nor is it the case that the human

17 "Situation" (1960), in *Parole* 2, 429. According to Chenu's own acknowledgement, much of the vocabulary here comes from Étienne Gilson, cf. *Le thomisme*, 6 ed. (Paris: Vrin, 1972), 241–54. For a more extensive presentation of the doctrine of the unity of body and soul in the history of Christian tradition, see F. Fiorenza and J.B. Metz, "Der Mensch als Einheit von Leib und Seele," in *Mysterium Salutis* II (Einsiedeln: Benziger, 1967), 584–636.

18 "Spiritualité" (1962), in *Parole* 2, 459, 456. Note the use of the term "nature" instead of "condition" or "situation" in Chenu's description. In connection with this, Chenu cites two texts from St. Thomas: "*Dicendum quod non tantum ab anima habet homo quod sit persona, sed ab ea et corpore, cum ex utroque subsistat*" (*In III Sent. disp. 5, q. 3, a. 2*) and "*Non quaelibet substantia particularis est hypostasis vel persona, sed quae habet completam naturam speciei. Unde manus vel pes non potest dici hypostasis vel persona, et similiter nec anima, cum sit pars speciei humanae*" (*Ia Pars, q. 75, a. 4, ad 2*). Chenu also refers to the chapter on the human person in the work of Jean Mouroux, *Sens chrétien de l'homme* (Paris: Aubier, 1948), 105–30.

person finds unity in an act of interiorisation that would dissolve all relations with the exterior world.[19]

Chenu emphasizes how St. Thomas, in the debate on the "unity of forms," rejected any division within the life of the mind, where the "higher" region of the mind would occupy itself with the contemplation of eternal and divine truths, and the "lower" area of the mind would focus on the knowledge and construction of the world. To employ another vocabulary, there would be an "intellect" in the pursuit of wisdom on the one hand, and a "reason" in the pursuit of science on the other, or else a *ratio superior* and a *ratio inferior.* Following in the footsteps of Thomas, Chenu is adamant: "There is no faculty of the divine."[20]

A dualism of this sort would carry serious consequences for any pastoral theology, social doctrine, or theological understanding of historical events. To the extent that these areas would fall under the rule of the Church's contemplative knowing – the ecclesial form of *ratio superior* – the integrity of the human situation in each area would be endangered. For Chenu, the soul is one and, by reason of its consubstantial unity with the body, may not escape the vagaries of history: "Of itself, a soul would gauge its own activity in the *aevum*; but, consubstantial with matter, *the human soul lives and acts in time; it never escapes from history.*"[21] With this, we touch on the implications of matter and corporality for a consideration of historicity and a recovery of time in a renewed anthropology.

The Recovery of Time: Human Historicity

The recovery of matter as an essential aspect of concrete human existence – namely, as human corporality – represents only one of the aspects of the human situation. Equally important is the fact that human

19 See "Spiritualisme" (1961), in *Parole* 2, 438: "*Ce n'est pas l'intelligence qui connaît et qui pense, mais l'homme, corps et âme, par son intelligence. Si l'homme est personne, et, au sommet de lui-même, dans la liberté et dans l'amour, ce n'est pas la seule intériorisation à soi-même, c'est, en même temps, et sans détriment pour cette décision suprême, par une relation à l'univers extérieur, qui entre dans la construction de la vie de l'esprit et dans l'identité personnelle.*"

20 "Situation" (1960), in *Parole* 2, 431. See also "Spiritualité" (1962), in *Parole* 2, 457; "Matérialisme et spiritualisme" (1948), in *Parole* 2, 462–3; cf. "Histoire du salut" (1968), 31: "*Au cours des siècles, sinon toujours en théorie, du moins en mentalité et en comportement, la 'spiritualité' chrétienne (le mot est significatif) a presque toujours penché, plus ou moins consciemment, pour l'existence d'une certaine région de l'âme échappant au corps pour être le lieu de la rencontre avec Dieu.*"

21 Ibid., Chenu's emphasis. Cf. St. Thomas, *De Pot.*, q. *3*, a. *10*, ad *8*: "*Anima mensuratur tempore, secundum esse quo unitur corpori, quamvis prout consideratur ut substantia quaedam spiritualis mensuratur aevo.*" See also *Ia-IIae*, q. *53*, a. *3*, ad *3*: "*Pars intellectiva animae secundum se est supra tempus, sed pars sensitiva subiacet tempori.*"

beings are situated in time. Together, corporality and temporality provide the coordinates for the human situation.[22]

This idea is the theme of a key article by Chenu, based on a talk given in 1958, entitled "Situation humaine: Corporalité et temporalité."[23] Historicity follows from the fact of corporality. In fact, human beings are in time because they have material bodies. "It is because he is consubstantially matter and spirit that man is in time and that history enters into the human fabric. An angel is neither in society nor in history."[24] Although temporality and corporality represent "the homogeneous coordinates of man's 'situation'," primacy lies with the material condition: "But the body is definitely the point of insertion into the world." The human condition is of "man-in-the-world," where the world is "corporal reality and existence in time par excellence."[25]

Historicity and the value of history in general are seen by Chenu as among the greatest discoveries of modernity. The achievement of the integration of historicity into the human sciences in the nineteenth century was an event of great magnitude whose echo still reverberates today: "Without doubt, awareness of his being-in-history, as of his being-in-the-world, is the most significant feature of the new man in modern civilization." It should be noted that, in praising the discovery and the integration of historicity, however, Chenu is also aware of the ambiguity involved in this "*prise de conscience*" and the errors and false perceptions it can evoke.[26]

---

22 Cf. "Présentation" (1964), in *Parole* 2, 11: "*corporéité et temporalité définissent uniment la situation de l'homme.*"

23 In the presentation of the volume of collected essays *L'Évangile dans le temps*, Chenu describes this article as "*sans doute la clef de l'ensemble*," (ibid., n. 3). The article was first published in 1960 and then appears in *Parole* 2, 411–36, under "Fidélité à l'Incarnation." It was reprinted once again in *Matière* (1968), 31–63.

24 "Une constitution pastorale de l'Église" (1966), in *Peuple*, 24.

25 "Situation" (1960), in *Parole* 2, 428; see also 431. In this context, Chenu cites with approval two aphorisms from M. Merleau-Ponty's *Phénoménologie de la perception* (Paris: Gallimard, 1945): "*Être au monde à travers un corps*" and "*Le corps n'est pas une chose, il est une* situation." 413. The two traits define a "*double et unique comportement*" where "*avoir un corps, c'est aussi et par le fait être dans le temps.*" See also Chenu's article "L'homme-dans-le-monde" (1963), 171–5.

26 "Présentation" (1967), in *Matière*, 9–10. See also "Devenir" (1947), in *Travail*, 78, where the integration of history in human knowledge is seen as "*l'incontestable grandeur du XIXᵉ siècle*". Together with socialization, it is "*un événement spirituel de première grandeur, dont nous mesurons désormais la portée pour cet humanisme total qu'appelle le monde du XXᵉ siècle.*" For the integration of historicity in Christianity, see the present chapter; for the integration of socialization, see chapter 4 of this book. For "*prise de conscience*" and its ambiguity, cf. "Une constitution pastorale de l'Église" (1966), in *Peuple*, 25. See also "Situation" (1960), in *Parole* 2, 427, where temporality is seen primarily as an essential coordinate of human existence in the world, but also "*comme l'indice de sa faiblesse sans doute, en sa condition de créature.*"

Historicity is not an accidental trait of human existence, but something intrinsic to the definition of human beings: "History is a dimension of the very being of incarnate spirit." Hence, it is not something that can be disregarded when analysing the characteristics of the human situation, or, if those characteristics are taken under consideration, something that can be interpreted as an unfortunate circumstance. Chenu refers to this view of historicity in terms of a growing awareness in his own theological development: "A conviction of greater and greater firmness and motive took root in me: time, far from being a stain, is part of the make-up of the life of the mind and enters into the understanding of things; historicity is an essential dimension of man." This characteristic of human existence is clarified by Chenu's preference for the term *condition* rather than *nature* when describing human existence and its fundamental structures. In this way, Chenu speaks of the human being as *situated* in time: "Man is *in history*, not by some accident but by his very nature, where time is a dimension of his being and a gauge of his action ... "[27]

It is the temporal dimension of human existence that orients the human being in terms of past, present and future. This orientation, which defines human perfectibility, operates in terms of a recapitulation of the past, an anticipation of the future, and a manifestation of action in the present. Human actions and hopes are thus articulated in terms of temporality: "[Man] finds stability and perfection in gauging his action, and his very hopes, against the movement of this world and of this society, (of which he is the personal and collective consciousness), by his capacity to recapitulate the past in the movement of the present, with a view to the future."[28]

When human historicity is seen in terms of an orientation towards human perfectibility, and when human existence is seen in terms of a condition of being-in-the-world, then human fulfillment is intrinsically related to the fulfillment of the world: " ... his perfection does not con-

---

27 "Spiritualisme" (1961), in *Parole* 2, 443; "Présentation" (1964), in *Parole* 2, 7; "Les événements" (1965), 18, Chenu's emphasis. The preference for the the term "condition" suggests a move away from the classical moralists and their consideration of "natural law" and other permanent structures of human existence: "*Sans rejeter certes cette nécessaire considération, nous sommes devenus plus sensibles aux limites de cette abstraction sous laquelle l'homme est présenté, sous couleur de haute spiritualité, comme toujours identique à lui-même, ne trouvant dans la mobilité des jours, que des variantes secondaires, avec des problèmes d'application, voire un indice de sa déchéance.*"

28 "Les événements" (1965), 18–19.

sist in overcoming existence in the world ... He fulfils himself in fulfilling the world." What was described as the measure of human action is thus the measure of a "destiny." Human temporality is not a succession of individual moments; rather, it involves a direction that is constitutive of history and that is located within "the eternal designs of a transcendent providence, made present in personal and collective consciousness."[29]

It is in this connection that Chenu explores the theme of the human person as co-creator with God in the building-up of the world: "He is a partner with God in the building of the world. The accomplishment of this potential of man implies correlatively the experience of reality as history. Man is unthinkable apart from history, even as he confers a historic dimension upon the universe." Human temporality, therefore, is that by which time receives meaning and becomes history. Through the human person, history becomes the project of progressive humanization: "Man humanizes nature. History is thus the human realm of Creation." This intimate relationship among the creator, the creature, and history is illustrated when Chenu refers to history as "this progressive realization of the image of God in the world."[30]

The history of humanity, for Chenu, is thus a progressive history. It is not an empty receptacle for the vagaries of fate. Temporality implies a content and a direction – an evolution. Chenu regards this progress as involving more freedom (i.e., personalization) and, at the same time, greater communion among the members of the human race (i.e., socialization). "This evolution takes on an always greater *freedom* to the extent that it accomplishes more and more *communion* among men, if it is true that, through the ages, for the human masses, the emancipation of persons has always been in proportion to communitarian commitment."[31] Chenu's option with regard to the project of historicity and the content of historical evolution is clear: "If a destiny is involved, we are in history. For history begins with the dawn of a collective consciousness."[32] And again: "Time, reality of history, is not the

---

29 "Spiritualité" (1962), in *Parole* 2, 458; "Création" (1974), 394; cf. "Body" (1979), 204.

30 "Création" (1974) 391–2, 393; cf. "Body" (1979), 201, 203. On the theme of the person as co-creator, see "Présentation" (1967), in *Matière*, 12. As the unity of matter and spirit, the human person carries the resources of spirit, intellect, and love, to the last posts of material reality: "*Le voilà l'homme coopérateur, nous dirions co-créateur (si le mot n'était ambigu) de l'univers.*"

31 "Devenir" (1947), in *Travail*, 78. The similarity with the views of Pierre Teilhard de Chardin is unmistakable. Chenu was familiar with his writings and recognized there an approach similar to his own; cf. "Une théologie pour le monde" (1967), 13.

32 "Les masses humaines, mon prochain?" (1966), in *Peuple*, 105.

amorphous and meaningless receptacle of actions that could just as well be instantaneous or eternal; it has a plot, a meaning, a guided extension."[33] The meaning of this "march of humanity" is "the solidarity of men." The movement of history represents the growth of humanity. It displays the "aspirations of a humanity in progress." When writing of this evolution, Chenu speaks of the "energy of history" and the "life of human societies": "[B]ehold it advancing and progressing, amidst the worst upheavals and despite humiliating failures, and the very chaos that it lives through emphasizes once again, in the long term, the cosmic determinism that seems to advance it."[34] The progress of history almost takes on a life of its own. Yet, in speaking of the humiliating failures of progress and the presence of chaos, Chenu does not give in to a blind optimism.

The Recovery of Others: Human Socialization

The preceding remarks on the content and direction of human temporality have brought to the fore the remaining characteristic of the human situation, namely, its social aspect. This is not to be seen as a separate trait lying over and against the first two; rather, it highlights what was already implied in the consideration of corporality and temporality. In fact, human existence as being-in-the-world is defined by all three factors: time, society, and matter.[35]

Chenu's Christian anthropology, following the Thomistic blueprint, displays these three co-essential attributes, which together define the human situation: the human being is so tied to the universe that the realm of matter becomes a part of human destiny; the human being is situated in time; and the human being is thus, by nature, social: "History, society, matter, the homogeneity is indissociable."[36]

---

33 Ibid.

34 "Devenir" (1947), in *Travail,* 79, 81, 77. See also "Fraternitas" (1973), 385–400.

35 Because of the importance of socialization, Chenu's treatment of its integration in Christianity deserves a separate chapter. However, because of the unity of the human situation as being-in-the-world, it is necessary to introduce the theme in the present chapter.

36 "Histoire" (1968), 31; cf. "Storicità" (1970), 150–1; "La teologia del lavoro" (1970), 311. See M.L. Mazzarello, *Il rapporto Chiesa-mondo,* 28: "*Più esplicitamente la sociabilità dell'uomo, richiamando la sua corporalità e la sua temporalità, concretizza la sua situazione nella storia. La storicità dell'uomo è, dunque, la dimensione del suo essere-spirito incarnato ed è l'espressione della sua condizione: essere-in-società, del suo essere, cioè, un essere-all'altro.*"

The description of human existence as being-in-the-world implies, for Chenu, a fundamental being-for-others. It is a central implication of human historicity. Self-consciousness is possible only in terms of human dialogue with the world and with others. Again, the reason for this is consubstantiality with matter, or human existence as incarnate spirit. Angels, as pure spirits, have neither social nor historical existence. Human beings, on the other hand, have self-presence only in relation to one another or to the world. "Man does not become a person except in a body; his 'incarnation' is at once the principle of individuality, of sociability, of historicity ... He is nobody until he is with somebody else; self-awareness is awareness of a self-in-the-world, an awareness of being with the rest of mankind. Thus the metaphysical structure of man includes a radical openness to history and a dependence upon history."[37] The social dimension of human historicity thus implies that the category of *neighbour* is to play a constitutive role: "[I]n truth, the condition for his presence to himself, for his dialogue with himself, is for the human being his dialogue with things and with his neighbour, his presence to the world."[38] It is also clear that this presence to the world will not be a neutral one. This idea is partially illustrated by the title of one of Chenu's articles published in 1965, "Les masses humaines, mon prochain?"

Social reality may not be seen as the juxtaposition of individual lives added together. The truly social realm is established by an original relationship between these individual lives whereby they evoke "a common density, objective beyond their interiority."[39] Thus social progress is measured by the passage from relationships of love – on an intersubjective level – to relationships of justice – on a level of social objectivity. Similarly, history may not be seen as a collection of individual biographics, but as a reality whose subject is civilization in its various epochs and ages: "[C]ivilization is measured by the establishment of rights,

37 "Création" (1974), 394; cf. "Body" (1979), 204–5; "Storicità" (1970), 150–1. In this context, Chenu makes references to Karl Rahner's *Hearers of the Word* (Tr. from the 2nd edition by Michael Richards, Montréal: Palm Publishers, 1969), 130–9, and to Edward Schillebeeckx's "Faith Functioning in Human Self-Understanding," in *The Word in History: The St Xavier Symposium*, ed. T. Patrick Burke (New York: Sheed and Ward, 1966), especially 43–4.

38 "Situation "(1960), in *Parole* 2, 413. The being-for-others character of human historicity is also described in terms of the importance of the neighbour in "Storicità" (1970), 151: "*ogni ritorno in se stesso non si opera che andando al di fuori nel mondo, un mondo che è volta a volta natura e storia, il mio 'prossimo'.*"

39 "Spiritualisme" (1961), *Parole* 2, 440.

rights of which not only the person, but the social body as such, is the subject, beyond the contracts of individuals and the reality of affections."[40] It becomes clear why Chenu was interested in drawing out the implications for Christianity not only of *homo artifex* but also of *homo economicus* and *homo politicus.*

In recovering the dimensions of matter, time, and society, Chenu witnesses not only to a renewed anthropology but also to a fidelity to the mystery of the incarnation, to the extent that the language of divine revelation is always that of the receiving subject.

THE GOSPEL IN TIME

For Chenu, this awareness of human historicity, indeed this discovery (*prise de conscience*) of a fundamental human characteristic, was a cultural phenomenon that Christianity could not ignore. An encounter between Christianity and the historical world-view was inevitable. Any major shift within the cultural matrix, such as a reorientation or deepening in the human consciousness of its situation in space and time, provokes a new understanding of faith, "a renewal in the understanding of the content of faith, as much in the architecture of its object as in [the] vivacity of its historical sensitivity."[41] This renewal of the *intellectus fidei* finds a parallel in the cultural ferments of the thirteenth century and, as in its the medieval antecedent, its coming to pass was not without controversy.

In essence, the projected renewal concerned the integration of the historical viewpoint and Christian theology. Chenu's interpretation of the incarnation as a continuing reality calling for new and creative theologies was explicitly formulated in response to the questions raised by the encounter of Christianity and historical consciousness. His writings on this matter contributed to the general historicisation of the Christian experience.[42] They emerged in various stages situated between the crisis

40 "Situation" (1960), in *Parole* 2, 434. This concern with a historical reality larger than the individual subject suggests one reason why Chenu tended to forego history seen as "*événementielle*" and focused on the "*longue durée*" in the context of a history of civilization.

41 "Théologie en procès" (1976), 693; the late date of this statement suggests that such clarity of judgment results from hindsight. The underlying question throughout all this, of course, concerns the authenticity of the historical viewpoint and that of its appropriation; see the critical reflection in the last section of this chapter.

42 Cf. G. Alberigo, "Christianisme en tant qu'histoire et 'théologie confessante'," in *Une école de théologie* (1985), 27.

of modernism and that of the *nouvelle théologie*. Chenu began with a positive evaluation of the modernist crisis as a major but flawed attempt to deal with the problem of history. This view was followed by a theological position making history legitimate but still subordinate and extrinsic to the act of theological reflection. It was in its turn superseded by Chenu's use of the historical method in the study of Thomism, in which a much more important and fundamental role is attributed to history. Finally came Chenu's attempt to articulate this more important role in what amounts to the beginnings of a theology of history.

Chenu and Modernism

Although officially condemned thirty years earlier with the promulgation of *Pascendi* in 1907, the spectre of modernism still hovered in the theological atmosphere. Polemical accusations and cries imputing heretical tendencies were frequent. Many elements of the crisis, particularly the question of history and dogma, remained unresolved and so became part of the theological agenda. Chenu's positive evaluation of modernist aspirations provides the necessary starting-point for his understanding of the task of theology as "reaping the fruits" of the historical method.

At the beginning of a chapter from *Une école de théologie* concerned with the spirit and method of Le Saulchoir, Chenu acknowledges the seriousness of the crisis by referring to a passage from Tyrrel: "It is not on this or that article of the Credo that we differ: we accept it all; we differ on the meaning of the word *credo*, on the meaning of the word *true* applied to dogma; it is the entire value of revelation which is at stake."[43] For Chenu, this crisis was a most candid witness to the intellectual and religious crisis besieging the Church of the time.

In his view, the crisis had less to do with this or that element of Christian revelation than with the very nature of revelation and the assent it required. The questioning went so deep that, for some, the very essence of Christianity was stood on end. Thus, the crisis had to do with the foundations of Christianity: "Suddenly, after a long incubation, the historical and philosophical foundations of the faith were called into question, and by this the entire structure of religious knowledge, from

---

43 Cited in *Une école de théologie* (1937), 35. The Tyrrel passage is from a letter to von Hügel dated 30 September 1904. The same passage is also cited in "Le sens et les leçons" (1931), 368.

elementary experience right up to scholastic theory, from the data of the Gospels right up to ecclesiastical formulas." Yet – and herein lies the significance of his position – Chenu sees the crisis in terms of growth for the Church: "Despite the dramatic seriousness of the situation, it was in truth growing pains in the Church, and thus for a healthy organization a normal happening."[44]

Chenu compares the history of the Church to the spiritual itinerary of the soul, which goes from total abandon in faith, with the exclusion of any human element that would stain the divine revelation, to the rational effort towards clarity and understanding that in turn clashes with the blind and enthusiastic obedience of faith. From the crisis of this antinomy, the soul moves to a reconciliation of faith and human wisdom, "with a view to a full speculative account of the faith and a pious elaboration of its data." Chenu applies this experience of growth, with its crises and resolutions, as a model for the understanding of the "collective christian thought." An early and significant example of such growth occurred with Clement of Alexandria and the Didascalia. A particular revolution in culture is seen by the Church as an adversary, is then assimilated, and finally becomes a tool of Christianity's self-expression. The initial effect of these periodic cultural renewals (*renouveaux de culture* or *renaissances*) on the Church is negative. Reconciliation comes slowly and painfully: "Every 'renaissance' … provokes a turning-in of the faith upon itself, and a crisis of theological speculation; it is only after a painful defensive reaction that a subsequent blossoming testifies to the permanent value of the faith and to the fruitfulness of theology."[45] Thus we had the Carolingian renaissance and "grammatical rationalism," a crisis through which grammar became an acceptable tool within theological investigation. Then the crisis was philosophy and the Aristotelian ideal of science. First Abelard, then Thomas Aquinas, introduced new rational instruments into theology. Each time, the renaissance was seen at first as a threat to faith and indeed, on each occasion, the danger of abuse was real.

Chenu sees an analogous situation with the advent of history in the modernist crisis. After grammar, after dialectic, and after science, his-

---

44 *Une école de théologie* (1937), 36, 38. In the 1931 article "Le sens et les leçons" (358), Chenu describes the crisis as "*une crise de croissance normale où la Providence divine permet, au service de la foi, les dangers et les souffrances de l'hérésie*".

45 "Le sens" (1931), 359, 369.

tory proposed to become theology's handmaiden. A critique of ideas is followed by a critique of facts: "After grammar, after philosophy – history. Reason, after the analysis of *words* and the critique of *ideas,* examines *facts.* Only those who believe facts to be simple realities, useless to the life of the spirit, would be astonished at this progression in three steps."[46] The modernist crisis was not limited to this issue, yet the advent of the historical method was its immediate cause: "It was even the most active leaven for the work in progress, as well as the immediate occasion of the doctrinal crisis."[47] Chenu does not dispute the correctness or the necessity of the condemnation of *Pascendi,* since in his view there were many abuses of the historical method, and the historicism of some had to be denounced. Yet – and here is the point of Chenu's attitude to modernism – the condemnation was only one aspect of the advent of the historical method in theology. Its fruitfulness for theology meant that the riches of revelation could be more fully discovered: "The condemnation of modernism was but the necessary condition and the negative aspect of a progress whose extreme interest we gauge today, and from which it remains but to draw all the profit."[48] The reaction of the Roman authorities was only "the flipside of a spiritual operation of great breadth and magnificent fruitfulness." The subject of this magnificent operation is faith, with its propensity for greater clarity and understanding, "faith, and, in it, theological learning, taking possession of new instruments of reason."[49] The task of theology after the modernist crisis would be, among other things, to "reap the fruits" of the historical method.

---

46 Ibid., 363–4. In "Position" (1935), in *Parole* 1, 129, Chenu gives the following statement as an example of the "simple" attitude to facts: "*L'Incarnation, après tout, ce n'est qu'un fait.*" Later, in *Duquesne* (1975), 38, Chenu identifies the author of the statement as Garrigou-Lagrange and comments, "*sa théologie courait le risque d'être seulement une métaphysique sacrée. Il était complètement étranger à l'histoire ... L'Incarnation le gênait parce qu'on ne pouvait pas la déduire métaphysiquement.*"

47 *Une école de théologie* (1937), 37; cf. also "Préface [Geffré]" (1968), 8, where the historical method is described as the "*dénominateur commun des problèmes et des novations,*" both for modernism and for the *nouvelle théologie.* It should be noted that the modernist crisis involved more than one view of history and historical method; on the variety of meanings during the crisis, cf. C. Théobald, "L'entrée de l'histoire dans l'univers religieux et théologique au moment de la 'crise moderniste'," in *La crise contemporaine: Du modernisme à la crise herméneutique* (Paris: Beauchesne, 1973), 7–85.

48 "Le sens" (1931), 367.

49 *Une école de théologie* (1937), 38; the passage is originally in italics.

Although it is not explicitly developed in this context, the law of incarnation grounds Chenu's evaluation of the modernist aspirations for the reconciliation of the historical viewpoint and Christianity. In effect, his position with regard to modernism reveals an effort to establish a historical status as constitutive for Christianity and to ground this status in the mystery of incarnation.[50] Already in the 1931 article "Le sens et les leçons d'une crise religieuse" Chenu refers to the incarnation as the doctrinal basis for the inclusion of history: "Theology, the science of God, is also the science of Christ. Here all of history comes in with its contingencies, here where we might have believed that only metaphysical principles reigned."[51] The incarnation is at the centre of Chenu's evaluation of modernism and, inasmuch as this evaluation is symptomatic of his own agenda, at the heart of his theological programme. One key difference between the modernists and Chenu, however, is that Chenu viewed the renewal of Catholic theology through the historical viewpoint as a task to be performed from within the neoscholastic framework. He saw the historical method as a means of returning to the original intuitions of the medieval vision. The particulars of this return will be clarified in the following section.

The Historical Viewpoint

What are the "fruits" from to be "reaped" from the use of the historical method? It is clear that the stakes in the debate about the historical viewpoint involve more than the mere use of the historical method as an additional tool for the investigation of faith. We have already suggested that Chenu's project ultimately involved the establishment of a historical status for Christianity and its grounding in the mystery of incarnation. Chenu's work was guided by a perception of the needs of the Church in the face of a profound shift in the cultural matrix of his time.[52]

There is a development in Chenu's thought from an extrinsic use of the historical method applied to the study of primary sources, to the progressive realization of historicity as an intrinsic dimension of the

50 Cf. G. Alberigo, in *Une école de théologie* (1985), 14, which describes as follows Chenu's theological project: "*Il s'agit en fait de reconnaître que le Christianisme a, de façon constitutive, un statut historique, enraciné dans le mystère même de l'Incarnation.*"

51 "Le sens" (1931), 364.

52 Cf. G. Alberigo, in *Une école de théologie* (1985), 22, who writes of Chenu's "*intuition des besoins de la condition chrétienne dans un contexte culturel en profonde mutation.*"

Word of God, by virtue of the concrete character of the Christ event.[53] This larger role of history is reflected in Chenu's references to the issue of "presence" and, later, to the fact that God speaks today and that the Word of God is "in act". The question, for Chenu, was no longer of legitimizing the application of the historical method in the sense of a history of dogma, but of understanding dogmas as "the expression of a reality incarnate in the succession of ages, an *economy*."[54] The shift is from history as method to history as truth, or at least to truth as historical. This theme is probably best illustrated in the very title *L'Évangile dans le temps*.

The entry of the historical viewpoint is first manifest in Chenu's reflections on the relationship of positive and speculative theology and in his renewal of this traditional division. Although he retained the two categories of theology right up to the Vatican Council, he progressively abandoned this formal model in favour of a reflection on the faith practice of the Church and a discernment of the signs of the times. Chenu's very early writings are marked by a reference to the Thomistic synthesis of faith and Aristotelian reason, as well as to the twentieth-century transposition of this synthesis as found in Ambroise Gardeil. The emphasis is clearly on an intellectual orientation, as distinguished from a practical orientation, which characterizes his post-conciliar writings. This progression parallels the growing importance given to the role of history and the historical viewpoint.[55]

From the scholasticism of the early decades of this century, Chenu inherited a form of theology based on the convenient divorce between positive and speculative theology. In practice, and even as a matter of principle, it separated theological construction from its sources in religious experience and history. Theological discourse is thereby reduced to a purely logical consideration, a game of abstract dialectics, whose task is to develop a logically coherent discourse on the basis of certain propositions that are held to be eternally true. It is reduced to a number

53 See "Préface [Geffré]" (1968), 8. Chenu also alludes to this development in his introduction to *Le déplacement de la théologie* (1977), 12: "*Aujourd'hui, voici le déplacement ... l'histoire est considérée un 'lieu' de la théologie, bien mieux comme l'exposant de tous les lieux théologiques.*"

54 "Théologie en procès" (1976), 693.

55 See especially Chenu's "Préface" to the 1932 edition of Gardeil's *Le donné révélé et la théologie*, reprinted in *Parole* 1, 277–82. Cf. Antonio Franco, "La teología de M.-D. Chenu: itinerario histórico-cultural" (*CT* 112 [1985]), 240: "*No se pone en tela de juicio el modelo sylogístico de teología a partir de las verdades de fe, que hacen el papel de principios. En estos años (1920–1932) no se encuentran todavía in Chenu ni un concepto dinamico de tradición ni una idea de revelación como economía histórica.*"

of atomized theses that are proven *ex scriptura, ex traditione,* and *ex ratione.* The function of history, in this model, is to provide a repertory of arguments for the usage of schools in the disputed conclusions. The study of history can provide only a set of opinions and witnesses, which are often disparate at that. History is unable to constitute an autonomous and organic theological knowledge; it cannot provide the certainty of a metaphysically grounded theological conclusion. For Chenu, this kind of theologizing by an autonomous and pure reason led only to juridicism and extrinsicism. The lack of any reference to the experience of faith (other than faith as obedience), to historical or religious experience, made this an ideological superstructure. It was perhaps true, but not meaningful. Furthermore, it was spiritually dead: the word of God was no longer heard through it.[56]

Such abstract theologizing about eternally valid propositions, with no regard for history, was partially responsible for leading the strong antimodernist reaction that was legitimized through the encyclical *Pascendi.* It was vigorously rejected by Chenu not only for reasons of intellectual integrity but, more fundamentally, for theological reasons. This is where incarnation comes into the foreground. Its role will be to mediate between the historicism of some and the "theologism" of others: "There was here not only, on the level of history, a misapprehension of a legitimate order of research, but theological error also, if it is true that God manifests himself by and in history, that the eternal is incarnate in time where only the spirit of man can reach it."[57] We have in this statement the main points of Chenu's theological position: the importance of history in a perspective of an economy of revelation, temporality as an essential characteristic of the human condition and therefore of human knowing, and the paradigmatic role of the incarnation.

The entry of history, triggered by the modernist crisis but already present previously, called into question the convenient separation between positive and speculative theology. In the name of history, Chenu appealed to the patristic notion of *oikonomia* and questioned the adequacy of an autonomous reason. The ultimate reason for the inadequacy of speculation and its failure with regard to the data of revelation is that

---

56 Clearly, this is the same theology typified in chapter 2 by Billot's position. Just as clearly, it is by means of a doctrine of faith incarnate in the human subject that Chenu resolves the difficulty. Cf. *Une école de théologie* (1937), 54–5.

57 *Une école de théologie* (1937), 37. Cf. "La théologie est-elle une science?" (1957), 111, where Chenu names the two errors: "*Historicisme et théologisme, excès opposés, furent le mauvais effet de ce schisme entre théologie positive et théologie spéculative.*"

these are available only in history, where the contingencies of historical fact have always been a scandal and a stumbling block to the reason of speculative systems. Between fact and system, the primacy always lies with the former: "[T]he smallest *fact*, from the moment that it is authentic, is a benchmark, and if a theological system cannot give place and reason in its theory to the fact, it is for the system to give way."[58] The type of intelligibility proper to theology is not like that of the philosophy which studies an eternal order of nature. The theologian's given, unlike that of the traditional post-Cartesian metaphysician, is available only in history. The theologian has no other object than the *auditus fidei* whose inventory is provided by the historian, under the guidance of the light of faith. This object is not a catalogue of propositions recorded in a Denzinger, "but a living, copious matter, always in act in the Church which is depository, pregnant with divine intelligibility."[59]

The theologian works on a history. The data of theology are not the nature of things or their ontological relationships. The object of theology is events corresponding to an economy whose realization is linked to time. That is the real world of the theologian, not the abstractions of a sacred metaphysics.[60]

The given is found only in history. This is the law of incarnation. The same theandric structure that governs the God-man and the faith-reason relationships, also governs the place of historical reason in the *intellectus fidei*: "It is in the name of this same theandrism of the word that the historical critique with all its apparatus will become the instrument proper to theology." The event of the incarnation provides the theandric structure for the understanding of history: "All of history goes by that route."[61] Clearly, it is a sacred history, but its sacredness does not dissolve the variety of contexts, which represent the stuff of human history. Otherwise, it would no longer be an incarnation.

It is important here, as Chenu underlines, to distinguish among the formal objects of the sciences, in order to avoid the confusion of mixed methodologies. The historical sciences – exegesis and the history of dogma – operate independently according to their own canons and under the light of their own resources. Positive theology differs in that it operates according to its own criteria, under the light of faith: "The

58 "Position" (1935), in *Parole* 1, 127.

59 *Une école de théologie* (1937), 55. The influence of the Tübingen theologians is evident.

60 Cf. *Une école de théologie* (1937), 61; see also "Position" (1935), in *Parole* 1, 128.

61 *Une école de théologie* (1937), 62, 61.

road from Athens to Piraeus is not the same as the one from Piraeus to Athens. If the discernment of these two paths seems quite abstract and their overlap subtle, it is because the overlap of the divine and the human in revelation – the revelation of the word of God at the summit of which is accomplished the revelation of the Word made flesh – is itself subtle to conceive of and to express."[62] The danger of any premature insistence on where the dividing line between sacred and human history lies is either spiritualism, where the historical is abandoned in favour of the preservation of the transcendent, or historicism, where there is a failure to recognize the theandric structure of history.[63] It is thus the doctrine of incarnation that resolves for Chenu the destructive dualism between speculative and positive theology, since "God manifests himself by and in history ... the eternal is incarnate in time where only the spirit of man can reach it."[64] More specifically, it is the doctrine of incarnation as perceived by the eyes of faith. History and speculation are incommensurate. They cannot simply be juxtaposed. It is faith that perceives the data of revelation in history, both positively and speculatively. Theology remains tied by faith to the theandric structure of revelation: "[B]ecause God speaks humanly, theology is in solidarity with the theandric mystery of this Word of God, Word made flesh."[65]

The development from history as extrinsic method to historicity as intrinsic dimension begins to appear in the renewal of Thomistic studies at Le Saulchoir. From the start of his theological career, Chenu was associated with the Dominican order and the theological faculty of Le Saulchoir. This meant doing theology within the Thomistic "school." Le Saulchoir was heavily involved in the revival of Thomistic studies as a result not only of the Dominican tradition but also of Leo XIII's encyclical *Aeterni Patris* (1879) calling for a return to the theology of Aquinas.[66]

Fidelity to the thought of St. Thomas was understood in a variety of ways, however. For Chenu and his colleagues, it meant remaining within

62 Ibid., 63. The methodological difficulty is noted but never elaborated in a systematic fashion.

63 The latter, for Chenu, was the error of the modernists who made history into an absolute whereas only faith is an absolute; see ibid., 62. See also 64: "*C'est la foi qui est un absolu, et échappe à l'histoire, la foi pure dans sa lumière infuse, et non pas le dogme,* auditus fidei *docile au* magistère."

64 Ibid., 37.

65 "La théologie est-elle une science?" (1957), 112.

66 See the literature on the encyclical and the revival of Thomistic studies by McCool, Poulat, and Schoof in the Bibliography of secondary sources at the end of this book.

"a body of master intuitions," rather than adhering to a rigidly defined system of propositions. These intuitions would be translated into conceptual systems "on the condition that they keep alive their light and that they submit them to a perpetual confrontation with an always richer reality." To be a Thomist implied fidelity to a certain spirit of invention, a presence to one's time, along with a sincerity "before a reality always new and always surprising." Unlike the theology of the manuals, this perspective meant that no "question" could be prejudged in favour of an already acquired "conclusion." The manuals "abuse their certainty and cheat, … they do not purely pose the problems, and play an artificial game in which the dice are loaded."[67] Chenu and the faculty of Le Saulchoir proposed a return to the consideration of the problems beyond the conclusion already reached. This return to an ever-fruitful source allowed for the grasp of the spirit of Thomas as it creatively struggled for a solution. Further, it made the appropriation of such a spirit possible. Through the historical method, in other words, the tension of the *quaestio* was maintained: "Historical study brings one back to the problem and maintains a state of questioning … Historical study maintains the presence, the return to the datum, which was the absolute, the primitive, the creative act – the restlessness of the philosopher, the sense of the gap between every reflection and the eternal truth, of which the system is as the temporal substitute."[68] Thus, the reconciliation of Thomistic docility with openness to the present reality was possible only through a return to the original sources, where reference to the original text became as important to theology as first principles to metaphysics. This approach meant a preference for the texts of St. Thomas himself as opposed to the presentation of his thought by later commentators. The purpose of the study was to grasp the very mind of Thomas through the exegesis of his texts, to reach the spirit of invention, as it were, as it struggled for the appropriate answer in the face of particular problems from its time: "To reunite with St. Thomas was first of all to rediscover this state of invention."[69]

67 *Une école de théologie* (1937), 45.

68 "L'étude historique" (1951), 737.

69 *Une école de théologie* (1937), 45. On the weakness of the commentary genre, cf. "L'étude historique" (1951), 736: "*Le commentaire se développe lui-même; le livre y est traité comme un conservatoire de vérités acquises, qu'il y faut retrouvé à n'importe quel prix. On fait des commentaires de commentaires. Le temps est évacué.*" Commentaries are not rejected outright by Chenu, of course, but they are situated in their time by means of the historical method; on Cajetan, see *Une école de théologie* (1937), 49.

The historical method, as used and developed by the exegete M.-J. Lagrange, was seen in Le Saulchoir as the ideal instrument for the fulfillment of this task. The presence of Père Mandonnet and the friendly cooperation of Gilson were also important in this regard. St. Thomas was thus read "in his time." No longer a timeless thinker as the commentators would have it, with no moorings in space or time, he was read and understood in the context of real time. Removed from the haven of eternal truths and propositions, where he was kept by a certain "baroque scholasticism" and its protective institution, he was temporalized. This shift was not motivated by an archeological interest for erudition, as in some of the historicism of the nineteenth century, but by the belief that there is a deep solidarity between a theology and the historical context that gave birth to it. This solidarity between thought and time is significant not only for the genesis of a particular theology or philosophy but also for its inherent intelligibility.[70]

Replacing St. Thomas in his own time implied a certain historical relativism. Yet there was no other way if intelligibility was to be achieved. "St. Thomas could not be explained entirely by St. Thomas himself, and his teaching, though it be ever so lofty and abstract, is not an absolute, independent of the era which saw its birth and the ages which have nourished it: an earthly conditioning of the spirit, by which historical contingencies and human accident insinuate and inscribe themselves into the most spiritual thought, and nuance with a discreet relativism the framework of the most coherent and unified systems."[71] In fact, to deny this historicity in the name of some unchanging truth or for the safekeeping of transcendence was to deny intelligibility. With characteristic vigour, Chenu says: "The absolutization of St. Thomas is a first-class burial."[72]

---

70 For an example of Lagrange's contribution, see his *La méthode historique: La critique biblique et l'Église*, Coll. Foi Vivante (Paris: Éditions du Cerf, 1966 [originally 1903]). Chenu never discusses the details of this contribution or how it applied to his particular field of study; cf. *Une école de théologie* (1937), 62–3. Cf. also "L'étude historique" (1951), 735: "*A un temps aplati et inerte, l'intuition historique substitue un temps réel.*" For the importance of the milieu, see also *Introduction* (1950), which is entirely based on this position; see, e.g., 6: "*La vérité n'est pas moins vraie pour être inscrite dans le temps.*"

71 *Une école de théologie* (1937), 48. This relativism was one of the points contested by the Roman authorities.

72 *Duquesne* (1975), 49. In the same passage, Chenu cites Péguy's remark about the fate of Aquinas in the Church: "*Un grand docteur considéré, célébré, consacré, dénombré. Enterré.*" In a similar vein, there is a sentence in *Une école de théologie* (1937), 76: "*Il ne fut pire disgrâce pour le thomisme, dont l'effort natif fut de fonder en Chrétienté un statut de l'intelligence humaine, que d'être traité comme une 'orthodoxie'.*" In response, Chenu was called to Rome in order to sign a form stating, among other things, that St. Thomas was orthodox.

However, the historical method as practised by Lagrange was insufficient for carrying out all the implications of situating St. Thomas "in his time." The necessary scope involved the reconstruction of all the facets of the human situation in which the Thomistic corpus was born: "It is the whole human fabric that one must reconstitute, upon which St. Thomas worked and in which he found at once his material, his techniques, his language, his means of expression, his ties and his liberty."[73] Chenu needed a new method in order to fulfill this task.

In this context, the decade of the 1930s was also the time when Lucien Fèbvre and Marc Bloch were laying the foundations of the *Annales* school of historiography. In reaction to a certain positivism of the singular historical fact, they introduced social and economic dimensions into cultural history. This approach to historiography took into account the economic causalities of history. From the beginning, Chenu was attracted to Fèbvre and Bloch, identifying his own approach to medieval studies with theirs. Proceeding to uncover the economic, social, and cultural underpinnings of Thomistic writings, he read Thomas from an economic viewpoint with the emancipation of the feudal system and the rise of corporations, from a social and political viewpoint with the constitution of the communes, and from a cultural viewpoint with the beginnings of the cultural communities we now call universities.[74]

The entry of history into theology contemplated by Chenu involved more than the use of historical method in the establishment of authentic texts and the recovery of the Christian past, more than an ancillary role for history. In fact, it heralded a revolution in the status, method, and object of theological reflection, a revolution whose impact is difficult for us to imagine.

Although discussion of the revival of Thomistic studies and the methodological disputes on the status of positive theology did contribute to integrating history into theology, the decisive factor was at a much deeper level. Our concern now is to establish some of the consequences and implications of saying that the object of theology is primarily an economy, which implies the entry of God into the sphere of history and temporality. In this case, what develops in and through time becomes a source for the intelligibility of this revelation. Far from being an

---

73 *Une école de théologie* (1937), 103, 105.

74 Cf. *Duquesne* (1975), 51–2. For some of the clearest passages expressing the proximity of Chenu's method to that of the *Annales* school, see *Théologie XIIe* (1957), 11–15. The theological implications of this method will be treated in the section on the signs of the times in Chapter 5. See also the moving address given by Jacques Le Goff at Chenu's funeral at Notre-Dame.

obstacle to understanding, human time becomes a source of theological understanding.

Dissatisfied with the conceptual inflexibility of neoscholastic theology for responding to the cultural shift from a classicist to a historical cultural matrix, Chenu looked for a more encompassing framework that would not only legitimize the use of historical method but make history a true and central *locus* for theological reflection. My contention is that Chenu found this larger framework in the concept of incarnation. It is accessible by a variety of routes and its fundamental structure from the viewpoint of history is recognized under many aspects: economy of revelation, history of salvation, continued incarnation, living tradition, new or successive Christendoms. Here we focus on the basic concept of economy and the related concept of tradition, leaving the remainder for the following chapter.[75]

In the context of the problem of history, the starting argument for incarnation is the same as in the first chapter. If God speaks to the human subject, it will be according to the human condition. If the human condition is historical, as the first section of the present chapter claims, then God's revelation will be historical. If the human condition includes the material realm, the reality of matter will also convey God's revelation. All this explicitly opposes docetic attempts to escape from the realism of the human condition. Thus, attempts to abstract from the concreteness of the historical situation, or to remove our relationship to God from historical reality, result in a "de-existentialization" of the human condition. On the pretext of a reference to a divinity there occurs a dehumanization.[76]

The implementation of the law of incarnation therefore involves a shift in the basic approach to the object of faith: "God is not God-God, but God who has come, who has descended into the human condition and who, to do this, has entered into history." Consequently, theology is

---

75 The ways in which "God speaks today," as well as the texts concerned with the present and future dimensions of living tradition, will likewise be left for Chapter 4. For the concept of cultural shift, which is borrowed from Bernard Lonergan, see the essays in Lonergan's *Second Collection*, edited by William F.J. Ryan and Bernard J. Tyrrell (London: Darton, Longman, and Todd, 1974).

76 Cf. "Pour une anthropologie" (1974), 85; *St. Thomas* (1957), 35: "*Dans le Christ, la Parole de Dieu m'est parlée en un dialogue consubstantiel à mon humanité*"; "*Storicità*" (1970), 151. See also "Histoire sainte" (1961), in *Parole* 1, 286: " ... *docétisme inconscient, dans la mesure où s'estompe une incarnation dont le temps est un des indices de réalité humaine, qu'il s'agisse de la Parole dans l'histoire sainte, qu'il s'agisse du Christ lui-même.*"

no longer "a sacred metaphysics" or a conceptualization of the religious instinct, but rather "the reflective and critical *prise-de-conscience* of an economy."[77] The advent of history and the development of historical consciousness lead to a re-evaluation of Christianity in terms of economy rather than in terms of propositions.

It was in 1935, in the important article "Position de la théologie," that Chenu explicitly acknowledged the irreducible and constitutive role of history in theology. Chenu explicitly ties the object of theology to a history: "[I]t is [not] the nature of things nor their intemporal forms; but events, answering to an *economy*, of which the fulfilment is time-bound." The *donné* is the works of God – the God of Abraham, Isaac, and Jacob – not of the pure act. The concreteness and the contingency of the principal work, the incarnation of Jesus Christ, are not reducible to any cosmic order of essences. The world contemplated by the believer, as well as by the theologian, is an order of salvation manifest in an economy. This economy has three levels, each one bound by some kind of irreducible contingency: the economy of creation, where divine providence is not answerable to, or determined by, any human cause; the economy of incarnation and redemption, where the gratuitous nature of the divine initiative remains absolute; and the economy of sacraments, where the actions of Christ are re-enacted in his Church.[78] Theology is realist to the extent that it is an understanding of the order of salvation in its history and its concrete realisation.

In this sense, the term "economy" implies that God's action is "*solidaire du temps de l'homme* (solidary of human time)". Following the path of the Greek fathers, whose return in the twentieth century coincided with the rediscovery of the concept of *oikonomia*, Chenu defines the very nature of Christianity as an economy of salvation. Christianity not only involves the teaching of certain truths, but, on the basis of these truths, it is the communication of divine life to humanity according to

77 "Théologie en procès" (1976), 692.
78 "Position" (1935), in *Parole* 1, 128, 129. On Christ's presence in the Church, see ibid., 130: "*reprise réele des actions du Christ.*" Cf. also *Une école de théologie* (1937), 61; "Histoire" (1968), 25: " … *la voie pour accéder à la transcendance passe par l'homme et par cette histoire en laquelle Dieu l'interpelle. Dieu parle par des événements.*" Again, this does not preclude the development of a theological science or even theological systems, but "*science et systèmes ont à capter une 'histoire sainte,' non pas un ordre des essences.*" See also *Introduction* (1950), 270, where Chenu says, "*L'incarnation rédemptrice constitue la substance même de l'économie …* " On the significance of the article "Position" in Chenu's development see A. Franco, "La teología de M.-D. Chenu," (*CT* 112 [1985]), 241–2.

stages laid out by God. The communication of divine life reaches its apex in the incarnation of the word of God and thereby sets the paradigm for all relations between the human and the divine realms: " ... but this word of God, following its course, is fulfilled in an incarnation: the Word is made man, at the centre of this divine history, and this event commands the time which precedes and the time which follows it, at the same time as it secures the authentic regime of the divine life in humanity." Chenu locates economy at the intersection of two concepts, in terms of their own content and in their relationship: "[T]he economy is at once mystery and history, that is mystery in history, and history in the mystery of Christ." Mystery, in this context, refers to the transcendent reality of divine life gratuitously offered to human participation. History refers to the gift as situated in time, unfolding in a pattern of preparation and fulfillment, within temporal forms that are not accidental but the inner stages of a divine plan solidary with human time.[79]

Chenu links the historicity of theology and its object to the related concepts of tradition and the Church as continued incarnation. With an explicit reference to the Tübingen school, for which he felt a great affinity, Chenu rejects a view of tradition as a quantum of *credenda*, according to an empiricist and static view of theological *loci*. Tradition, for him, refers to the living presence of the Spirit in the Church, which takes its theandric structure from Christ. It is not only a conservation of dogmatic formulas, acquired as a result of decisions taken in the past, but a creative principle of intelligibility and an inextinguishable source of new life. Tradition is not an aggregate of traditions, but a principle of organic continuity whose interpreter is the Church. In this view, the task

---

79 "Les sacrements" (1952), in *Parole* 1, 324–5. Chenu also writes at 324: "*Non pas seulement un enseignement de vérités, mais, grâce à cet enseignement,* la transmission de la vie divine à l'humanité selon les étapes disposées par Dieu" (Chenu's emphasis). In a footnote, Chenu cites with approval the following passage from Henri de Lubac's *Histoire et esprit* (Paris: Aubier, 1950), 380: "*Le mystère chrétien ne nous a pas été livré dans une série de définitions intemporelles, sans rapport à une situation historique précise, quitte à se laisser revêtir par la suite à notre gré d'images bibliques, à titre d'illustrations.*" On the paradigmatic character of the incarnation for all Christian action, see "Anthropologie" (1947), in *Parole* 1, 309, where Christianity is called "*une économie où l'Incarnation et l'assomption humaine que celle-ci réalise sont devenues le prototype de tout acte chrétien ...* " Cf. "Histoire" (1968), 28, where Chenu stresses the irreducible and gratuitous character of the divine initiative: "*[N]i la nature ni l'histoire n'ont capacité de révéler le mystère de Dieu: sa Parole vient 'd'en-haut' ... La grâce est grâce, et l'histoire profane n'est pas source de salut.*"

of theology is to discern the living tradition in action, by being present to one's time.[80]

Here again, the shift is from historical method as applied from the outside to historicity as an internal dimension of the object. Tradition is the expression of a reality incarnate in the unfolding of time. In this context, the concepts of tradition and economy overlap. Tradition is living, in that it corresponds to the ever actualized presence of God in the Church. It concerns less a past that has been carefully preserved, than the authentic emanation of the definitive incarnation in light of contemporary events in the world, perceived with the eyes of faith. In this sense, it is concerned no less with the present and the future than with the past.[81]

HISTORY AND THE LAW OF INCARNATION

Chapter 2 pointed to incarnation as the law governing the relationship between faith and reason and presiding over the origin of theological science. The aim of the present chapter, in accordance with our gradual approach, has been to explore the meaning and function of incarnation by removing a set of brackets and extending the scope of analysis to include the historical viewpoint. I have divided this task into three stages, two of which have been completed in this chapter.

First, it was important to obtain an overview of the human situation as the *locus* for incarnation. We have done this from Chenu's own understanding of the situation. The presentation here is limited in that the analysis is primarily theoretical and abstract, in the realm of anthropology and existential structures, even though its focus is the rise of

80 Cf. *Une école de théologie* (1937), 66–7, where Chenu acknowledges the debt to the Catholic theologians of Tübingen (Drey, Möhler) and Scheeben, even in the use of their vocabulary. He adds: "*Avec eux, c'est l'intellectualisme abstrait de l'Aufklärung et son indifférence à l'égard de l'histoire, que nous repoussons: péchés connexes, qui ne furent pas sans contaminer la scolastique moderne, candidement solidifiée dans la foule de manuels, même thomistes.*"

81 Cf., for example, "Théologie et recherche" (1970), 71, 74–5: " ... *une lecture toujours actuelle de la Parole de Dieu, intégrant aujourd'hui tout le passé, dans l'Église, communauté hiérarchique et magistérielle, à la fois animée par l'Esprit et immergée dans le langage contemporain*"; "Histoire" (1968), 26–7; "Storicità" (1970), 155. The "perception with the eyes of faith" will be explored further in Chapter 5, where the question of appropriate criteria for this "re-lecture" will have to be discussed. See "Théologie en procès" (1976), 695: "*Ainsi la Parole de Dieu ne se rapporte pas seulement à l'histoire du salut qui s'est déroulée dans le passé, mais aussi à l'histoire du salut qui s'accomplit dans le présent et dans l'avenir.*"

historical consciousness and the promotion of the concrete. Although the text alluded to the pastoral situation of the French Church in the face of dechristianization and the challenge of modernity, especially as a historical context for the emphasis on the concrete and the existential, the particulars of the human situation were left untouched. The discussion was limited to a critique of the destructive and alienating dualism found in the spiritualist approach, and to Chenu's attempt to overcome this position with the triple recovery of corporality, temporality, and intersubjectivity.

Second, we approached the necessary confrontation between the historical viewpoint and Christianity as "reaping the fruits" of the historical method in the name of the law of incarnation. Chenu's evaluation of modernism as a significant but flawed attempt to integrate the historical viewpoint into Christianity was followed in our examination by his own contribution to the historicization of the Christian experience. This was described as a general movement from the extrinsic use of the historical method to historicity as an intrinsic dimension of Christianity when seen as an economy of salvation. For Chenu, this movement was grounded in the mystery of the incarnation.

Third, we must include the social dimension of human existence within the scope of the process of ongoing incarnation. This task remains to be done. With it, our discussion will accomplish the turn to the concrete situation. The phenomenon of socialization will be the partner of Christianity in the encounter, and the process of ongoing incarnation will involve the shift in the Church's self-understanding from "new Christendom" to a "state of mission."

What can be said about the meaning and function of incarnation for Chenu up to this point? The first two chapters presented incarnation as a law or principle analogously derived from the incarnation of Christ. The precise nature of the analogy was never clarified. Thus, the law of incarnation has been invoked to preserve the integrity of the human in its relationship to the divine. As the theandric paradigm, the incarnation of Christ is the cause of the peculiar structure of theology, which somehow participates in the original mystery. To the extent that theology is faithful to its theandric structure, where faith is incarnate in human reason, the word of God abides in its discourse. It was in this sense that Kuhn's aphorism was meant to be understood: "No theology without a new birth."[82]

82 Quoted at the head of "Position" (1935), in *Parole* 1, 115.

The present chapter has pursued the theme of temporality and history, with the result that the incarnation now serves as the explicit doctrinal basis for the inclusion of history in theology. The law of incarnation becomes the principle for actualizing the nature of Christianity as God's presence in time: *L'Évangile dans le temps*. It is the methodological manifestation of a reality that continually assumes unto itself new dimensions of the human situation as they are uncovered in the unfolding of time. To follow the law of incarnation means to participate in living tradition and to be a member of the Church as continued incarnation. In conjunction with all that has been said about the direction and content of history, incarnation will encompass the progressive humanization of history as the way of divinization. This perspective will be confirmed in chapter 4, with Chenu's analysis of socialization as a sign of the times.

If this perspective is correct, an underlying question must now be brought to the fore. As the process of incarnation is tied to the progressive uncovering of deeper dimensions of human consciousness, what serves as the criterion of authentic development in the progress of humanization, particularly in light of problems of error and moral evil? In other words, how are deviations from authentic humanization, such as ideological distortions, distinguished from occasions for incarnation? The question cannot adequately be answered until the concrete situation is explicitly included in our discussion. Then the question will be: What is an authentic sign of the times? Is evil a reality that must be assumed and integrated, or one that must be rejected? With this in mind we now remove the last set of brackets and turn to the concrete.

4

Church, Society, and Mission

IN CONTINUING the task of tracing a perspective of incarnation as the underlying pattern in Chenu's theology, we now turn to the concrete situation of the Church in the modern world. Whenever a major stand is to be taken, a decision to be made, or a choice to be declared, the law of incarnation serves as a guide and a basic strategy. It thus offers a model for both theological understanding and pastoral action.

The present chapter corresponds to the removal of the third and final set of brackets in our gradual approach to the meaning and function of incarnation. That is, our analysis will no longer be primarily theoretical and abstract, but concrete. Although the turn to the concrete began in the previous chapter, it remained on the level of formal existential structures such as corporality, temporality, and intersubjectivity. Socialization will form the focus of the present analysis, not only in terms of formal structures but as it appeared within the pastoral situation of the French Church. The basic horizon of this situation is formed by the questions commonly associated with dechristianization and the challenge of modernity. The partner in the encounter of Christianity with the human situation will no longer be the historical viewpoint as a stage in theological method, but "the civilization of work". That encounter involves a shift in the self-understanding of the Church from new Christendom to state of mission, and a shift in pastoral strategy from conquest to presence and witness.

We begin by broadly mapping out the question of dechristianization as it is found in Chenu and echoed in a variety of positions. We then turn to an analysis of the key elements of the new situation, and end with the appropriate response to that situation. The presentation is limited to highlighting Chenu's position and, even then, only those aspects that clarify the meaning and function of incarnation. Thus the presentation of Chenu's theology of work, his social thought, and his theology of mission is not exhaustive; each of these is examined solely with the aim of understanding incarnation.

DECHRISTIANIZATION AND THE PASTORAL SITUATION

The final context for Chenu's confrontation with the modern situation finds its concrete expression in what has been called the phenomenon of dechristianization. Such is the name given to the great challenge facing the French Church in the first half of the twentieth century. Dechristianization was the most explicit manifestation of the cultural shift, and the Church's painful introduction to the world of modernity – what has been called "the merciless confrontation with social reality."[1]

Dechristianization represented a set of questions that was on everyone's mind. The pastoral situation of the Church set the agenda for the theologians and acted as a ferment for their work. Chenu's theology of incarnation appeared as a response to the cultural shift made manifest in the massive dechristianization of the working class. The fruitfulness of this period for the Church was due in large part to the uninterrupted dialogue between the theologians and those involved in pastoral field work. The cross-fertilization between the pastoral activity of the Church and theology was noted by the historian of French Catholicism René Rémond, among others. Rémond wrote of the close link between speculative thought and practical experience: "It is because during these thirty years theology was taken up with all the problems the apostolate posed for it, and because in return reflection on the Church fed pastoral and missionary activity, that this period shall remain a period rich in grace and outstanding in fruitfulness in the history of the Church."[2]

1 The phrase "*impitoyable confrontation avec la réalité sociale*" is from J.B. Duroselle's *Les débuts du catholicisme social en France (1822–1870)* (Paris: PUF, 1951), 548. It is used by E. Poulat in *Naissance des prêtres-ouvriers* (Paris: Casterman, 1965), 11, in reference to problems facing the Church in the 1930s and 1940s. Poulat comments, in a footnote: "*Juste observation d'historien, qui est aussi, mais sur un autre plan, un lieu idéologique de première importance dans l'histoire moderne du catholicisme.*" Adrien Dansette's treatment of the period is a likely candidate for Poulat's criticism; cf. Dansette's *Destin du catholicisme français 1926–1956* (Paris: Flammarion, 1957) and Poulat's "Religion et politique" in *Église contre bourgeoisie* (Paris: Casterman, 1977), 63–79.

2 "Préface" in Jean Lestavel's *Les prophètes de l'Église contemporaine* (Paris: Éditions de l'Épi, 1969), 9.

This intimate relationship between theology and pastoral activity, between theory and praxis, suggests that we can no longer ignore the set of questions arising from the pastoral situation. Indeed, most of Chenu's writings can in one way or another be characterized as a reflection on some aspect of the Church's situation in the modern world.[3]

To begin, Chenu points to the inadequacy of the contemporary vocabulary used to describe the phenomenon. The term "dechristianization" or "apostasy" not only contains a failed diagnostic of the situation but, more importantly, illustrates a hidden motive that is expressed in such a characterization. A more historical perspective and awareness will prevent the use of a past event or era (e.g., the restoration of Louis XVIII) as the sole criterion for the understanding and evaluation of the present situation. A historically informed view will also allow for a certain openness of the gospel proclamation vis-à-vis the novelty of the present developments.[4]

In speaking of the "apostasy of the masses" or of "dechristianization," we do not mean the sin of just a few individuals who have somehow become more numerous on account of unfortunate circumstances. We refer, rather, to a life environment, a *milieu*, which undergoes the inevitable influence of a particular set of determinisms. This supra-personal dimension is essential to Chenu's evaluation. Entire dimensions of collective existence that previously carried at least an implicit reference to Christ have seen their structures emptied of any religious meaning in the traditional sense. In no way are we dealing with the personal fault of some individual or group of individuals. Chenu speaks of "the objective denaturing of entire blocs which ... were desacralized." If the term "apostasy" were to be used at all, it would refer not to a personal sin multiplied by a large number of individuals but to something on a much larger and all-encompassing scale: "Apostasy ... characterizes entire social milieux, in the irrepressible determinism of their human

3 This is the case even if Chenu wrote little on actual dechristianization. The problem is presupposed by his whole theological enterprise. His so-called historical writings can also be included in this category to the extent that they originated from a nest of contemporary concerns.

4 Cf. G. Le Bras, "Déchristianisation, mot fallacieux," *Social Compass*, 10 (1963), 445–52; E. Poulat, "Déchristianisation du prolétariat ou dépérissement de la religion," in F. Bédarida and J. Maitron (eds) *Christianisme et monde ouvrier* (Paris: Les éditions ouvrières, 1975), 67–78. For another point of view, based on a perspective of *longue durée*, see J. Delumeau, "Déchristianisation ou nouveau modèle de Christianisme," *Archives des sciences sociales des religions*, 40 (1975), 3–20. On the "*disponibilité*" of the gospel in face of new cultural values, see the section Paradigms for a New Encounter: Mission and Witness in the present chapter, on the mission of the Church.

condition." We must not confuse "apostasy" with the change and development of new social structures such as the world of work. Similarly, "dechristianization" implies the undoing of a formerly religious reality, the breakdown of an "established Christendom." It is therefore often confused with various forms of atheism. Chenu questions such implications and strives to make the necessary distinctions to avoid rampant confusion: "No, there was no preexisting faith, for the express reason that this world of work – of which (with the technical revolution) the original structures would appear thenceforth as constitutive of the civilization of tomorrow – this world of work, I say, was a never-before-seen reality in a massively evolved universe. It was a reality which traditional faith could not foresee, any more than classical economics or liberal sociology could foresee it." This is much more than a minor question of semantics, since it radically affects our understanding of what is going on and, thus, of what needs to be done. The proponents of the term "dechristianization" refused to acknowledge the fundamental mutation undergone by society, and the human revolution implied by the revolution in technology. For Chenu, the situation implied a real change in the human condition, with its hierarchy of values and its consciousness, not merely a change in the exterior trappings of life. To judge these values and these hopes in terms of a negative reference to a past situation is to falsify the view of reality. It precludes the possibilitity of originality; it reads the situation from back to front and misses the creative element. Even worse, it excludes the possibility of future dialogue and understanding from the start: "We doom ourselves ahead of time to being ineffectual, because from the start we render dialogue – elementary condition for true speech, including the Word of God – impossible."[5]

5 "Déchristianisation ou non-christianisation?" (1960), in *Parole* 2, 247–9. This is Chenu's basic article on the issue. This text should not be classified as a case of excellent hindsight because of its relatively late date. Chenu's awareness of the novel character of the situation, "*une réalité* inédite *dans un univers massivement évolué,*" dates from the late 1930s, as this chapter will demonstrate shortly. In the same article, on 249, Chenu quotes a 1954 statement from Mgr Garrone supporting the view that dechristianization was indeed the negative aspect of something novel: "*Cet état se traduit dans les structures par l'absence radicale et normale de toute imprégnation, non seulement chrétienne, mais religieuse. C'est du tout neuf. Cet état se traduit dans les consciences par toute une portion d'existence que la lumière de la foi n'éclaire pas. La foi est devenue étrangère. C'est donc moins une déchristianisation que l'apparition de quelque chose d'étranger, et non de soi hostile, au christianisme.*" Cf. Louis and André Rétif, *Pour une Église en état de mission* (Paris: Librairie Arthème Fayard, 1961), 52–3. It should be noted that all these ills resulted from a lack of historical consciousness or – what ultimately amounts to the same thing – from the presence of a historical bias and blindspot. The same bias denied the human dimension of faith (refer to chapter 2) and historicity (chapter 3).

Before we move on to Chenu's characterization of the new reality manifest in the phenomenon of dechristianization, it would be useful to contextualize the thrust of his answer. Both Chenu's view of dechristianization as the dawn of a new age in the history of humanity and the implied criticism of an established Christendom are part of a much wider discussion in the French Church. This discussion both supports his view and shows the consistency and originality of an approach based on incarnation. The range of attitudes to the phenomenon of dechristianization is visible in the responses to the 1933 survey by *La vie intellectuelle* on the then-current reasons for unbelief. In many ways the survey was really asking for the reasons for dechristianization, so it admirably fulfills our present purpose of evoking the intellectual context in which Chenu formulated his position.[6] One common charge against Christianity often reported by the respondents to the survey as a cause of unbelief concerned its disregard for the problems of this world: "[What] Catholics are reproached with, in a thousand and ten thousand different ways, is being concerned but little with this world and being preoccupied only with the other." To the extent that this world had increasingly become the centre of interest and, indeed, the focus of a new religion, Christianity was perceived as being opposed to any sense of progress.[7] At the extreme, Christianity was seen as anti-human.

One of the respondents was Pierre Teilhard de Chardin. His answers are particularly significant for us because of the proximity of his position to that of Chenu. This proximity was not accidental; Chenu often refers to Teilhard in relation to his ideas on progressive humanization and the laws of the "social becoming." Teilhard clearly rejected mass apostasy as the cause for dechristianization and placed the burden on the rise of a new religion of the world. He called on Christianity to embrace this new object of human adoration: "The World is being spontaneously converted to a kind of natural Religion of the Universe which turns it away unduly from the God of the Gospel: it is in this that its 'unbelief' consists. Let us convert this conversion to an even higher degree, by showing through our whole lives that only Christ, *in quo omnia constant*, is capable of animating and leading the newly perceived progress of the Universe; and from the extension of what makes con-

---

6 This choice is further supported by the close association between Chenu and the Dominicans of Juvisy, where both *La vie intellectuelle* and *Sept* were published; cf. *Duquesne* (1975), 86–9.

7 Jean Lacroix, "Réponse à l'enquête … ," *La vie intellectuelle*, 24 (1933), 216. Cf., 214: "*Le catholique est opposé au progrès.*"

temporary unbelief will arise perhaps the faith of tomorrow."[8] Note the religious interpretation of the phenomenon, the sense of dynamism, and particularly the sense that something new is perceived to be going on. Finally, for Teilhard the road to the faith of tomorrow did not lie in the rejection of this new situation but in its acceptance. Only by acknowledging the value of the new reality can the Christian hope to bring about an even deeper conversion to Christ.

In 1933, there also appeared in *La vie intellectuelle* an anonymous article warning against the dangers of a facile and naïve optimism about the new situation and calling for a serious examination of conscience on the part of Christianity. Too many people, it claimed, were refusing to believe in the dechristianization of the country or else were minimizing its extent. The writer's analysis of the situation was particularly blunt: "The working masses are no longer Christian; all investigators affirm it." The massive rallies and demonstrations organized by Church authorities should not hide the statistical reality and the social composition of the participants: "Religion appears to be the prerogative of one class, the bourgeoisie." Economic or even religious reasons for this state were not sufficient; it was inadequate to blame laicism or the legacy of the Revolution. A critical self-examination was more necessary than accusing phantom enemies: "To begin with, Catholics on the whole have been unaware, are unaware still, of the misery of workers ... How often, in response to accounts of lamentable misfortune, have such reflections been heard: 'We did not know'? All right, but there is an ignorance which is guilty." This ignorance was coupled with an inability or a refusal to read the new and complex aspirations of the working population. The social mutation went by unnoticed or else opposed in the name of the past. The author continued his flow of rhetorical questions aimed at a stirring of conscience: "While in all domains, an evolution had occurred (or was occurring) from the regime of mastership to that of collaboration, have we not obstinately retained the theories of another era, and canonised decrepit institutions? Have we not confounded religious principles with social and political organizations? Have we drawn out the 'essence of Christianity' from the fleeting individuations in which it may for a time have become incarnate?" The issue of religion

---

8 P. Teilhard de Chardin, "Réponse à l'enquête ... ," *La vie intellectuelle*, 24 (1933), 222; the answer is reprinted in his *Oeuvres complètes*, vol. IX (Paris: Éditions du Seuil), 147–53. The similarity between the positions of Teilhard and Chenu is noted by Congar in "Le Père Chenu", 789: "*Ce que le P. Teilhard a perçu pour l'ensemble du cosmos et la totalité de son histoire, le P. Chenu l'a perçu pour la dimension historique et sociale de la vie humaine.*"

had been transformed in the minds of the workers into a question of social class. Catholics were perceived as being too often opposed to popular claims in the name of a Christian doctrine "which is most often no more than a system built up by their own fancy." To be fair, unbelievers also contributed to the growing gulf by exploiting Christian principles in order to maintain positions of privilege and oppose just reforms. The result was to be expected: "How can one be surprised, under these conditions, that workers associate Church and social caste and that religion becomes a question of class?"9

Other respondents to the 1933 survey were also led to an examination of conscience. They reflected on their own intellectual, social, and political conduct as contributing factors in the generalized state of unbelief. Reflections of this kind were not limited tothe actions of individuals, but took the Church as their object as well. They considered the Church to be at fault on two major points: first, in fostering an attitude of defense and a ghetto mentality, rather than presenting a basis of assimilation, and second, in contracting social and political alliances that were later found to have been compromising. Both errors had led to an impoverishment of Christianity and its isolation within modern society and its problems. When addressing unbelievers, or merely indifferent outsiders, the Church offered less a constructive interpretation of events than a "catalogue of errors." Even in so doing, the Church more often than not presented a caricature of the true doctrine of Christ rather than the real thing.10

9 See Anon., "Crise religieuse et crise sociale," *VI*, 19 (1933), 182–212, 357–81; the citations are from 183, 186, 363, 361–2, 367; see also 379: "*Le peuple a donc abandonné et détesté un catholicisme dont il n'avait rien à attendre et qui semblait se faire complice de ses ennemis, ne fût-ce que par son silence.*" The article was published in pamphlet form the same year by the Dominicans of Juvisy. For comments, see Émile Poulat, *Naissance des prêtres-ouvriers* (Paris: Casterman, 1965), 146–7; Poulat claims the author is Colonel André Roullet, a frequent lecturer at the *Semaines sociales*.

10 See Charles Dutroncy, "Les responsabilités des catholiques," *VI*, 30 (1934), 12–13. Dutroncey does not, for all that, completely reject the use of authority, cf., 16: "*Certes, il faut parfois recourir, pour protéger les idées, aux moyens de défense immédiats, mais il est dangereux de s'en tenir là et de faire de la pure répression la garantie unique de l'orthodoxie.*" See also André Boyer and Bernard de Solages (eds), "L'enquête dans les milieux de l'Enseignement Primaire," *VI*, 32 (1934), 189, where the authors speak of "*La difficulté, pour ne pas dire l'impossibilité, qu'il y a pour des incroyants, indifférents ou anticléricaux peu importe, à reconnaître la doctrine du Christ, et sa doctrine dernière dans les caricatures que trop souvent nous, catholiques, leur en présentons.*" The responses are often short on the historical details of such errors and "compromising" alliances. At this stage, it is the general perception that is important, rather than the historical accuracy of the responses.

The question of Christian responsibility for the sorry state of affairs was treated at length by Henri Guillemin in the 1937 article "Par notre faute," which caused quite an uproar upon publication. The article did not limit Christianity's shortcomings to the previous hundred years; instead, it pointed to a general state of decay lasting more than ten centuries: "The times are far distant from mediaeval Christendom ... One must look the truth in the face ... for more than ten centuries, the Catholic faith has not ceased decreasing ... Perhaps it is not useless to strive to measure with courage the extent of our guilt in this great drama of destitution ... Alas, it is not enough to say, It is Calvin's fault, It is Voltaire's fault. There again one must ask whether our betrayals did not precede these revolts, and whether it was not thanks to us that Luther or the *philosophes* received such a hearing. God entrusted us his name and his love for us to spread them. The story of what we have done with this duty is sad and sometimes frightful."[11]

For Guillemin, any remedial effort had to begin with a recognition of Christianity's own fault, including a repudiation of the alliances contracted in the previous century that resulted in the alienation of the masses. The Church had to admit to its role in the "great scandal of the twentieth century." Only in this way would it be able to offer a truer picture of itself to the outside world. To the extent that there was already movement in this direction, one could speak of the Church's fault as a *felix culpa*. The editorial accompanying Guillemin's article suggested as much: "Without the frightful scandal which, in the twentieth century, saw the poor lost by the Church of the poor, would we have been spectators to the miracle of the JOC?"[12]

An even more important document for our purposes, and the last one we will consider in this section, is Yves Congar's "Conclusion théologique"

---

11 Henri Guillemin, "Par notre faute," *VI*, 51 (1937), 326–2, the citation at 326–7. Although it is beyond the scope of the 1933 survey, the article is thematically related to our topic in a significant way. In a short biographical notice at the end of his *Les catholiques dans la France des années 30* (Paris: Éditions Cana, 1979), 266, René Rémond comments on Guillemin's style: "*La vigueur de l'investigation s'allie à la verve du polémiste et la ferveur à la détestation passionnée.*" Rémond's book was originally published under the title *Les catholiques, le communisme et les crises: 1929–1939* (Paris: A. Colin, 1960).

12 "Église, corps de péché," *VI* 51 (1937), 322–5, signed Christianus. On the two articles and the furor they created in Rome, see René Rémond, 232–8. The difficulties originated partly with the date of publication – only a few days after the closure of the Dominican journal *Sept* by Church authorities. The upshot of the reprimand to *La vie intellectuelle*, as quoted by Rémond, was that "*le censeur aurait dû censurer.*" The assigned "censor," it was later found out, was Chenu; cf. *Duquesne* (1975), 87–8.

in the 1933 survey on unbelief. Its value lies not only in its discerning clarity and perceptiveness, but also in the proximity of the author's position to Chenu's on the meaning and function of incarnation. The article is also of use to us for Congar's clear articulation of his starting point, "the fact of a generalized state of unbelief," and his emphasis on the "very largely social character of the motives of unbelief."[13]

Congar pointed to the divorce of faith from life and to the general privatization of religion as the main causes of contemporary unbelief. He described the gulf between faith and life as contrary to the "totalitarian" nature of faith, which involves all of human life, both private and public, inner and outer, and which generates "an order of Christendom" and "the creation of a Christian culture." Faith is a "total principle" where "that which is human is as a whole found to be taken up and transfigured, where all that was simply of man comes to be of Christ, and in Christ, of God, so that in all things God might find his glory." The crisis of unbelief would remain urgent to the extent that faith did not succeed in assuming this human whole, to the extent that the humanization of faith did not take place. In the present situation, according to Congar, faith had become separated from a number of key domains of human activity; it had become private and personal and thus violated its own nature. It was no longer the law of the whole of life: "Faith appears no longer as something *particular,* something *apart* and cut off from life." A substitution of a faith *whole* by a purely human and secular *whole* had taken place. Such was the rise of a new "totalitarian" order outside the sphere of faith: "In parallel and at the same rate as a spiritual world (of which Christ was no longer the principle) was built up alongside the Church, the Church itself (pulling itself together and tightening itself up under the attack, even as it became more interior and perhaps spiritually purer) specialized and was reduced to a particular group. Thus it appeared, before a human 'whole' sufficient for the development of life, as a *part* – as a closed, special and antiprogressive *party.*" In short, a separate and secular reality had arisen, acting like a "totalitarian" order in competition with the "totalitarian" claims of faith while, at the same time, relegating faith to a subordinate position. With the progressive laicization of the Christian state, more and more activi-

---

13 Y. Congar, "Une conclusion théologique à l'enquête sur les raisons actuelles de l'incroyance," *VI*, 37 (1935), 214–49. In his preface to B. Besret's *Incarnation ou eschatologie? Contribution à l'histoire du vocabulaire religieux contemporain 1935–1955* (Paris: Éditions du Cerf, 1964), 14–15, Chenu applauds the use of Congar's conclusion as the starting point for a contemporary history of the term "incarnation." The citation is from 214–15.

ties formerly under the aegis of the Church were now constituted outside the Church. Thus, charity had become "benefaction," and the poor were no longer the members of Christ but ordinary citizens with a right to government assistance. Religion had now been declared to be a private matter. It was no longer the Church that represented the "whole" of the human order, but "man and the purely human creations of man."[14]

Many critics of the situation would have stopped here and placed the entire blame for the Church's crisis on the forces of laicism. The reality was more complex; its understanding required more vision and discernment. The Church's loss of position in society and in the ordering of human activity represented only the underside of an equally positive operation. Congar saw the affirmative side of the process of secularization: "the constitution of a purely human spiritual dimension outside of Christianity." It involved belief in the self-sufficiency of reason and science, and in the possibility of an indefinite progress in the midst of this world, "the sufficiency of man in the midst of an evolving universe at once infinite and contained."[15]

For its part, the Church reacted negatively and isolated itself in face of laicization and growing rationalism. It developed a so-called "ghetto mentality." The fear of modernism in theology led to a narrow conformism whose result was the creation of a world apart from the world for the Church. Faith was stripped of a context in which to live and thrive. The result was a failure in the basic mission of the Church: "From that time, an immense portion of human activity, a whole growth in humanity, of human flesh – modern life with its Science, its sorrows,

14 Ibid., 216, 220, 224, 228; see also 227–8: "*Ainsi petit à petit, tous les gestes humains, toutes les réalités humaines se créent leur statut en dehors de l'Église et se soustraient à la foi.*" Chenu would call this the end of the Constantinian era, or simply the end of an "*état de chrétienté*"; cf. *Parole* 2, 17–36. In many ways, the "totalitarian" aspect corresponds to a description of intransigent catholicism; on this see Yves Tranvouez, "La fondation et les débuts de *La vie intellectuelle* (1928–1929): Contribution à l'histoire du catholicisme intransigeant," *Archives des sciences sociales des religions*, 42 (1976), 57–96, esp. 57–9. This is why Chenu advocated incarnation and mission in the world rather than the building of a Church next to the world; see the section Paradigms for a New Encounter in this chapter. On all this material, see B. Groethuysen *Origines de l'esprit bourgeois en France. L'Église et la bourgeoisie.* (Paris: NRF, 1927; Gallimard, 1956).

15 Y. Congar, "Une conclusion théologique ... ," 228, 235. Congar speaks not only of a new spiritual dimension but also of a "*mystique humaine (bientôt humanitaire).*" The reference to Teilhard is undeniable; cf. *Oeuvres complètes*, vol. IX (Paris: Éditions du Seuil, 1965), 147–53. We are dealing with a "*nouvelle révélation*," a religion of the human reality, with its appropriate faith and conversion.

its loftiness – did not have the incarnation as such of the Word; the Church did not give soul to the body that was stretched out and which, like every human value, should have received communication of the Spirit of Christ so as to become Christ's Body and give glory to God." Congar thus read the modern situation in terms of an incarnational presence of faith or the lack of it. The separation of faith and life was in fact, a deficit of incarnation. The Church had a duty and a need to extend constantly the scope of this incarnation: " … everywhere where there something of man, of humanity, there must be a mystical Body, an extension of the redemptive Incarnation." Every human value, every human progress in knowledge or activity, every "growth in humanity," had to be answered by a "growth in the Church, an incorporation of faith, an incarnation of grace, a humanization of God … " Otherwise, the result would be a Church appearing to oppose the values of human life rather than assuming them into its fold. The Church would appear no longer as the ark where everything of value was redeemed, but as a party moving to protect its own interests, which were often associated with a particular class or culture. "Faith does *not appear* any longer as the *whole* of man and as the very light of *life* in Christ; it appears not so much suprahuman as inhuman – alongside that humanity in which, nonetheless, our Saviour clothed himself."[16]

In such a situation, the task of the Church will clearly be to renew its presence in the world. Incarnation will be at the heart of this renewal. Faith must recover its place among the activities of life; it must become present to the human dimension in life: "Faith must become humanly present, like Christ."[17]

In the aforegoing, we can discern what may be termed a "boomerang effect." A survey of the causes of contemporary unbelief begins with a look at the outside influence of secularism and generally ends with an examination of conscience.[18] There is general agreement as to the existence of the problem, but a wide disparity of opinion as to its causes, its history, and its remedies.

---

16 Ibid., 241–2, 245. For the creation of a Church as a world apart from the world, see a similar argument in M.-D. Chenu, "Le sens et les leçons d'une crise religieuse" (1931), 356–80.

17 Y. Congar, "Une conclusion théologique … ," 248.

18 Cf. Émile Poulat, *Naissance des prêtres-ouvriers* (Paris: Casterman, 1965), 115: "*L'interrogation va ainsi faire boomerang et, jaillie chaque fois d'un regard sur les* païens, *va se retourner vers la* chrétienté *au sein de laquelle va s'instaurer une contestation réciproque d'attitudes divergentes.*"

ELEMENTS OF THE NEW SITUATION

The concrete pastoral situation characterized by dechristianization heralded the development of something new, rather than merely the breakdown of existing pastoral strategies. We now turn to a closer analysis of the key elements of the new situation.

The new situation is fundamentally characterized by the advent of what Chenu called the "civilization of work." It comprises a new set of social and economic factors for which, according to Chenu, there exists no adequate theological understanding. Chenu's description of the new situation and his efforts to develop a theology proper to the civilization of work inevitably involve a critique of previous approaches. The position of moralism, the "pious moralism" of the nineteenth century, is inadequate here, because it fails to take into account either the social structures involved or the specific and unique properties of the new phenomenon of work seen primarily as a social reality. The inadequacy of older, existing approaches to the human situation is most visible with the phenomenon of work where the *novelty* of the situation finds its most concentrated form.

The Church's reaction to the revolution in technology exactly parallels its reaction to modernism and the introduction of new rational procedures in the understanding of faith. The first reaction, always one of conflict and trouble, is followed, after further reflection, by a human presence witnessing to the fact that, despite all impurities and the presence of evil and ambiguities, the new reality is already redeemed in Christ and must be directed to its final end.[19] Chenu sees a parallel between the rise of Aristotle's *homo naturalis* in the Middle Ages and the *homo oeconomicus* of modernity. The difference is that modernity has not yet found its Thomas Aquinas to integrate the new image of humanity with Christianity. Such is the continuation of incarnation.

---

19 Cf. "Pour une théologie du travail" (1952), in *Travail*, 51, where Chenu speaks of the new situation as "*ce nouvel objet, impur, hélas, comme l'est toute génération humaine, mais terre rachetée d'avance et qu'il faudra conduire à sa fin divine.*" See also 54: "*c'est dans un conflit douloureux et obscur que grâce et nature se nouent, tant dans le secret des âmes que dans les constructions du savoir et dans les entreprises de la société.*" In an article entitled "Religious Beliefs and Praxis: Reflections on Catholic Theological Views of Work," in Gregory Baum (ed.) *Work and Religion* (*CON* 131 [1/1980], 102, n.15), Francis S. Fiorenza criticizes some of the views of Chenu but admits that "he is more aware than others of the negative qualities of industrialised labour."

Underlying this view of the relation of Christianity to the developing self-understanding of humanity (first detachment, then involvement) are the seeds of a theology of history. There is a conviction in Chenu that the dispensation of grace occurs not only through space geographically but also through time historically. The dialectic of nature and grace is no longer formulated according to a static conception of a certain abstract and rationalistic theology, but according to the rhythm of humanity's development in time. Herein lies Chenu's perspective of continued incarnation: "We would be wrong to imagine that grace, incarnate once for all in Christ, by this fact constitutes an immobile capital alongside a humanity whose earthly itinerary and steps undertaken are utterly unconnected with salvation (except by the piecemeal intermediary of certain persons). No. Grace is diffused in time." By rejecting a static conception of the dialectic of nature and grace and by locating the "diffusion" of grace in time, Chenu is committed to a dynamic view of God's involvement in human history wherein the incarnation is oriented towards an eschatological fulfillment in the endtime. In this perspective, the rhythm of history will contribute to a fuller development of incarnation. From now on, the stuff of history matters. It is not merely accidental, but central to an understanding of the divine economy: " … we know very well that history itself, in its sacred development, is divided into two periods – the one preparing Christ's coming, the other fulfilling the pleroma of the incarnation, – and this in a perspective of the end of time, where history will be fulfilled in grace."[20] History has now reached a critical stage of development. Christianity is faced with a technological revolution that radically changes human self-understanding and brings to light a new dimension of existence.

One major element of this novelty concerns the shift from tool to machine. It is significant because medieval accounts of *homo artifex*, based on the activity of the craftsman, are no longer adequate. Prior to the advent of technology, the theme of *homo artifex* was developed as an integral element of our relationship to nature, that is, in terms of microcosm. The advent of the machine introduces new factors that make the older vision difficult to preserve without any changes.

Socialization, the second major element of the new situation, is the direct product of technological society. For Chenu, it is of importance

---

20 "Pour une théologie du travail" (1952), in *Travail*, 50–1; Chenu goes on, "*la grâce envahit les choses dans le temps, et elle y trouve elle-même sa plus impressionnante dimension.*" See also "Dimension" (1937), in *Parole* 2, 89.

to theology because it manifests a decisive and authentic stage in the collective development of humanity. By bringing about socialization, work is a factor of humanization. It is for this reason that Chenu's evaluation of the new situation focuses on the phenomenon of work.

The Phenomenon of Work: From Tool to Machine

Beyond a moral evaluation of intentions, what is needed, according to Chenu, is an analysis of work as an object in itself, "in its own density, in its economic function, in its historical role." One approach to the task in question, labelled by Chenu as simply a case of "bad theology", is fundamentally extrinsicist: it finds value in work but this value originates outside of work, in the intention or attitude of the worker, not in the process of work itself. The effect, says Chenu, basically ratifies a sense of alienation. In contrast, Chenu wants to look at work on its own terms, discovering its own nature, its material and human processes, in order *then* to make a Christian judgment about its internal laws and spiritual exigencies.[21] Only in this way can we uncover the true structures of *homo artifex*.

Along these lines, a theology of work will be a reflection – under the light of faith – on the human activity of work, which thereby directly or indirectly enters the economy of salvation. Chenu laments the absence of a true theology of work in the theological circles of his time.[22] The dominant view was that work represented something only accidental, having no intrinsic value other than being an amorphous matter open to moralization and sanctification in the name of civic duty. In the words of a somewhat later vocabulary, there was no sense of work as a terrestrial reality.

The lack of a true theology of work results generally from a failure to recognize the novelty of the situation and the changes it implied in the understanding of work. At best it is the result of hope that existing

---

21 "Pour une théologie du travail" (1952), in *Travail*, 10, 12. This is already the basis of Chenu's later distinction between the deductive and inductive approaches in theology; the latter is consonant with an incarnation perspective. See also "Travail" (1959), in *Parole* 2, 545, where he distinguishes along the same lines between *théologie* and *mystique* and where the latter's "sentimental" approach has sometimes merited the Marxist charge of alienation. Throughout this discussion on the phenomenon of work, it is clear that Marx is the very prominent partner in Chenu's conversation. Chenu was the first to organize a course on Marx at Le Saulchoir in the 1930s; cf. *Duquesne* (1975), 66.

22 "Pour une théologie du travail" (1952), in *Travail*, 11–12.

patterns of theological reflection are sufficient for the new situation, whose radically new character is overlooked. In other words, there is a new situation for which the existing models of theological reflection on work are inadequate. A new dimension of human existence is in the process of being uncovered, and it calls for a new incarnation on the part of the Church. The new incarnation will first take the form of a new Christendom, then renew its self-understanding in terms of an ongoing state of mission.[23] The name given to the new understanding is socialization, the "coming-to-consciousness"[24] of the social dimension of human existence. Chenu speaks of it in terms of a natural law of "*devenir social*" which, by virtue of the incarnation, must become a divine law.

Socialization will be treated separately in a later section of this chapter, but a few words are necessary here. First of all, it is not a deductive principle but the product of an analysis of concrete conditions. Specifically, socialization is seen as the result of a revolution in social conditions, a revolution crystallized in the phenomenon of work as it appears in the age of modernity. Work in the modern age is characterized by the shift from tool to machine, and this shift carries momentous consequences. Work is now the privileged manifestation of the new dimension of existence and hence the privileged locus of new incarnation. It is "the endeavour which is situated the most exactly at the point where the individual enters into the community." As such, work is the vehicle and the herald of socialization. It is a factor of humanization in that it allows humanity to move forward in its collective march.[25]

The perception of this new dimension of humanity forms the ground for a "*nouvelle chrétienté*." The new reality is not acknowledged either by "baroque scholasticism" or by what Chenu calls the moralism of the

23 See the section Paradigms for a New Encounter on the response of the Church to the new pastoral challenge.

24 This is the equivalent of the French expression *prise de conscience*. The hyphenated form is preferred to the simple form "consciousness" in order to underline the dynamic character of the event and its relation to a historical process. In the next chapter, the expression is rendered as "differentiation of consciousness" to underline the interior dimension of the same phenomenon.

25 "Dimension" (1937), in *Parole* 2, 99. See *Travail*, 22: "*Le travail est facteur d'humanisation en devenant le pivot d'une 'socialisation' grâce à laquelle l'humanité franchit une étape décisive dans sa marche collective.*" See also *Spiritualité du travail* (1941), 7: "*Car le travail, croyons-nous, est l'un des éléments les plus sensibles de l'émergence spirituelle de nouvelles couches humaines, mal conscientes jusque-là de ce qu'elles portaient, de corps et d'âme.*"

nineteenth century. It is the context for Chenu's retrieval of the patristic maxim, "What is not assumed is not redeemed." The corollary, as it were, refers to what is *not* assumed, yet still remains a human good as a failure of the law of incarnation or at least of its application.

The new dimension is the advent of socialization, the coming-to-consciousness of the social dimension of existence. For Chenu, this event is a direct by-product of technological civilization. The concept of *homo artifex* had a place in medieval scholasticism as an integral element of the human relationship to nature; with the shift from tool to machine, it is no longer represented in theology. The advent of the machine introduces new factors making the older vision difficult to sustain and preserve. The existing theology is oriented to *homo artifex* as craftsman in terms of conditions that are no longer applicable to the modern worker and are thus inadequate. The inadequacy is not because of pastoral or pedagogical inaptitude, but because the older vision ignores the fundamental revolution in the human condition brought about by the advent of the machine. The older vision is anachronistic; as such, it fails in its mission.[26]

The older theology is also open to the Marxist critique of alienation. Under its aegis, the Christian would be an exile in his own land in the midst of a new world. The incarnation would have failed. Hence it is essential to recognize what is going forward in the revolution incurred by the civilization of work. Socialization must be integrated into the work of grace: "Because a human good is involved – a human good of very high quality and immense extension – and because humanity takes on new dimensions there, the divine life must constitute its material. The incarnation of Christ must continue." Clearly, it will be necessary to show whether every aspect of the socialization process is equally eligible to be called a human good. As a matter of fact, it will be shown that socialization, as brought forward in the developments of the civilization of work, is riddled with ambiguities. An essential part of the Christian work of incarnation and witness will be to denounce the evil and promote the good in the civilization of work. The underlying questions are what socialization is and precisely how it is made manifest in work. When

---

26 Chenu calls this older form of theology "*une expression artisanale … de la Parole de Dieu*"; see "Travail" (1959), in *Parole* 2, 550. For the relationship of technological advancement to socialization, see, for example, "Civilisation technique" (1948), in *Matière*, 66: "*La civilisation communautaire* [i.e., socialization] *est l'effet d'une civilisation mécanique née des applications de la science aux sociétés.*"

Chenu refers to socialization in terms of revolution, in what exactly is the Christian invited to participate?[27]

Socialization manifests a pervasive and intrinsic structure of the human condition. It is no mere juxtaposition of individual activities and achievements that would be more effective through their coming together. It is, rather, a case of the whole being larger than the sum of its parts: "it is the concentration, into a collective density, of committed human values, above and beyond individuals." It is evident that some form of social consciousness existed prior to the advent of mechanization. The revolutionary character of socialization lies in the fact that the consciousness of belonging to a collective grouping where human values are encountered did not previously exist to such a degree. Against the social conservatism proclaiming that there will always be workers and employers, Chenu attempts to recognize the specific role of work in terms of the evolution of humanity.[28]

There always was work, but only in the nineteenth century did it come to be accompanied by a consciousness of its social ramifications. Only then did something like a collective consciousness of work come into being, allowing for an observation of its laws, its ends, and, ultimately, its role in history. This coming-to-consciousness coincided with a radical change in the reality of work that affected not only the level of human life but also its essential quality. The transformation centred on the shift from tool to machine and ushered in not only a phase in the economy but a new age in the history of humanity: "[One] must know anew this new human soil which work makes up, having become, in the age of the machine, a reality without common measure with what it had been for millenia – transfigured in its function and its end as much as in its structure." The advent of the machine caused not only a quantitative intensification of work but – what is more more important – a qualitative transformation of lifestyle. The human encounter with nature was forever modified – it now came under the aegis of rationalization: "In transforming work, [the machine] inaugurated a new era of man in the universe."[29]

---

27 "Dimension" (1937), in *Parole* 2, 95. Socialization is called a revolution in "Révolution communautaire" (1944), in *Parole* 2, 363: "*une révolution est en cours.*" As an example of the relevance of Marxist critique, see "Travail" (1959), in *Parole* 2, 545, where Chenu speaks of the older vision "*méritant parfois la critique du marxisme qui l'accuse d'aliéner les hommes.*"

28 "Devenir" (1947), in *Travail*, 93. Cf. "Pour une théologie du travail" (1952), in *Travail*, 9.

29 Cf. "Pour une théologie du travail," 14, 20. At 14, Chenu also writes: "*Le passage de l'outil à la machine a non seulement ouvert une nouvelle phase de l'économie, mais inauguré un nouvel âge de l'humanité.*"

The machine reinforces human dominion over nature (cf. Gen 1:26) by means of rationalization. The human creative activity of *homo artifex* thereby reaches a major new stage of its vocation: "The worst failures and the guiltiest wrongdoings could not condemn this destiny." The mechanization of this dominion does not destroy its mystery. As he did in the case of the new methods and techniques of rational procedure in the quest for understanding, Chenu rejects the facile opposition between sacred and rational as applied to the phenomenon of work. More than anything else, the machine is a symbol of such rationalization. Notwithstanding a critique of a certain naïve optimism, Chenu welcomes the machine as a rational product and chastises those who reject the age of the machine in the name of some mystification that is not always wholly disinterested.[30]

The truly revolutionary character of the shift from tool to machine becomes manifest when we consider that work is productive of something more than profit. Work is that through which a new social consciousness is brought into the world. The spiritualists denounce work not only for its rationalization but also for the material, economic, and demographic concentration of people and resources it entails. Yet it is this very concentration that brings people together and fosters the collective consciousness wherein human solidarity as a distinct value finds expression. Through a process of interiorization, there develops a sense of belonging to a common enterprise, a common project – a consciousness of participating in a common good of order. In this law of community, a new freedom is found: "Instead of the opaque juxtaposition, the brute, 'objective' presence of individuals one to another, it is a spiritual presence, in a fraternal instinct which develops a hitherto imperceptible social temperature."[31]

Chenu is not naïve enough to suggest that all work situations in the age of the machine are *de facto* conducive to community. He points to the rise of the proletarian class and the development of class consciousness as unfortunate fruits of the revolution. Yet, he says, we cannot deny the nature of things on the basis of their perversion by human malice. The Christian will not be surprised at such a perversion, since ours is a fallen condition and a sinful state. Like all human reality and endeavour including love, work and its associated developments must be redeemed: " ... depersonalizing collectivism is but the human perversion, in a catastrophic interlude, of an operation which will, in the end,

30 Ibid., 18; cf. 19.
31 Ibid., 23.

manifest the *social* nature of man, on that level which today is privileged. Once again, work reveals the depths of this nature."[32] Human nature, of course, has not changed. The human condition, however, has undergone a radical transformation.

The birth of the proletariat, the working class, is the bitter first fruit of the laws at work in the process of socialization. The fruit is bitter because it came into being through conflict and violence. Chenu believes that only when social consciousness will bear its real fruits – i.e., peace and fraternity – will socialization become truly authentic. However, such a development can only come about through the influence of small communities that will be "the spiritual link of a similar interiorization, and therefore of this human promotion of persons and liberties."[33] Clearly, this is a reference to the task of witnessing taken up by the communities of the Mission de France and the Mission de Paris – the task arising from the Christian response to the new situation.

Likewise, Chenu does not pass over the fact that the world of work is "the nerve of positive atheism." As long as human alienation is present, that is, as long as the human dimension is lost, so too the religious reference to God will be overshadowed: "Work could no longer have a religious meaning, because it no longer had a human meaning." The Christian task will be to recover the cosmic meaning of work, wherein the human role of co-creator is restored to its rightful place. The stage for this task is at the intersection of human existence and the universe or, more simply, at the intersection of the individual and society.[34]

The revolutionary character of the new civilization of work and the radical nature of the mutation it introduces can best be seen in terms of changes in the human relationship to the universe. This relationship has now come to be dominated by the human desire to be responsible for humanity's own creation: "In way that was previously unthinkable, man no longer lives the life of nature, but a guided, rationalized life, a life which he creates for himself, which he invents for himself." What is involved in this previously unheard-of way of life is a new form of humanism, a new promotion of the human creative endeavour, with the machine as the proper instrument of that creative activity. In this sense, what emerges in the civilization of work is a new dimension of life. The effect runs much deeper than any political revolution. To be sure, this

---

32 Ibid., 24; cf. 22–3.
33 Ibid., 24.
34 Ibid., 28.

change, too, involves the human condition alone, not human nature as such.[35]

A unique perspective on this analysis of work is offered through the happy and fruitful coincidence of thirteenth-century theology with the specific problems of the industrial revolution in twentieth-century France. The coincidence is especially visible with regard to values in the order of secondary causes. In this sense, modern theology is far from being without resources in face of the challenge of the new civilization of work.[36]

The shift from tool to machine has shed new light on the medieval analysis of the relationships among worker, work, and nature. In this perspective, work is no longer seen primarily as a natural extension of the human relationship to the universe, and hence as defining only a human end (*finis operantis*). Work is not an activity subject to the intentions and morality of the worker. On the contrary, it is primarily the production of an objet (*oeuvre*) with an autonomous value. Work is thus defined in terms of an objectivity (*finis operis*). More precisely, it is through this very subordination to the object of work – that is, to work as an object – that human perfection is found in the phenomenon of work: " … it is in producing a work, in subordinating himself to it, in submitting himself to its laws in matter, that man at work finds his perfection as man."

The effect of the machine and of industrialized work in general was to heighten the gulf between the worker and the work produced. This depersonalizing and even materialist moment was cause for scandal for a certain spiritualist position: " … industrialized work has provoked – and continues to provoke – the bewilderment of religious consciousness as well as the (less interesting) protests of literary or philosophical snobbery." The promotion of the object of work as a separate entity responds to the fundamental law manifest in the phenomenon of work. A premature introduction of moral questions would violate this law and ignore the distinction between *finis operantis* and *finis operis*. It would, in short, ignore work as a terrestial reality. Good intentions do not displace the nature of things.[37]

---

35 Ibid., 32; cf. 37, where Chenu refers to the new "*humanisme du travail.*"

36 In his analysis of work and its doctrinal treatment in scholastic theology, Chenu relies heavily on Jean Lacroix, "La notion de travail."

37 "Pour une théologie du travail," 33. In "L'homo oeconomicus et le chrétien" (1945), *Travail*, 48, Chenu lays out the philosophical implications: "*L'homme au travail. L'homme trouvant dans le travail le moyen de se réaliser lui-même. L'homme enfin devenant homme.*" It is here that the rival metaphysical claims of Marxism are to be met. Cf. also "Travail" (1959) in *Parole* 2, 547: "*L'homme se fait homme en transformant le monde, en le travaillant.*"

In the name of the principle of the consubstantiality of matter and spirit so central to all Thomistic anthropology, Chenu criticizes those who displace the autonomy of work as a *perfectio operis*. The superiority of the human spirit is not such that it can fulfill itself independently of this *perfectio operis*. Chenu opposes the rejection of terrestrial reality in the name of safeguarding the transcendent orientation to the love of God. The reality of work carries an authentic value of its own independent of human spiritual finality. It is not a mere instrument of perfection: "Work, the 'civilization of work', is of worth in itself, for its own truth, for its original effectiveness, for the building up of the world, for the historic destiny of humanity; not, to be sure, that it is a supreme end, by which man is definitively fulfilled, ... but this work is truly an end in its own order, a secondary end, and not an instrument of perfection, a simple bundle of uses, advantages, prosperities, to be moralized by pious intentions." Far from any scandalous effect, the advent of the civilization of work represents an opportunity and a demand for a further incarnation of grace. The common good involved in terrestrial reality is no longer, as in the sacralized order of the Middle Ages, a merely instrumental function, "but an order of values come of age, in its own goodness and its specific effectiveness."[38]

Socialization: A New Dimension of Existence

The Church's effort to sanctify the individual without sanctifying the social structures of existence was useless and contrary to the basic laws of the Christian economy, since the vocation of individual human existence is lived only within a social dimension. These social structures of existence appeared as something new, something that had not existed before, at least not in terms of consciousness nor on such a massive scale. Hence we speak of the *advent* of socialization to describe the massive increase in the general awareness and, specifically, the internalization of the social structures of existence. These social structures must be sanctified. They must be addressed by the Christian proclamation for two main reasons. First, they represent constitutive elements of human existence, which according to the law of incarnation is assumed in its entirety. Second, they have not been previously addressed and until recently have remained on the outside of mainstream Christendom.

38 "Pour une théologie du travail," 35–6, 37. In this context, Chenu makes a reference to the "prophetic" pages of Jacques Maritain's *Humanisme intégral* (Paris: Aubier, 1968; c1936), especially to chapter 6, "*Des chances historiques d'une nouvelle Chrétienté.*"

Hence, it is more appropriate to speak of the non-christianized segment of the population than of the dechristianized masses.[39]

A refusal of the legitimacy of the social dimension is a "*faux spiritualisme*" of the type already encountered with regard to the cognitional activity of faith. It would be an error resembling the glorification of the individual by liberalism. It would be contrary to the laws of the divine economy, which proceeds by way of incarnation. In any case, the social dimension can hardly be evaded. It was not a political or economic theory that was making the rounds of academia, but an effort to understand an all-pervasive reality that could not be denied without at the same time denying human nature.

Yet the denial did occur for a large segment of Christianity, which enclosed itself in a ghetto and thereby condemned an even larger segment of the population to the realm of the unreligious, the unchristian, and, ultimately, the unredeemable. A certain form of Christianity approached the working world as something strictly foreign or at best accidental and tangential to the essence of its message and its mission. The net effect was that the working world did in fact become a foreign land estranged from the Church. Once the Church was faced with the fact of a massive non-christianized population, it had to re-evaluate the social and historical situation and, in that light, its own mission. The new situation called attention to itself, and forced the Church to realize its own disincarnate state before it could interpret the changes in the situation as something to be assumed in the name of incarnation and according to its law of realism.

The denial came in the form of an emphasis on the individual person and the individual quest for perfection and holiness. Very often, the strategy was to protect the individual against his or her environment by creating an "artificial" milieu where the person could live out the Christian virtues within a closed circle, protected from the pagan or atheist world. For Chenu, such "spiritual protectionism" may have been necessary during certain periods, but its inevitable result was a Christianity cut off from life, from daily struggles and the reality of social classes, a

---

39 See "Dimension" (1937), in *Parole* 2, 92: "*Si l'Incarnation n'arrive pas à assumer cela, c'est une tranche d'humanité qui est rejetée au déchet. Sanctifier l'individu sans sanctifier l'homme social, c'est vain travail. Vain en fait, comme une maladresse; vain en droit, comme une erreur. Car c'est incohérence dans l'économie du salut; c'est consentir implicitement à faire échec à la loi de l'incarnation.*" Cf. "Liberté et engagement" (1938), in *Parole* 2, 347: "*Le chrétien ne se sanctifie pas par une évasion mystique hors du social.*" On dechristianization see "Déchristianisation ou non-christianisation?" (1960), in *Parole* 2, 248–9, as well as the section Dechristianization and the Pastoral Situation in this chapter.

Christianity without boldness or courage. In short, the result was a disincarnate Christianity, which abandoned the proletariat to its misery in the name of its pagan character. This was not only a tactical but also a doctrinal error. In effect, the Church's message was that a key area of life, in fact *the* key area among the proletariat, was outside the concern of religion, that the main hopes and struggles of their lives fell outside the limits of what is redeemable. Redemption would be available in proportion to the denial of these areas of life. Chenu's verdict is unambiguous: "A sin against the realism of the Incarnation."[40]

The articulation of socialization within theology came after the concrete reality of the desertion of the Church by the working class. First came the crisis of dechristianization, which was then interpreted as nonchristianization. Only later did the hopes and aspirations of the new reality come to be seen in terms of a growing socialization. The discussion of socialization is therefore set within the context of a concrete experience. The formerly abandoned and non-christianized masses had to be interpreted as part of a comprehensive growth towards ever-greater community. Socialization itself came to be characterized as, among other things, the arrival of the phenonemon of the masses. Specifically, Chenu's reflections on the effects and meaning of socialization were fuelled by the 1936 strikes of the factory workers and the election of the Front Populaire government. The experience of the war further contributed to the sense of urgency in the Christian mission.[41]

---

40 Cf. "Dimension" (1937), in *Parole* 2, 97: "*[C]hristianisme désincarné, c'est-à-dire à la lettre sans incarnation, abandonnant à sa misère la masse damnée et honnie du prolétariat paganisé.*" See also Chenu's remarks about the "pharisaic fear" to get one's hands dirty through involvement with the world, in "Corps de l'Église et structures sociales" (1948), in *Parole* 2, 163.

41 Cf. *Une école de théologie* (1937), where the phenomenon of the masses and their effective and irrepressible presence in public life is discerned as a sign of the times. See also "Les masses humaines, mon prochain?" (1965), in *Peuple*, 99–128. On Chenu and the strikes, see the comments of Olivier de La Brosse in *Le Père Chenu: La liberté dans la foi* (Paris: Éditions du Cerf, 1969), 71–2: "*Lui qui avait vu vivre les militants ouvriers et connaissait de près leur action, décrivait, un an après les événements [de 1936], cette 'dimension nouvelle de la chrétienté', cet espoir qu'avait fait germer dans la classe ouvrière la grande crise sociale qui devait préluder aux réformes de l'après-guerre.*" On the war, see "Chrétien, mon frère ... Pourquoi la guerre?" (1939), in *Parole* 2, 225–30. This is an excellent example of the concrete character of Chenu's theology as well as a good starting point for his reflection on the problem of evil. His position involves a rejection of a certain apologetic and its argument for rational credibility since it remains extrinsicist, "*[elle] n'introduit point dans la connaissance effective de Dieu, ne nous met en dialogue avec lui, 'notre Père'. Elle est non moins extérieure à la vie réelle et concrète de notre esprit.*" He continues, "*tenons donc à niveau la réponse et la question, et ne cherchons pas ici une réponse abstraite et rationnelle à une question où toute notre vie, avec le sort de l'humanité, est engagée.*"

Thus, the fact of the revolution in social structures caused not only a crisis in society but also a crisis in the Church, wherein fundamental structures of the Church were put in question.[42] In cases where the relationship between the Church and society becomes problematic and troublesome, the focus shifts to the principles underlying that relationship. A normal state of affairs exists when the Christian community receives the basic form of its organization from the existing social structures in civilization. Such a state of affairs is thrown into turmoil when those social structures undergo a sudden and rapid evolution. In such moments of history, the displacement can become almost violent, and the very discontinuity between Church and society becomes the focus of our efforts to understand. An opportunity is created for deeper insight into the laws and principles underlying the unfolding of the Christian economy. The early decades of the twentieth century offered such an opportunity to the French Church.

On this subject, Chenu begins by acknowledging the Church as mystery. Its innermost reality is hidden within the communion of faith established by the mystery of Christ in the Holy Spirit: "It is the mystery of Christ carrying out in humanity his eternal plan of divine life, achieved once for all in his death and resurrection."[43] Through faith, we become contemporaries of this reality. Chenu stresses, however, that this is not a faith reducible to the psychology of religious experience, but a faith referring to the presence of the Holy Spirit, God's witness within us. This faith remains above the vagaries of historical accident and the societal dimension, for it is merely the figure of this world that passes away.

Yet history is not thereby abandoned. Christ's drama did not occur outside history; likewise, the Church has a historical existence within time: "Nonetheless Christ is in time, and the Church has a body which is humanity itself, spread throughout history." By becoming a history of salvation, the destiny of humanity as a whole is the form, as it were, of

42 Cf. "Corps de l'Église et structures sociales" (1948), in *Parole* 2, 159, where Chenu speaks of the "*mise en question presque brutale de ses propres comportements, tant dans l'organisation intérieure de ses diverses communautés que dans les formes de son apostolat.*" The three major works associated with the surveys of religious practice in the French Church are H. Godin's *France, pays de mission?* (1943), F. Boulard's *Problèmes missionnaires de la France rurale* (1945), and G. Michonneau's *Paroisse, communauté missionnaire* (1946). To this list, Chenu adds J. Loew's *En mission prolétarienne* (1946) and, in terms of a concluding synthesis, Cardinal Suhard's pastoral letter *Essor ou déclin de l'Église* (1947).

43 "Corps de l'Église et structures sociales" (1948), in *Parole* 2, 160. This starting point is pedagogical and sets the basis for an affirmation of social and historical reality. It should not be taken as a first step in a dogmatic deductivist approach.

this communion of faith. Salvation is still a personal matter, but it is not available outside the human community. The incarnation structure is paramount: "Yes, to be sure, the Church is the supersacrament ... whose vicissitudes are not past events to which I associate myself in memory, but the recurrence in me of the mysteries of Christ died and risen again; nonetheless, this mystery of Christ dying and rising in me is, precisely, accomplished by an incarnation, a coming of God in time – and thus not by an eviction of history, but by a recapitulation of every creature. The coming of Christ, the intervening space between the comings of Christ, is the transformation of the world, the divinization of man in the transformation of the universe." In light of such an arrangement, it is not surprising that Chenu keeps a close eye on developments in the society surrounding him. For Chenu, the progress of the human world is not a matter of accidental or tangential importance. Its developments are important not in any secondary fashion but as part of the reality of ongoing incarnation. The whole progress of humanity through time is now included in the mystical body of Christ by virtue of the scope of the economy of salvation. The laws of human development become the laws of the ongoing incarnation. The structures of human life will be the "substructures of the divine life," not according to empty paradox but according to the basic set of relationships established by the law of incarnation.[44]

Having laid the groundwork, we can now ask about the nature of these structures. In what do they consist? How are they revolutionary? The fundamental structure of socialization is first manifested in an act of consciousness whereby the human person becomes aware that the least human act is always already involved in a network of social relations. This social network is present as an overarching framework dominating every human action and penetrating its most secret and private meaning. In every pursuit of the private good, we are already somehow involved in the general fate of the common good. This social dimension cannot be evaded: "I cannot pass by the smallest marketplace, claim the most modest salary, settle the briefest contract, without right away, from the most immediate reflection, feeling encircled on every side – and supported as well – by economic, social, juridical and politi-

44 Ibid., 161. Chenu continues: "*La grâce est sociale. L'humanité devient le corps mystique du Christ, et la prise de possession du monde, en laquelle l'homme accomplit son destin de créature, entre matériellement dans le développement mystique de la divine entreprise ... Le paradoxe n'est pas celui de Kierkegaard, c'est le paradoxe de l'Incarnation, engagement et liberté d'un Dieu fait chair pour que toute chair ressuscite en Lui.*"

cal solidarities which make up the space of my contract, of my work, of my business, prior even to my intentions. And this, in a sort of musical chairs which, from one end of the world to the other, multiplies endlessly an inextricable and invincible network … Social life surrounds me narrowly and incessantly. Constraint? Resource also? Both, no doubt." The striking element in this description of the coming-to-consciousness of the social dimension of reality lies in the inevitability of the condition. We recognize here the *facticity* of life as taught by the existentialist philosophers. The social dimension precedes and places limits on our creative possibilities. We find ourselves "encircled on all sides" in a way that is "inextricable and invincible." Thus, the negative moment of social consciousness is emphasized first. Yet, Chenu adds, we also perceive the social network as a support. Juridical, political, and economic relations are not only limitations but also the basis for various solidarities and natural communities.[45]

Through the internalization of these solidarities we come to belong to and participate in something larger than ourselves. Socialization in this sense implies no mere juxtaposition of individual lives, but the consciousness of a reality belonging to a different order. This new reality is both larger and other than the sum of its parts. It involves "the concentration of committed human values into a collective density, above and beyond individuals … Thus, not interindividual exchanges, but multiplication, or better yet community totalization of an energy of which the group as such becomes the subject and the promoter."[46] Socialization thus induces a major shift in the basic understanding of the subject, from individual to member of a humanity in the midst of progress.

The error of liberalism lies, among other things, in a failure to see the social phenomenon as anything more than a coalition of individual liberties. Socialization destroys the extreme claims of liberalism by bringing about a new revolution: "The revolution of the twentieth century denounces mercilessly the illusions and mystifications of 1789." Socialization is termed revolutionary because the opposite values of liberalism

---

45 "Dimension" (1937), in *Parole* 2, 89–90. He also writes: "*[L]e moindre acte humain comme la plus menue réalité sont engagés dans un régime sociétaire qui les commande et de toutes parts les pénètre.*" For a classic statement of the pervasiveness of the social dimension of reality, see Peter L. Berger and Thomas Luckmann, *The Social Construction of Reality. A Treatise in the Sociology of Knowledge* (Garden City, NY: Doubleday, 1966; Anchor Book edition, 1967). See on this "Les communautés naturelles, pierres d'attente de cellules d'Église" (1965), in *Peuple*, 129–43.

46 "Devenir social" (1947), in *Travail*, 93; cf. 92–6.

were so pervasive and deeply ingrained. As liberal individualism con-
quered the viewpoint of many Christians in the nineteenth century, the
authentic human value in socialization became difficult to discern. The
dominant tendency among Christians was to sanctify the individual
while denying any autonomous value to the social dimension, or even to
sanctify the individual against the social dimension. This mystical escapism from social reality was parallel to the error of liberalism and was
rejected by Chenu: "Thus we do not in the least accept a disjunction
between the person and the social – the person a spirit to sanctify, the
social merely the external matter of holiness. Would this be possible absolutely speaking? It is not, at any rate, the dispensation willed by God,
which is fulfilled in an incarnation." It was for having accepted more or
less such a disjunction that Christianity bore the brunt of Marx's violent
critique. In this context, Chenu admits the truth of the Marxist saying:
"It is easy to be a saint if one gives up being human." Chenu counters
with the doctrine of incarnation and the resulting mode of being in the
world: "That sanctity is false and vain which does not recognize the radical conditions of human life. Now, the Christian recognizes them, and
this, not as a concession, but because he knows that his God, Christ
incarnate, accepted and consecrated and took them on – not simply by
virtue of the Incarnation, but in the inaugurated regime as well, the
mystical Body which is the Incarnation continued. This communion, or
supernatural 'collectivism' provides the climate for an ordered exercise
of freedom and determines the temporal mission of the Christian." The
references to incarnation and to continued incarnation bring out the
central character of this issue and the basis of Chenu's approach to the
question. They also provide the clue for the practical directives needed
for the challenge of Christianity's temporal mission.[47]

It will be clear by now that the advent of socialization carries a number of ambiguities. Not every expression of the social bond between persons is fully adequate to the nature of the human individual. The value
of the social entity can easily be promoted to the detriment of the person. Yet the perfection of the human being can be achieved only in a
social context. Human freedom is exercised and fulfilled within a community. This fact is not eliminated by the threat of a glorification of the
masses. The dangers of a certain naturalism or naturalistic mysticism –
what used to be called laicism at the turn of the last century – do not dis-

47 "La pensée contemporaine" (1960), in *Parole* 2, 173; "*Liberté et engagement*" (1938),
in *Parole* 2, 347–8.

qualify the basic truth of socialization. The potential error of horizontal-ism does not call for the denial of the human value of social existence. It was the failure to make such distinctions that led to confusion between socialization and socialism in the eyes of many Christians. Chenu, for his part, refused to reject the insight of Marx with respect to socialization despite the materialist philosophical stance of Marxism.[48]

Clearly, the human person has always been a social animal. The social dimension of existence has been ever-present; it did not appear for the first time in the nineteenth century. In this sense, socialization is a fact of the human condition. Yet the incredible intensity in the development of social consciousness in the latter half of the nineteenth and the beginning of the twentieth century warrants our use of the term "revolu-tion." Still, the discontinuity implied by this shift in the collective consciousness is not without precedent.

In order to illustrate the interaction between Church and world in the context of the movement of history, Chenu chooses examples from the past. History is thus "an experiential mistress of truth."[49] Chenu ex-amines the renewals of the early Middle Ages with the aim of uncover-ing the *laws* of social evolution and the Church's response to them.

Chenu's favourite such historical reference was the social and cultural renaissance of the twelfth and thirteenth centuries, "one of the social cycles which makes up one of the most organic and suggestive periods of the march of history." This period of history involved the disappear-ance of serfdom through the passage from a feudal regime to the com-munes and the corporations. It also saw the rise of the universities. Chenu aptly summed up the spirit of the times in the definition he gave for "commune": "[I]t is the prise-de-conscience of a common good, in which one and all see themselves in solidarity, by a collectivism in which material interests are the fabric of spiritual commitments." A new social

---

48 See "La pensée contemporaine" (1960), in *Parole* 2, 173: "*[I]l ne faut pas oublier que, de soi, c'est par la prise de conscience des communautés dans lesquelles elle est engagée, que la personne humaine trouve les ressources de son épanouissement, de sa liberté même.*" See Duquesne (1975), 102–8. Chenu believes that after so many years of verticalism it is only natural to err a little on the side of horizontalism. In fact, it may even be necessary, if the new phenomenon of socialization is to be preserved from stillbirth. It should be clear by now that Chenu's reac-tion to socialization is the same as his reaction to the modernist crisis. See also "Corps de l'Église" (1948), in *Parole* 2, 166. For evidence of the pastoral reason for this position, see *Pour être heureux* (1942), 4: "*L'homme est un esprit incarné. Nous préférerions céder à l'apparence d'un matérialisme historique, plutôt que d'oublier, dans un pseudo-moralisme, les dures conditions concrètes d'une économie du travail, – le sort des travailleurs.*"

49 "Réformes de structure" (1946), in *Parole* 2, 38.

class arose that found its strength and meaning in association, substituting for the vertical and personal relations of serfdom a horizontal network of relations in "a regime in which everyone becomes aware of his participation in a common good which gathers together and which he has freely chosen in the body of his choice."[50]

The Church's attitude towards this "new world" was at best uncertain; in fact, in many ways the Church was downright opposed to the changes. The basic reason for its opposition was that the new emancipation threatened the old order of feudality, to which the Church was ideologically linked. The Church was not only the support and the guarantor of the old order but also its chief beneficiary: "the temporal presence of clerics in all of the machinery of the institution was the normal condition of its spiritual effectiveness." It was thus negatively inclined to the aspirations disturbing the established order, "and the solidarity which bound together prelate and lord in the bonds of the same tradition, reinforce[d] its moral resistance with economic interests."[51]

The encounter between the established Church and the aspirations of the new type of humanity was therefore not an easy one. The Church experienced "a sort of displacement which for a moment left it at once pulling back and aspiring." It was not equipped with the instruments necessary for dealing with the new realities of emancipated associations and corporations. On the other hand – at the risk of becoming alienated from a certain established clericalism – some elements in the Church reacted more positively, "to recognize in this new humanity a fine subject for Christian grace."[52]

Thus arose the reform of the twelfth century. St. Francis and St. Dominic combined fidelity to the Church with trust in the values of the new social order. Theirs was both an institutional and an apostolic reform by means of a return to the gospel. The original friction led to a renewal of the Church's presence to its time. A return to the gospel did not mean a refusal of the new values in the name of some spiritual purity. On the contrary, following the paradox of incarnation, it meant a solidarity with the new values, the advent of a new *chrétienté*: "From this point the 'reforms' are no longer only moral purifications or salutary reparations; by a return to the Gospel, they are the advent of a new

---

50 "Devenir social" (1947), in *Travail*, 88, 86; "Réformes de structure" (1946), in *Parole* 2, 47.

51 "Réformes de structures" (1946), in *Parole* 2, 48.

52 Ibid., 49–50.

Christendom, in the historical, geographical and spiritual unity of a Church that is one, holy, catholic." Chenu belonged to a generation which believed that the Church of the twentieth century was faced with a similar situation. The nineteenth century had uncovered new dimensions of humanity expressed in a consciousness of socialization. That, in turn, called forth a new *chrétienté*.[53]

Reference to the revolutionary ferment in the twelfth century serves to emphasize a deeper continuity in the midst of discontinuity. The upheaval of the twentieth century is not the "first time." The longer perspective places our limited viewpoint within the larger rhythm of the history of humanity. Indeed, the relations between grace and human nature in its developmental aspect have on various occasions been experienced in terms of conflict.[54] The classic example is the encounter of an established Christendom with the philosophy of nature and Aristotelian anthropology. Despite the potential dangers of naturalism and rationalism, the new developments found a status and a refuge in the theology of St. Thomas. As we have noted, for Chenu, the developments of the twentieth century are still in search of their Thomas. The details of the encounter with the twentieth century, however, bring us to the next section.

PARADIGMS FOR A NEW ENCOUNTER:
MISSION AND WITNESS

Having examined the new situation and the revolutionary developments in a new humanity, we can now ask about the details of Christianity's approach to these matters. As socialization becomes acknowledged as a potentially authentic development requiring a new incarnation on the part of the Church, how will this incarnation take place? What will be its fundamental characteristics? How will its principles and strategies be applied in concrete terms?

We begin with a clarification of the term *chrétienté* and the relationship to history and civilization implicit in it. Next we examine Chenu's reflection on Action catholique and its strategy of conquest, acknowledged as the first explicit form of the necessary new incarnation. In the

53 Ibid., 53.

54 Cf. "L'homo oeconomicus" (1945), in *Travail*, 49: "*Ce n'est pas la première fois qu'émerge un 'homme nouveau' dans l'histoire de l'humanité.*" See also the way historical precedents are used in the appraisal of the modernist crisis, "Le sens et les leçons d'une crise religieuse" (1931), 356–80.

final section we see the inadequacy of this strategy and consider the efforts that saw it succeeded by the strategy of presence.

"Chrétienté" *and* "Nouvelle Chrétienté"

The term *chrétienté* requires some interpretation, thanks to a certain ambiguity as to its usage.[55] There is, first, a negative use of the term referring to the earthly commitments and burdens of the Church throughout the ages and pointing to those attachments tying the Church to the so-called establishment and stifling its evangelical ferment. Such a use of the term is undeniable, yet not exclusive. However, the term also carries a positive meaning in connection with the necessity for the Church to become incarnate in the civilization in which it finds itself. It is for this reason that the use of the term seems ambiguous.

In the presentation to *L'Évangile dans le temps*, Chenu addresses the issue of the meaning of *chrétienté*. He does not offer a technical definition but acknowledges both the ambiguity and the centrality of the concepts involved: "The term 'Christendom' is not without ambiguity. Sometimes it denotes the established institution, with all its weight, enwrapping the living Church in the networks of a sacralization of profane structures. Sometimes it proclaims advantageously, in the historic movements of human societies, the imbuing of the Gospel, the regime of incarnation – in the Church as in Christ – according to the very condition of man and the new dimensions of society." In short, the term refers to the concrete and historical forms of Christianity at any given time in history. This said, it sometimes refers to the established institutions and temporal structures binding the Church; at other times it is used positively to describe the ways in which the Church is present to its time. In the latter usage, *chrétienté* refers to the Church's incarnation in a particular time and culture, within a particular society and civilization.[56]

Chenu uses the term *chrétienté* to describe the basic form taken by the Church in its succession of different incarnations throughout history. It

---

55 For a discussion of the history of the term and the possibilities of its contemporary use, see Giuseppe Alberigo et al., *La chrétienté en débat: Histoire, formes, et problèmes actuels* (Paris: Éditions du Cerf, 1984); see especially the historical contribution by Daniele Menozzi, "L'Église et l'histoire. Une dimension de la chrétienté de Léon XIII à Vatican II," 45–76.

56 "Présentation" (1964), in *Parole* 2, 10. Cf. "Réformes de structures" (1946), in *Parole* 2, 46, where the term is used to refer to "*l'engagement de l'Église dans les sociétés profanes qu'elle sanctifie.*"

is thus associated with the historicity of the Church and its rootedness in an incarnational structure. The following passage illustrates this usage: "Let us say, if you like, that the Church – the one Church – the mystical Body of Christ – is constituted in time and in space, consisting of Christendoms, in which the growth of humanity becomes the subject of the earthly growth of divine life."[57] In case this was not sufficiently clear, Chenu stresses that the Church's existence and development through successive *chrétientés* is not an accident to be regretted but the essence of its mission to make the love of Christ and the freedom of the Spirit present to the world of its time: "In truth, the Church, the mystical Body of Christ and sanctuary of the Spirit, does not live or subsist except by and in the Christendoms which, over the ages, have embodied the charity of Christ and the freedom of the Spirit in successive human societies." The development of the Church in relation to various times and societies is seen in terms of a succession of *chrétientés*, which represents a continuation of the one incarnation. The succession represents the way in which the Church, as the mystical body of Christ, effectively assumes the whole of humanity as it develops and grows in time.[58]

Still, it would not be accurate to stress only the positive meaning of the term *chrétienté*. It is true that, in the history of the usage in the first part of the twentieth century, it came more and more to be associated with the Constantinian age of the Church, an age whose death knell was by then being proclaimed. Yet even in the midst of overcoming the established and establishment *chrétienté*, Chenu speaks of a "*nouvelle chrétienté*." He maintains this terminology throughout those critical moments when a particular "incarnation" of the Church and its historically established form come into question and are challenged by rising new developments in self-understanding and social consciousness. The advent of socialization and *homo oeconomicus* is not so much a threat to the established *chrétienté* as an opportunity for growth and a chance for it to fulfill

57 "Révolution communautaire" (1944), in *Parole* 2, 367. For the solidarity of *chrétientés* with revolutionary human developments, see "La foi en chrétienté" (1944), in *Parole* 2, 115: "*La communauté mystique de l'Église, sacrement du Christ, se réalise en des* Chrétientés successives *qui sont solidaires de l'histoire et de ses révolutions. Aussi, je ne suis pas surpris, mais je triomphe, au contraire, en voyant la chrétienté de 1944 solidaire en quelque manière de la révolution humaine qui est en train de retourner ce siècle; et j'ose espérer que cette fois, mieux que dans les années 1500, les chrétiens resteront présents.*"

58 "Réformes de structures" (1946), in *Parole* 2, 37. On continued incarnation as a process of assumption, refer to the subsection in chapter 5, Theological Meaning of the Signs of the Times.

its mandate of continuous incarnation: "If the divine life had to stop before *homo oeconomicus* and give up the idea of taking him up into its economy of grace, then Christianity – as Marx dogmatized and as certain Christians have believed! – would be done for, for it would be the failure of the Incarnation itself, in which the whole mystery of our faith resides. So far, then, from seeing here the failure of Christendom, we discern more still a magnificent opportunity for growth of the community."[59] Although Chenu speaks of a "magnificent opportunity for growth" using the same basic categories, a shift towards the different terminology of mission is noticeable. Yet the qualities ascribed to the Church of mission are fundamentally the same as those of the *nouvelle chrétienté*.

The Strategy of Conquest: Action catholique and
Jeunesse ouvrière catholique

The pioneers in the building of the new Christendom were the teams of the specialized movements of Action catholique. Groups such as Jeunesse ouvrière catholique (JOC) sought new ways of effectively proclaiming the gospel message in a secularized world. As their name suggests, the particular focus of their action was the working class. More specifically, their pastoral conquest was aimed at the new social dimension of existence manifest in the phenomenon of work.[60]

In the work of such groups, more than anywhere else, it was evident that practice precedes theoretical elaboration. The activity of the JOC teams required a new theological context. In their view, the existing context was too closely allied to an obsolete social order and was generally ill-prepared to meet the modern secular world. The pastoral experience called for a renewal of traditional Catholic teaching with a new sensitivity for the existing social, cultural, political, and economic situation.[61]

On the other hand, certain tendencies in theological reflection were proving to be particularly fruitful on the pastoral level and in fact contributed to the success of the various pastoral experiments. Such was the

59 *Spiritualité du travail* (1941), 42.

60 On the pastoral importance of the social dimension, see "Dimension" (1937), in *Parole* 2, 92–3: "*C'est là précisément que je suis menacé d'être le plus misérable, en ce XXe siècle, où tout en moi est pénétré de vie sociale. C'est donc là que la Chrétienté nouvelle devra organiser sa conquête apostolique.*"

61 From 1932 onwards there were regular retreats for JOC teams at Le Saulchoir. On their significance for Chenu, see "La JOC au Saulchoir" (1936), in *Parole* 2, 271–4. See also Y. Congar, "Le Père Chenu," 782.

case with the ecclesiological reflections on the mystical body of Christ and the popularization of the doctrine of the incarnation. Thus one JOC chaplain recalled the early years of his pastoral activity: "I centred all of my spirituality on the Incarnation and the mystical Body. There was Mass, and there was charity. Above all it was imperative to put the emphasis on the *Incarnation*. We had so much to react against a too-'disincarnate' religion! ... Among the people, we were much reproached with having neglected the problems of the earthly city, concerning ourselves only with 'the other world'! ... The mystery of the Incarnation was truly the preferred mystery of the nascent JOC."[62] Reciprocally, it was in the praxis of the JOC that Chenu saw the basis for a renewal of theology in general and of the teaching on incarnation in particular.

For Chenu, the JOC represented the Church militant in its fidelity to the law of continued incarnation. The centrality of incarnation is immediately apparent in the very concept of pastoral ministry, which Chenu characterizes as "the conquering expansion of the incarnation and of Christ's sacraments." Within this broad definition of pastoral activity, not all ministries fell under the banner of Action catholique. This follows from the fact that the individual and the family could no longer be the only focus of the Church's activity. The revolution of socialization had brought into view a social dimension of existence that could not be reduced to an aggregate of individuals or families. The parish, which was the corresponding pastoral instrument, was no longer sufficient: "The family as social cell is insufficient; the family as Christian cell is insufficient, and with it the apostolate entrusted to it. To the extent that the parish, that community of families, has for its object the supernatural growth of families – not exclusively, of course, but as the object proper to it and for which it is exactly adapted in terms of apostolic technique – to the same extent will it be adequate to the task of sanctifying ulterior social structures. It is here that work, for example, will henceforth find its status." Chenu in no way denies the validity and necessity of parish ministry; he merely draws attention to its limitations in face of the new dimensions brought to light by socialization. The parish was still very well equipped to administer to the needs of the individual. Yet the issues raised by socialization were located not on the level of

---

62 J. Ball, "Pour une spiritualité eschatologique (Lettre d'un ancien aumônier jociste)," *MO* 7 (1945), 29; quoted in B. Besret *Incarnation ou eschatologie?* (Paris: Éditions du Cerf, 1964), 41. See the remark by historian René Rémond in his preface to Jean Lestavel's *Les prophètes de l'Église contemporaine* (Paris: Éditions de l'Épi, 1969), 9, on the reciprocal fruitfulness of speculative theology and pastoral action.

individuals but on the level of institutions and social and economic *milieux*: "Apostolate of the milieu, that is of the natural, homogeneous, and at the same time of the daily, habitual milieu: the one which makes up concrete life in the workshop, the office, the factory, in the neighbourhood, on the playing field or in recreation, where (as is the case everywhere) the same trades, the same hopes, the same servitudes, the same ways of feeling and thinking exert their collective pressure." As such, the specialized movements of Action catholique should not be seen as an extension of existing parish structures and methods or as an addition of lay personnel in response to a clerical shortage but rather as "coming from the very essence of the kingdom of God and from the deepest nature of the Church, an extension of the Incarnation to a new societal regime of Christendom." The focus of this new incarnation is the world of work, where the societal dimension of human existence is most visible. The ministry of the JOC became the prototype for all the specialized movements of Action catholique. The old theme of a Christian glorification of work took on a completely new meaning. It was not merely the individual worker as an isolated unit who was the target of sanctification, but the collective reality where every worker was committed, involved, and perhaps crushed. In other words, it was the *milieu* of work that was primarily to be sanctified.[63]

Consequently, pastoral efforts directed at individual ascetic practices, at the development of personal spirituality and prayer life, at the exercise of charity in its various forms, did not constitute movements in Action catholique. Although such efforts are highly profitable on both the individual and the social levels, their primary and immediate goal is not to incarnate the life of grace in the various social milieux and institutions of the contemporary world. Along somewhat similar lines, Chenu divided the active ministry of the Church into parishes and other works, each having its proper objective and the means of achieving it.[64]

---

63 "Dimension" (1937), in *Parole* 2, 94, 95, 96, 98. It should be noted, as Chenu points out, that the decisive dimension was indeed "*la participation du laïc à l'apostolat hiérarchique de l'Église.*" See also *Une école de théologie* (1937), 67–8, where he calls the ACO a typical structure of the new *chrétienté*.

64 Cf. "Dimension," 101: "*Une association qui a pour but de défendre les libertés chrétiennes sur le plan civique ne s'insère évidemment pas aussi intimement au coeur de l'Action catholique, qu'un groupement patronal ou ouvrier prenant en charge la sanctification de son milieu et y constituant l'armature caractéristique d'un 'état de grâce' du travail ou du métier.*" For the question of parishes, see also "La révolution communautaire et l'apostolat" (1944), in *Parole* 2, 376–7; on the social dimension of spiritual practice, see "Dimensions collectives de l'ascèse" (1951), in *Parole* 2, 379–87; "Paroisses et oeuvres. Les exigences de l'Action catholique" (1934), 343–58, especially 354–7.

Finally, it should be noted that, for Chenu, it was movements such as the JOC that would break the hold of Marxism on the discovery and pro-motion of the dignity and solidarity of the working class. Marxism had triggered and deformed the *prise de conscience* of the working class into an instrument of class conflict.[65] The Christian task would be to free this consciousness from terms of class conflict and redirect the historical de-velopment of socialization towards a Christian consciousness of human dignity.

The Strategy of Presence: The Church "en état de mission"

The development of pastoral strategies from the 1930s to the 1940s can be generally characterized as a movement from conquest to presence. The watershed that gave rise to the new developments is often said to be the work by Abbés Henri Godin and Yvan Daniel, *France, pays de mission?* The publication of the book in 1943 was a bombshell in the French Church. Its message was that all the efforts to penetrate the world of the working class had in effect failed. The gulf separating the Church from the new world was much larger and more impenetrable than originally expected.[66]

The use of the term *mission* emphasized that the areas to be evange-lized represented new territories where the gospel was not yet preached, even though they were in fact situated within the boundaries of Chris-tendom. The term suggested the necessity of going out beyond one's own boundaries in more than a geographical sense. The new reality of the secular world required a properly missionary attitude on the part of

65 Chenu here quotes extensively from Jacques Maritain's *Humanisme intégral*, particu-larly from chapter 6, *"Des chances historiques d'une nouvelle Chrétienté."* For example, see Mar-itain, 238: " ... *le gain historique dont nous parlons ici, c'est la prise de conscience de la dignité du travail et de la dignité ouvrière, de la dignité de la personne humaine dans le travailleur comme tel ... C'est la tragédie de nos temps qu'un gain d'ordre premièrement spirituel comme celui-là paraisse soli-daire d'un système athée comme le marxisme."*

66 Cf. "En état de mission" (1958), in *Parole 2*, 238: "*Les contemporains n'oublieront jamais l'émotion apostolique et* doctrinale *alors éprouvée, et tout d'abord par le cardinal Suhard, qui en fut littéralement, et demeura, boulversé.*" See also "L'Abbé H. Godin" (1944), in *Parole 2*, 243–6. On all this, see Émile Poulat, *Naissance des prêtres-ouvriers* (Paris: Casterman, 1965), who stresses among other things the importance of the war for the realization of the gulf that still existed between the Church and working people. See also the more recent works by Oscar L. Arnal, *Priests in Working-Class Blue: The History of the Worker Priests (1943–1954)* (New York: Paulist Press, 1986), especially 115–23 on the place of the incarnation and re-lated terms in the reflection of the worker-priests; id., "Beyond the Walls of Christendom: The *Engagement* of the Mission de France and its Seminary (1941–1954)," *Contemporary French Civilization*, 7 (Fall 1982), 41–62.

the Church. Only such an approach effectively translated the Church's situation vis-à-vis the world. The missionary model acknowledged the novelty of the situation and the Church's position in an alien and pagan land: "The missionary act par excellence is the Word of God addressed to a pagan; it is the *true* dialogue of God's envoy, of a God who speaks to men in the language of men; it is the completely fresh meeting between the Gospel and as-yet unknown values, newly emerged from a world in transformation: it is a vital communion with human communities whose collective existence is determinant even unto the most elementary reflexes; it is, as it first bursts forth, a presence to the world, thus at the frontier of where the Church and the world meet."[67] So it is that mission became the new paradigm for the encounter between Church and world. Indeed, the term came to be applied not only to certain specialized pastoral projects such as the Mission de France or the Mission de Paris but to the state of the Church in general. It referred to more than particular actions of the Church on the periphery of its establishment in order to enlarge its domain. It suggested a state of mind that would be reflected in all of the Church's dealings with the world: *Une Église en état de mission*. The missionary model was offered as the most adequate and appropriate expression of the Church's self-understanding in a secularized world: "The Church is missionary by nature and has been since Christ's commissioning, since the gift of the Spirit. However, established Christendom left as an appendix, as a complementary task, that which was and is (in its first inspiration) a proper and permanent quality ... Mission is the operation by which the Church comes out of itself – out of 'Christendom' – to speak to the non-believer, to encounter 'those who are far away'."[68] For Chenu, the Church was constituted as missionary from the very beginning and in its very essence.

The shift from the *nouvelle chrétienté* of the 1930s to the mission of presence in the 1940s can also be described as a progressively more rigorous interpretation of the exigency of incarnation. The growing secularization of society caused the gradual abandonment of any categories associated with the Constantinian era. Even the category of *nouvelle chrétienté* was seen as too narrow to do justice to the autonomous values represented by the new reality. Or, rather, the term itself was seen as too closely related to the dangers of the Constantinian *chrétienté*. The task of the Church had to be distinguished more and more from any notion of

67 "En état de mission" (1958), in *Parole* 2, 238–9.
68 "Fin de l'ère" (1961), in *Parole* 2, 32–3.

sacralization. The way of incarnation must be from below, not from above; from the inside, not from the outside.

The movements of Action catholique were seen as moving from above. At least, the effect of the pastoral action of the JOC was often a "*déclassement*" (class displacement) in which the elites trained from the milieu found themselves alienated from the very milieu to which they were to return. The mentality of conquest was too close to an apologetic from above and from the outside; it was more of a proselytizing condescension than an incarnation. The missionaries of work wanted something closer to the concreteness of the milieu. The tendency of Action catholique to move from above was corrected in the 1940s by the adoption of a missionary model for the Church whose strategy was based less on conquest than on presence and witness. Sanctification of the milieu should not work by taking someone out of the milieu, but rather by transforming the milieu from the inside.[69]

The key expressions that clarify these spatial metaphors (i.e., inside vs. outside, from below vs. from above) of the missionary model are "presence" and "witness." The new terms express the way of incarnation for a Church in a secularized world: "Henceforth the Church, before a profane world, is as it were constrained to be missionary, a witness to the Word of God among neutral organizations, and no longer a privileged institutional competitor. If it comes to that, simple 'presence' is the major (if not sufficient) apostolic act. 'To live with', as a sign and accomplishment of fraternal love, even unto communion of spirit – more difficult than communion of heart: it is the very pure and very effective expression of the Word of God, which always proceeds by incarnation."[70] The way of Christian witness after the Constantinian era carries a more explicit allowance for the autonomy of secular reality: "Taking charge

---

69 Cf. "Corps de l'Église" (1948), in *Parole* 2, 162: "*Non pas adaptation du dehors, par une espèce d'apologétique partisane ou de religion condescendante; mais de l'intérieur, extension d'une incarnation par laquelle se réalise le mystère total du Christ*"; see also ibid., 163, where Chenu speaks of the necessity of a "declericalization of grace" in order to break the tendency to move from above. The contrast between the conquest of Action catholique and the mission of *présence* should not be exaggerated. The term "conquest" is also used of mission; e.g., "L'Abbé H. Godin" (1944), in *Parole* 2, 243: "*Voici un dizaine d'années que le vieux mot chrétien de mission retrouve, sur des objets nouveaux, son dynamisme de conquête.*" Cf. Jn 17: 15, which Chenu quotes in this context: "I do not pray that thou shouldst take them out of the world, but that thou shouldst keep them from the evil one."

70 "Fin de l'ère" (1961), in *Parole* 2, 34. See Oscar Arnal, *Priests in Working-class Blue*, 115–23, for comments on such expressions as *présence*, *vivre avec*, *témoignage*, and *communauté de destin*.

spiritually has, to be sure, not diminished; but it is accomplished in a tak-
ing-on of the human machinery itself: the more grace is a grace of incarnation, the more it touches by its very purity the totality of man,
according to the tonality of human nature, without confusion or admix-
ture, without reduction or turning aside."[71] In other words, witness has
replaced conquest. The Christian is in the world bearing witness to the
God of incarnation precisely because he is the God who became flesh
and dwelt in a human society. Likewise the priestly ministry is first defined in terms of witness to the faith and only later in terms of sacramental function: "How can one baptise a civilization without entering into
it?"[72] In the act of witness, the Christian is not aiming primarily to convert the other through argumentative persuasion but rather to manifest
the truth of Christian being: "*Être visiblement ce que l'on est*" (To be visibly
what one *is*). "We insist endlessly today on the movement of faith in apostolic expansion: it is not an imperialist expropriation, it is not a conquest, it is not even a conquest, it is not even first of all a 'doctrine'
taught from a pulpit; it is first of all a witness."[73] Doctrinal formulation of
faith and its communication are not thereby excluded, but they *are* seen
as a later development that should not eliminate the primacy of witness.
The moment of witness is personal, historical, and often ambiguous.
That, says Chenu, is the price we must pay for its truth. Chenu is clearly
not blind to the problem, since he acknowledges the ambiguities in the
process of socialization and the need for redemption. The continuation
of incarnation will thus include redemptive *praxis* that confronts evil and
promotes the Christian good of faith, hope, and charity. Between the
moment of Christian witness and the impact of committed action lies the
reading of the signs of the times. Such discernment will be the form of
theological science in an age of historicity and secularization.

71 "Corps de l'Église" (1948), in *Parole* 2, 167; note the allusion to the Chalcedonian
formulation.

72 "Le sacerdoce des prêtres-ouvriers" (1954), in *Parole* 2, 280. Chenu does not distinguish two kinds of priestly ministry, but grounds one function in the other; see ibid., 276:
"*[N]ous refusons de limiter le sacerdoce à ses fonctions sacramentelles et cultuelles, parce que ces fonctions mêmes supposent comme leur fondement et leur principe vital le témoignage de la foi, comme premier acte de l'Église du Christ dans le monde.*" Cf. "Liberté et engagement" (1938), in *Parole* 2,
349: "*Encore une fois, nous rencontrons l'Incarnation, et non ce Dieu distant à qui son infini inter-
dirait tout contact.*"

73 "Témoigner, c'est être visiblement ce qu'on est" (1963), in *Communauté chrétienne*, 6
(no. 31, 1967), 74. This article, originally published to celebrate the thousandth issue of
Témoignage chrétien in 1963, is Chenu's most explicit treatment of witness. Note the double
denial of "*conquête.*"

5

Word as Sign

AS SOON AS THE ACT OF WITNESS IS GIVEN PRIMACY, the question of criteria of authenticity becomes unavoidable. How can I tell if my witness is true? When a theology becomes concrete and historical, the question of authenticity moves to the foreground and must be included in any consideration of the law of incarnation. The question is still one of faith and theology, but it is now complicated by an explicit confrontation with the historical and social dimensions of human existence. What is the method involved in the pastoral doing and the theological thinking of a Church "situated in the world"? What is the *praxis* that corresponds to the state of continuous incarnation? If we reject a strategy of "opportunistic accommodation," what is the way towards the practical implementation of continuous incarnation? How is this implementation to be achieved and maintained?

In the first place, the phrase "situated in the world" must be clarified. The historical context of Chenu's later writing now comes to the fore. The Vatican II document *Gaudium et Spes* represented the major document for this period of the Church. It was the focus of most of Chenu's theological activity. The Church of *Gaudium et Spes* was faithful to the exigency of incarnation because it was a Church "situated in the world." Furthermore, the material for *Gaudium et Spes* was prepared through, among other things, the reading of the signs of the times. This prophetic reading becomes the method appropriate to a state of being in the world and in a state of mission. It is the theological reflection that corresponds to the act of witness. In our analysis of this reflection, we shall see the problem of evil emerging as a matter for the interpretation of the signs of the times. We close the chapter by examining the actual task of thinking, discerning, and living according to the law of incarnation, with the focus on *praxis* as the locus for theology.

TOWARDS A THEOLOGY OF THE WORLD

The implementation of the idea of Church as continuous incarnation requires the basic dualism between Church and world to be overcome. A new theoretical framework is necessary as a result of the exigency of incarnation. It is as though following the path of incarnation brings with it the development of new ideas or the rediscovery of forgotten theological doctrines. Thus, in the previous chapters we saw the refurbishing of the pastorally powerful idea of the mystical body and the concept of living tradition. Here we begin by examining the new relationship between Church and world that resulted from taking the historical situation seriously. The new openness to anthropological values further suggests a renewal of the ideas of community and creation. The description of the Church as a messianic people of God is then interpreted as a concrete statement about the Church's place and task in the world.

The New Paradigm of Gaudium et Spes*: Church in World and World in Church*

The differentiation in consciousness that led to the triple recovery of materiality, sociality, and historicity was officially included in the Vatican Council document *Gaudium et Spes*. This pastoral constitution articulated the principles of a Church founded on incarnation. For the first time in history, there was talk of the Church *in* the world, not merely of the Church *and* the world: "It is the very mystery of the Incarnation, of God made man and come into history, which continuing from age to age by and in the Church determines the being of this Church."[1]

In face of massive dechristianization, the Church had been put in question and was being forced to rediscover the laws of its being. The reflection thus instituted led to a consciousness of being in a state of mission, seen in terms of fidelity to a continued incarnation. Much remained to be said, however, about the content of this mission. The desacralization or secularization of modern culture forced the Church into a new mode of presence in the world and a new form of efficacy for

---

1 "Une constitution pastorale" (1965), in *Peuple*, 15. Chenu emphasizes that the document in question was not a "decree" but a "constitution" having to do with the very being and nature of the Church; cf. 14: "*Non, il s'agit bien, au sens le plus formel du mot, d'une 'constitution,' c'est-à-dire d'un ensemble d'énoncés sur la structure même de l'Église, communauté hiérarchique du Peuple de Dieu dans le monde.*" He also notes that the successive versions of the redaction of *Gaudium et Spes* relied increasingly on the centrality of the incarnation, giving more and more room to Christ.

Christian action. No longer attempting to sacralize the political or economic structures of society, the Church welcomed and encouraged the
autonomy of the new "profane" reality. It had to leave behind its "stop-
gap" supplementary role in the world and turn to its more proper role
of witness to the incarnation. The context for that role is a humanity autonomous in its various functions, even under the influence of grace.
Such is the Church's mission.[2]

The distinction between sacred and profane reality was useful in terms
of analytic procedures. But the distinction dissolves in light of the mystery of Christ and his grace at work in human history. The history of
salvation does occur in "profane" history. However, it occurs not in terms
of the sacralization of the political or the economic reality, but rather in
terms of the sanctification occurring through the recapitulation of all
earthly values and meanings in Christ: "A separation of the two domains
is failure to the Incarnation, to the very knot of the mystery."[3]

It was not so much that a pre-established faith position was applied to a
political or economic situation; rather, the political and economic experience provoked a re-examination of faith. This approach implied an entirely different perspective for the situation of the Church. The Church
was no longer to be found outside of the world, it was now *in* the world.[4]
The new perspective led Chenu to speak of the mutual inclusion of the
two poles: the Church was in the world and the world was in the Church.

Chenu does not deny the character of mystery found at the very heart
of the Church. Yet the nature of this mystery is precisely incarnational.
This characterization means a clear rejection of any remaining neo-
Platonist schema in which the emanation and return of the Church
occurs with a rejection of history: "Yes, to be sure, the Church is the
supersacrament ... whose vicissitudes are not past events to which I associate myself in memory, but the recurrence in me of the mysteries of
Christ died and risen again; nonetheless, this mystery of Christ dying
and rising in me is, precisely, accomplished by an incarnation, a coming
of God in time – and thus not by an eviction of history, but by a recapitulation of every creature." The question of Church and world is not an

---

2 "Condition nouvelle" (1960), in *Parole* 2, 469: "*Dépassé le temps des suppléances, elle est
'missionnaire'.*" For more on the sacred-profane pairing in Chenu, see M.L. Mazzarello, *Il
rapporto Chiesa-mondo*, 58–65.

3 "Préface" to G. Casalis (1970), 10. On recapitulation, see the subsection Theological
Meaning of the Signs of the Times in this chapter.

4 Cf. *Duquesne* (1975), 78: "*[L'Église] n'a son existence que dans le monde. À la limite, il faudrait dire que l'Église, c'est le monde lui-même en tant qu'il porte en lui une capacité à entendre la
Parole de Dieu.*"

abstract one. It is the Church in the world of today, the contemporary world, hence a world that has discovered its social dimension. The law of incarnation is also active in this area. The economy of salvation is not played out beyond the boundaries of human history but in its very midst. Human progress through history becomes the very stuff for a continued incarnation, always new and always dramatic. For Chenu, the social dimension may not be excluded from this action, for it represents the very consummation of the process of incarnation. Such is the paradox: the structures of human existence become, in the economy of incarnation, "the substructures of divine life, in communities as in individuals." A law of human existence becomes the law of grace.[5]

A major consequence of the Church's incarnate state was the development of a community consciousness in the Church in response to socialization. Only thus could the social dimension of human existence be assumed into the economy of incarnation. A horizontal collegiality at the Council appeared as one effect of the new consciousness. The use of the term "people of God" to describe the Church was probably the most visible manifestation of the new sense of community. Commenting on the document *Lumen Gentium*, Chenu notes the definition of the Church both as people of God and as hierarchic community. The emphasis is on community first and only then on the hierarchic dimension, which belongs more properly to the term society: "Thus ... are we able to say that the Church is above all a 'community', of which the horizontal dimension finds its consubstantial statute in the vertical structures of 'society'."[6]

5 "Corps de l'Église et structures sociales" (1948), in *Parole* 2, 161. Chenu goes on: "*La grâce est sociale. L'humanité devient le corps mystique de Christ, et la prise de possession du monde, en laquelle l'homme accomplit son destin de créature, entre matériellement dans le développement mystique de la divine entreprise.*" See also "Foi en Chrétienté" (1944), in *Parole* 2, 114, where Chenu speaks of human structures becoming "*les structures de la vie divine,*" and suggests that the communal life may be even more important than the individual one, as the latter may not live outside a community. He continues at 115: "*La croissance terrestre de l'Église, corps mystique de Grâce, sera selon la croissance de l'humanité même*"; cf. "Dimension nouvelle" (1937), in *Parole* 2, 92.

6 "L'Église, peuple messianique" (1964), 31. In a recent interview ("La foi d'un homme libre, le Père Chenu" [1985], 62), Chenu recalls one of the conciliar debates on *Lumen Gentium*, where a bishop suggested that the horizontal emphasis of "hierarchic community" be replaced by the more vertical orientation of "*societas perfecta*": "*Je dois à la vérité de dire que l'archevêque en question était celui de Cracovie, Mgr Wojtyla.*" For more on Chenu's use of the distinction, first put forward by Tönnies, between society and community, and on the shift from one to the other, see *Duquesne* (1975), 111–12. See also "Vie conciliaire et sociologie de la foi" (1961), in *Parole* 1, 375: "*La cohérence institutionnelle et spirituelle de l'Église ne s'établit pas seulement par une relation verticale des cellules locales au pontife suprême, mais simultanément et non moins nécessairement par les relations horizontales des cellules entre elles, dans le corps unifié.*"

The social phenomenon of contemporary civilization therefore carried serious repercussions for the Church and precipitated a differentiation in the consciousness of the Church as a people of God. Chenu has no wish to exclude the dimension of Church as society. On the contrary, he stresses the complementarity of the two aspects, but with a certain priority on the side of community. For Chenu, the community dimension of the Church is highlighted in our age because the Church's relation to the world and its various developments is based on the law of incarnation. It was in our age that the technological revolution spawned the phenomenon of socialization, which in turn created a consciousness of community. It is a sign of the Church's incarnate state that the one-sided emphasis on individual spirituality and asceticism was finally overcome through the general phenomenon of socialization.

It is precisely in terms of such an event in consciousness that Chenu describes the relationship of Church and world as it manifested itself in the progressive redaction of *Gaudium et Spes*: "[S]eized by the internal logic of a *prise-de-conscience*, the Church, looking into itself, looks into the world." The pastoral constitution became the official record of this effort to determine the principles and the laws of a Church "of which the very being, begotten of Christ the God-made-man, is involved in the world and in history."[7]

It is thus in the very nature of the Church to be situated in the world – not in any world but in the world of today, in the contemporary world that belongs to history and its vicissitudes and is marked by specific discoveries. The Church is not to coexist side by side with the world, as two societies completely foreign to each other, "but by a mutual inclusion, a will to live together (*Mitsein*), under the difference of their object and their end."[8]

This last remark also shows how Chenu would be led to criticize the distinction proposed at the Council by Cardinal Suenens concerning

---

7 "Une constitution pastorale" (1966), in *Peuple*, 12, 13. In a note on 12, Chenu quotes a 1963 address by Cardinal Montini as evidence of this new relationship: "*Au concile, l'Église se cherche elle-même; elle tente, avec une grande confiance et avec un grand effort, de mieux se définir, de comprendre elle-même ce qu'elle est. Après vingt siècles d'histoire, l'Église semble comme submergée par la civilisation profane, comme absente du monde actuel. Elle éprouve alors le besoin de se recueillir, de se purifier, de se refaire, pour pouvoir reprendre avec une grande énergie son propre chemin ... Tandis qu'elle entreprend ainsi de se qualifier et de se définir, l'Église cherche le monde, tente de venir en contact avec cette société ... Et de quelle manière réaliser ce contact? Elle raccroche le dialogue avec le monde, lisant les besoins de la société où elle opère, observant les carences, les nécessités, les aspirations, les souffrances, les espérances qui sont au coeur de l'homme.*"

8 Ibid., 15. Chenu continues with an explicit reference to the mystery of incarnation as the ground for this mutual inclusion.

the Church *ad intra* and *ad extra*. Although originally beneficial in that it allowed a great deal of reflection about the Church's situation in the world, the distinction was ultimately dualistic, or at least potentially ambiguous. The Church is both interior and exterior at the same time. The proposed distinction tends to overshadow the unity of the Church's being and its mission in the world. We are not dealing with an inner Church, constituted by the community of believers, and an outer Church, constituted by the missionary enterprise. The moment of witness is not a "concession" to the situation; it is intrinsic to the nature of the one Church. Once again, the overcoming of dualism stresses the constitutive character of the missionary moment as opposed to any opportunistic pastoral adaptation to changing circumstances.[9]

The extent of this "mutual inclusion" is far-reaching. What sometimes appears a facile accommodation to the liberal mores of the time in fact concerns the very nature of the Church. Such is the case with laws of society becoming laws of grace. The developments of socialization in the field of communication have revolutionized the corresponding structures of the Church. Through the incarnational process of assumption, the Church takes on these developments as its own: "All that sociologists say based on the nature of societies, the theologian must take up analogically, based on the nature of the Church, according to the original laws of the mystical Body of Christ, in history."[10] The grounds for this procedure, for the establishment of "mutual inclusion," are to be found in the concept of continued incarnation.

The Church displays the structures of both a society and a community. In so doing, it follows the dictates of sociological axioms. The Church is a society as a result of the vertical organizational structures of authority. This societal dimension functions as a backbone for the Church's existence as community. The authority of the Church is at the service of the community in its faith witness. As a community, as a "people," the

9 Cf. *Duquesne* (1975), 79. Cf. also "Une constitution pastorale" (1966), 136, where Chenu clarifies the idea of dialogue between the Church and the world as between "*deux entités non pas étrangères, mais intérieures l'une à l'autre.*" See also "L'opinion publique dans l'Église" (1970), 132: "*Il n'y a pas deux Églises, ni deux fois: la même foi est communion au Christ et témoignage dans le monde. Contre une certaine image de la chrétienté, nous tenons désormais qu'il ne s'agit pas là d'une extension fervente, en second temps, quand on a fait le plein chez soi, comme une besogne supplémentaire, en appendice. C'est tout d'une pièce.*"

10 "L'opinion publique dans l'Église" (1970), 125. Chenu continues: "*L'Église requiert en ses membres la communication, l'information, le droit à l'information, – non par une concession au libéralisme d'un monde démocratique, ni par le seul fait qu'elle est société, comme les autres, mais pour une raison spécifique, tirée de sa* nature." Cf. 124; these matters concern "l'être *théologique* lui-même de la Communauté chrétienne."

Church is subject to the sociological laws of what is called "horizontal communication": participation, freedom of access to information, etc. This is a basic effect of the socialization of our modern culture on the Church.

The sociological characterization of the Church is an example of the idea of mutual inclusion. Yet there is a properly theological reason for being open to sociological determinisms. It is the same reason that saw contemplation finding its home in the psychological structures native to the human person, and faith finding adequate expression in the technical procedures of the human mind. The word communicated in the Church is the word made flesh and present in history. The presence of the word is creative of community. The incarnation is a *sacramentum audibile*: "God speaks, and his Word is immanent in his people, gathered and constituted by his Word. The Word creates its community. Where the Word is, there is the Church. The Church is the realm of the Word. The *sensus fidei* of the People of God, and the authority which guarantees from within its authenticity, are simultaneously grounded in this realism of the Christian economy."[11] Such is the theological grounding of Church as community, society, and hierarchic community. The *sensus fidei* is the theological correlate to the sociological category of community. On this level, what was termed "horizontal communication" becomes the act of the witness of faith in the world.

The concept of *sensus fidei* is perfectly traditional, yet Chenu notes that it was inadvertently obscured and forgotten in the previous four centuries of the Church's history. Only in the twentieth century, through the advent of socialization, did the Church rediscover its heritage in this area. Through a development in the world's self-understanding, the Church recovered a lost balance.[12]

As noted earlier, events and developments in the world are the occasion for further differentiations in the consciousness of the Church. These *prises de conscience* are not purely introspective procedures in which the Church turns its contemplative gaze *ad intra*. They depend on some kind of input or even shock from the outside. They imply a contact with an "other." It is by means of the relationship with the other in any society that a person becomes himself or herself. This is true on the psychological level, but is even more applicable on the ecclesial level to the extent that "the Church is a coming of divine life, not only once

11 Ibid., 127.
12 Cf. "La Chiesa communità nella fede: esigenze e compiti del popolo di Dio" (1967), 112–14.

upon a time in that being who was Christ, Son of God come in history, but also today in the world." The world is the determining trigger for ecclesial consciousness on the psychological level, whereas the word comes from above: "The meeting of the two is this impact of the *prise-de-conscience.*"[13] The events of the world in its changing conditions thus play a constitutive role in the make-up of the Church. The law of incarnation allows the world to have such an impact on the being of the Church community.

Against a more or less conscious idealism, which in the human person tends to separate the supratemporal spirit from the material realm, Chenu maintains that the Church exists *in* the world "according to the logic of the Incarnation, from which it emanates mystically and sociologically." If this is the case, then the various shifts and changes in the world, not only in terms of technology or economics but in terms of the human condition, contribute to the inner growth of the Church. The history of salvation is no less a history for being sacred: "The Church is not an epiphenomenon laid over a heterogeneous humanity, any more than grace is. It defines itself in defining its relation to the world."[14]

Beyond a mere mention of the law of incarnation, Chenu asks about the law of emergence, which governs the differentiations of consciousness and their ground in history. For an answer, he looks at the dialectic between the continued and assured fidelity of the Church and the historical mutations in the perception of Christian truth. Thus, the process of socialization and its particular manifestations in the phenomenon of work have given the gospel's universal law of love a new concreteness. Work environments are privileged contexts for human relations. Despite the dangers of dehumanization, work creates a ground for community. Technological progress brings forth new exigencies for the Church to realize the true measure of its mission: "Technical and economic progress yield ... matter, possibility, a universal standard, to the brotherhood born of the Gospel, in the construction of the world ... By periodic upheavals, at the rhythm of revolutions – whether it be by liberation from slavery, and the abolition of serfdom, or today by going

13 "L'opinion publique dans l'Église: Débat" (1970), 138. This is one of the most explicit texts on the nature of the *prise de conscience*. It is particularly useful here because it relates the phenomenon of consciousness to the incarnation and to its continuation in history and in the world of today.

14 "Pour une lecture théologique du Syllabus" (1965), 44. See also 46: "*C'est en rencontrant le monde que l'Église prend conscience d'elle-même, et non dans une déduction abstraite des principes dits éternels.*"

beyond class and by the liquidation of the proletariat (the proletariat of nations after that of individuals) – Christians have gauged better the dimensions of messianism and of the Incarnation." The generalized and irreversible process of socialization has forced the Church to recognize not only the economic but also the political measure of Christian charity. The universalization of human problems – racial, cultural, economic – and the emancipation of formerly colonized peoples call on the Church to forgo a decidedly western alliance tied to a Constantinian age now past, and to become truly "catholic." The lesson of history and of tradition is clear. Like nature, history is not destroyed but perfected by grace.[15]

The Church as Messianic and Prophetic People

We have seen that "people of God" was a fundamental description of the Church at the Council; however, this is not the place to review the massive literature on the subject. Nor is it the place to review all that Chenu wrote about it. The particular focus of this section is to highlight one characteristic associated with a people of God, one bringing out the importance of incarnation in the context of the relation of Church and world. The characterization of the Church as a *messianic* people of God is a fundamental statement about the Church's place and task in the world: "In the world, the Church (Body of Christ and People of God) is the messianic people, witness to promises since Abraham, bearer of the hopes of men – at those times when those hopes rise to men's consciousness – and peacemaker."[16]

15 "Un peuple messianique" (1967), 176. Cf. "Pour une lecture théologique du Syllabus" (1965), 45: "*La grâce trouve dans la nature (et dans l'histoire, nature en marche) des complicités auxquelles elle donne consistance divine au delà d'elles-mêmes*"; cf. "Travail" (1959), in *Parole* 2, 567; "Un pontificat entré dans l'histoire" (1963), in *Parole* 2, 193: "*La promotion à l'échelle mondiale des problèmes, des tâches … c'est un extraordinaire élargissement des frontières économiques et mentales à l'intérieur desquelles vivait jadis chaque atome humain. Dilatation physique, culturelle, spirituelle, de chacun de ces atomes, dans une solidarité massive, qui risque, hélas, de l'opprimer, mais qui, de soi, le fait accéder au niveau de l'homme total, disons à la 'catholicité'.*" See also "La pensée contemporaine, pour ou contre Dieu" (1960), in *Parole* 2, 183: "*l'Église est obligée, par le mouvement du monde, d'être, à la lettre, catholique.*"

16 "L'Église, peuple messianique" (1964), 32. The immediate effect of calling the people of God "messianic" is to bring out the inherently eschatological dimension of the Church's existence in history; cf. "Un peuple messianique" (1967), 165: "*C'est toute l'ancienne alliance qui nourrit ainsi le mot. C'est toute l'expérience séculaire de l'Église, après l'avènement du Christ, que récapitule ce mot. C'est toute l'espérance – espérances personnelles, espérances collectives plus encore – qui gonfle ce mot de son dynamisme eschatologique, déjà en acte dans le temps présent.*"

For a long time, the messianic view of Christianity was overlooked in favour of another perspective, in which Jesus was seen primarily as God-made-man and much less as messiah. The result was a neglect of the intrinsic potential of messianism as the "line of force of the Community of believers and of the peace of the world." Chenu believed the time was ripe for a recovery of the meaning and function of this idea. He acknowledged that messianism had been taken over by all sorts of movements and ideologies throughout history, often in less than felicitous ways. The greater the distortion of eschatological myths, the greater the need and urgency for a recovery of the authentic meaning.[17]

Human hope is the primary area affected by the recovery of the true meaning of messianism. It is through the relationship between Christian hope and human hope that messianism reformulates the Church's role in the world: "Men are carried along, haunted by the hope of liberation and the love of peace ... A messianic people, Christians have to build the Kingdom of God, in a fraternal love which finds matter to work on well beyond interpersonal relations, in the many undertakings of the world and of civilization. Messianism is part of the definition of the relations between the Church and the world."[18] The hopes of humanity are of the highest relevance to the Church. As a messianic people of God, the Church is the carrier of these hopes and the witness to their fulfillment. The relationship is dialectical, yet not heterogeneous. The Christian economy is inserted into the dynamics of human history. The mystery is in history.

Following the maxim *"Distinguer pour unir,"* inherited from Jacques Maritain, Chenu maintains the analytical difference between the two kinds of hope: "temporal, so exalted and so fascinating, and Christian, so often discussed and forgotten." The distinction sometimes even leads to a rival eschatology, based on naturalism or scientism, claiming to lead humanity towards an immanent end based on its own resources. Christian hope stands as an absolute against any such exaltation of terrestrial aspirations. Yet the two kinds of hope are not foreign to each other; they

17 Cf. "L'Église, peuple messianique" (1964), 32: *"Il est temps de rendre sens et efficacité, sens doctrinal et efficacité apostolique, à ce capital premier de l'économie judéo-chrétienne."* Chenu continues, pointing out the inherent fragility: *"Plus le 'messianisme' est détourné et accaparé par les jeux terrestres, plus il est capté par des idéologies condamnables, plus aussi nous devons lui rendre, avec sa santé, sa pleine vérité. Ce à quoi nous renonçons en pareille conjoncture tourne contre nous, dans notre existence même."*

18 Ibid., 32. Note the characteristic emphasis on a context larger than that of the individual's salvation. On the hope for liberation, see "Liberté évangélique et mythe de la libération" (1971), 22–7.

are not related heterogeneously. The principle of mutual inclusion is also active here: "There again, and in all of this, the coming of the Word in humanity implies (as a test of its truth) that the creation of the Word itself be brought to term in the hopes of men – with the poor at their head. From now on, human history is a sacred history, in the fulfilment of the messianic promises." For Chenu, the theme of messianism is consubstantial with the Christian economy. Despite the possible distortions – with the millenarian temptation on the side of Christianity and with materialistic ideologies on the other side – the messianic theme remains the nourishment of the human masses, "obscure hope which is one of the most gripping signs of this time."[19] Despite all difficulties of discernment and dangers of abusive interpretations, the people of God cannot forsake their messianic character: "Messianism remains the springboard of the People of God, earthly springboard to the very extent that it is an eschatological springboard." The very fact of incarnation preserves the transcendent character of the promised fulfillment. The presence of time and historical development within the fulfillment of the messianic promises is not an accident but concerns the very substance of the Christian economy: "Since messianism develops in history, the laws of history become its own laws. The history of salvation, of the messianic deliverance, finds its 'subject' in history, just as faith – the light from above – is expressed, exercised, built in the mental fabric of man who is its 'subject' ... Messianism is not a heterogeneous density superimposed from without upon the historic humanization of the world, just as faith is not a light shed upon an intellect alien to it."[20] For faith as for messianism, divine gratuitousness encounters a natural desire and consents

---

19 "Une constitution pastorale de l'Église" (1966), in *Peuple*, 31–2. Chenu goes on: "*Mais aussi savons-nous que, sous peine de mystification, ces deux espérances non seulement ne s'opposent pas, mais embrayent l'une sur l'autre, la terrestre appelant l'autre, la chrétienne nourissant la première: donner un sens à l'existence de l'homme, lutter contre la faim dans le monde, instaurer la justice, la fraternité et la paix, promouvoir l'unification ordonnée et pacifique des nations ... *" Cf. also, ibid., 18, n. 3, where Chenu quotes a speech of Paul VI from 3 February 1965, on the centrality of Christ in relation to human hopes: "*Gesù è al vertice delle aspirazioni umane, è il termine delle nostre speranze e delle nostre preghiere, è il punto focale dei desideri della storia e della civiltà, è cioè il Messia, il centro dell'umanità, colui che dà un senso agli avvenimenti umani, colui che dà un valore alle azioni umane, colui che forma la gioia e la pienezza dei desideri di tutti i cuori.*" Chenu notes that *Gaudium et Spes*, n. 45, picks up the text almost literally but regrettably without the important reference to messianism; cf. "Une constitution pastorale de l'Église" (1966), 33. See also "L'Église, peuple messianique" (1964), 32.

20 "Un peuple messianique" (1967), 166, 168. Chenu also defines the terms of the dialectic of interpretation and warns against premature "spiritualization" of the messianic texts: "*Dialectique dont l'équilibre est fort instable, sous la coordination des deux pôles, dans le dépassement du processus créateur dans l'histoire temporelle, par la libération rédemptrice en histoire du salut.*"

to its native laws and structures. The human ascent remains an openness to the gratuitous nature of the promise. The transcendence is preserved and the humanity is not violated: "Grace is grace, and profane history is not a source of salvation."[21]

By the fact of its presence in history, messianism is dynamically oriented towards the future and towards the inscrutable ways in which the future impinges on the present. The messianic people of God are located between the two comings of Christ: "The Messiah *has come*, the Messiah *will come*. This is saying that he *comes* – permanently."[22] The whole process of discernment is given an urgency that is only heightened by the process of socialization. The eschatological end of time is not situated in a linear fashion *after* the present but is a dimension *of* this present; it is a reality present in history, calling the Church to be true to its own mission.[23] This is the meaning of Chenu's often-repeated phrase, *"Dieu parle aujourd'hui."* The messianic era, which has arrived with Christ, proclaims the access to eternity "not by an escape, but by an incarnation in time."[24] To live in terms of messianic hope is something far more and far different than moral resignation in the face of adversity. It is the certainty of the eternal, perceived and lived in the present.

THE SIGNS OF THE TIMES

Being present to one's time is central to the theological task. It is in a very real sense the subjective counterpart to the process of continued incarnation. Ultimately, for Chenu, the theologian's *locus* is the life of the Church in history. The Church in act is the *locus* of theology

---

21 "Une constitution pastorale de l'Église" (1966), 26; this is an often-repeated phrase in Chenu and has the function of a foundational principle.

22 "Un peuple prophétique" (1967), 608. Cf. M.L. Mazzarello, *Il rapporto Chiesa-mondo*, 75, n. 254: "*La legge costitutiva della Chiesa è evidentemente la dialettica, nella storia stessa, di un'esperienza già realizzata nell'avvento del Cristo e tuttavia tesa verso la ricapitulazione del secondo avvento.*"

23 See "Un peuple messianique" (1967), 176, where Chenu suggests that in this context signs of the times will be "*les critères des discernements opportuns, à la jonction de la transcendance et de l'immanence du Royaume.*"

24 "Un peuple prophétique" (1967), 609. It is this eschatological "endtime" that provides the horizon for historical discernment; cf. 610: "*La fin des temps commande de l'intérieur les étapes du temps et les discernements de l'histoire ... les chrétiens, en perdant le sens de l'histoire, avaient perdu par là même le sens de leur incarnation.*"

because it is the home of tradition, the vital and communal development of scripture.[25]

For Chenu, tradition refers to the living presence of the Spirit in the Church. The economy of salvation is not limited to the events of the past. Theology is also concerned with the salvation history that occurs today and that points to the future fulfillment according to the eschatological promise. The incarnation continues; God speaks today. As new dimensions of humanity rise to consciousness, they are assumed into Christianity. They become the field for new exigencies of incarnation. Not only geographically but also temporally, the Church is in a state of mission.

This is the context in which we can speak of theology as a reading of the signs of the times. The God of Christianity has assumed the human condition. He has entered history. The task of theology, consequently, is not the definition of ontological natures and their relationships, but reflection on an economy in the process of becoming. Wherever there is an emergence of progressive humanization in the course of history, there the theologian will find the activity of the word of God. The theologian is attentive to an economy made of events, not propositions. These events are more than examples; they are the very field of God's self-communication. God speaks today, as Chenu likes to repeat. He speaks in a witness which is not superimposed in the events of history, but which gives them their ultimate meaning. The task of the theologian is to discern this meaning, to read the signs of the times. Inasmuch as these signs point to the eschatological fulfillment of the promise, their interpretation involves a prophetic function.

The analysis of the signs of the times is presented as the method most appropriately corresponding to the being of the Church as defined in the pastoral constitution *Gaudium et Spes*. The portion of the document where the expression was officially enshrined reads as follows: "[T]he Church has always had the duty of scrutinizing the signs of the times and of interpreting them in light of the gospel. Thus, in language intelligible to each generation, she can respond to the perennial questions which men ask about this present life and the life to come, and about the relationship of the one to the other."[26] "Signs of the times" thus refers to a fundamental category defining the relationship of Church and world in an age of newly discovered historicity. The signs of the times

25 See the interview with Chenu in *ICI* (1965), 30.
26 *Gaudium et Spes*, no. 4, in Walter Abbott ed., 201–2.

are the markers by which the Church orients itself and its activity in the world.

The entry of the expression into the vocabulary of the Church was somewhat sensational. Its ease of usage should not, however, seduce us into minimizing the difficulties of defining its precise meaning. The first meaning suggested concerns the human reference to time. Beyond the systematic and abstract analysis of human nature, the consideration of the particular temporal situation as the context for the development of that nature takes on equal importance. The expression, in other words, intends human historicity.[27]

After some background on the history of the expression, we will examine Chenu's view of both its sociological and its theological meaning. Lastly, we consider the ambiguity of the signs of the times, the possibility of error in light of the problem of sin and evil, and the ability of Chenu's perspective to cope with these difficulties.

Historical Background

The history of the expression "the signs of the times" – with respect to its more authoritative usages – goes back to scripture. The word "sign" belongs to the basic categories of biblical language, which all later usages must acknowledge and to which they must refer. The Judeo-Christian religion is an economy located in the development of history whose progress is marked by the presence of "signs": "Thus having recourse today to signs of the times is not the doing of pastoral opportunism, but of the objective understanding of God's Word."[28] The problem

---

27 Cf. "Les signes du temps" (1966), in *Peuple*, 36: "*Le temps est à considérer comme une valeur coessentielle, modifiant la vie de l'esprit non seulement dans son mécanisme, mais dans sa substance. C'est toute la problématique de l'historicité de l'homme.*"

28 Ibid., 37. On the roots of the term, see ibid., n. 1, where Chenu quotes from Congar's *Le Concile au jour le jour. Troisième session* (Paris, 1965; 84): "*Qui dit signes des temps avoue qu'on a quelque chose à apprendre du temps lui-même. Il est vrai: cette catégorie des signes des temps demanderait à être précisée, car on doit honorer sa référence biblique, christologique et eschatologique. Mais c'est la visée impliquée dans ce vocable qui est le plus intéressant. Il s'agit de reconnaître pleinement l'historicité du monde, de l'Église elle-même en tant que, distincte du monde, elle lui est cependant liée. Les mouvements du monde doivent avoir un écho dans l'Église, au moins pour ce qu'ils posent de questions. On n'aura pas de réponses pour toutes, du moins de réponses toutes faites et adéquates. Du moins saura-t-on qu'il ne suffit pas de répéter les leçons de toujours.*" On the biblical background, see especially Mt 16: 1–4 and Lk 12:54–6. See on this K. Füssel, "Die Zeichen der Zeit als locus theologicus. Ein Beitrag zur theologischen Erkenntnislehre," *Zeit. für Phil. Theol.*, 30 (1983), 259–74.

with using the expression is to maintain the biblical reference yet not to remain locked into what Chenu termed biblical positivism, but instead to move to an actualization of the meaning for the Church of today.

It was Pope John XXIII who brought the expression into the official language of the modern Church. In the encyclical *Pacem in Terris* (1963), "the signs of the times" was not used as an embellishing or decorative expression – as a superficial reading might suggest – but as "a basic category in the construction of thought."[29] Each of the four main sections of the encyclical ended with an enumeration of the signs of the times, that is, a manifestation of Christian values at work within the very movements of history: socialization, the promotion of the working class, the entry of women into public life, the emancipation of colonized peoples, and so forth. These parts of the text were the result of a particular reading of the current historical movements, a prophetic perception at work in the front lines of Church and world. In the agenda of John XXIII, their analysis was to become the basic material for the work of the second Vatican Council, the stuff of *aggiornamento*.

The Sociological Meaning

In a sociological sense, the signs of the times refer to phenomena that, by their generalization, their great frequency, and the imprint they leave on the collective consciousness, characterize a certain age and express the needs and aspirations of contemporary humanity. The expression contains a primary reference to history, as opposed to natural or conventional signs. Signs of the times are inscribed in historical facts, in events, which have, by their texture and human context, a meaning that overflows their materiality.

The expression refers to historical events that not only carry their immediate meaning but, beyond this, point to another reality, to another order of meaning.[30] An example is the taking of the Bastille. As one action among many by Parisian rioters in the summer of 1789, it was

---

29 Ibid., 38. Chenu rightly notes that the expression is not found in the original Latin text of *Pacem in Terris* but only in the subtitles of the various translations. It appears for the first time in the convocation bull of the Council *Humanae salutis* of 25 December 1961; see "Les signes des temps. Réflexion théologique" (1967), 206. See *Pacem in Terris*, nos. 39–45, 75–9, 126–9, 142–5.

30 See "Signes" (1965), in *Peuple*, 40: "*Mais il y a aussi des signes historiques, dont la contexture est originale et la portée différente; il s'agit d'un 'événement', accompli par l'homme, et qui, outre son contenu immédiat, a valeur d'expression d'une autre réalité.*"

not particularly important. But this miniscule fact became and was "significant," of a different order, to the point of serving as a symbolic rallying-point and crystallization for revolutionary movements for over a century.

The point, for Chenu, was not to establish as precisely as possible what happened in an event belonging to the past, but to discern in that event the hidden power animating it and somehow, through a transformation, promoting it to the symbolic order. Beyond the positivism of the bare fact, what was important in the event was "the *prise-de-conscience* that it set in motion, capturing the energies and hopes of a human group, beyond the relective understanding of this or that individual." This conception is not unrelated to Hans-Georg Gadamer's *Wirkungsgeschichte*, translated as history-of-effects, based on the idea that history is brought forward primarily through events in collective consciousness whereby the human spirit progressively discovers further dimensions to its existence.[31] The laws of history, the "*devenir social*," are ultimately founded upon these differentiations of consciousness.

Although such events capture the imagination of many, and in this sense are properly called events in the collective consciousness, their deeper significance is at first perceived by only a few, who are "so immersed in their communities that they read the destiny of these communities by an overall presentiment of successive key moments." These are the prophets. They read the significance of the events not through sophisticated methods of analysis but through affective communion with the aspirations of their people. The signs of the times are the points of impact of their insight.[32]

This model is particularly evident in the religious sphere. Thus the Judeo-Christian economy is continuously marked by the intervention of prophets in the context of the coming or the fulfillment of the messi-

31 Ibid. On the efforts of French historiographers to overcome the positivism of the bare fact, and on the birth of the *longue durée* school of historiography, see Paul Ricoeur's Zaharoff lectures, later included in *Time and Narrative*, vol. 1 (Chicago: University of Chicago Press, 1984), at 91–225. Cf. Hans-Georg Gadamer, *Wahrheit und Methode* (Tübingen: Mohr, 1960).

32 "Signes" (1965), 41. Yet it is also true that the task of discerning the signs of the times belongs to the whole Church. See *Gaudium et Spes* no. 44, in Walter Abbott, ed., 246: "With the help of the Holy Spirit, it is the task of the entire People of God, especially pastors and theologians, to hear, distinguish, and interpret the many voices of our age, and to judge them in the light of the divine Word. In this way, revealed truth can always be more deeply penetrated, better understood, and set forth to greater advantage."

anic kingdom. Historical events are the signs of this movement without ever losing their so-called terrestrial reality. So it was that the exodus from Egypt, the stay in the desert, the exile, and so forth, occurred.

Like these Old Testament signs of the times, events are not signs in isolation from other events. Rather, they become significant, as signs, in the context of a wider constellation or network of events that, through their particular association and through their repercussion in time, become enmeshed in the consciousness of a whole generation. Such is the case, in our age, with the phenomenon of socialization. A variety of disparate circumstances, such as technological innovations, political and economic regimes, social determinisms, cultural exchange on a global level, all contribute to the significance of socialization as a sign of the times. That is, taken together, they express the needs and aspirations of humanity because, together, they are the source of a shift in the collective consciousness (*prise de conscience collective*).

Now the business of reading this deeper significance in events or chain of events is no easy matter. The meaning of the signs of the times must remain immanent to the event. Otherwise history becomes expendable. If Christians claim to read historical events in terms of their reference to the gospel, they may not do so through a process of spiritualizing history and abstracting from the concreteness of history. It is historical events *as* historical events that become signs, that become, for the Church, subjects of grace. If there are signs to be discerned, they will be found, and kept, within the reality of time, without any premature sacralization that would rob them of their moorings in space and time. Socialization is not a sign of the times because it presents an occasion of Christian charity, which had always been proclaimed. It is not a question of finding new areas for the application of old principles. Rather, it is the very shock of a social mutation that is a sign of the times, and a call to a new dimension of communal existence enlightened by the gospel.

The Theological Meaning

Beyond the sociological sense there is also a properly theological meaning to the expression "the signs of the times," a doctrinal context to which it belongs. The clue comes from Chenu's description of the signs of the times as "preparations for the Gospel in the rise of civilizations" and, more importantly for our present purposes, as "seeds of the creating

Word as pledge of the incarnate Word."[33] The discernment of the signs of the times will occur, therefore, within a renewed understanding of creation and its relation to the economy of incarnation.

Chenu went to great pains to emphasize that the text of *Gaudium et Spes* did not represent a set of "solutions" given *ex cathedra* to be applied to the problems of the world. It was not extrinsicist. Faithful to a perspective based on incarnation, Chenu saw an inductive procedure at work. Yet even incarnation does not proceed in a vacuum but presupposes the work of creation. The pastoral constitution represented a concrete stand based on the gospels and inspired by the word of God, yet at the same time "taking on the values inscribed by the Creator in human nature, expansion of earthly civilizations."[34] This is one example of Chenu's understanding of the relationship between creation and incarnation.

The so-called terrestrial values find their true home in a renewed doctrine of creation, where they are assumed anew in an economy of incarnation. The doctrine of creation, as a home for human values, becomes truly manifest only in light of the God-man. Christ reveals human nature to itself not by means of a superimposed grace, but by the fulfillment of humanity's inner capabilities. Humanity possesses these potential capacities by virtue of being created in God's image. In other words, it is through Christ that the signs of the times are deciphered. They are indeed *praeparatio evangelica*, but they are revealed as such through the incarnate word: "The Word, in becoming incarnate, reveals the Creating Word. In history, Creation and Incarnation are homogeneous, in a selfsame mystery. By the Incarnation, a new creation is accomplished. The Church, the Body of Christ in ongoing incarnation, is immediately ordered to the achievement in history of this lordship of Christ over creation." *Gaudium et Spes* curbed the tendency in theology to represent the main elements of salvation history (i.e., creation-sin-redemption) in an abstract and linear fashion. The result was the rediscovery of the cosmic dimension of the incarnation. Chenu thus refers to the function of incarnation in recalling creation to its status of being

---

33 "Orthodoxie-orthopraxie" (1974), 56. See "Valeur chrétienne des réalités terrestres" (1965), 248, where Chenu identifies the "*juste valeur des réalités terrestres*" and the "*pierre d'attente de la grâce*" with the signs of the times. This is important for matching a continuity in thinking with a changing vocabulary.

34 "Une constitution pastorale de l'Église" (1967), 15. Chenu continues: "*Double et unique problématique, selon laquelle la grâce accomplit la nature, en régime d'Incarnation, au rythme de l'histoire.*"

in the image of God. Creation is in continuity with the economy of the redemptive incarnation. Creation and redemption are solidary by virtue of the solidarity between the human creature and creation, between the God-man and the creative Word, and between "all men who undertake in Christ the salvation of the entire creation." The construction of the world and the fulfillment of all human temporal tasks both enter "in the development of a creation wholly recapitulated in Christ."[35]

The reference to the construction of the world and to temporal tasks prevents this doctrinal development from becoming another abstraction. At stake is the unity of creation against any possible dualism. Chenu directs repeated efforts at denouncing the dualism so common among Christians when conducting social, political, and economic affairs, yet so foreign to the nature of Christianity. In this dualistic perspective, terrestrial realities are nothing more than "occasions" for the action of grace; they remain indifferent, amorphous matter with no relation to the kingdom of God: "Mere provisional scaffolding for the so-called 'supernatural' construction of the City of God."[36] Against this popular position, Chenu claims that no earthly reality in human existence is indifferent. All reality is either good or evil. If it is good, then, implicitly or explicitly, it will contribute to the construction of the kingdom. In other words, it will be recapitulated in Christ, who is both creative Word and redeemer. The lordship of Christ is not limited to the so-called supernatural world: "The incarnation brings creation to term, creation in which man, through Christ, fulfils in himself the image of God, by the very fact that he cooperates in this creation throughout history."[37]

Creation is not seen in isolation, as "pure creation", but in relation to Christ. Every creature is *capax dei* or *capax Christi*. Christ's coming brings creation to fulfillment. This is the properly cosmic dimension of incarnation. This emphasis is clear in another text by Chenu: "The Incarnation of Christ develops and consumes itself in an incorporation in which

35 Ibid., 28, 29. Chenu elaborates a little on what he means by continued incarnation in the context of a theology of creation: " ... *l'humanité du Verbe incarné – et non la providence abstraite des déistes – s'incorpore de génération en génération la communauté des hommes en acte de coopérateurs de la création.*" Cf. 27; "*Ainsi l'homme-Dieu révèle l'homme à lui-même, non par une superimposition de la grâce, mais par l'accomplissement, dans une rencontre gratuite, de capacités internes qu'il portait en lui de par sa création comme image de Dieu. L'incarnation mène à son terme la création.*" In a footnote to this context, Chenu recalls the plan of St. Thomas' *Summa* where the third part (incarnation) unfolds in the movement opened up by the first part (creation).

36 "Valeur chrétienne des réalités terrestres" (1965), 248.

37 Ibid., 248–9. On the whole theme of the overcoming of the dualism between creation and incarnation, see Maria Luisa Mazzarello, *Il rapporto Chiesa-mondo*, 44–52.

every reality, every human value becomes part of his Body – his Body in which all creation will be 'recapitulated' ... The incarnate, redeeming Logos accomplishes the work of the creative Logos: personal identity which does not allow the redemptive work to be separated from the creative work, and gives the Incarnation its cosmic dimension, where creation finds its unity."[38] In other words, for Chenu, creation and incarnation do not exist as two separate and isolated movements. Against the usual tendency for Christians to begin with the incarnation, with God's entry into this world, Chenu reminds us that "the Incarnation is situated within the phenomenon of Creation ... it is a new Creation, and to understand it completely, I must refer to the Creation."[39] It is not the case that creation and the natural order exist on the one hand, with the mystery of redemption as the superimposed supernatural order on the other hand. Nor is the natural world on one side and the supernatural Church on the other, as two competing realities with more or less peaceful boundaries. Furthermore, is not the case, on the one hand, that construction of the world is without interest or value for the kingdom and, on the other hand, that the kingdom of God is without meaning or value for the construction of the world: "No, creation and incarnation are grasped in a reciprocal involution."[40] The redemptive incarnation is fulfilled by means of a recapitulation of all that is good, all that is true, with all human meanings and values at work in the project that is creation. We do not have two disjointed mysteries, following the order of grace and the order of nature, where the reality of redemptive incarnation is juxtaposed onto creation. Rather, the two are mutually implied. The Church is not outside of the world because the incarnation occurs in creation. Hence, human events, values, and the project of constructing a world, all are of interest to the Church.

Chenu uses the Chalcedonian formula for resolving the dialectic of creation and incarnation as well as for justifying the presence of the Church in the world. He grounds the two elements in the unity of the divine person. Just as Christ cannot be "a case apart" within the realm of creation, so too the Church cannot be "a case apart" within the world. Christ is truly human and his human nature is a real human nature.

---

38 "Les laïcs et la 'consécration du monde'," in *Peuple* (1967), 87–8. L.A. Gallo, in *La concepción de la salvación*, 54, calls this "*un texto-síntesis.*"

39 *Duquesne* (1975), 73. The same argument is used throughout *Gaudium et Spes* to ground the Church's presence in the world; see ibid., "*De telle manière que l'Église, communauté qui découle de l'Incarnation, s'inscrit à l'intérieur du monde, de la Création.*"

40 "Le rôle de l'Église dans le monde contemporain" (1968), 426.

Likewise, creation cannot be considered on its own, as self-fulfilled and theologically complete, without reference to the incarnation. Following the Chalcedonian model, the properties of each nature are preserved, "*salva proprietate utriusque naturae.*"[41]

This unity, with the distinction of natures but without mixture, is the very condition for a synthesis of creation and incarnation. The hypostatic union is therefore, at least indirectly, the doctrinal basis for the autonomy of terrestrial values, for the involvement of lay people in the Church, for the presence of the Church in the world. In this context, Chenu warns against a contemporary form of idealistic monophysitism that views the created world only as matter for a possible sacralization.[42]

Signs of the times are thus located in the intersection of the two orders: construction of the world within creation and messianic economy within a liberating incarnation.[43] It is this doctrinal context that allows terrestrial or secular values to be related to the Christian economy. Chenu calls such values "toothing stones" (*pierres d'attente*). They may also be "stumbling blocks" (*pierres d'achoppement*), but they would be so by distortion and not by nature. Their nature is to remain open to be assumed for purposes of redemption.[44]

Correspondingly, incarnation brings creation to its fulfillment. The economy of redemption is here expressed in terms of restoration and

41 Denziger, 148. Chenu's reading of Chalcedon is based on F. Malmberg's interpretation (*Über den Gottmenschen* [Freiburg im Brisgau: Herder, 1960]) of the Augustinian expression: "*Nec sic assumptus homo est ut prius creatus post assumeretur, sed ut ipsa assumptione crearetur*" (PL 42, 688). Cf. "*Consecratio Mundi*" (1964), 616. See also "Le rôle de l'Église" (1968), 441, where Chenu links this to the two moments of healing and conservation in the economy of salvation. The differences between the two realms of nature and grace are preserved in the union of the two natures in Christ: "*Dans la participation de l'homme à Dieu s'achève l'humanisation, c'est-à-dire la création de l'homme … Cette conservation [des différences] s'est accomplie par l'union suprême de la nature avec Dieu qui la pose et l'affirme. Le monde s'achève en tant que monde dans sa déification.*"

42 See "*Le rôle de l'Église dans le monde contemporain*" (1968), 440: "*Dans cette théologie de l'Incarnation, la distinction des deux natures, pures de tout mélange, est la condition même de la synthèse … Cette distinction des deux natures permet à la nature humaine de fournir tout son contenu positif, pour la construction de la synthèse qui doit relier le monde et Dieu.*" See also "*Consecratio mundi*" (1964), 616.

43 Cf. "Un peuple messianique" (1967), 175: "*C'est dans les implications nécessaires et délicates de ces deux économies que la foi va exercer son discernement et observer les* signes des temps, *lieux historiques de l'impact de l'économie du salut sur les réalités terrestres de l'humanisation du monde, 'matière du Royaume des cieux'* (Const. past., n. 38)."

44 This is Chenu's transposition of the medieval *potentia obedientialis* whereby creatures have a natural capacity for the supernatural order and to the reception of grace.

recapitulation, in relation not only to the meanings and values of humanity, but to all the works of humanity. All of creation longs to be freed from corruption and to participate in the glory of the children of God. The biblical text underlying all this discussion is the often-quoted Rom 8:18–23: "For the creation waits with eager longing for the revealing of the sons of God ... the creation itself will be set free from its bondage to decay and obtain the glorious liberty of the children of God. We know that the whole creation has been groaning in travail together until now ... " According to this rediscovered Pauline doctrine, the human person cannot be redeemed by being separated from nature. Against false spiritualism, Chenu writes that "Christ did not come to save souls, but to save men, and not only men, but the whole world." Christ came to restore creation in its totality. No part of creation is destroyed in the process of redemption; rather, all is brought to fulfillment where "the all-gracious gift of divine life, in Christ the God-man, gives nature back to itself in liberation from evil; restores it and *perfects* it, to be entirely open to divine participation in a communion of love."[45]

The theme of recapitulation, as a basic dimension of redemption, is central to the dialectical synthesis of creation and incarnation. All human works and values, especially the project of constructing a human world throughout the centuries, are recapitulated in Christ: "Assimilated into his Body, they enter also (like all creation) into his work, into his *mystery*. The believer knows how to read and to live here the death and resurrection of Christ."[46]

Christ's work of recapitulation is dynamic. This dynamicism gives concrete expression to the belief that the mystery of incarnation is not

45 "Théologie du travail" (1959), in *Parole* 2, 568, 569. There is here a basis for the development of an ecologically sensitive theology. For the centrality of Rom 8:18–23, see "Le rôle de l'Église dans le monde contemporain" (1968), 425–6, where Chenu refers to this passage as providing "*les dimensions du mystère*," beyond any "*opportunismes apostoliques.*" See also "Valeur chrétienne des réalités terrestres" (1965), 250, where Chenu refers to the signs of the times as "*interpellations de Dieu à travers les événements*" and adds: "*Dieu 'fait signe'. Et la création attend la révélation des fils de Dieu. 'Expectatio creaturae'* (Rom 8:19)." Cf. "Un peuple messianique" (1967), 181, where the "groaning in travail" of Rom 8:22 provokes the following: "*Enfantement: il y a donc continuité.*"

46 "Théologie du travail" (1959), 569. Chenu continues, saying that all works involved in the personal and communitarian project of humanization "*sont ainsi élevés à la qualité divine de la louange, de l'offrande, de la libération, qui sont les trois caractères du sacrifice, accompli dans l'acte pascal de Jésus-Christ.*" See also "Valeur chrétienne des réalités terrestres" (1965), 251: "*L'incarnation aboutit à une consécration dont l'homme est le ministre.*"

limited to a corner of Judaea 2000 years ago, but that it continues.[47] The actualization of incarnation, its development, and its consummation are realized in a continued historical incorporation by which all human values and meanings are dynamically assumed in Christ, through his body the Church.[48] Incarnation as recapitulation is not the superimposition or juxtaposition of the supernatural value onto the natural, but the "taking on of a nature open to this divine promotion, open, individually and collectively, to a history that transforms it."[49] By means of the dynamic recapitulation that it brings forward, the incarnation brings the creative enterprise to its divine consummation. At the same time, the messianic dimension of the incarnation colours the humanization of God with joyful and sometimes painful human hopes. Such is the coherence of the Word, which is both creative and incarnate.[50]

For Chenu, the Chalcedonian interpretation of incarnation allows for the recovery of all human reality into the zone of salvation. All human contributions to the project of continued creation are taken up into the mystery of continued incarnation: "Far from being emptied, and as it were crushed by the grace of a redeeming incarnation, these works of the creation that is continued by man (cooperating with God) are recapitulated beneath Christ's messianic and cosmic kingship. Thus authentic catechesis restores earthly activities, destinies – *by situating them in the economy of the Incarnation* – not only to moralize them but, much more radically, to give them (in their very being) their humano-divine dimension."[51] Terrestrial values discerned as signs of the times are thus located within the project of continued creation and recapitulated as part of the mystery of continued incarnation.

47 See "Dimension nouvelle" (1937), 89.

48 See "Liberté et engagement du Chrétien" (1938), in *Parole* 2, 352: "*Si Dieu s'incarne pour diviniser l'homme, il faut qu'il prenne* tout *dans l'homme, du haut en bas de sa nature; ne serait pas racheté, ne serait pas libéré ce qui, dans l'homme, resterait en marge de son emprise, de son assomption.*" To limit this process of God's humanization, in the name of transcendence, is false reverence and doceticism.

49 "Théologie de la mutation" (1970), 86. On the fulfillment of creation, see M.L. Mazzarello, *Il rapporto Chiesa-mondo*, 48: "*La venuta di Dio nella storia rivela dunque la consistenza di una creazione che trova il suo svolgimento nella storia e il suo compimento nella recapitulazione in Cristo.*"

50 See "Paradoxe de la pauvreté évangélique et construction du monde" (1963), in *Parole* 2, 402–3.

51 "Théologie du travail" (1959), in *Parole* 2, 544. See M.L. Mazzarello, *Il rapporto Chiesa-mondo*, 49, n. 156: "*In altri termini, Il P. Chenu intende dire che l'Incarnazione del Verbo implica un'assunzione della materia nel processo di divinizzazione che si compie per e nell'uomo.*"

The Problem of Evil and the Interpretation
of the Signs of the Times

Once we agree that certain aggregates of facts and events have a deeper layer of meaning – in other words, once we agree that there are such things as signs of the times – we are still left with a major problem of interpretation. The existence of evil and, more simply, the ambiguity of history make it impossible to rule out error and distortion in the reading of the signs of the times. Not every set of values captivating the collective consciousness at any given time is necessarily a contribution to the progressive humanization of history. In addition to movements of progressive humanization in history, there are movements of regressive dehumanization. This ambiguity may ultimately make the use of a category such as the signs of the times impractical.

When the expression was introduced in the language of the Council, certain observers complained of an unfounded optimism attaching to it. In a report to the preparatory commission working on the pastoral constitution at Vatican II, the pastor Lukas Vischer made some important remarks.[52] He noted that we have no clear criteria for distinguishing the voice of God from another, misleading voice. The world is an ambiguous place where evil is mixed with good and where sin belongs to the order of things. Although the ultimate victory does not belong to it, evil is still a reality to be dealt with. Its efficacy is frightening, its presence all-pervasive, and its successes far more frequent than the proclamation of the kingdom. It is not only the presence of God that has inhabited the values of societies in history; there have also been the dark and destructive voices of principalities and powers.

It is in light of these matters that theologians such as Jürgen Moltmann have pointed out that alongside the messianic view, there is also the apocalyptic approach. In the latter viewpoint, signs of the times are seen as ominous portents preceding the approaching end-time. The emphasis is on the crisis that precedes the parousia.[53] To the extent that

---

52 Following Chenu, I am relying on J.-P. Jossua, "Discerner les signes du temps," *VS,* 114 (May 1966), 546–69, here 555, 561–2.

53 See Jürgen Moltmann, *The Church in the Power of the Spirit* (London: SCM, 1977), 37–50. Moltmann's treatment of the signs of the times is part of a larger project on ecclesiology. He ultimately rejects the category of signs of the times, both messianic and apocalyptic, on the grounds of insufficiency of theological criteria. In a note (368, n. 64), he remarks that Chenu "only talks about the positive signs of salvation and the longing for salvation found in world history."

the positive interpretation of signs of the times follows from the law of incarnation, Henri de Lubac's comment, though from a different perspective than Moltmann's, is also relevant to this discussion. He warns against a reductive interpretation of Christianity's assumption of human values in which we forget that the mystery of Christ is one not only of incarnation, but also of crucifixion and resurrection: "Our incarnate God is a crucified God. The Word made flesh is a God dying in the flesh and reborn 'in the Spirit'."[54] Both Moltmann and de Lubac seem more sensitive than Chenu to the problems associated with the question of evil. The interest of theologians in the critical theory of the Frankfurt school is also oriented to the thorny issues of distorted interpretation and the problem of evil.[55]

With the emphasis on witness, the question of authenticity in the interpretation of development becomes more important than ever. Chenu is not blind to the problem, since he acknowledges the ambiguities involved in the process of socialization and the need for redemption. The continuation of incarnation will thus include redemptive *praxis* that confronts evil and promotes the Christian good of faith, hope, and charity. Between the moment of Christian witness and the impact of committed action lies the reading of the signs of the times. Such discernment will be the form of theological science in an age of historicity and secularization.

The issue of evil and the presence of sin in our world is particularly topical in light of Chenu's infectious optimism. Yet he openly acknowledges the dramatic presence of violence in our societies. With particular reference to his theology of work, developed in the late 1940s, Chenu looked back on his early synthesis and described it as "my Promethean diagnosis, still enticed by the discovery of fire."[56] Various social crises such as the conflict of ideologies, the rise of consumerism, and the failure of adequate transfer between First and Third World countries have renewed the reflection on human fragility and even on the "old theme" of original sin. Thus, the signs of the times are ambiguous not because of an intrinsic evil in their "value" but because of the pride or idolatry of the interpretation. Instead of an emphasis on condemning error, Chenu advocates for the Church not only the discernment of terrestrial values in the signs of the times but also the promotion of these values

---

54 H. de Lubac, *Paradoxes, suivis de Nouveaux paradoxes, Nouvelle édition augmentée* (Paris: Éditions du Seuil, 1959), 45; cf. 44: "*Le Christ n'est pas venu faire 'oeuvre d'incarnation'; mais le Verbe s'est incarné pour faire oeuvre de rédemption.*"
55 See, for example, some of the writings of Fiorenza, Lamb, Metz, and Schillebeeckx.
56 "Trente ans après" (1975), 75.

when they are absent. As history teaches us, the ambiguity of the world is not new. Incarnation is therefore always in the form of redemption: "But yet, the grace of Christ has always been confronted with similar ambiguities, in humanities dramatically upset by the problems these ambiguities posed. *Every incarnation takes place by and in a liberation from evil, a redemption*, as we say; and grace is at once divinizing and purifying, healing the values which it wishes to take on, in a difficult discernment."[57] The assumption of human values discovered in the process of history is therefore not merely a neutral and morally blind procedure. Incarnation implies liberation from evil.

The problem of sin and evil also appears in the context of messianism and the various attempts at the fulfillment of human hopes. These attempts include failures and much suffering. In this context, Chenu reminds us that the messiah, in Isaiah's prophecy, was a suffering messiah. Here again, the passion and death of Christ become central, and the theme of recapitulation receives an added dimension: "By the mystery of God-made-man, failures themselves enter into the recapitulation of Christ, and derive meaning and effectiveness in the passion and death of Jesus the Saviour." For Chenu, in the relationship between the Church and the world, here is the most mysterious as well as the most meaningful point in the dialectic of love, "in this God-made-man, of whom the Church carries out the witnessing, in its failures and destitution as much as in its successes."[58]

PRAXIS AS THE NEW LOCUS FOR THEOLOGY: ELEMENTS OF A CRITERIOLOGY

We finally come to the actual business of discernment and the practical implementation of the law of incarnation. The previous section has made it plain that this is no easy task. The danger of distortion is always present; we can never assume it has been eliminated. Chenu does not offer a prescription for correct interpretations, nor does he develop a system of theological criteria by which signs of the times can be discerned and plans for action followed. He does, however, suggest certain guidelines based on the very nature of signs of the times.

---

57 "Un Concile à la dimension du monde" (1962), in *Parole* 2, 635, emphasis added. Cf. "Les signes du temps" (1965), 46. On the ambiguity of signs of the times in Chenu, see also Carlos N. Salgado Vaz *O compromisso temporal liberta o cristao*, 156–61.

58 "Une constitution pastorale de l'Église" (1966), 33.

The fuller meaning of events cannot be reached by a kind of superimposition of an ideal interpretation or a pre-established theology. The complexity and density of history must be preserved. It cannot be spiritualized or de-temporalized. If the socialization of various sectors of life is seen as a sign of the times, it cannot be understood as such by an analysis of the social nature of the human being or by the influence of socialist ideology; both are ideological superstructures. Socialization is a sign of the times by virtue of the scientific and technological development of an industrial society. To approach socialization by way of the ideology that may have influenced it, or even directed it, may result in a blindness to the historical movement that carried it. Many generations of Christians have misread the fact of socialization by rejecting socialist ideology. Peace movements are often regarded with suspicion for the same reasons. Terrestrial values discerned as signs of the times are toothing stones for grace, for the kingdom and the life of God. They are obediential potencies. But they can also be stumbling blocks in the construction of the kingdom. They are ambiguous. Yet even in their ambiguity they have a deeper meaning for they are "in waiting" (cf. Rom 8:19, *expectatio creaturae*). The differentiation of historical movements and ideologies therefore must necessarily become a principle in the interpretation of the signs of the times.

From the Christian point of view, the values thus discovered in history take two basic forms. First, there are values that take their place in the economy of creation, inasmuch as this is not an event of the past but a continuous presence and action on the part of God. Further discoveries in science and technology are human contributions, in terms of "secondary causes," to the fulfillment of the creative process. Second, there are terrestrial realities that are more aptly related to the redemptive economy of incarnation, to the extent that these values may contribute to human liberation and the dissemination of Christian love. In discerning these two dimensions of the signs of the times, the Church can discern the creative and liberating presence of God in the world. It is the very autonomy of terrestrial values that guarantees the transcendence of the divine presence.

Chenu's contribution to the development of rules for interpreting the signs of the times can be seen as identifying elements for a criteriology of incarnation. The remainder of this chapter focuses on Chenu's understanding of *praxis* as a basic locus of theological reflection, on prophets as agents of theological interpretation, and on the Holy Spirit as mediator of God's presence in the world. Each is an essential element in the reading of the signs of the times and therefore contributes to our understanding of the meaning and function of incarnation.

Orthodoxy and Orthopraxis

It is important to recognize that, for Chenu, the emphasis on *praxis* does not represent a *new* locus for theology. At best it is a "recovered dimension."[59] The relatively new usage of the term *praxis* belongs to a much older, established set of dialectical relationships – indeed, one about which Chenu wrote early in his career.

One relatively recent location for the new emphasis on *praxis* is in the relationship between the doctrinal and pastoral dimensions of the second Vatican Council, between *Gaudium et Spes* and *Lumen Gentium*, or more specifically in the relationship between the pastoral and the doctrinal aims of *Gaudium et Spes* itself. This duality of aims is not a dualism. *Gaudium et Spes* was proclaimed pastoral without being a set of practical directives, without being a plan for a practical adaptation of previously established doctrinal principles.[60] In this sense, the Council was a vindication of Chenu's own campaign against "pastoral positivism."

It was with the same intention of overcoming the dualism between the life of the mind and the concrete situations of daily life that Chenu entered the discussions on the nature and method of theology in the 1930s. His staunch rejection of a discontinuity between *théologie spéculative* and *théologie pratique* in the name of the one process of incarnation on the part of faith now led Chenu to enter the discussions on the dialectical relations between *praxis* and *theoria*. The implication in both cases is that the concrete and historical life of the Church becomes the place where the presence of God is to be discerned. The life of the Church is "*l'Évangile en acte*": "It is saying that the concrete and historical

---

59 See "Orthodoxie-orthopraxie" (1974), 51, where Chenu refers to the article by C. Dumont, "Des trois dimensions retrouvées en théologie: eschatologie, orthopraxie, herméneutique," *NRT*, 92 (1970), 561–91. For this whole section, see also Chenu's "Theoria y praxis en theologia" (1972). Paul Ricoeur is reputed to have once quipped that *praxis* is a German word.

60 See the explanatory note, part of the official text, appended to the title of *Gaudium et Spes*, in Walter Abbott ed., 199: "The pastoral constitution ... is made up of two parts; yet it constitutes an organic unity. By way of explanation: the constitution is called 'pastoral' because, while resting on doctrinal principles, it seeks to explain the relation of the Church to the world and modern mankind. The result is that, on the one hand, a pastoral slant is present in the first part, and, on the other hand, a doctrinal slant is present in the second part."

life of the Church-Community is, for the believer, a place to listen to the Word of God, the human ground of revealed truth – from the proclamation of the Gospel (the kerygma) right up to its encounter with cultures, and with the problems then posed for the expression of faith. To take up again the old categories, *praxis* comes in and plays a role in a permanent dialectic with the *theoria*." The category of "right-ness" (*ortho-*) belongs not just to *theoria*, which would then be applied in some neutral *praxis* through the manipulation of an already received truth. This would be pastoral positivism. "Right-ness" belongs intrinsically to action: "There is an *orthopraxis* – which is even to the profit of orthodoxy; while this *praxis* involves neither conceptual formulation nor authoritative imperative in its concrete and singular operation." There is action that manifests Christian faith, that is "a realm of its existence and its truth," and this manifestation is not merely a pragmatic application of previously established directives.[61]

Already in the 1930s, Chenu refers to the need for an authentic science of Christian action constructed inductively. He sets this moral theology in opposition to a "legalism" that is no more than a collection of individual cases acting as a catalogue of possible choices for behaviour, "a collection of questions of conscience, posed with reference to precepts, and resolved according to the degrees of extrinsic probability of the authorities adduced."[62] He rejects such legalism because of its extrinsicist nature, in the same way that he rejected a model of theology based exclusively on a Denzinger collection of propositions. Any action that manifests faith is part of the theologian's *donné*.

The emphasis of *Gaudium et Spes* also included the rejection of a conceptualism based on principles arrived at by a process of deduction. If the life of the Church – that is, its *praxis* – is a locus for the word of God, clearly it is there that we must begin our analysis. Chenu therefore notes the importance of inductive analysis of the human condition in today's world at the beginning of the pastoral constitution. Such an analysis is quite ordinary for the historian or the sociologist. For the theologian, it is "exceptionally decisive" if it truly becomes the basis for the construction of Church doctrine. It is in such a context that Chenu notes the passing of the traditional "social doctrine" developed deductively on the basis of natural law, appropriated and applied by the Church outside

---

61 "Orthodoxie-orthopraxie" (1974), 53, 52. Note the incarnational overtones of the expression "*le sol humain de la vérité révélée.*"
62 *Une école de théologie* (1937), 72.

the concrete situations of history. In its place, *Gaudium et Spes* proposed an inductive analysis respecting the autonomy of societies and cultures. Criteria for Christian living are to be developed on the basis on the Church's situation in the world: "*Praxis* becomes the immediate rule of collective awarenesses of faith."[63]

A theology based on *praxis* does not mean that theology must refer to concrete situations in order to discover new questions or new approaches to old problems. For Chenu, this kind of reference to the concrete remains "on the outside"; to a certain extent the texts of Vatican II were limited in this way. *Praxis*, if it is a true (*ortho*) expression of the ecclesial life of faith, must play a normative role in theological understanding. Yet Chenu does not wish to eliminate deductive discourse entirely; he does not claim that the induction based on *praxis* is the only possible discourse of faith. *Orthopraxis* does not exclude orthodoxy. It is the perduring presence of orthodoxy that prevents reflection on *praxis* from becoming hopelessly entangled in a circular argument. Deduction remains without being necessarily charged with ideology, keeping its power of conceptualization and doing the work of theological reason. Induction and deduction are in a dialectical relationship, with a particular emphasis on *praxis* because of the particular circumstances of contemporary history.[64]

If the emphasis on *praxis* and the corresponding inductive analysis is fundamental and decisive for the construction of doctrine, it is not something altogether new. The reference to the inductive analysis of *Gaudium et Spes* is not an argument from authority for Chenu, but rather an "authentic ratification of a communion and of reflections already underway for a long time."[65] The reality of *praxis* has been around for a long time, either explicitly or implicitly, with either greater or lesser prominence in theological reflection.

Much of the development of twentieth-century Catholic theology was directed at the recovery of a more integral understanding of the life of faith in all its dimensions and in the variety of its expressions. The pastoral practice of the Church was clearly a basic source here, which, along

---

63 "Orthodoxie-orthopraxie" (1974), 54. Cf. 53: "*S'il est vrai que la* praxis *de l'Église, Peuple de Dieu dans l'histoire, est un lieu de la Parole de Dieu, il en ressort que l'analyse de ce champ de la Parole est la première opération à mener, une fois consentie la lumière de la foi.*" Note the role of faith in the analysis of the human condition.

64 Cf. "Théologiens du tiers monde" (1981), 42. This is an important qualification that tends to be overlooked in the evaluation of Chenu's writings.

65 Ibid., 55.

with other factors, contributed to the understanding of the theological task as "the understanding of the mystery whose object is the history of salvation" rather than a "sacred metaphysics."[66] The growth of existentialist philosophy contributed to the recovery of elements not easily included in rational constructions. In the first place, the primary category of existence made its way into theology after a long absence. Both on the individual and the collective level, the concrete reality of existence is manifest in *praxis*.

This awareness of concrete reality becomes particularly evident in the case of liturgy. For Chenu, liturgy is a privileged area where the Church fulfills itself as mystery in act. The result is that the doctrinal moment is displaced as a fundamental category for understanding cultic activity: *Lex orandi, lex credendi* (the law for prayer is the law for belief) where "*praxis* is light."[67] In *Une école de théologie*, Chenu already spoke of the priority of the given, and of the need to remain "present to the datum revealed in the present life of the Church and the current experience of Christendom." This "datum" is the presence of the Spirit in the Church and what Chenu calls living tradition as "principle of intelligibility and inexhaustible source of new life."[68]

As in the establishment in theology of autonomous status for reason and its various procedures, the ruling principle here has to do with incarnation: "*Praxis* is not an administrative contrivance; it is an embodied expression, a discovery of comportments required by an authentic communion in the mystery." This is the case not only in the sense of the Church's situation as incarnate in the world, but in the more doctrinal sense as well. Various forms of Christian *praxis*, such as the pastoral

66 Ibid., 56. Chenu's rejection of "sacred metaphysics" seems directed to a particular historical form of baroque scholasticism, which still survives and which, he claims, distorts the theological task because of its break with the living data. Chenu is not thereby rejecting all forms of ontological reflection. Cf. "Homélie" (1970), 44, where he writes about "doing what is true" (Jn 3:21; 1 Jn 1:6): "*La vérité évangélique sera donc d'un autre ordre que la vérité métaphysique, même si nous récusons une incompatibilité entre théologie de la Parole et philosophie de l'être. Le mot même de 'vérité,' dans la langue biblique … est saturé d'une densité originale: vérité, c'est fidélité, justice, certitude, paix, droiture.*"

67 Ibid., 56–7: "*En cela, l'activité cultuelle a sur la théologie une priorité de fait, et, à ce titre, le doctrinal n'est pas la catégorie fondamentale grâce à laquelle on pourrait d'emblée et sans l'amoindrir saisir le culte comme réalisation de l'Église par elle-même.*"

68 *Une école de théologie* (1937), 67, 66. Cf. Y. Congar, *La tradition et la vie de l'Église* (Paris: Éditions du Cerf, 1963), 62: "*La Tradition est vivante parce qu'elle est tenue par des esprits qui en vivent dans une histoire qui est activité, problèmes, mises en questions, confrontations, apports nouveaux, exigences de réponses.*"

presence of base communities, are the theological source for further understanding of the mystery of incarnation. In the dramatic struggle for liberation there is present "a realistic theology of the redeeming Incarnation, purged of the liberal nonsense of a certain piety."[69]

The very nature of Christian truth is such that it requires the coordination of saying and doing; it calls for the unity of *theoria* and *praxis*. The Church is called to practise what it preaches: "The cognitive element and the practical element are indissociable. There is no purely intellectual deploying of the truth of Christ in a philosophico-theological system, but 'the man whose life is true comes to the light' (Jn 3:21). Not merely a true judgment, but a liberating event ... Orthodoxy is not of worth in itself. The message must be lived, carried, to be understood – to be 'true'."[70] Orthodoxy is not thereby rejected. Rather, it is situated within a broader relationship to truth in such a way that it finds its proper objectivity in relation to the field of *orthopraxis*.[71] That broader relationship finds its justification in the economy of the word and its incarnational structure. The word of God is expressed in human words, those of individuals, those of societies, those of cultures: "Once again, *praxis* makes up the fabric of this '*intellectus fidei*'. A pure, abstract orthodoxy would be no more than an axiom stripped of vitality."[72] With such a broad field of investigation, for Chenu the theologian's primary partner is the people of God as a whole, rather than just the magisterium of the Church. Such is the context for the theologian's activity of discernment. It corresponds to Chenu's view that the magisterium is not a source of faith, in the sense of scripture and tradition, but only an

69 "Orthodoxie-orthopraxie" (1974), 57, 58. He adds: "*Orthopraxie plus délicate, certes, que les orthodoxies théoriques.*" See also "Théologiens du tiers monde" (1981), 42–3.

70 "Orthodoxie-orthopraxie" (1974), 59–60. Chenu would also no doubt agree that such is the nature of all human truth. H.-G. Gadamer's resurrection of the medieval *applicatio* as the term of all understanding is only one confirmation of this insight. Chenu acknowledges his debt, here, to Walter Kasper's chapter on the truth of the gospel in *Dogme et Évangile* (Paris: Éditions du Cerf, 1967).

71 Cf. ibid., 61: "*L'orthodoxie, avec ses propositions, trouve sa fidélité, son objectivité, son assurance, dans le terrain d'une orthopraxie.*" In a footnote to this passage, Chenu remembers the controversy surrounding E. Le Roy's publication of "Qu'est-ce qu'un dogme?" during the modernist crisis, noting Le Roy's emphasis on the practical meaning of dogma.

72 Ibid., 61. Cf. *Une école de théologie* (1937), 53–4, for a similar rejection of a theology that has broken its links to the living faith in the name of syllogistic clarity. At the end of the "Orthopraxie" article, 63, Chenu cites a passage from Maximus the Confessor to illustrate his understanding of the relationship between the two elements: "*La pratique est la réalité de la théorie, la théorie est la nature intime et mystérieuse de la pratique.*"

institutional condition of the expression of the truth. This is one of the points of Chenu's remarks in the introduction to the 1986 "Instruction on Christian Liberation" of the Congregation for the Doctrine of Faith issued by the Vatican: "Just as well, then, here in the case of liberation theology, if orthodoxy has opportune occasions to apply itself, the normal regime is orthopraxy. The criterion of orthodoxy is not of an authoritarian or juridical order, but dwells in the communion of the community (local – i.e., base community – or general), which manages the spontaneity of charisms."[73] Liberation theology continues in the direction of *Gaudium et Spes* in rejecting a spiritualist anthropology of the Augustinian type and in opting for a less dualist view of the human condition. The transformation of the world in a Christian *praxis*, where the discernment of the signs of the times is a daily experience, is part of the building of the kingdom.

Reading the Signs of the Times: The Theologian and the Prophet

The task of discernment, according to Chenu, belongs properly to the prophets. It also belongs to the theologians inasmuch as they share in the charism of prophecy. Once again, time is the source of intelligibility. Time is not an exterior, contingent conditioning of the meaningful event. Rather, its concreteness is the point of emergence of a consciousness that decides the significance of the event. It is through this consciousness that a historical event becomes a sign of the times. We are not dealing here with a deductive act based on a theory, but with an inductive act emanating from a perception provoked by an *engagement* in a *praxis*. Such is the prophet's communion with the hopes, aspirations, and dramas of the world.[74] Nor are we dealing with the articulation and adaptation of theoretical principles aimed at a Christian ordering of temporal realities, as in the Church's social doctrine. Rather, it is a matter of discerning the calls, the exigencies, the failures even, of human hope in travail. The subject was presented thus in the pastoral constitution on the Church in the modern world: "The People of God believes that it is led by the Spirit of the Lord, who fills the earth. Motivated by this faith, it

73 "Introduction" (1986), v-vi.

74 Cf. "Un peuple prophétique" (1967), 605: "*La communion aux problèmes, aux espérances, aux drames du monde est le test de la vérité humaine et divine d'une Église missionnaire.*" This is the ground of the truth in the witness of the worker-priest, namely, his "*communion aux destins des travailleurs auxquels il s'assimile.*" It is also the basis for the argument against the distinction *ad intra* and *ad extra*.

labors to decipher authentic signs of God's presence and purpose in the happenings, needs, and desires in which this People has a part along with other men of our age. For faith throws new light on everything, manifests God's designs for man's total vocation, and thus directs the mind to solutions which are fully human."[75] For Chenu, *praxis* is the privileged locus for the exercise of this discernment. The interpretation of the signs of the times occurs in and through a *praxis* oriented by faith.

The prophet stays close to the movement of history.[76] In the sometimes dramatic and ambiguous struggles for peace, justice, and liberation, the prophet perceives the exigencies of the future, precisely because he or she is situated in the perspective of a future promise in the process of realization. The prophet identifies with the hopes of the poor and the oppressed, because, paradoxically, it is they who have a sense of history's progress. By their situation, they witness to the obsolescence of social and economic structures. By their hope and struggle for emancipation, they remind history about the true source of eschatological promise. The poor and the oppressed are "the effective hearers of the great News of liberation, and thus the qualified witnesses of the messianic message."[77] The prophet is the voice of these silent masses.[78] The prophet denounces the false spirituality that relegates matters of justice to the eternal world for fear of a contamination of the divine. By being present to the concerns of the time, the theologian as prophet is a prospector for the future, in the belief that the building of the kingdom must begin on Earth, or else not at all.[79] The theologian's critique

---

75 *Gaudium et Spes*, no. 11, in Walter Abbott ed., 209.

76 See "Signes" (1985), 44: "*En tous cas, le prophète est plus réaliste que le docteur, parce qu'il lit dans l'histoire. Il perçoit les signes du temps, au-delà des énoncés de principe.*" See also "Prophètes et théologiens dans l'Église" (1963), in *Parole* 2, 209: "*Aussi [le prophète] est-il en communion passionnée avec les curiosités et les aventures de son temps. Parce qu'il a le sens de ce que va être demain, il a l'intelligence d'aujourd'hui.*"

77 "Théologiens du tiers monde" (1981), 43. See also "L'Église des pauvres" (1965), 9–13; "Les masses pauvres" (1965), 169–76.

78 Cf. "Rôle du prêtre dans la civilisation industrielle: Prophétiser avant d'évangéliser" (1969), 113, where Chenu lists the prophetic task as one of the primary functions of contemporary priesthood: "*Prophétiser avant d'évangéliser, évangéliser avant de catéchiser, catéchiser avant de sacramentaliser: telles sont les étapes … Le critère de toutes ces opérations, en valeur évangélique et en efficacité ecclésiale, est la rencontre, aussi spontanée que possible, avec les pauvres. C'est le signe par excellence de la venue du Messie, et non pas seulement l'objet d'une prédication moralisante.*"

79 Cf. *Duquesne* (1975), 23: "*[J]e ne puis pas concevoir que les théologiens ne soient pas à leur manière, prophètes, prospecteurs d'avenir. Bien sûr, tous les théologiens ne peuvent l'être exactement, mais l'ensemble du corps des théologiens doit intégrer cette dimension prophétique.*"

of social, economic, and political structures is joined, by means of a creative imagination, with a witness to new ways of being in the world.

The witness of the prophet is often disturbing, just like the parables of Jesus. Its realism calls into question the established order or disorder of institutions. It questions the alliance between the religion of the promise and the political state of conservation and maximization of profits. Because the prophet perceives the eternal in time, he or she prefers symbolic actions to the conceptual distinctions between spiritual and temporal, between grace and nature.[80] It is thus not surprising to find that prophets are generally not quiet, conforming people. The Church has had mixed feelings about their charism, which it has both desired and feared.[81] Yet their charism is recognized as such – that is, for the good of others – provided that it follows the criterion of community.[82] An important point in the discussion of Vatican II concerning the signs of the times had to do with who would do the interpreting. Chenu quite clearly states that, on the basis of the Council documents, the whole Church is called to this task of discernment. The whole Church is the prophetic people of God: "Not just a few individual prophets either, announcing the future coming of a liberator-Messiah, but this people itself, manifesting the present coming of the Messiah in the hopes of men."[83]

The functions of prophet and theologian are not identical for Chenu, even though they belong together in the community of the Church. The theologian cannot evade the voice of the prophet. The properly theological task is not rendered obsolete through the witness of the prophet. Prophecy does not eliminate the conceptual statement, the pursuit and development of theological knowing, the construction of theological systems, and the general work of the human mind in the light of faith. Chenu is aware that, just as anti-institutionalism is dangerous, so too anti-intellectualism can lead to the depreciation of the

---

80 Cf. "Un peuple prophétique" (1967), 607: "*Le prophète ne s'exprime pas en concept, il ne construit pas de système, ni ne rationalise de règle de vie; il recourt aux symboles et aux gestes, et ses 'paraboles' ne se résorbent pas en raisonnements ... C'est un 'sage' qu'il transmet, et il est le héraut du Messie, venu et à venir.*"

81 Cf. *Duquesne* (1975), 22: "*Bien sûr, tous les prophètes sont toujours un peu extravagants et toujours un peu marginaux. Il y a donc des tensions.*"

82 Cf. "Un peuple prophétique" (1967), 608: "*Ainsi l'institution garantit la vérité du mystère communiqué.*" Chenu refers at this point to Paul's position on the variety of spiritual gifts in the one community; cf. 1 Cor 12.

83 "L'Église, peuple messianique" (1964), 32. Cf. also, on the question of who does the discerning, "Les signes du temps: Réflexion théologique" (1967), 223–5.

Christian tradition. His position is clear: "Theologians and prophets dwell together in a Church that is in good health."[84]

The prophet's witness must be translated in terms of the Church's mission. The theologian must produce a second-order discourse that follows the first-order witness of the prophet. The messianic hope of the prophet becomes an essential element of theological rationality "to bestow on him [the theologian] a co-essential dose of passion."[85] This theological translation, however, will be very different from the speculative deductions of yesterday's theological systems. Chenu has not completed such a theology. He acknowledges that the pursuit of justice and the building of the kingdom are not identical, but he has not systematically clarified this relationship of continuity and discontinuity. Given the choice, he would rather err on the side of continuity. In this sense, he is sometimes more of a prophet than a systematic theologian. Perhaps the reason for this impression lies in the fact that we have not yet forsaken our love for the security of systems and that we still fear the disturbing insecurity of the prophet.

Incarnation and the Work of the Holy Spirit

The law of incarnation is intimately related to the mission of the third person of the Trinity. Chenu has not written a great deal of explicit material about this, yet the mission of the Holy Spirit is so central to his understanding of the economy of incarnation that it warrants a separate section of its own.[86] As we have repeatedly said, the history of salvation is not something that occurred only in the past. It also occurs in the present and will be fulfilled in the future. The mystery of incarnation in the person of Jesus Christ occurred once and for all. Though historically unique, it must be presented as reality that can be actualized and verified in the present situation. The task of theology is to make this reality manifest in both social and ecclesial contexts. The effica-

---

84 "Un peuple prophétique" (1967), 608. See also Chenu's comments on the relationship in sixteenth-century Spain between the prophetic Las Casas and the Salamanca theologian Vitoria, "Prophètes et théologiens dans l'Église" (1963), in *Parole* 2, 212: "*[C']est avec complaisance que nous observons la parfaite cohésion de deux charismes essentiels, celui du prophète et celui du théologien. Sans aucun doute, l'un n'aurait pu sans l'autre avoir sa vérité et son efficacité.*"

85 "La théologie en procès" (1976), 696. Chenu adds: "*Serait en échec une théologie qui ne ferait pas profit d'un charisme prophétique, pour lire les 'signes des temps'.*"

86 See, for example, "Réveil évangélique et présence de l'Esprit au XIIᵉ et XIIIᵉ siècles" (1976), 167–71, and "Le réveil de l'Esprit" (1976), 9–12. As a general rule, the more explicit references to the Holy Spirit occur in the later works of Chenu, although they are not entirely absent from the early material.

cious actualization and the real anticipation of the eschatological promise in the historical conditions of the human situation are in fact the
work of the Holy Spirit. They therefore lie at the heart of any implementation of the law of incarnation.[87]

It is the Spirit that makes Christ present and that makes the gospel a
living word. Without the Spirit, Christ would be only in the past, and the
gospel would remain a dead letter. The awareness of this fact in the
present moment of Church history constitutes the re-awakening of faith
in the Holy Spirit. Among other contributing factors, Chenu credits the
interventions of the eastern prelates at Vatican II, with their emphasis
on a Trinitarian personalism that effectively helped to reduce the latent
tendencies towards deism still present within Latin western theology.[88]
With this in mind, he follows the traces of the re-awakening of the Spirit
in the concrete life of the Church.

To begin, Chenu notes that we have access to an understanding of
God's inner life through the two missions of the Son and the Spirit and
their realization in history: "The unsearchable mystery of fruitfulness
and love in God is unveiled for us by the two 'events' of the Incarnation
of the Son and the sending of the Spirit."[89] The Church is thus both the
body of Christ and the communion of the Holy Spirit. For the theologian to take note of the re-awakening of faith in the Holy Spirit is to
discern the work of the Spirit.

The liturgical renewal is one area where the activity of the Spirit is
particularly visible. From the *epiklèsis* now explicit in the eucharistic
prayers to the proliferation of small spontaneous prayer groups, a long-
lost dimension is resurfacing. The emphasis on the priority of witness
over catechesis, with all the dangers of ambiguity and subjectivism
found in experience, reflects an awareness of the power of the Spirit op-
erating in the actions and lives of Christians devoted to the service of
others. The rehabilitation of pastoral work as a true *locus* for the incarnation of the gospel and the construction of the Church has contributed to the recovery of tradition as living. Tradition is thus not only a
matter of faithful memory but also presence, "realm where the synthesis
takes place between the transmission and the present experience, where

87 Cf. "Théologie en procès" (1976), 694–5, where Chenu relates the absolutely
unique event of incarnation to the statement "*Dieu parle* aujourd'hui," then relates both to
the work of the Holy Spirit.

88 Cf. "La conscience nouvelle du fondement trinitaire de l'Église" (1981), 30.
Chenu's own emphasis on the living presence of God in history, manifested in an economy,
is reflected in his frequent reference to both Dionysius and Maximus the Confessor.

89 Ibid., 32.

the Spirit is at work."[90] Finally, the Vatican II characterization of the Church as people of God resulted in a renewal of the idea of charism as special gift from the Spirit for the good of the community. All these factors point to a practical understanding of the twofold mission of the Son and the Spirit.

Chenu finds it appropriate that the present awakening of the Spirit comes on the heels of the rediscovery in the twentieth century of the humanity of the God-man. The fact of the historical and social differentiations of consciousness has contributed to a new understanding of the incarnation as historical humanization of God. It fits the logic of this operation that the rediscovery be followed by an awakening of the Spirit. Such is the internal dynamism of the Christian economy, where the mission of the Spirit follows the mission of the Son.[91] What distinguishes this particular re-awakening of the Spirit, for Chenu, is the decidedly social character of charism as opposed to the more individual concept of gift of the Spirit. The object of the Spirit in the age of socialization is not so much the individual soul as the people of God moving forward in history.[92]

In speaking of the presence of the Spirit in us and in the Church, Chenu is led to an "ontology of the Spirit." This presence is radical in the sense that it is not merely "alongside" our various operations of thinking and loving, but is rather "the very law of our being and our doing." The presence of the Spirit, while homogeneous with the action of Christ, implies a relationship of a different sort. Not only does it penetrate the various levels of our subjectivity – in terms of our consciousness and our freedom – but beyond these its field includes the psychological, social, and political dimensions of human history, "the body of Christ working towards the total incorporation of all human undertakings."[93]

---

90 Ibid., 35. On small groups, see "Carismi e gruppi spontanei" (1970), 431–45.

91 Cf. "Le réveil de l'Esprit" (1976), 9; cf. Jn 16, where Jesus, having finished his mission and about to return to the Father, promises to send the Spirit "who will guide you into all the truth."

92 Cf. "Réveil évangélique et présence de l'Esprit" (1976), 170, where Chenu links the social and political dimension of Christian love, *fraternitas*, to the action of the Spirit: "*La seule loi absolue de l'Évangile est l'amour fraternel, qui, y compris dans sa dimension politique, est le signe de la présence de l'Esprit.*"

93 "L'Évangélisme de saint Thomas" (1974), 400; cf. also "Lex fundamentalis, lex nova" (1972), 43–8; "La rénovation de la théologie morale: la loi nouvelle" (1969), especially 291–2. See *Gaudium et Spes*, n. 26, in Walter Abbott ed., 226: "God's Spirit, who with a marvelous providence directs the unfolding of time and renews the face of the earth, is not absent from this development."

Such is the new law in the regime that fulfills the old covenant. The Holy Spirit is in many ways in charge of the "management" of the continued incarnation. Chenu speaks of "the law of this incarnation which inaugurates and fulfills the presence of the Spirit in humanity."[94] The very movement of history implies the presence of the Spirit, and the most severe discernment of historical movements and ideologies will not destroy that presence in the emergence of the new creation.[95]

The Signs of the Times and Contemplation

It should hardly be surprising that, in an interview shortly before his death, Chenu spoke of his preference in praying to the Holy Spirit. This presence of the Spirit in the world was precisely the object of his contemplation. There is a clear relationship between contemplation and the reading of the signs of the times.

The link can be seen in Chenu from his earliest writings. The object of contemplation, according to some of the early retreat texts, can be described in general terms as the work of incarnation, or better, as the incarnation at work. However, only in later writings does this object become clear in relation to the the task of theological reflection.

The 1988 article "De la contemplation à l'engagement" provides clear evidence for the link between the discernment of signs of the times and a contemplative life. Given the context of the article, as well as its title, the link is unmistakable and quite intentional. Furthermore, the shift to a more evangelical standpoint, to which Chenu refers in other articles, retreat texts, and conferences – though the actual word "evangelical" is absent from the article in question here – is also clearly within his understanding of contemplation: "[A]gainst the position of an atemporal scholasticism, engagement in the world is a factor of contemplative life." The activity of the Holy Spirit in the various missionary movements is the objective element of Christian experience to which the gifts of the Spirit in the contemplative act are the subjective counterpart. The missionary element – here Chenu has in mind the young teams of the JOC in the late 1920s – was the sign of the times, that is, a particular experience was being read in terms of its underlying theological significance. A pastoral

94 "Liberté et engagement du Chrétien" (1938), in *Parole* 2, 352.

95 See "Chrétien, mon frère" (1969), 297: " ... *l'Esprit-Saint, qui renouvelle la face de la terre, est présent à ces transformations, dans un aggiornamento permanent ... pour conduire à maturité le Corps du Christ, pour manifester la puissance de la Résurrection.*"

experience was regarded as propitious terrain for the intelligence of faith: "It is probably one of the most precious graces of the Spirit to keep us present there where he exercises his creativity for opportune innovations in a world of change."[96]

The familiar theme of the Church's relation to the world is thus linked to the contemplative dimension of faith. The shift from the individualism of *The Imitation of Christ* to the social consciousness of the Church seeking the world does not imply an abandonment of contemplation. Contemplation never occurs in a vacuum, but in the world. Such is the vocation of all contemplatives, especially those whose vocation is the Dominican mixed life. For Chenu, "the world is the object of my faith's complacency, and the events which weave its history are the carriers of a capacity of divinisation." Here, "complacency" is a technical term referring to the activity of contemplation, the exercise of the virtue of faith. Such exercise takes the form of a discernment of the signs of the times, and this discernment is thus rightly described as "one of the resources of contemplative life where the gifts of the Holy Spirit are present in sociological insights, such as the coherence of nature and grace in the Christian economy which follows history."[97]

The rootedness of the reading of the signs of the times in contemplation, and the necessary relationship to the gifts of the Holy Spirit, are crucial to the understanding of Chenu's theology. Without them, the activity of discernment would remain abstract and subject to the variety of subjective and ideological biases. While the presence of bias is not thereby eliminated, the activity is given a concrete foundation and an objective theological setting.

As long as the signs of the times are discerned and assumed into the history of salvation, theological reflection remains "in waiting." The inconclusive character of our remarks on the interpretation of the signs of times and on the elements of a criteriology have to do with the nature of a theology committed to the concrete and the historical. The lack of certainty on the level of historical action is the price for respecting the integrity of the human situation, as well as an acknowledgement of the problem of sin and evil.

Still, the waiting is not without direction and orientation. The Church, as the messianic and prophetic people of God, is the witness to the

96 "De la contemplation à l'engagement" (1988), 101.
97 Ibid., 102.

eschatological promise. It is a carrier of all human hopes for fulfillment and liberation. Through the mediation of the Holy Spirit, the eschatological end-time is active as a dimension of the present. God speaks today. The discernment of that word by means of a prophetic reading of the signs of the times rooted in contemplation is what theology is all about.

6

Incarnation and Christology

ON 15 NOVEMBER 1980 at the Dominican house of St. Jacques in Paris, Chenu gave the homily during the mass in celebration of the feast of St. Albert. It was a dramatic occasion. He began by complaining about his incompetence on the subject, proceeded to offer a wonderful homily full of insights about St. Albert, and concluded with several revealing remarks about his own long journey in the Church and in theology.

After sketching the historical context of St. Jacques at the time of St. Albert, Chenu pointed out the two areas that had attracted the saint's attention: nature, in all its physical complexities, and the mystery of God's transcendence, which Albert pursued in his reading of Denys. Far from being torn in two different directions, Albert had demonstrated a clear desire to pursue both the understanding of nature with all the trust in the power of human reason that it implies, and the mystery of God. "I still do not quite know how he would articulate this. One or another among you may be able to see how. How does one articulate this naturalism at the limits of empiricism, and this penetration, this investment by the transcendence of God?"

Chenu drew a twofold conclusion. In the integration of confidence in the powers of human reason and the sense of God's transcendence, St. Albert had been successful, while Chenu himself was not. He thus ended the homily by giving a "decidedly subjective testimony" about his own "incompetence," which came to light "these last days."

This moving conclusion has somewhat the quality of a confession about it. First, with reference to his early work on *La théologie comme science*, Chenu detects a certain rationalism, which today he would write differently: "I would situate it within the sense of mystery, that the sense of mystery might have all its weight." Not that he now rejects his confidence in the role of human understanding, but he does admit that in his youth he may have been a little too intrepid: "I admit that I am much more surrounded by a sense of mystery these days. I do not regret the understanding of faith with all its demands, but at some moments I find it a little inadequate before the sense of mystery; I feel a bit like a man in a tunnel, who barely sees a small light and who feels his way along the wall. It is as though the mystery of man, which I feel very strongly, increased the mystery of God in me. It is not a temptation against faith, but a sort of dimness. I think that this was St. Albert's destiny to some extent, in a sort of extraordinary health." This intrepidity also played in Chenu's pastoral commitments. Three times he was carried away by "a sort of lyricism before the events of the Church, and each time I was a bit disappointed afterwards." Three times, he says, he thought the kingdom of God would come, only then to be disappointed: first in 1936, with the social involvement of the JOC; then, after the war, with the launching of the Mission de France and the birth of the worker-priests; and finally, with the second Vatican Council. Every time, he felt elation followed by disappointment. Unlike the spirituals of the Middle Ages, who believed that the age of incarnation would give way to the age of the Spirit, eliminating history and everyday reality, Chenu now wishes to maintain, along with St. Albert, the place of rationality within faith and also "the sense of the modest reality of the Incarnation."[1]

At the end of our journey through the writings of Chenu, it is precisely this "sense of the modest reality of the Incarnation" that raises questions. There is no doubt that it is the all-pervasive structure in his theology. What is its exact status and meaning? Surely it is more than a metaphor or a structural device for organizing his theology. But what exactly is the relationship between incarnation as process or law and the event of the incarnation? Given the centrality of incarnation in Chenu's theology, where the law of incarnation is considered as ruling the whole of history and especially the role of the Church in the world, why is there relatively little specific reference to Christ? The issue becomes paradoxical when we consider that Chenu's whole effort was devoted to the integration of the historical dimension of existence into theology – that is, the concrete character of existence in space and time – which is precisely where the role of Christ should have its greatest impact. Finally, is there any connection between the relatively little room given to Christ and the lack of a sense of mystery in Chenu's early writings?

1 "*Homélie prononcée à la messe de saint Albert le Grand*" (1981), 106–13, here 111–13.

A starting point for an answer to the last of these questions lies in Chenu's contribution to a longstanding problem in the study of St. Thomas, namely the plan of the *Summa Theologica*. It may seem at first that this matter is of greater concern for arcane textual studies than for the fundamental christological option. Yet, as Chenu himself declares, "The plan of St. Thomas' *Summa* is a means of access to his mind."[2] A study of Chenu's contribution to this problem of Thomistic studies should, therefore, reveal something of Chenu's own position on theology, especially with regard to the relationship of theological science to the particular events of salvation history. Chenu was, after all, not only a historian of the Middle Ages but also a disciple of St. Thomas for whom the thought of the *doctor communis* remained a living source.

CHENU'S POSITION ON THE PLAN OF THE *SUMMA*

It is generally recognized that Chenu's 1939 article on the plan of the *Summa* was a ground-breaking advance in Thomistic studies. As Torrell has pointed out, however, it was not until after 1950, the year of Chenu's *Introduction à l'étude de saint Thomas*, which included an expanded version of the 1939 article, that contemporary studies on the subject began appearing.[3] The significance of Chenu's contribution lies in his approach, which considered both the understanding of the role and tasks of theology and the place of historical events and their inevitable contingency within theological science.

First of all, Chenu recognized the specific nature of the literary and theological genre of the *Summa*. As he demonstrated elsewhere, the growing autonomy of theology as a discipline in the twelfth century meant a greater need for systematization and an effort of conceptualization: "in becoming a 'science' – be it in a relative sense – theology tended to organize its goal and its objects, and so to construct them on the basis of architectonic principles taken from the rational structures of the mind, set to work under the light of faith."[4] Beyond the standard commentary on Peter Lombard's *Sentences* (an analytic compilation of biblical and patristic texts written in the twelfth century), the synthetic

2 *Introduction*, 258.

3 The original article was "Le plan de la Somme" (1939), 93–107. The expanded version appears on 255–76 of Chenu's *Introduction*. See Jean-Pierre Torrell, *Initiation à saint Thomas d'Aquin* (Paris: Éditions du Cerf, 1993), 219ff.

4 *Introduction*, 256.

aspect of theological reflection became more prevalent. The goal of the *Summa* was thus threefold: to present in a concise and abridged fashion the whole of a particular scientific area, to organize synthetically the object of study beyond a piecemeal analysis, and finally to accomplish these goals in a pedagogically effective way. The term *ordo disciplinae* characterized this effort at once encyclopaedic, synthetic, and pedagogic. Neither the scriptural *lectio* nor the *quaestiones disputate* lent themselves to the construction of theological science. They lacked "that freedom in which understanding can promote its master intuitions and embody them in adequate systematic arrangements."[5] In studying the plan of the *Summa*, there is more at stake than the order of logical structure and classification of questions. What is important is the interior movement animating that structure, revealing the intellectual options which give primacy to this or that part. Thus, following Chenu's example, it is not a matter of mere classification that the treatise on grace (at the end of *Ia-IIae*) precedes the one on Christ (*IIIa Pars*): "No, we have here the effect of a deliberate plan whose reach we cannot overemphasize." It is for this reason that Chenu can say that the plan of the *Summa* of St. Thomas provides "a means of access to his mind."[6]

The task of constructing a systematic body of knowledge is always faced with the resistance of the data to be systematized. This is especially so in the case of theology where the data – the word of God – are unified only in the mind of God, whereas the human mind is always discursive and complex. Here, more than anywhere else, the system is the sign of the inherent weakness of human reasoning, as well as of its greatness.[7] The creation of the *summas* in the thirteenth century struggled with this very challenge: how to transform a sacred history into an organized science.

With St. Thomas, the pursuit of an *ordo disciplinae* corresponded with the developing notion of science, whose technical requirements were becoming more clearly perceived and applied, though not always without controversy: "an organic knowledge in which (in the search for *raisons d'être*) the elaboration of the data of experience and of thought

---

5 *Introduction*, 257. Chenu continues: "*Ordo disciplinae, dit saint Thomas: aussi bien une telle construction est requise par l'objet même du savoir, qui ne se livre point à l'esprit sans cet ordre secret hors duquel les plus exacts énoncés ne seraient, scientifiquement parlant, que matière informe et opaque.*"

6 *Introduction*, 258.

7 See here Chenu's article on the psychology of the act of faith in the thirteenth century, in which he analyses the relationship of assent and *cogitatio* in the one act of faith.

develop in a series of analyses and syntheses – by the composition, division and coordination of abstract notions. The extension and comprehension of these abstract notions serve as a base for the constitution of an order where natures find their realm of intelligibility in logical classifications: henceforth, such will be the schema – reduced to its simplest expression – of any knowledge claiming the name of science."[8] The case of theology presented a particular difficulty for scientific construction. Its data are a history of events, a series of contingent facts, "works of divine liberty and of human liberty, unconditioned (consequently) both in their existence and in their succession, irreducible to a series of *raisons d'être* as to a chain of deductions."[9] The challenge was to present and organize the various elements in such a way as to preserve their proper character of contingent events within the economy of revelation, yet at the same time to place them within a speculative order that would produce intelligibility.[10]

To introduce an *ordo disciplinae* into sacred history, St. Thomas went beyond the Aristotelian schema of science and borrowed the Platonic theme of emanation and return: "Since theology is knowledge of God, all things shall be studied in their relation to God, whether in their production or in their finality: *exitus* and *reditus.*" Chenu goes on to comment: "It is a magnificent resource of intelligibility: that all things, every being, every action, every destiny be situated, known, judged in that supreme causality where its *raison d'être* is totally revealed, in the very light of God." More than a science, theology is wisdom, where the emphasis is on universal order: "admirable portion of Neoplatonism – whether pagan or Christian matters little for the moment – which (in continuity with the epistemology of the Greek philosophers) develops virtue beyond its reach, so as to know the evolution of the creature. It is a universal order where diverse natures, analyzable in terms of genus and species, take their place, but which brings intelligibilty to the common root of all nature."[11] This schema, Chenu claims, is open to history, indeed to sacred history. That history begins, in fact, with a description of the emanation of the world, whose entire destiny and that of its creatures, by way of a desire for happiness, is a return to God.

---

8 *Introduction*, 259.

9 *Introduction*, 260. As a point of comparison, see the methodological difficulties raised by history in Bernard Lonergan's *Method in Theology* (New York: Herder and Herder, 1973).

10 Cf. *Introduction*, 260: "*Bref, comment, sans les sortir de leur économie originelle, disposer les éléments du donné révélé selon un ordre spéculatif qui exprimât une authentique intelligibilité?*"

11 *Introduction*, 261.

Such is the plan of the *Summa* and its interior movement. The *Ia Pars* is about emanation, where God is seen as principle. The *IIa Pars* considers the return, where God is seen as end. The *IIIa Pars* examines the "Christian" conditions of that return.[12]

It is clearly in the neo-Platonic Christians, and especially in the then-strong Dionysian tradition, that St. Thomas found the *exitus-reditus* schema. Yet the double movement of procession and conversion was far from the particular philosophical context of a Plotinus. It had to be purged of its cosmic determinism and its idealist dialectic, which were radically opposed to a Christian economy of creation and salvation based on divine freedom: "Thus the apparent paradox is burst – the paradox of the insertion and exposition of a sacred history within a representation of the universe which originally (and more than any other) wished to eliminate all history."[13]

Now, the *exitus-reditus* schema is not used as an conceptual framework where the matter of sacred history can easily be disposed and organized, "but truly as an order of knowledge, creator of intelligibility at the heart of the revealed datum."[14] This is the "very original intelligibility" that is the object of the theologian's pursuit. All the tools of the theologian's reason, as powerful as they are, remain ordered to the data given. Theological reflection can make an argument of *convenientia*, but it can never deduce its necessity. And it is this argument of "convenience," so common in the *Summa*, that brings out the full interplay of system and history. "Now, there is a secret marriage between this very particular type of intelligibility (which yields for the theologian the argument from fittingness – so despicable to Aristotelian epistemology, but so essential to theological epistemology) and the schema of emanation and return where, at decisive moments, the divine freedom governs the rhythm of its development." Respect for the concrete character of history is here met by the desire for order generated by the discipline, and both history and order are governed by faith. "Sacred history and *ordo disciplinae* find here their proper interference under

---

12 Cf. *Introduction*, 261: "*et parce que, de fait, selon le libre et tout gratuit dessein de Dieu (c'est l'histoire sainte qui nous le révèle), ce retour s'est fait par le Christ homme-Dieu, une* IIIa Pars *étudiera les conditions 'chrétiennes' de ce retour; l'histoire évidemment, ici plus qu'ailleurs, sera maîtresse, car elle sera, au sens fort du mot, révélatrice; et la spéculation trouvera sa vraie valeur à se modeler sur les suaves contingences de l'amour divin.*"

13 *Introduction*, 263. Chenu thus calls the *exitus-reditus* schema, as used by St. Thomas, "*extrêmement appauvri philosophiquement parlant.*"

14 *Introduction*, 263.

the jurisdiction of faith which leads both to the absolute of God, there giving them their definitive intelligible consistency. The plan of the *Summa* is truly a theological plan, that is, a plan where the knowledge of God is formally and spiritually the principle of human knowledge, furnishing it at once with its object, light and necessity."[15]

In calling the *exitus-reditus* schema truly "theological," Chenu refers to its inherent capacity to bring theological knowing beyond the particularities of the economy of history to the divine reasons ruling over it.[16] Here is the decisive step: the primary object of theology is not history but God. "Indeed, the object of theology is not first and foremost that economy where in fact man receives grace and faith from Christ; it is [rather] God in his very reality; all of his perfections, throughout the course of history, all the works of creation and recreation, ... are treated of and judged formally *sub ratione Dei* [according to the mind of God]. The plan of the *Summa Theologica* and its divisions are taken from the very nature of the object of theology. It could not be more suitable."[17] In this sense, theology remains a religious knowing in its very structure. In its most rational construction, it is a *doctrina sacra*. The *exitus-reditus* schema in theology refers all objects, all actions, all events and destinies under its consideration, to God as principle and end.[18] Everything is considered in relation to two causes: the efficient cause of God as creator and conserver (*Ia Pars*), and the final cause of the beatifying and glorified God (*IIa Pars*). Moreover, the two movements are intimately linked together. The procession of beings from God gives an ontological ground for their conversion and the return to their principle of production, thus forming a single path of correspondence between form and end based on the one plan of the efficient cause.[19]

15 *Introduction*, 263.

16 Cf. *Introduction*, 263–5: "*Car ... ce plan tend* de soi *à conduire le savoir théologique, au delà de l'économie qu'il considère, jusqu'aux raisons divines qui la commandèrent.*"

17 *Introduction*, 264. The significance of the *de facto* place of Christ in theology in relation to theology's primary object is discussed below.

18 Cf. *Introduction*, 264, where Chenu quotes from St. Thomas' *Commentary on the Sentences* (*In II Sent., prol.*): "*Creaturam consideratio pertinet ad theologos et ad philosophos, sed diversimode. Philosophi* enim *considerant creaturas secundum quod in propria natura consistunt; unde proprias causas et passiones rerum inquirunt. Sed* theologus *considerat creaturas secundum quod a primo principio exierunt et in finem ultimum ordinantur qui Deus est; unde recte divina sapientia nominatur, quia altissimam causam considerat, quae Deus est.*"

19 In this connection, Chenu argues for the unity of dogmatic and moral theology. Speculative and practical theology are but two aspects of one reality. Human actions are seen as "steps" on the way of the return. Cf. *Introduction*, 267.

The *IIIa Pars* is likewise seen in terms of the same plan and belongs to the movement of return as the *de facto* means of conversion: "The Incarnation, the centre of this economy, does not enter into this dynamic except as the means willed by God."[20] Chenu readily admits that the place given the incarnation has been the source of most of the objections to the plan of St. Thomas. Theology seems already entirely constructed by the time Christ enters the scene. The redemptive incarnation seems an afterthought. The real history of salvation appears to be a contingency with no relation to an abstract metaphysics of God, grace, and virtues. Humanity is first of all presented, not as the mystical body of Christ, but as an element of cosmology. And, eliciting what is probably the most emotional objection, there is a treatise on grace without any mention of *Christian* grace, and there is a treatise on charity without any mention of the one who revealed the love of God.[21]

Chenu recognizes the absence of christological reference in the first two parts of the *Summa* and defends the plan of his master: "In truth, the incarnation is a contingent event: in the cycle of *exitus* and *reditus* it does not come into the picture except as an absolutely gratuitous work of God. The predestination of Christ is principal in fact, it does not come by right into this economy; it is impossible to situate it *a priori* in the dialectical series of divine decretals."[22] The centrality of the incarnation is not denied. But a distinction is made in the order of knowledge and intelligibility. The very gratuity of the Christ event excludes it from the *a priori* consideration of divine decrees. Here intelligibility is of the first order; accordingly, the event of Christ is understood as a means. "The vision of God is not fulfilled save by and in Christ, but the knowledge of God must be analysed in its exigencies and its comportment, before the most precious modalities. The redeeming incarnation makes up the very substance of the economy, but its primary intelligibility

20 *Introduction*, 266: "*L'Incarnation, centre de l'économie, ne rentrera dans ce circuit que comme le moyen voulu par Dieu.*" Cf. 268–9, where Chenu says, using more traditional vocabulary, "*de ce retour le Christ médiateur est l'artisan, il est la 'voie'.*"

21 See *Introduction*, 269.

22 *Introduction*, 270: "*C'est que, en vérité, l'incarnation est un événement contingent: dans le cycle de l'exitus et du reditus, il ne rentre que comme une oeuvre absolument gratuite de Dieu. La prédestination du Christ est capitale de fait, elle n'entre pas de droit dans cette économie; il est impossible de la situer a priori dans la série dialectique des décrets divins.*" As Chenu points out, we recognize here the characteristic positions of the famous controversy between Thomists and Scotists on the motive for the incarnation and the absolute primacy of Christ. He notes that the doctrinal position of St. Thomas is reflected in the plan of the *Summa*. See note 51 below for Hans Urs von Balthasar's comment on this passage.

resides no less in its role as a means; it is not to minimalise its admirable history to see it thus situated in an ontology of grace."[23] In this sense, it is the very commitment of Thomas to the ideal of theological and scientific intelligibility, the *ordo disciplinae*, that allows him to maintain the events of the Christian economy as an object of history: "This is a paradoxical success of theology, which can join, to a sense of God's transcendence, knowledge of the necessary and respect for the contingencies of a love that is always free."[24]

CRITICAL REACTIONS TO CHENU AND LATER FORMULATIONS

Chenu's *Introduction à l'étude de saint Thomas* was generally well received in the critical reviews. The chapter on the plan of the *Summa*, however, sparked much discussion. In one review, the Jesuit Henri Rondet took issue with the placement of christology and the apparent secondary importance given to the incarnation as contingent event: "Probably this conclusion will stimulate many discussions. Christ is the way, but he is also the destination; one cannot oppose the mystery of Christ to the mystery of God; it is in Christ that God reveals himself to man, and indeed it is for Christ that all things were made."[25] To bring home the point, Rondet called upon the subalternation of the sciences, which Chenu himself had worked out previously. As long as no science usurps the place of the superior science and remains coherent within itself, the whole edifice of human knowing culminates in the affirmation of a fact: "the primacy of Christ, in whom all things find their consistency by the will of God: *Christus, in quo omnia constant* [Christ, in whom all things hold together] (Col 1:17)."[26] Such a perspective in no way diminishes the scientific character of theology; rather, it highlights the multiple aspects of theological reflection. "Here it notes the necessary links between things, having recourse to general categories of thought; else-

---

23 *Introduction*, 270. Chenu goes on: "*La transition de la IIa à la IIIa Pars représente le passage de l'ordre nécessaire aux réalités historiques, du domaine des structures à l'histoire concrète des dons de Dieu.*" In a note, he adds that just as Christ does not become the *object* of theology, so too, against a modern tendency influenced by deism and the opposite extreme, we cannot have a theology where the God of Abraham and the biblical and gospel history would disappear.

24 *Introduction*, 271.

25 "Bulletin de théologique historique," *RSR*, 38 (1951), 144–57; here, 154. Rondet is referring to Chenu's *Introduction*, 270.

26 Ibid., 155.

where it is content with arguments from fittingness, showing the harmony of the divine plan and the agreement between nature and grace. However, the more it deepens its object, the more it finds itself in the presence of mystery, in the presence of the revealed *fact* – which one must accept not as a unit which reason cannot assimilate, but as a light. It is a light which, from above, enlightens that which one had already believed one possessed perfectly."[27] Rondet did not believe that we should oppose biblical theology and speculative theology, or history and science, but that we should strive to organize this knowledge within the framework of salvation history while maintaining scientific structure within the various phases of theological reflection. To this Rondet believed Chenu would answer that theology should speak of God as he is in himself, not of our own history, and would himself reply to Chenu: "But is this not forgetting that God has not revealed himself to us except through the history of salvation? Moreover, it seems to us that the great theological geniuses of the future will take up again the work of the Angelic Doctor and – without doing it any violence – will arrange it more conspicuously around the mystery of Christ who is at once the Way, the Truth and the Life."[28] This last remark makes it clear that Rondet took issue not so much with Chenu the historian as with Chenu the Thomist, in that he regarded Chenu's interpretation of St. Thomas to be a contemporary theological contribution.[29] It is in light of contemporary theology that Rondet criticized Chenu's interpretation.

Another Jesuit theologian, André Hayen, also took exception to the place given to Christ in Chenu's interpretation of St. Thomas. In a section of his *Saint Thomas d'Aquin et la vie de l'Église* entitled " 'Réalisme théologal' et la théologie,"[30] he took up the question of the plan of the *Summa*. For him, the main division is not between the first and the

27 Ibid., 155, Rondet's emphasis. In a note, Rondet defends the autonomy of science and philosophy and stands clear of any confusion between the domains of philosophy and theology that could be introduced in the name of the primacy of Christ: " *Que le Christ soit l'achèvement de la création, cela ne change sans doute rien aux lois mathématiques ni aux principes généraux de la métaphysique, mais cela permet de finaliser les sciences de la nature, l'histoire de la vie et surtout l'histoire humaine. Faut-il nécessairement pour cela opter entre la thèse thomiste et la thèse scotiste sur le motif de l'Incarnation ([cf. Chenu, Introduction,] 270)? Nous ne le pensons pas, et des thomistes authentiques s'efforcent de dépasser ici la problématique habituelle.*"

28 Ibid., 156.

29 Cf. ibid., 145: " *Historien de la pensée médiévale, le P. Chenu est aussi un thomiste fervent pour qui l'oeuvre étudiée n'est pas une pièce de musée, mais une doctrine vivante et capable de susciter la vie.*"

30 André Hayen, *Saint Thomas d'Aquin et la vie de l'Église* (Louvain: Publications Universitaires, 1952), 77–100.

second parts, corresponding to Chenu's *exitus-reditus*, with the third part as the means willed by God. Rather, Hayen saw the main break as occurring just before the third part. The first and the second parts together constitute an abstract treatment of theology, while the third turns to the concrete: "Passing from the two first parts of the *Summa* to the third is thus not a purely conceptual passage from emanation to return to God. It is a 'real' passage, from the abstract consideration of the universal truth of God and his work to the concrete knowledge of the singular Person of Jesus Christ in his historical contingency – that is, in his being situated in the history of the world."[31] The focus of Hayen's critique is the placement of Christ. He reacts especially against the "*ultérieurement* [subsequently]" used by Chenu to qualify the place of Christ and our filial adoption in him in relation to the study of grace.[32] One consequence of this division is that the natural desire for God is seen not in *a priori* terms, but as a "reality recognized in the concrete activity of existing nature," which itself is "created in Christ (Col 1:16)": "Concretely, it does not carry out its activity independently of Christ and of the supernatural influence of the Father who draws the whole world to his Son, our only Saviour."[33] Hayen concludes: "What we have just said allows us to specify exactly the place of Christ in the thought of St. Thomas. This place is total. It is more total than P. Chenu would grant when he writes that adoptive sonship in Christ will follow 'subsequently' upon the nature of grace, or that if 'the predestination of Christ is principal in fact, it does not come by right into this economy (of the return to God); it is impossible to situate it a priori in the dialectical series of divine decretals'."[34]

31 Ibid., 86.

32 Ibid., 90: "*Le mot que nous venons de souligner [*"ultérieurement"*] choquera plus d'un lecteur. Il serait inadmissible, s'il s'agissait d'une antériorité réelle, chronologique ou simplement ontologique, de la grâce sur le Christ: y a-t-il moyen de penser, dans toute leur réalité surnaturelle, la grâce et la vision béatifique sans référence au mystère trinitaire de la génération du Verbe, de la procession de Saint-Esprit et de la mission des Personnes divines.*" This occurs in the treatment of the first part of the *Summa*. Hayen uses this argument for the abstract-concrete distinction and division.

33 Ibid., 93.

34 Ibid., 95. References are to Chenu's *Introduction*, 270. In a short review of Hayen's book in *BT* (8, 2 [1947–53], 771–2), Chenu admits to a certain "*gêne spirituelle*" before St. Thomas' interpretation of the incarnation and welcomes a debate on the issue. He accepts Hayen's distinction between abstract and concrete, and recognizes that the use of "*ultérieurement*," which he calls "*un adverbe fâcheux et équivoque*," "*durcit évidemment la pensée de S. Thomas.*" Yet he adds: "*La 'christianisation' de la* Prima Pars *et de la* Secunda *ne se fait pas cependant, me semble-t-il, sans une accommodation qui, pour favoriser la ferveur, amollit quelque peu les analyses rationnelles.*"

According to Hayen, when St. Thomas speaks of God, there is always a reference to Christ: "For a Christian, to speak of God means to speak of Christ."[35]

For some, the issue of the place of Christ centres on two basic options in the conception of theology and the place of the incarnation. In reviewing the contribution of Per Erik Persson[36] to this debate, Chenu writes: "The rejection into the *IIIa pars* of the 'history' of Christ is, to be sure, a debatable opinion; but if it is done, it is the consequence of a position of the *Ia pars* and *IIa pars*. This position (quite apart from Neoplatonist sources which are more or less at arm's length) is of weight in itself – with its ontological, cosmic, anthropological densities – against another position in theology. For the latter position – always appealing – the fact of the Incarnation is the axis for understanding of the economy of God."[37] Yet the issue, as we have seen Rondet noting above, is not to be reduced to the choice between Thomist and Scotist ideas of theology. Besides, the acknowledgement of a plurality of options in so basic a theological issue is somewhat of a defeat for a system claiming to account for everything *sub ratione Dei*. One wonders – and I will return to this later – whether Chenu the historian is not in tension with Chenu the theologian on this point.

Mario Serenthà also focused on the relationship between the plan of the *Summa* and the place of christology, doing so especially in light of some more recent affirmations by Chenu.[38] He noted that, as late as 1982, Chenu's position had hardly changed since the original article of 1939. Indeed, even the wording is almost identical. This is significant in

35 Ibid., 96. Hayen continues: "*Aussi saint Thomas pourrait-il répondre au P. Chenu, nous semble-t-il, que le Christ historique est nécessaire*, necessitate ex suppositione, *de la même nécessité, concrète et* ontologique, *qui fait que Socrate est nécessairement assis tant qu'il est assis et que l'univers est nécessairement immortel tant que l'immuable volonté de Dieu veut le créer. Mais la réalité singulière de Jésus, pas plus qu'une autre, n'est 'directement' connaissable à notre intelligence. Pour la connaître, il faut une réflexion,* per conversionem ad phantasmata, *et cette réflexion n'arrive à une connaissance entièrement déterminée du singulier qu'en s'achevant en un acte de libre adhésion au Christ.*"

36 "Le plan de la Somme théologique et le rapport 'Ratio-revelatio'," in *RPL* 56 (1958), 545–72.

37 *BT*, 10 (1957–59), 470. On this issue, see also H.-M. Féret, "*Creati in Christo Jesu*. Essai de critique théologique," in *RSPT*, 30 (1941–42), 96–132.

38 "A proposito di recenti affermazioni di M.-D. Chenu riguardanti il piano generale e la cristologia della 'Summa'," *La Scuola cattolica*, 111 (1983), 89–95. The "recent" refers, among other items, to Chenu's "Introduzione" to an Italian anthology of texts from St. Thomas entitled *La conoscenza di Dio nella Somma Teologica* (Padua: Edizioni Messagero, 1982), 5–42.

view of the discussions that arose precisely on the basis of Chenu's original proposal. In these, lines were drawn between, on the one hand, those who saw in the *Summa* a primarily christological plan, a plan that would have Christ in the centre even if the explicit treatment of christology occurs in the third part, and, on the other hand, those who claimed that the neo-Platonic schema of *exitus-reditus* lies at the origin of the *Summa*. Serenthà further noted that Chenu had always maintained that this schema is open to history and to the particular historical dimension intrinsic to Christian revelation. This assertion is underlined by the christological treatise of the *IIIa Pars* and its examination of the mysteries of Christ's life culminating in Easter. Such a treatment of the historical event of Jesus is completely absent from the theology of the manuals. This distance between the biblical account and theology is unknown to St. Thomas.[39]

Serenthà focused on Chenu's claim that, in the *Summa*, the life and works of Christ are treated within the framework of a theology of the two natures.[40] He pointed out that such a theological reading of the gospel is significant precisely in its distance from a biblical view, which stresses first the concreteness of the life of Jesus of Nazareth. Referring to the introduction of the concept of "the singularity of Christ" in recent christology as a point of access to the mystery of Incarnate Word, he wrote the following: "Such an introduction wishes precisely to express the fact that the fundamental point of reference for a correct reading of the whole reality of Son of God made man is not first of all the theology of the two natures, but rather it is the concreteness, the unrepeatability, the 'singularity' of the event of Jesus, in which and through which is revealed the face of God and that of man, the two 'natures' contemporaneously present: these natures are implied in those, emerge from those, find here their definitive manifestation, they must be read in the frame that this singularity decided, and not vice versa."[41] Chenu's reading does not permit one to speak of a "biblical theology" in the

39 In this connection, Serenthà refers to Chenu's criticism of Garrigou-Lagrange, in his emphasis on the necessary and his ignorance of history, and his other Roman teachers who would skip the particulars of Christ's life (cf. *III*ᵃ 27–59) and jump to the conclusions. Cf. ibid., 92.

40 Cf. "Introduzione," 32: "*Tutta la vita e le opere di Cristo, nella terza parte, saranno inquadrate nella teologia delle due nature – umana e divina – che aiutano a capire il Cristo all'interno del mistero teandrico. Si tratta, in concreto, d'una lettura teologale del vangelo. Storia sacra e riflessione su Dio, epistemologicamente disparate, vengono composte in un solo sapere.*" This passage does not figure in the *Introduction* of 1950 or in the original article of 1939.

41 "A proposito di recenti affermazioni," 92. Serenthà believes that such a confrontation between Chenu's affirmations and recent christological developments is "*senz'altro legittima*" since Chenu maintains his position in 1982.

Summa, especially in relation to christological discourse. If Chenu's interpretation of Thomas is correct, according to Serenthà, the distance with regard to a biblical perspective is clear. Furthermore, to say that the mystery of incarnation and recapitulation is read within creation seems to run counter to the New Testament affirmations about "creation in Christ" and about the fulfillment of the first Adam in the last Adam.

Serenthà was obviously aware of Chenu's repeated emphasis on the openness of the Thomistic system to history and on its rootedness in the reading of scripture. The divergence in judgment with Chenu lies in the latter's terms of comparison. Chenu was comparing the historical and biblical character of St. Thomas, with regard to the plan of the *Summa* and the place of christology, to the theological tradition that followed Thomas, especially the manual tradition of theology. Compared with the "baroque" christology of Chenu's teachers in Rome, that of St. Thomas does appear to be more sensitive to historicity. From this greater historicity, Chenu deduces the scriptural foundation of St. Thomas. Serenthà's objection was that such a deduction cannot be taken for granted.[42] In light of this difficulty, he believed that the question of historicity and scriptural foundation in St. Thomas, especially in relation to christology, ought to be reconsidered.

One of the most recent treatments of the matter has appeared in Jean-Pierre Torrell's *Initiation à saint Thomas d'Aquin*.[43] Noting the importance of Chenu's 1939 article in giving the "opening salvo" in the whole discussion of the plan of the *Summa*,[44] Torrell recognized the principal difficulty of Chenu's proposal as lying in the weakened position given to christology. As an alternative, he proposed the solution of M.-V. Leroy.[45] The *exitus-reditus* schema is still valid provided that it is limited to the economic section of the *Summa*, not to the theological section, following the old patristic division.[46] Whereas the dominant

42 Cf. ibid., 94: "*Ora, precisamente questa no può e non deve essere dato come immediatamente 'scontato': da una maggiore 'storicità' nei confronti del manuale non scaturisce ancora direttamente una immediata biblicità.*"

43 Jean-Pierre Torrell, *Initiation à saint Thomas d'Aquin* (Paris: Éditions du Cerf, 1993).

44 Ibid., 219.

45 Cf. M.-V. Leroy in *RT* 84 (1984), 298–303, reviewing the work of A.-M. Patfoort, *Saint Thomas d'Aquin. Les clés d'une théologie* (Paris, 1983). See also the article by Patfoort, "L'unité de la *Ia Pars* et le mouvement interne de la Somme théologique de S. Thomas d'Aquin," *RSPT* 47 (1963), 513–44.

46 Cf. Torrell, 222: "*La 'théologie' correspond au début de la* Prima Pars *(QQ. 2–43), où il s'agit bien de Dieu en lui-même; alors que l'"économie' regroupe tout le reste de la* Somme *(à partir de la* Ia Q. *44), cet ensemble de 393 questions étant lui-même à comprendre selon le schème exitus-reditus.*"

movement of the first part is still the emanation, the second and third parts of the *Summa* are in the movement of return as it applies to the human creature, reasonable and made in the image of God. The movement of return finds its fulfillment when the human creature attains perfect resemblance in communion with God through the mediation of Christ: "Complete and nuanced, this explanation seems to correspond well to to what St. Thomas did."[47]

Torrell went on to confirm the explanatory value of this schema by examining the place of the incarnation. Using two texts overlooked by Chenu,[48] he found that, far from being "a piece added after the fact," the role of the incarnation for St. Thomas was to fulfill the movement of *exitus-reditus*. "It is that much more unfortunate that P. Chenu did not have these texts in mind at the moment he wrote his first essay, for they clearly show that, in the thought of St. Thomas, not only does the incarnation not introduce continuity into the schema of *exitus-reditus*, but on the contrary it is only in the incarnation that this movement reaches its fulfilment."[49] Chenu's emphasis on the centrality of *exitus-reditus* for the plan of the *Summa* would seem finally to be vindicated. Yet the vindication carries a noteworthy corrective with regard to the place of christology in the *Summa*. How serious is this corrective? The judgment of the critics is that Chenu's proposal for the plan undervalues the central place of Christ. The underlying judgment flowing from this is that the very value of the historical is put into question. Can these judgments legitimately be generalized to apply to the whole of Chenu's theology? In other words, does Chenu's proposal for the plan of the *Summa* indeed give us access to the heart and spirit of his theology?

There is no doubt that Chenu's approach is more theological than christological, or rather, more theocentric than christocentric. In this sense, the law of incarnation, to use Chenu's key phrase, would refer to the general movement of emanation-return as a whole, in which the event of the incarnation is the chosen and wonderful means. There seems to be a cosmological overtone that, while thoroughly theological, somehow overshadows, perhaps even prevents, the development of a christology.

Chenu's position here was criticized by many authors, and he softened some of his formulations as a result.[50] Specifically, the place of Christ in

---

47 Ibid., 223. He adds, with Leroy, that the *exitus-reditus* schema, before being neo-Platonic, is simply Christian.

48 Cf. *Sent. III Prol.* and *Compendium theol.* 201.

49 Torrell, *Initiation*, 226–7.

50 See the notes in the third edition of Hayen, *San Tommaso e la vita della chiesa oggi, Nuova edizione Italiana a cura di Inos Biffi* (Milan: Jaca Book, 1993).

the *Summa* was re-affirmed and given more prominence by other inter-perters of St. Thomas.[51] Still, my question on this matter has not been primarily related to the place of Christ in St. Thomas, but to the place of Christ in Chenu's interpretation of Thomas. And Chenu's placement of the event of incarnation, while perhaps not fully representative of St. Thomas' position – as shown by the various criticisms of Chenu's position – is quite instructive and revelatory of his own theology.

However, a difficulty seems to arise. We are left with the impression that Chenu, more than many of his contemporaries, was especially com-mitted to the entry of history and historical consciousness into theologi-cal reflection.[52] Yet if the emanation-return schema is indeed dominant, it might lead to an undervaluing of the historical fact in its singular and concrete character, with an emphasis on its formal or even exemplar significance over its uniqueness.

THE PLACE OF CHRIST IN CHENU'S THEOLOGY

It is now necessary to ask bluntly: Is there a place for the personal Christ in Chenu's theology? Does the plan of the *Summa* really provide "a means of access to his mind"? Is the emanation-return schema ulti-mately an abstract conceptual structure that blocks access to a personal God? Is Chenu's commitment to historical consciousness ultimately pre-vented from reading the sign of the times above all signs of the times?

The interpreter of Chenu is quickly reminded of the occasions when the author uttered a retraction, saying his earlier writings were too "ra-tionalist." Fundamental questions are therefore raised about Chenu's understanding of the nature of theology. There are several instances in

51 See Torrell's section "La place de l'Incarnation" in his *Initiation à saint Thomas d'Aquin*. See also, among others, Hans Urs von Balthasar, *The Theology of Karl Barth*, trans-lated by Edward T. Oakes (San Francisco: Ignatius Press, 1992), 264, n. 17, where he com-ments on the place of the *singularia* as *exemplum vitae* in St. Thomas (*ST Ia, q. 1, a. 2, 1 c*): "In regard to this text one must ask whether even the *singularia Christi* (from which indeed all the other *singularia* of revelation get their singular character) are subsumed under this interpretation – a question which we must unconditionally answer with a No if Christ's life as such is to be the truth and not merely an example for life (*exemplum vitae*) or an author-itative witness to a doctrine which in itself is timelessly true. The teaching against which we here take our stance, as indeed we do in this entire book, has recently been advocated in M.D. Chenu, O.P. with a – it seems to us – frightening clarity." There follows a quotation from Chenu's *Introduction*, 270, where Chenu explains the *de facto* contingency of the incar-nation event.

52 It is only necessary to recall how Chenu criticized Garrigou-Lagrange's statement, "*L'incarnation ce n'est qu'un fait.*"

Chenu's writings where he speaks of his conception of theology in terms of one option rather than another. The subject in question is usually the object of theology, creation, grace, or simply theological anthropology. We have already discussed how much of his anthropology is quite explicitly set up in opposition to what he calls the Augustinian form of theology, which he usually labels as a form of dualism that is always seductive. The question can also be raised whether his emphasis on emanation-return in theology makes it difficult for Chenu to embrace the concrete event.

The nature of theology, for Chenu, is centred on the task of searching for reasons, for the intelligibility inherent in creation from the point of view of God's plan. Basic to the task is the search for laws manifested in particular events. The emphasis is on the intelligibility of particular events, both in the Church and in the world, on the search for a deeper meaning than appears on the surface of things. Chenu is thus always looking at things in terms of the big picture. The danger is that the particularity of the concrete experience or event will be swallowed up in the articulation of intelligibility, that the event will be seen as an instance of law. Chenu is aware of the danger, but is not always immune to it. It is likely that this is what he has in mind when he admits to a strain of rationalism in his theology.

Chenu notes the strong reaction to pre-conciliar projects on the part of the Council fathers, when they rejected a scholasticism of abstract propositions in favour of a theology where the emphasis lies in the "realism of an economy where Christ is the centre and the recapitulation of every thought and every action."[53] The implication of this choice was a rejection of Thomism, with its emphasis on the order of intelligibility in creation. It seemed like a replay of the old dispute between Thomists and Scotists about the object of theology: God or Christ. Yet Chenu insists that Thomism was open to history, and indeed goes on to embrace the "christological" Council.

In the words of Paul VI, the Council opted for a theology that is concrete and historical. The pre-conciliar texts, supported by one faction of the Council fathers, emphasized abstract and atemporal propositions. A different conception of the concrete came forth from another faction of Council fathers, according to Chenu, which emphasized a theology of creation, along with the traditional "seeds of the Word" and the autonomy of terrestrial realities: "For some, the irreducible

53 "Saint Thomas, chrétien pour notre temps," (1965), 247.

originality of the Christian mystery and of its positive economy; for others, intelligibility, included among the 'reasons' which (in the contingence of history, sacred and profane) reveal the permanent values which creative Wisdom establishes." Chenu sees an echo here of the old school controversy about the object of theology and the appropriate method for the study of that object – a historical-biblical method for some, a speculative and doctrinal method for others. In this light, Chenu says, the theology of St. Thomas is compromised; that is, his option in favour of the *ordo disciplinae* is questioned. There follows a reference to the plan of the *Summa*: "We know moreover that the very arrangement of the *Summa* – seeking the intelligibility of the divine undertaking in an emanation and a return of the creature, where Christ, in the third part, is considered as the path of return – *does not satisfy the absolute primacy of the fact of the redeeming Incarnation and favours the law of essences.*"54

How does Chenu respond to this challenge to St. Thomas? By saying that we must also read his commentaries on scripture where the value of the historical is asserted and preserved. However, these are precisely what Chenu rarely refers to in his own theology. His own way to the historical is from within or sometimes even in spite of his Thomism.55

Chenu embraces many of the Vatican II statements about the historicity of the human condition and the historicity of revelation. For example, he often quotes or refers to the orientation of *Dei Verbum*, where it is said that the "definitive" character of the revelation in the time of the gospel is not only not incompatible with the idea of development but actually implies it: "The mystery of Christ is always in act, not only by shedding an old light on new situations, but by an immanent presence in the community of his Body. The Church is the historical form taken by grace." The many references in Chenu's writings to "God speaks today" are here given a clear christological ground: it is Christ who speaks today. Later Chenu says, "Every development, in thought and in action, is within the total truth of Christ and his Gospel."56 There is no absolute rejection of metaphysics; however, in line with his emphasis, Chenu states that the problem of "ontological relations" is to be met not outside but within historical reality.

54 Ibid., 248, my emphasis.

55 In this context it is interesting to note that the third edition of *La théologie comme science au XIIIe siècle* (1957) differs from the earlier editions by, among other things, a wish for greater reference to the biblical commentaries of St. Thomas.

56 "Histoire du salut et historicité de l'homme" (1968), 24, 26.

For Chenu, the constant emphasis on historicity, in terms of both anthropology and Christian revelation in general, lies in the very nature of the economy of revelation. That is, it corresponds to the method of God's self-communication to us: "God, in speaking to man, speaks the language of men – according to the geography of civilizations and the developments of history, as much as he speaks according to the psychology of individuals." This classical theological position was already articulated by Augustine: "*Deus hominibus loquens more hominum loquitur* [God speaks to men after the manner of men]" (*De civ. Dei.* XVIII, 6, 2).[57]

The resulting interest in theological *loci* and the signs of the times is simply the practical consequence of taking the concrete circumstances seriously, since it is in them that God's word is present. This approach is at the root of both the Council's *aggiornamento* and theology's renewal in light of historical consciousness. The question remains whether "the signs of the times" is a sufficient category to encompass all that is meant by the concrete, especially when considering the person. Chenu's anthropology, though not systematically developed, carries three fundamental characteristics that take this renewed consciousness into account: the importance of social relations, the link to matter, and the situation in time and history. His anthropology is very much in line with that of St. Thomas, as well as with the christological vision of the universe of Vatican II. Yet even if all three characteristics can be traced in one way or another to the writings of Thomas, it does not mean that they exhaust his anthropology. Several traits remain undeveloped in Chenu, which would, if present, provide a more balanced view. Perhaps Chenu's mistrust of a theology focused on the individual and the individual's interiority, which he derisively calls "*spiritualisme*," can account for this.

An important component allowing the reader to find some unity between Chenu's earlier and later writings is contemplation. The newly rediscovered historical dimension of the economy of salvation, which corresponds to a more cosmic christology, has become an object of contemplation. "It is an admirable convergence, for the delight of the theologian, of the lines of mystery grasped and contemplated in history: while a new light shed on man today lends support to a rediscovery of the Incarnation as a historical humanization of God, Christianity's Christological centre of gravity places man in a new light as well. Anthropology and Christology, Christology and anthropology, together become (the one by the other) the geometrical realm of theology in

57 Ibid., 28.

the full understanding of mystery." Chenu's longstanding battle against monophysitist and docetist reductions of christology leads him to embrace the new light coming from historical consciousness.[58]

In an important 1970 article on historicity and immutability in Christianity, "Storicità e Immutabilità," the importance of christology is once again apparent. This focus first appears with a reference to the structure of *Gaudium et Spes*, where the emphasis is on the temporal "recapitulation" of Christ, the "perfect man" who "entered in the history of the world."[59] Along with the accent on the Church in the *modern* world, it marked a shift in the approach to thinking about God's action in relation to the world, from a deductive approach flowing from previously grasped eternal principles that are then applied or projected onto particular circumstances of history, to an inductive approach starting from the scrutiny of the very same circumstances, a reading of the signs of the times.

A key element in Chenu's theology is the relationship between Christ and the Church. In Christ, the word of God entered history. This word is present in the Church. It is in act in the people of God. The history of salvation in act in the people of God is thus grounded in Christ, in whom the word entered history. Christ is not absent from this presence of the word in history through the Church. "The mystery of Christ is always in act ... through an immanent presence of his body in the community. The Church is the historical form of grace." The "act" of the Church includes its proclamation of the word and the liturgical celebration of the eucharist, which manifests the recapitulation of human and cosmic history in Christ incarnate. As further support for this position on the Christian economy, Chenu alludes to *Dei Verbum*, which presents revelation as the word of the living God today rather than as a inventory of truths held in a deposit.[60]

Also significant for an understanding of signs of the times, but from a different perspective, is Chenu's use of the classical formula *fides ex auditu*. Christian faith is a theological virtue, unlike the moral virtue of religion, which proceeds from human efforts. That is, it proceeds from "hearing" the word of God. It is no longer seeking God that is involved; rather, it is God, a personal God, entering into a relationship with us where divinization occurs through a humanization of God. Using the categories of history, God's "entry" is an "event"; the same term is used is describing the object of the signs of the times.

---

58 Ibid., 31.
59 *Gaudium et Spes*, no. 38.
60 "Storicità e immutabilità della realtà cristiana" (1970), 147.

Chenu's position on christology is most evident when we consider the relationship between Christ and history as a whole or, put another way, the relationship between the doctrines of incarnation and creation. His interest is global: history as it relates to the order of creation. Christ's recapitulating role functions in relation to the whole of creation. In this sense, the incarnation of Christ brings the new creation to fulfillment. Not surprisingly, Chenu refers to the *Adversus haeresis* of Irenaeus to support his view of Christianity as economy and the recapitulating role of Christ. This is obviously not a new teaching, and the reference to tradition lends support to Chenu's particular objective, namely, a renewed theology of creation. Throughout the 1950s and earlier, a renewed teaching on the goodness of creation was seen by many as the most important contribution by Christian theology in an age marked by massive departures from the Church. The alternative, duly pointed out by Marxist critics, was a religion of alienation and a false idealism based on an escape from the world. Chenu's position is clear: "The coming of God into history thus reveals the consistency of a creation whose history is development. The Incarnation is like the terrestrial connection, through the incarnate Word, of the creative work of the Word unfolding in the world, *Logos prophorikos.* Creation and Incarnation are not two superimposed operations, but two emanations which envelop each other permanently. Their coherence, divine and human, which finds its material in time, is affirmed in the one eschatology, in the 'fullness of time'."[61]

The mutual interplay between a theology of creation and a christology is well illustrated in Chenu's contribution to a theology of work. In a 1959 contribution on religious education, "L'enfant et son avenir professionnel. Esquisse d'une théologie de la création et du travail,"[62] Chenu begins with a preamble in which he summarizes the basis for the current renewal in the Church, which in turn will ground any renewal in catechesis. The pivot of this renewal is clearly the re-valorization given to the *economy* of salvation, "that is to say, of the divine arrangement of the governing facts which punctuate 'Sacred History', of which the major and governing fact is the incarnation of God-made-man – prepared by the Old Covenant in the people of Israel, continued by the New Covenant in the Church."[63] The object of theology, in this perspective, is not

---

61 Ibid., 150.
62 Paris: Édition de Fleurus, 1959, 11–47; reprinted in *Parole* 2, 543–70 under the title "Théologie du travail."
63 "Théologie du travail," *Parole* 2, 543.

a system of thought, but the Word of God communicating with human-kind according to the rhythm of the economy in which it is bound. Co-operating with the creator in a continued creation, the human destiny in the world is given new value. Human hopes are preserved and ful-filled: "Far from being emptied, and as it were crushed by the grace of a redeeming incarnation, these works of the creation that is continued by man (cooperating with God) are recapitulated beneath Christ's mes-sianic and cosmic kingship. Thus authentic catechesis restores earthly activities, destinies – *by situating them in the economy of the Incarnation* – not only to moralize them but, much more radically, to give them (in their very being) their humano-divine dimension."[64] The article takes this theological framework as its structure. In the first place, the role of *homo artifex* is underlined in light of a doctrine of continued creation, but also in light of technological advances in contemporary civilization. Despite its ambiguities, brought on by the distortions of original sin, a new era of humanity is heralded, new dimensions of humanity are uncovered that are also "matter for the grace of Christ, in his ongoing incarna-tion."[65] In a renewed theology of creation, beyond the initial act of God *in principio*, the task of theologians and catechists is clear, "*one must restore the exact sense of the reference to God included in the very being and in the evolu-tion of things*, whether according to the genesis of nature or by the hand of man."[66] Chenu goes on: "It is a living reference, established not in an annihilating passivity, but in the autonomy of that freedom which is the supreme gift of a creator who desires collaborators. A God who commu-nicates, therefore, in an emanation (the mediaeval theologians were not afraid of the word) of his love – if it is true that love wants to bestow upon the beloved the capacity to respond freely to its own total gratu-itousness."[67] The human task of cooperation with the creator is thus the

---

64 Ibid., 544. In n. 2, Chenu notes the insufficiency of a catechism of "perseverance," to which he opposes "*une catéchèse où le monde du travail soit situé dans une économie totale du mystère du Christ.*"

65 Ibid., 552. The term "incarnation" here probably refers to the grace of Christ as its subject.

66 Ibid., 555. Chenu's emphasis.

67 Ibid., 555–6. In a note, Chenu offers the following clarification, which addresses the earlier criticism about the lack of explicit reference to biblical data: "*Pour rester bref, nous lais-sons à ces théorèmes leur énoncé abstrait. Mais il importe de savoir qu'ils n'ont été énoncés et élaborés dans les écoles que sous la pression d'une lucidité religieuse extrêmement fervente, et dans la méditation des textes bibliques. Et cette ferveur religieuse est communicable aux simples, hors l'abstraction de l'école, dans la lecture de l'Écriture et l'émotion de ses formes figurées*" (Chenu's emphasis). Still, religious does not mean christocentric, despite the earlier reference to continued incarnation.

response to the loving emanation of God. In this task, there is no dualism between worldly profession and religious vocation. Chenu rejects the position that, in the name of a certain supernaturalism, would assign profession to nature and reserve vocation to the realm of grace. Just as we are both matter and spirit, so too the construction of the world falls within our vocation, in terms of solidarity and fraternal charity.[68]

The article on religious education ends with a section entitled "La récapitulation dans le Christ."[69] Here, the emanation-return schema becomes most explicitly apparent, even to the Christian conditions of this return. Chenu summarizes the path taken so far and introduces the place of Christ: "We have considered work as man's free and active participation in God's creation and governance of the world. At the same time as man fulfils himself in thus confronting nature, he brings nature itself back – powerful demiurge that he is – brings it back to its completion, to its destiny, in bringing it back to God, in his understanding and his love. Now note this, then: it is by and in Christ that man can effect this return."[70] Arguing against "a cramped conception of Christ's undertaking in his incarnation," and exploiting the larger view of salvation economy made available through the renewal of biblical studies, Chenu maintains that "Christ came to restore all of creation (according to its structures coordinated and arranged into a hierarchy in man), by a

---

68 In a corrective note, ibid., 567, Chenu adds the following: "*On veillera ainsi à bien équilibrer l'homme-au-travail ... dans la perspective eschatologique, entre un pessimisme radical, pour qui est futile en définitive la besogne terrestre, et un optimisme utopique, selon lequel la cité temporelle chrétienne, au terme de ses progrès, serait la Cité de Dieu.*" There follows a reference to Yves Congar's *Jalons pour une théologie du laïcat* (Paris: Éditions du Cerf, 1953). The nature of this corrective note most likely results from the controversy between incarnational and eschatological tendencies in the 1950s. For a helpful review of the controversy, see Bernard Besret, *Incarnation ou eschatologie? Contribution à l'histoire du vocabulaire religieux contemporain, 1935–1955* (Paris: Éditions du Cerf, 1964).

69 "Théologie du travail," 568–570.

70 Ibid., 568. There follows an explanatory note showing the parallel between the present development and the plan of the *Summa*: "*Sans l'avoir décidé a priori, nous nous trouvons reprendre le plan de la vision chrétienne du monde que présente saint Thomas dans sa* Somme théologique*: l'émanation de la créature est l'effet de l'amour de Dieu, entraîné à pareille extase, et la création, image et vestige de Dieu, porte, par cet amour, dans sa nature, les lois de son développement. Mais le retour à Dieu ne s'accomplit que par la grâce du Christ ... Il est évident cependant que ce plan est* doctrinal, *avec ses paliers d'abstraction qu'il implique. Pédagogiquement, le fait du Christ (dans l'Écriture, dans le mystère de la célébration liturgique) restera premier. Autant ces deux voies sont opportunément différentes, autant il faut en coordonner les ressources selon les conditions et les circonstances éducatives*" (Chenu's emphasis). Note that the primacy of Christ is affirmed in terms of pedagogy.

grace which is incarnate in human nature; human nature which is itself in solidarity with, and which enjoys the fruits of, all nature."[71]

In this perspective, an interest in the progress of terrestrial economies – cultural, social, and physical developments – is far from being an obstacle to faith. Rather, it is a resource when we show "the all-gracious gift of divine life, in Christ the God-man, [give] nature back to itself in liberation from evil; [restore] it and [*perfect*] it, to be entirely open to divine participation in a communion of love."[72] Chenu goes on: "At this point, all of man's works – and at the summit, his great work of the construction of the world throughout the ages – are *recapitulated* by Christ. Assimilated into his Body, they enter also – along with all creation – into his work, into his *mystery*. The believer knows how to read and to live here the death and resurrection of Christ. All of the current ethics of work; all of the rootedness of profession in man, in the universe, in the community; are thus elevated to the divine quality of praise, offering, and liberation, which are the three attributes of sacrifice accomplished in the Pascal act of Jesus Christ."[73] Again, he stresses the cosmic implications of the Christ event with a reference to Pauline texts, especially to Rom 8:18–23.

Similarly, in another text, where Chenu writes about the Council's rediscovery of terrestrial values and the positive nature of secularisation, he reminds his audience of the role of Christ. He cites Paul's letter to the Colossians in Col. 3:22–3, "All is yours, but you are Christ's," and continues with a strong statement about Christ: "As much as we must involve ourselves in the discernments called for both by the progress of history and by the transcendence of God's Kingdom, we must hold, equally as much, that beneath these formal discernments (necessary for the truth of doctrine and the effectiveness of action) the divine and human reality of Christ's grace embraces completely the totality of existences and destinies."[74]

The emphasis on the role of Christ and his grace remains, along with the rejection of all easy dualisms whereby we separate temporal and spiritual, secular and sacred – in short, nature and grace. Underlying these

71 Ibid., 568. He adds: "*Vision cosmique, où la résurrection de la chair est le test significatif, au noeud de la matière et de l'esprit, de la vérité humaine et terrestre de l'incarnation*" (568–9).

72 Ibid., 569, Chenu's emphasis.

73 Ibid., 569, Chenu's emphasis. With its reference to the cross, the resurrection, and the threefold aspect of the paschal sacrifice, this is one of his most explicitly christological texts.

74 "Valeur chrétienne des réalités terrestres" (1965), 248.

distinctions is often a notion of history wherein the concrete is merely the "occasion" for Christians to work out their salvation, but where the circumstances remain neutral or indifferent, without any intrinsic relation to the kingdom of God. The result is a notion of the supernatural where the grace of Christ is to be found outside of daily circumstances. Chenu comments:

Against this one must maintain that no reality in human existence, whatever it may be, is indifferent. Either it is good, or it is evil. If good, it enters (deliberately or not) into the building up of the Kingdom; it is 'recapitulated' by Christ. Christ's Lordship is not limited to the so-called 'supernatural' world. Christ is the Word made flesh, and the same Word is creator and saviour. The incarnation brings creation to completion, that creation in which man fulfils in himself by Christ the image of God, by the very fact that he cooperates with this creation throughout history. The evolution of the world by and in man, in brotherly love, is the very ground of the Kingdom of God. The final fulfilment will embrace the totality of the universe and of history; and this eschatological hope already imbues every human reality: 'When I am lifted up, I will draw all men to myself.' (Jn 12:32).[75]

This powerful statement hits most of the right christological notes. Moreover, the value of the concrete – the singular and the particular – is emphatically affirmed and grounded christologically. None of this can be denied. Yet similar statements do not occur frequently in Chenu's writings. They stand out because they are so few and remain somewhat isolated; they are not really an integral part of his discourse. Chenu's tendency is to affirm the autonomy of the secular in light of the incarnation; hence the emphasis on the value of creation and its relation to the incarnation.

The issue of the relationship of nature and grace dominated much of the theological debate in the first half of the twentieth century. In many ways, it remained one of the central outstanding issues after the modernist controversy.[76] It underlay the discussions on the relations of faith and reason, theology and philosophy, faith and experience, Church and culture, gospel message and terrestrial realities, as well as many other key areas of theological reflection.

75 Ibid., 248–9.
76 See on this whole issue Gabriel Daly, *Transcendence and Immanence: A Study of Catholic Modernism and Integralism* (Oxford: Clarendon Press, 1980).

Chenu never wrote a treatise on grace. The relationship of nature and grace nevertheless occupies a central place in all his theological preoccupation. In *La théologie au XIIe siècle*, he writes: "A word to anyone who may one day write the history of the theology of grace in the Church of the twentieth century: it is assuredly not in some controversy between a Paleothomist and a Neomolinist that the real and interesting content of this theology is to be found. One must find it in the position of the problems of nature and grace renewed by the birth and development of Catholic Action, or by essays in the theology of history."[77] The passage is significant in giving us a glimpse of the context in which Chenu viewed the entire relationship of nature and grace. My purpose here is not to review his position on the issue, but once again to raise the question of the place of christology in the context of the nature-grace relationship. This re-examination is particularly apt in light of the objection raised about the placement of the treatise on grace in the plan of the *Summa*.

In Chenu's collected essays *La Parole de Dieu*, "grace" appears only four times in the thematic indices of the two volumes.[78] The first mention occurs in the context of an article on sacraments. There is a clear reference to the incarnation of Christ in the setting of the basic problem: "In an economy where the Incarnation, and the lifting-up of humanity that it accomplishes, have become the prototype of every human act, the truth and force of a liturgy reside in a 'sacramental' regime – that is to say, in symbolic arrangements where grace is expressed and transmitted through human acts ritualized to that end. Here more than elsewhere, it would be an error to superimpose the sacred upon the profane, grace upon human nature; nature is consecrated in itself, according to all the realism of efficacious symbols. The utter gratuitousness of grace in no way implies the evacuation or reduction of the laws or behaviour of the human subject; according to the very intentions of Christ, the author of the sacraments, it is this human subject who is the

---

77 "Moines, clercs, laïcs. Au carrefour de la vie évangélique," in *La théologie au XIIe siècle*, 225. The English translation reads slightly differently; it is the only passage Chenu altered: "The scholar who will someday write the history of the theology of grace of the twentieth century will certainly not find the real and interesting substance of that theology in some neo-scholastic controversy, in polemics between some paleo-Thomist and a neo-Molinist. He will have to find it in problems concerning nature and grace newly raised by young Christian thinkers aware of the changes taking place in the fundamental structure of society, aware of economic developments, and of new conceptions of the world and of history that are in the process of formulation." See *Nature, Man, and Society in the Twelfth Century*, 202; see also the "Translators' Note," v.

78 The actual occurrences of the term "grace" are, of course, much more numerous.

basis for the distribution and the symbolic expression of grace."[79] According to this text, the sacramental character of the liturgy derives from the incarnation as "prototype of every Christian act." Following a pattern already well-established in other writings, the relationship of nature and grace is seen not in terms of "superposition" but in terms of incarnation; that is, the laws of the human subject serve as the basis for the expression of grace. The gratuitous character of grace is not thereby diminished in any way.

A much different context is present in the second passage where grace is mentioned, from "La révolution communautaire et l'apostolat" of 1944.[80] Chenu here is writing about the Christian implications of the social revolution in which humanity discovers its communitarian dimension. He asks rhetorically whether the grace of Christ has anything to do with this reformation of humanity. The pastoral consequences of the answer to this question are clear. As can be expected, Chenu's answer will be set in opposition to any form of escapism from terrestrial reality in the name of some false spiritualism or "*eschatoligisme*." Hence, he will write of the "earthly commitment of grace."

The re-creation of grace, which represents the destiny of humanity, does not occur outside the context of the first creation. It would be not only awkward practice but doctrinal error if the Christian apostle were to proclaim salvation at the cost of some essential feature of human reality. The doctrine in question is that of creation. The vocation of the baptized must embrace the human vocation and all the tasks it involves. But, Chenu adds, the sanctity of the apostle, which includes the reference to human matter, occurs "in and through Christ."[81] The task of the apostle, then, is to watch human reality in all its evolutions, in the worst crises, beyond its fragile and agitated surface, in order to grasp its deeper layer where the aspirations of the human soul are revealed: "To develop supernatural force, the apostle is no less subject to this universal law of spirit and action." To understand the nature of the apostolic task, therefore, we must reach the internal determinisms underlying all human reality, where "collective phenomena exert an almost irresistible hold," because it is there that "according to the human and divine law,

79 "Anthropologie et liturgie" (1947), in *Parole 1*, 309. See also 315 in the same article, where there is mention of the liturgy as providing the necessary communitarian basis for the "*promotion de la grâce.*"

80 "La révolution communautaire et l'apostolat" (1944), in *Parole 2*, 363–78.

81 Ibid., 364: " … *la sainteté de l'apôtre comporte de soi, dans la vérité même de sa grâce propre, la référence à la matière humaine que, dans et par le Christ, il doit embrasser.*"

grace must find its points of entry."[82] The precise nature of this human and divine law is further explained. It concerns the very truth of the Christian economy: "The divine life does not increase in us by esoteric means, but truly according to the very structures of our being, individually and collectively; its forces ... embrace our faculties in their native elasticity and borrow their dynamism. *Faith* follows, in its cogitations, the laws of our intellect; *hope* flows in our desire for happiness; *charity* takes hold of all our love's expressions and manners of acting. Such is the spiritual branching-out of grace ... If it is so, it is not only the laws of human nature in general – eternal and metaphysical laws – that will explain the behaviour of grace and manifest its paths; but also the concrete states of this nature and its present conduct in the evolution of societies and the variety of civilizations."[83] Now the grace in question is clearly the grace of Christ, "the royal and chief grace of Christ,"[84] according to Chenu. And it is Christ's work of recapitulation, the continued incarnation, that follows this law.

The next passage follows a similar argument. It comes from a 1953 article, "La ville. Notes de sociologie apostolique".[85] Here again, it is the concrete state of humanity in a social and urban context that becomes the subject of divine communication. Grace is not juxtaposed on the individual or collective subject, but enters "inside": "Poured thus into the spiritual frame of men, grace is conformed to this frame's functions and organic distributions without prejudice to its own law; just as [*tout comme*] the Son of God is wholly incarnate in the functions of human life, without prejudice to his divine personhood."[86] As elsewhere, the relationship of nature and grace is stated in terms of the law of incarnation. Everything here depends on the interpretation of the "just as" in Chenu's text. What functions as the paradigm? Is the incarnation of the son of God an example, albeit the highest one, of the general law of incarnation? Are we dealing with a theological or a christological paradigm?

82 Ibid., 366.
83 Ibid., 366. In this sense, Action catholique is defined (377) as "*le régime communautaire de la grâce.*" See also "Dimension nouvelle de la chrétienté" (1937), *Parole* 2, 92, where a similar analysis of the law of incarnation leads Chenu to conclude with the aphorism, "*Loi de nature qui devient loi de grâce.*"
84 "La révolution communitaire et l'apostolat" (1944), 368.
85 "La ville. Notes de sociologie apostolique" (1953), in *Parole* 2, 515–36.
86 Ibid., 531.

A decisive step in dealing with this issue comes with the shift in the very concept of nature. Moving away from a metaphysical view, which would remain ignorant of the concrete state of humanity in its social and cultural context, Chenu opts for a decidedly historical view of the human condition. The whole area of the discernment of the signs of the times represents, as it were, Chenu's theology in action. This is where the underlying structure of his theological enterprise, as enterprise, is most visible. The task of reading the signs of the times was already seen in an earlier chapter as an expression of the ongoing structure of incarnation. There the weakness of the theology of the signs of the times was said to be the lack of an adequate criteriology, especially in relation to the problem of evil. Now the signs of the times must be examined from a different perspective, namely, their relation to the schema of *exitus-reditus* and their concept of the historical concrete. This re-examination is all the more urgent in light of Chenu's statements in the homily for the feast of St. Albert. The three occasions when he thought the kingdom was about to arrive were examples of the signs of the times. Yet somehow, his discernment led to disappointment.

Here, once again, the problem is one of emphasis. Chenu repeatedly stresses that human reality is *capax dei*, according to the traditional formula. This capacity for God is present not only in human nature, but in that nature as it develops in space over time; not only in the human person, but in the phenomenon of socialization. This "not only ... but" formulation, motivated by a valid reaction against a one-sided individualism, necessarily places the emphasis on the second half of the disjunctive proposition as the needed corrective.[87] The question then arises: In his desire to include the whole concrete, does Chenu not thereby miss the concrete by placing the emphasis on a dimension of the human subject rather than on the subject whose characteristics include these crucial dimensions?

Chenu was always a vociferous fighter, a "theologian of the trenches," as he sometimes liked to refer to himself. His battles were numerous, as were the theological ideas that he fought as distortions of true Christianity. Examples were the various tendencies, reminiscent of the christological heresies such as docetism and monophysitism, which he discerned

---

87 See, for example, "Valeur chrétienne" (1965), 250 and "Les signes des temps" (1965), 36: "*Car l'homme est, au sens fort du mot, 'sujet' de la grâce,* capax Dei, *non seulement dans sa nature radicale, mais dans sa nature développée, non seulement dans sa personne, mais dans sa sociabilité.*"

in the fideistic and conceptualist denial of history. He saw that Marxist criticism and other forms of atheism were correct if Christianity was conceived as an abstract system alienated from human existence. But this was not the Christian faith that he learned from St. Thomas or that he lived with his Dominican brothers at Le Saulchoir.

For Chenu, in the end, it was a matter of realism. The abstract conceptualism of Garrigou-Lagrange was completely incapable of dealing with the reality of history. This was not merely an academic dispute about the methodological reaches of the theological discipline; it touched on the very heart of Christianity. The word of God is precisely present in history, and as long as we are blind to history we also miss the word. The word of God chooses history and historical presence as a means of self-communication to us, substantially present in Christ and proclaimed in the Church by the presence of the Spirit. Garrigou-Lagrange and his scholasticism indubitably tried to articulate the truth of Christ. Yet, Chenu would reply, the mystery revealed in Christ is not only one who says the truth, but one who is the truth. "In this way, in the end, the question of truth comes down to the question of knowing who the very person of Jesus is ... Thus the truth is a strongly Christological concept."[88] This, then, is the true object of Chenu's discernment of the signs of the times.

Revelation is given to us not primarily through propositions that can be grasped through a series of logical rules, but through a person that can be known through an event, the event of the incarnation, death and resurrection, as well as through the event that is the presence of the Church in the world.

---

88 "Vérité évangélique et métaphysique wolffienne à Vatican II" (1973), 639–40.

Conclusion

THE CONTRIBUTION OF MARIE-DOMINIQUE CHENU to theological renewal came at a crucial time when the Church was in the midst of a painful struggle with the advent of modernity. The issue was to find a theological language that could speak to the concerns and aspirations of the modern world, yet could also overcome the shortcomings of the modernist proposals and be acceptable to the Church.

It was through a determined and unwavering focus on incarnation that Chenu was able to negotiate successfully the major cultural shift facing the Church at the turn of the previous century. It was by remaining faithful to what he called the law of incarnation that Chenu could identify the weakness of "baroque scholasticism," the urgency of the modernist questions, as well as the inadequacy of the modernist solution. He was able to develop the centrality of incarnation in a number of areas, all of them relating to the issue of human historicity.

Chenu's theological vocation, as he saw it, was to be a witness to the mystery of incarnation in all its implications for the nature of theology, the meaning of Christian existence, and the role of the Church in the modern world. The law of incarnation is thus simply the consequence of what is at the heart of Christianity, namely God's entry into history. All docetic, nestorian, and monophysite tendencies that attempted to keep the incarnate word beyond the vicissitudes of history and the concreteness of the human situation were constantly opposed by Chenu. Incarnation therefore became the centre of all his theological writings, the basis for renewing all the old problems inherited from a different age, and the ground for staking out new claims in the mission of the coming age.

Chenu believed that each age in the history of the Church has been given a special insight into one aspect of the divine mystery. For him, the insight granted to the twentieth century concerns the mystery of incarnation as God's humanization. Following the medieval category of *convenientia*, incarnation is especially appropriate for our own age, in which the Church faces a world that appears to be opposed to anything Christian. The world of modernity in which the Church finds itself proclaims the centrality of the anthropological, which is seen as an emancipation from the alienating belief in God and the institutional expression of this belief. To place and maintain humanity in the centre seems to require the destruction of all "anti-human" structures such as Christianity. The Church has become associated with forces opposed to the emancipation of the human in the world. As long as this association remains in force, the Church's voice has little chance to be heard. In such a situation, where human consciousness has been discovering the new dimensions of historicity and socialization, a supratemporal onto-theology or a "sacred metaphysics" can make little headway. One result of the situation has been the birth and growth of a non-Christianized working class. Like nothing else, the new emphasis on incarnation has offered the Church the opportunity to be itself and to address the modern world without appearing to deny humanity's deepest aspirations. The Church is now in a state of mission, proclaiming the salvation of *homo artifex* as well as *homo sapiens.*

The first major consequence of this emphasis on incarnation has been the affirmation of the human element in Christianity. There is in Chenu a repeated preoccupation to preserve the integrity of the human in its encounter with God. The human subject, according to Chenu, is at home in the world. He was thus always suspicious of a theology that proclaimed the salvation of the soul in terms of an interiority ignoring the facticity of the human situation. The human subject is not redeemed through a denial of what is properly human. Chenu did not forego interiority, but he knew it must include the subject's encounter with the material universe and the world of other subjects. There can be no encounter with God if it means the destruction of something genuinely human. This applies to the autonomy of human reason in the pursuit of theological understanding, as well as to the social dimension of human existence as it is made manifest in the phenomenon of work. Both are aspects of the one *expectatio creaturae*. In all cases, the inclusion of the human element is by virtue of the law of incarnation.

The affirmation of the human dimension also leads Chenu to make more room for the subjective pole in the experience of faith. The role of faith in theological knowing is given a constitutive role. The theory of subalternation in the discussion on the scientific character of theology breaks the destructive duality between mysticism and theology, between religious experience and its rational expression in theological understanding. That first epistemological question and its resolution serve as a model for the overcoming of many other forms of dualism in Christianity, which can be just as destructive.

Finally, the affirmation of the human takes on a much wider context through Chenu's recovery of a theology of creation. The effect is to give the human project of constructing the world a place in the economy of salvation; terrestrial values contribute to the building of the kingdom. Theologically, this idea is portrayed in the continuity between the creative word through which all things have their being, and the incarnate word that brings creation to its fulfillment through the redemptive recapitulation of all created goods. This is the closest that Chenu comes to a theological exposition of the process of continued incarnation.

Another consequence of the emphasis on incarnation bears on the role of historical method and the place of history in theology. A major reason for the success of Chenu's use of the concept of incarnation arises from its basis in the tradition of the Church. Chenu's proposal for renewal originates from within neoscholasticism and appeals to a return to Thomistic sources. His *retour aux sources*, to the questions behind the ready-made solutions, is made possible by his use of the historical method, whose use in theology Chenu justified on the grounds of incarnation. It was this historical recovery of St. Thomas, beyond the commentaries and manuals of scholasticism, that contributed to breaking the deadlock between modernism and neoscholasticism.

The introduction of historical methods points to the larger issue of historicity and its effect on theology. Chenu's writings are heavily marked by the particular set of circumstances from which they arose. Most of his articles were written as a result of invitations to speak to various groups in different contexts. In other words, his theology is *situated* in history. Through all the apparent disparity of themes, Chenu's concern for the historical status of Christianity recurs repeatedly. Making room for history is not just a matter of admitting a new member into theology's collection of methods. Historicity lies at the heart of Christianity. The object of Christian faith is not so much the God of eternal truth, but the God who enters into human history. Christianity is primarily a *history* of salvation; hence, the recovery of the important notion of *oikonomia* so vigorously advocated by Chenu. God is therefore to be discovered and known, not through an escape from the realities of space and time into the realm of the eternal, but through an *engagement* in history. One immediate application of this reasoning was the bridging of the gulf between pastoral action and theological reflection as well as the more prominent role given to *orthopraxis*.

What, we must ask at the end of this book, is the bottom line on the meaning and function of incarnation in Chenu's theology? Despite the undeniable contributions of his theology, a number of questions about it remain. For example, how christological is Chenu's use of the term "incarnation"? Is "continued incarnation" a part of christology or ecclesiology? What is the precise nature of the analogy? Throughout the preceding chapters, it was pointed out that the use of incarnational language is difficult to circumscribe in a precise way. It would not be fair to judge this merely as vagueness or purposeful obfuscation. The lack of precision, which is never denied by Chenu and is sometimes even exploited by him, seems to be the cost of a certain prophetic, even poetic, force in Chenu's theological language.

There can be no denying that Chenu fails to clarify in a sufficiently systematic way the precise relationship between the unique event of incarnation in the person of Christ and the actualization of this event in the history of the Church, which Chenu calls "continued incarnation." Clearly this is not a case of the same unique event somehow continuing through history. The Church does not in this sense have a human and a divine nature, but it does have a human and a divine element, a visible and an invisible element.[1] The relationship of faith and reason is more precisely defined thanks to Chenu's use of the theory of subalternation. Yet even in the case of theological knowing he will speak of the "[d]ouble theandric mystery, or better yet, the unique mystery, which is the very mystery of Christ, in whom the human and the divine are one."[2] When Chenu alludes to the one mystery, he is referring to the divine initiative that is manifest uniquely in the person of Christ yet is also present in history through the mission of the Church. The same mystery is present in the encounter between faith and reason in the theological act of understanding. In either case, if the mystery is to be known it will be according to the conditions of human knowing:

---

1 For this kind of *mise au point* of incarnational language, see the nuanced and useful remarks by Yves Congar in "Dogme christologique et ecclésiologie: Vérité et limites d'un parallèle," in *Sainte Église. Études et approches ecclésiologiques* (Paris: Éditions du Cerf, 1964), 69–104, especially 102–4.
2 *Une école de théologie* (1937), 61.

Cognita sunt in cognoscente ad modum cognoscentis (Things known are in the knower according to his manner of knowing).

The relations between christology and the various implementations of the law of incarnation lack systematic differentiation and thematization in the writings of Chenu, yet they proved eminently fruitful for the development of theological method and for the *aggiornamento* of the Church. It is with explicit reference to the mystery of incarnation that Chenu gave autonomy to the operations of human understanding under the guiding light of faith and made human experience a valid locus for theology. It is in the name of the same mystery that he introduced the historical-critical method into theological reflection.

Similarly, in the area of ecclesiology, it is in the name of incarnation that Chenu was able to integrate a reflection on the pastoral practice and the missionary tasks of the Church with the self-understanding of the Church. Out of an underlying soteriological concern, he was able to address directly the phenomenon of socialization and thereby uncover new dimensions for the Church to assume – since what is not assumed is not redeemed. Yet even here the analogy between the incarnation and the Church-world relationship has its limits. Its force lies in the application of the Chalcedonian category of "distinct yet not separate" towards the overcoming of dualisms between faith and reason, grace and nature, eternity and time, kingdom and history. Just as Christ has a human and a divine nature, so too the Church has a visible and an invisible dimension. Against all docetic, nestorian, and monophysite tendencies, Chenu maintained that the Church's being was in the world. Although he failed to make the necessary clarifications in his plea for continuity between the quest for justice in the world and the building of God's kingdom, his emphasis served to foster an attitude of love and acceptance instead of suspicion towards the world. That attitude became official with the publication of *Gaudium et Spes*.

This brings us to the question of optimism. Like Teilhard de Chardin, Chenu seemed, at times, to ignore the presence of evil in the world. In a world living under the threat of nuclear destruction, Chenu's optimism appears unwarranted from the viewpoint of common experience. Particularly in light of recent developments in hermeneutics and critical theory, Chenu's insufficient methodological sophistication in the task of discernment feels out of step with the modern concern about the problem of evil. Chenu did not ignore the sinful condition of the human situation, but clearly opted to emphasize the process of divinization. His understanding of redemption acknowledged difficulties and discontinuities, but he left to others the details of particular developments and applications.

Yet we should heed Chenu's lesson about historicity and recall that a reflection on the Church's situation in the world historically preceded and made possible a reflection on the Church's critical function in the world. Were Chenu to begin his theological writing today, his partners in dialogue would undoubtedly include critical theorists, but his theology would remain focused on the end to which we are all called. Chenu's so-called "optimism" is firmly grounded in the realism of Christian hope. His writings are always close to the history of the Church in action, accompanying front-line pastoral workers in the discovery of their mission and the ferment of their hope. In the context of a concrete historical rootedness, Chenu opted for prophetic presence rather than the critical emphasis that can lead to a prophecy of doom. Vatican II has shown that it was the right thing to do at the time. Prophetic writing does not replace hard theological thinking, but without it theology has much less to think about.

Abbreviations

A *Angelicum*

AC *L'Ami du clergé* (Langres)

AD *Année dominicaine*

AFP *Archivium Fratrum Praedicatorum* (Rome)

AHDLM *Archives d'histoire doctrinale et littéraire du Moyen-Age* (Paris)

AN *Antonianum* (Rome)

B *Blackfriars [and New Blackfriars]* (Oxford)

BC *Bulletin du Cange* (Brussels)

BIR *Bulletin d'information et de recherche* (Paris)

BSFEM *Bulletin de la Société française d'études mariales* (Paris)

BT *Bulletin thomiste* (Le Saulchoir)

BTAM *Bulletin de théologie ancienne et médiévale* (Louvain)

C *Cîteaux. Commentarii cistercienses* (Westmalle)

CC *La civiltà cattolica (Rome)*

CD *Cahiers du droit* (Paris)

CF *Ciencia y fe* (Buenos Aires)

CHM *Cahiers d'histoire mondiale* (Paris)

CJ *Cité et justice* (Paris)

CO *Communio* (Granada, Seville)

COM *Communion* (Taizé)

CON *Concilium* (Paris)

CR *Criterio* (Buenos Aires)

CSD *Cahiers saint Dominique* (Paris)

CT *La Ciencia tomista* (Salamanca)

CUC *Cahiers universitaires catholiques* (Paris)

DC *La documentation catholique* (Paris)

DO-C *Documentatie centrum concilie* (Rome)

DT	*Divus Thomas* (Piacenza)
E	*Études* (Paris)
EC	*Études carmélitaines* (Paris)
EE	*Équipes enseignantes* (Paris)
EH	*Économie et humanisme* (Lyon)
ER	*Études religieuses* (Liège, Paris)
ES	*Esprit* (Paris)
ET	*Esprit et technique* (Brussels)
ETL	*Ephemerides Theologicae Lovanienses* (Louvain)
EV	*Église vivante* (Louvain)
G	*Gregorianum* (Rome)
H	*Humanitas* (Brescia)
I	*IDOC International* (Paris)
ICI	*Informations catholiques internationales* (Paris)
IDO-C	*Information documentation sur l'Église concilaire*
JE	*Jeunesse de l'Église* (Paris)
L	*La lettre* (Paris)
LTP	*Laval théologique et philosophique* (Québec)
LV	*Lumière et vie* (Lyon)
MaD	*La Maison-Dieu* (Paris)
MD	*Memorie domenicane* (Pistoia)
MO	*Masses ouvrières* (Paris)
MSR	*Mélanges de science religieuse* (Lille)
ND	*Notes et documents* (Milan)
NIC	*Nouvelles de l'Institut catholique* (Paris)
NRT	*Nouvelle revue théologique* (Paris)
NS	*New Scholasticism* (Washington)
P	*Pensiamento* (Madrid)
PeM	*Parole et mission* (Paris)
PM	*Paroisse et mission* (Lyon)
PP	*Il pensiero politico* (Firenze)
R	*Il regno* (Bologna)
RAM	*Revue d'ascétique et de mystique* (Paris)
RD	*Recherches et débats* (Paris)
RDO	*Revue dominicaine* (Montréal)
RDSR	*Revue des sciences religieuses* (Strasbourg)
REL	*Revue des études latines* (Paris)
RFN	*Rivista di filosofia neo-scolastica* (Milan)
RHE	*Revue d'histoire ecclésiastique* (Louvain)
RHS	*Revue d'histoire de la spiritualité* (Paris)

RJ   *Revue des jeunes* (Paris)
RLT   *Rassegna di letteratura tomistica* (Naples)
RPL   *Revue philosphique de Louvain* (Louvain)
RSCI   *Rivista di storia della Chiesa in Italia* (Rome)
RSR   *Recherches de science religieuse* (Paris)
RSPT   *Revue des sciences philosophiques et théologiques* (Le Saulchoir)
RT   *Revue Thomiste* (Toulouse)
RTAM   *Revue de théologie ancienne et médiévale* (Louvain)
RTL   *Revue théologique de Louvain* (Louvain)
RTM   *Rivista di teologia morale* (Bologna)
RTP   *Revue de théologie et de philosophie* (Lausanne)
S   *Scriptorium* (Brussels)
SA   *Sapienza* (Rome)
SC   *La scuola cattolica* (Milan)
SCH   *Scholastik* (Freiburg)
SD   *Sacra doctrina* (Milan)
ST   *Studium* (Rome)
T   *Teologia* (Brescia)
TC   *Témoignage chrétien* (Paris)
TH   *The Thomist* (Washington)
THU   *Terre humaine* (Paris)
TQ   *Theologischer Quartalschrift* (Tübingen)
VC   *Verbum Caro* (Taizé)
VI   *La vie intellectuelle* (Paris)
VP   *Vita e Pensiero* (Milan)
VS   *La vie spirituelle* (Lyon)
VSS   *La vie spirituelle. Supplément* (Lyon)

In addition, the following abbreviations referring to Chenu's works are used in the text and in the biliography.

Duquesne   *Un théologien en liberté. Jacques Duquesne interroge le Père Chenu.* Paris: Le Centurion, 1975.
Matière   *Théologie de la matière.* Paris: Éditions du Cerf, 1968.
Parole 1, 2   *La Parole de Dieu.* 2 vols. Paris: Éditions du Cerf, 1964.
Peuple   *Peuple de Dieu dans le monde.* Paris: Éditions du Cerf, 1966.
Théologie   *La théologie au XIIe siècle.* Paris: Vrin, 1957.
Travail   *Pour une théologie du travail.* Paris: Éditions du Seuil, 1955.

Bibliography of
Marie-Dominique Chenu

1921

1 "De l'oraison." [Partial translation of John of St. Thomas, *Compendium totius doctrinae catholicae*]. *VS* 3, no. 27 (December 1921): 219–28.

2 "Un traité de spiritualité." [Review of Mgr Waffelaert, *La colombe spirituelle* (Paris: 1919)]. *VS* 3, no. 17 (February 1921): 398–400.

1922

3 "Le bon frère Thomas." *RJ* 1 (1922): 521–7.

1923

4 "Contribution à l'histoire du traité de la foi. Commentaire historique de la IIa-IIae, q. 1, a. 1." In *Mélanges thomistes. Coll. Bibliothèque Thomiste*, no. 3, 123–40. Paris: Vrin, 1923. [Reprinted in *Parole* 1, 31–50.]

5 "Ascèse et péché originel." *VS* 9, no. 41 (February 1923): 547–51.

6 "Aux incroyants." *VS* 9, no. 49 (October 1923): 93–5.

7 "Bulletin d'histoire des doctrines chrétiennes." *RSPT* 12 (1923): 214–35, 250–3.

8 "Chronique de théologie mystique. Idéal monastique et vie chrétienne." *VS* 7, no. 40 (January 1923): 441–5.

1924

9 "La raison psychologique du développement du dogme." *RSPT* 13 (1924): 44–51. [Reprinted in *Parole* 1, 51–8.]

10 "Bulletin d'histoire des doctrines chrétiennes." *RSPT* 13 (1924): 221–39, 255–63.

11 "Review of P. Rotta, *S. Tommaso e il pensiero classico* (ed., *S. Tommaso d'Aquino. Pubblicazione commemorativa del sesto centenario della canonizzazione*, Vita e Pensiero, Milano 1923, 51–83)." *BT*, no. 3 (July 1924): 75.

12 "Review of A. Legendre, *Introduction à l'étude de la Somme Théologique de Saint Thomas d'Aquin* (Blond, Paris 1923)." *BT*, no. 3 (July 1924): 72–4.

13 "Review of A. Thiery, *Commentaire du Traité de l'Ame d'Aristote. Traduction française du texte latin de S. Thomas d'Aquin commentant le traité de l'Ame laissé par Aristote.*" *BT*, no. 2 (May 1924): 52–3.

14 "Review of A.G. Pealez, *El patriotismo y la moral segun S. Thomàs* (in *CT*, September 1923, 171–85)." *BT*, no. 5 (November 1924): 172–3.

15 "Review of F. Macler, *Ile de Chypre. Notices de manuscrits arméniens* (in *Revue de l'Orient chrétien*, XXIII (1922–23), 172–98)." *BT*, no. 2 (May 1924): 51–2.

16 "Review of F. Pelster s.j., *Zur Forschung nach den echten Schriften der hl. Thomas von Aquin* (in *Philosophisches Jahrbuch*, XXXVI (1923), 36–49)." *BT*, no. 2 (May 1924): 54–5.

17 "Review of G. Bardy, *Notes sur les sources patristiques greques de S. Thomas dans la 1ère Partie de la Somme Théologique* (in *RSPT*, 1923 (XII), 493–502)." *BT*, no. 3 (July 1924): 76.

18 "Review of J.B. Kors o.p., *La justice primitive et le péche originel d'après S. Thomas. Les Sources. La Doctrine* (Bibl. Thomiste II, Le Saulchoir, Kain 1922)." *BT*, no. 3 (July 1924): 76–7.

19 "Review of R. Schultes o.p., *Introductio in Historiam Dogmatum* (Paris, 1923); Idem, *De definibilitate conclusionum theologicarum. Conspectus historicus doctrinae scolasticorum* (*CT*, mai 1921, 305–333); F. Marin Sola o.p., 'Respuesta a un estudio historico sobre la conclusion teologica' (*CT*, septembre 1921, 165–194); R. Schultes o.p., 'Responsio ad «Respuesta a un estudio historico»' (*CT*, mars 1922, 168–176); F. Marin Sola o.p., *La evolucion homogenea del Dogma catolico* (Madrid, 1923)." *BT*, no. 3 (July 1924): 79–83.

1925

20 "*Authentica* et *Magistralia*. Deux lieux théologiques au XIIe et XIIIe siècles." *DT* 28 (1925): 257–85. [Reprinted in *Théologie au XIIe*, 351–65.]

21 "Bulletin d'histoire des doctrines chrétiennes." *RSPT* 14 (1925): 217–47.

22 "Jacques de Brescia." In *Dictionnaire de théologie catholique*, vol. 8, 291–2. Paris: Librairie Letouzey et Ané, 1925.

23 "Jacques de Lausanne." In *Dictionnaire de théologie catholique*, vol. 8, 298–9. Paris: Librairie Letouzey et Ané, 1925.

24 "Jacques de S. Dominique." In *Dictionnaire de théologie catholique*, vol. 8, 299–300. Paris: Librairie Letouzey et Ané, 1925.

25 "Janssenboy Corneille." In *Dictionnaire de théologie catholique*, vol. 8, 531. Paris: Librairie Letouzey et Ané, 1925.

26 "Janssenboy Nicolas." In *Dictionnaire de théologie catholique*, vol. 8, 531–2. Paris: Librairie Letouzey et Ané, 1925.

27 "Javelli." In *Dictionnaire de théologie catholique*, vol. 8, 535–7. Paris: Librairie Letouzey et Ané, 1925.

28 "Jean de Fribourg." In *Dictionnaire de théologie catholique*, vol. 8, 761–2. Paris: Librairie Letouzey et Ané, 1925.

29 "Jean de Montenero." In *Dictionnaire de théologie catholique*, vol. 8, 791. Paris: Librairie Letouzey et Ané, 1925.

30 "Kilwardby." In *Dictionnaire de théologie catholique*, vol. 8, 2354–6. Paris: Librairie Letouzey et Ané, 1925.

31 "Klapwell ou Clapwel, Richard." In *Dictionnaire de théologie catholique*, vol. 8, 2357–8. Paris: Librairie Letouzey et Ané, 1925.

32 "Knippenberg." In *Dictionnaire de théologie catholique*, vol. 8, 2360–1. Paris: Librairie Letouzey et Ané, 1925.

33 "Koellin." In *Dictionnaire de théologie catholique*, vol. 8, 2370–2. Paris: Librairie Letouzey et Ané, 1925.

34 "Labat." In *Dictionnaire de théologie catholique*, vol. 8, 2386. Paris: Librairie Letouzey et Ané, 1925.

35 "Laberthonie, Pierre Thomas." In *Dictionnaire de théologie catholique*, vol. 8, 2387. Paris: Librairie Letouzey et Ané, 1925.

36 "Labye." In *Dictionnaire de théologie catholique*, vol. 8, 2392–3. Paris: Librairie Letouzey et Ané, 1925.

37 "Lafon." In *Dictionnaire de théologie catholique*, vol. 8, 2446–7. Paris: Librairie Letouzey et Ané, 1925.

38 "Lambert." In *Dictionnaire de théologie catholique*, vol. 8, 2470. Paris: Librairie Letouzey et Ané, 1925.

39 "Las Casas." In *Dictionnaire de théologie catholique*, vol. 8, 2620–1. Paris: Librairie Letouzey et Ané, 1925.

40 "Pro fidei supernaturalitate illustranda." In *Xenia Thomistica*, edited by P. Sadoc Szabó, 297–307. Rome: Typis Polyglottis Vaticanis, 1925.

41 "Review of A. Bernareggi, *S. Tommaso d'Aquino e la repressione dell'errore* (in *SC*, July-September 1924, 54–86)." *BT*, no. 3 (May 1925): 289–90.

42 "Review of A. Michel, *Justice originelle* (*Dictionnaire théologique catholique*, volume VIII, Paris 1925, coll. 2020–2042)." *BT*, no. 5 (September 1925): 345–7.

43 "Review of A. Wautier D'Aygalliers, *Ruysbroek l'Admirable* (Perrin 1923)." *BT*, no. 4 (July 1925): 308.

44 "Review of A.A. Fredelghens, *Doctrine de S.Thomas d'Aquin au sujet du sacre-ment de Pénitence et de la Confession aux laiques* (in *Miscellanea Tomista (Est. Franc. XXXIV)*, Barcelona 1924, 302–325)." *BT*, no. 3 (May 1925): 287–8.

45 "Review of D. Lallement, *Commentaire de S. Thomas d'Aquin. La doctrine sacrée* (in *Lumen*, 1923 (IV), 30–43, 98–115 and 163–73)." *BT*, no. 1 (January 1925): 199.

46 "Review of F. Marin-Sola o.p., *La Evolución homogénea del Dogma catolico* (Madrid 1923); Idem., *L'évolution homogène du Dogme catholique* (Fribourg-Paris 1924, 2 ed., 2 vols.); R. Schultes o.p., *Introductio in Historiam Dogmatum* (Paris 1923)." *BT*, no. 1 (January 1925): 196–8.

47 "Review of H.X. Arquilliere, *Jacques de Viterbe* (in *Dictionnaire de théologie catholique*, Paris 1925, volume VII, coll. 305–309)." *BT*, no. 3 (May 1925): 294–5.

48 "Review of J.-B. Kors, *La justice primitive et le péché originel d'après S. Thomas. Les Sources. La Doctrine* (Bibl. Thomiste II, Le Saulchoir, Kain 1922); Van der Meersch, *De distinctione inter justitiam originalem et gratiam sanctificantem* (in *Collationes Brugenses*, 1922 (XXII), Extrait de 20pp.); N. Sanders o.m., *De oorspronkelijke gerechtigheid en de erfzonde volgens S. Thomas* (in 'De Katholieke Missiën', 1923, 400–10); J. Loppens, *Une controverse récente sur la nature du péché originel* (in *ETL*, 1924 (I), 185–91); G. Huarte s.j., *De distinctione inter justitiam originalem et gratia sanctificantem* (in *G*, 1924 (V), 183–207)." *BT*, no. 1 (January 1925): 220–1.

49 "Review of M. Cordovani o.p., *Ciò che manca alla gloria di S. Tommaso* (in *MD*, 1924 (XLI), 93–6; and in *L'attualità di S. Tommaso*, Milano 1924, 122–6); A. Bernareggi, *Ciò che manca alla gloria di S. Tommaso* (in *SC*, July-September 1924, 190–4); M. Grabmann, *De metodo historico in studiis scholasticis adhibenda* (in *CT*, 1923 (XXVII), 194–209)." *BT*, no. 4 (July 1925): 321–2.

50 "Review of M. Grabmann, *La Somme théologique de S. Thomas d'Aquin. Introduction historique et pratique* (Paris 1925)." *BT*, no. 5 (September 1925): 332–5.

51 "Review of M. Grabmann, *De Summae D. Thomae Aq. theologicae studio in ordine Fratrum Praedicatorum jam seculis XIII et XIV vigente* (in AA. VV., *Misc. Dom. in memoriam VII anni saecularis ab obitu S. Patris Dominici*, Rome 1923, 151–61); Idem., *Hilfsmittel des Thomasstudiums aus alter Zeit (Abreviationes, Concordantiae, Tabulae) auf Grund handschriftlicher Forschungen dargestellt* (in *DT*, 1923 (I), 13–43, 97–122, 373–80); Idem., *La scuola tomistica italiana nel XIII e principio del XIV secolo* (in *RFN*, 1923 (XV), 97–155); Idem., *Eine Ungedruckte Verteidigung der theologischen Summa des hl. Thomas von Aq. aus der ältesten Thomistenschule (Cod. Vat. lat. 4287)* (in *DT*, 1924 (II), 270–6); I. Taurisano o.p., *Discepoli e biografi di S. Tommaso* (in AA.VV., *S. Tommaso d'Aquino. Miscellanea storico-artistica*, Rome 1924); A. Walz o.p., *Ordinationes Capitolorum generalium*

de S. Thoma ejusque cultu et doctrina (in *Analecta S. Ordinis F. Praedicatorum,* 1923 (XXXI), 168–73)." *BT*, no. 3 (May 1925): 290–2.

52 " 'Maître' Thomas est-il une 'autorité'? Note sur les deux lieux théologiques au XIIᵉ siècle: Les *auctoritates* et les *magistralia.*" *RT* 30 (1925): 187–94.

1926

53 "Bulletin d'histoire des doctrines chrétiennes." *RSPT* 15 (1926): 422–46.

54 "Le *De spiritu immaginativo* de R. Kilwardby, O.P. (+ 1279)." *RSPT* 15 (1926): 507–17.

55 "Ledesma, Barthélemy de." In *Dictionnaire de théologie catholique,* vol. 9, 126. Paris: Librairie Letouzey et Ané, 1926.

56 "Ledesma, Martin de." In *Dictionnaire de théologie catholique,* vol. 9, 126. Paris: Librairie Letouzey et Ané, 1926.

57 "Ledesma, Pierre de." In *Dictionnaire de théologie catholique,* vol. 9, 126–7. Paris: Librairie Letouzey et Ané, 1926.

58 "Lemos, Thomas." In *Dictionnaire de théologie catholique,* vol. 9, 210–11. Paris: Librairie Letouzey et Ané, 1926.

59 "Leone, Denis." In *Dictionnaire de théologie catholique,* vol. 9, 427. Paris: Librairie Letouzey et Ané, 1926.

60 "Lopez, Louis." In *Dictionnaire de théologie catholique,* vol. 9, 934. Paris: Librairie Letouzey et Ané, 1926.

61 "Lorens, ou Laurent d'Orléans." In *Dictionnaire de théologie catholique,* vol. 9, 934–5. Paris: Librairie Letouzey et Ané, 1926.

62 "Loth, Louis-Bertrand." In *Dictionnaire de théologie catholique,* vol. 9, 939. Paris: Librairie Letouzey et Ané, 1926.

63 "Maflix." In *Dictionnaire de théologie catholique,* vol. 9, 1509–10. Paris: Librairie Letouzey et Ané, 1926.

64 "Magalhaens." In *Dictionnaire de théologie catholique,* vol. 9, 1510. Paris: Librairie Letouzey et Ané, 1926.

65 "Marcel d'Ancyre." In *Dictionnaire de théologie catholique,* vol. 9, 1993–8. Paris: Librairie Letouzey et Ané, 1926.

66 "Marchese." In *Dictionnaire de théologie catholique,* vol. 9, 2007. Paris: Librairie Letouzey et Ané, 1926.

67 "Mariales." In *Dictionnaire de théologie catholique,* vol. 9, 2335–6. Paris: Librairie Letouzey et Ané, 1926.

68 "Review of A. Landgraf, *Das Wesen der lässlichen Sünde in der Scholastik bis Thomas v. Aquin. Eine dogmengeschichtliche Untersuchung nach den gedruckten und ungedruckten Quellen* (Bamberg 1923); Idem., 'Partes animae normae gravitatis peccati. Inquisitio dogmatico-historica' (in *Bogoslovia,* 1924 (II), 97–117); Idem., 'De necessaria relatione caritatis ad bonitatem moralem

actuum humanorum' (in *Bogoslavia Vestnik*, 1924 (IV), 35–50, 127–44, 212–25)." *BT*, no. 4 (July 1926): 119–20.

69 "Review of A. Meozzi, *Tommaso d'Aquino. De Regimine principum. Traduzione e introduzione* (Lanciano 1924)." *BT*, no. 1 (January 1926): 39.

70 "Review of A. Pirotta o.p., *S. Thomae Aq. In Aristotelis Librum de Anima Commentarium* (Torino, 1925)." *BT*, no. 1 (January 1926): 32.

71 "Review of C. Boyer s.j., *S. Thomas et S. Augustin* (in *SC*, July-September 1924, 22–34); F. Marcos del Rio o.s.a., 'El conocimento segùn S. Tomàs y S. Augustin' (in *Ciudad de Dios*, 1925, n. CXL, 401ff.; 1925, CXLI, 163–201; 1926, CX–IV, 355–87; 1926, CXLV, 5–29); A. Gardeil o.p., 'Le 'Mens' d'après S. Augustin et S. Thomas d'Aq. (in RSPT, 1924 (XIII), 145–61); M. Grabmann, *Der göttliche Grund menschlicher Wahrheitserkenntnis nach Augustinus und Thomas v. Aq.* (Münster 1924); J. Sestili, 'Utrum Deus moveat immediate intellectum creatum. Ia P. q. 105, a. 3' (in *Xenia thomistica*, Typis Polyglottis Vaticanis, Rome 1925, vol. II, 155–85)." *BT*, no. 3 (May 1926): 97–100.

72 "Review of E. Flori, 'Il trattato 'De Regimine Principium' e le dottrine politiche di S. Tommaso' (in *ST*, July-September 1924, 134–169); M. Bloch, *Les rois thaumaturges. Étude sur le caractère surnaturel attribué à la puissance royale particulièrement en France et en Angleterre* (Strasbourg 1924)." *BT*, no. 2 (March 1926): 62–3.

73 "Review of E. Hocedez s.j., *Richard de Middleton. Sa vie, ses oeuvres, sa doctrine* (Louvain-Paris, 1925)." *BT*, no. 5–6 (September-November 1926): 205–6.

74 "Review of F. Herle s.j., 'L'agostinismo e l'aristotelismo nella scolastica del secolo XIII. Ulteriori discussioni e materiali' (in *Xenia Thomistica*, Typis Polyglottis Vaticanis, Rome 1925, 517–88); F. Pelster s.j., 'Der älteste Sentenzenkommentar aus der Oxforder Franziskanenschule. Ein Beitrag zur Geschichte des theologischen Lehrbetriebs an der Oxforder Universität' (in *SCH*, 1926 (I), 50–80); M.-D. Chenu o.p., 'Kilwardby (Robert)' (in *Dictionnaire de théologie catholique*, vol. VIII, Paris 1925, coll. 2354–2356); Idem., 'Klapwell (Richard)' (in *op. cit.*, coll. 2357–2358)." *BT*, no. 3 (May 1926): 102–4.

75 "Review of F.A. Blanche o.p., 'Les mots signifiant la relation dans la langue de S. Thomas d'Aquin' (in *Revue de Philosophie*, 1925 (XXV), 363–8); E. Gilson, 'Note pour l'explication de quelques raisonnements scripturaires usités au Moyen Age' (in *Revue d'Histoire Française*, 1925 (II), 350–60); J. Webert o.p., 'L'image dans l'oeuvre de S. Thomas et spécialement dans l'exposé doctrinal sur l'intelligence humaine' (in *RT*, 1926 (IX), 427–45); O. Lottin o.s.b., 'Le droit naturel chez S. Thomas et ses prédécesseurs. Commentaire historique de la Ia-IIae, q. 94' (Bruges 1925); A. Michel, 'Justice originelle' (in *Dictionnaire de théologie catholique*, vol. VIII, Paris 1925, coll. 2020–2042)." *BT*, no. 5–6 (September-November 1926): 217–19.

76 "Review of J. Mathis, *Divi Thomae Aq. De Regimine principum ad Regem Cypri et De Regimine Judaeorum ad ducissam Brabantiae* (Torino 1924)." *BT*, no. 1 (January 1926): 31–2.

77 "Review of J.-B. Destrez o.p., 'La 'pecia' dans les manuscrits du Moyen Age' (in *RSPT*, 1924 (XIII)." *BT*, no. 1 (January 1926): 27–8.

78 "Review of J.-B. Destrez o.p., 'Les disputes quodlibétiques de S. Thomas d'après la tradition manuscrite' (in *Mélanges thomistes* (Bibl. Thom. n. 2), Le Saulchoir 1923, 49–108); P. Synave o.p., 'La question disputée 'De sensibus sacrae scripturae', quodl. VII, a. 14–16 (avril 1256)' (in *Revue biblique*, 1926 (XXXV), 50–2)." *BT*, no. 2 (March 1926): 61.

79 "Review of M. Grabmann, *La Somme théologique de S. Thomas d'Aquin. Introduction historique et pratique* (Paris 1925); M. De Wulf, *Histoire de la philosophie médievale*, vol. I: 'Des origines jusqu'à Thomas d'Aquin' and vol. II: De Thomas d'Aquin jusqu'à la fin du Moyen Age' (Louvain-Paris, 1924–1925, 5 ed.)." *BT*, no. 3 (May 1926): 84–6.

80 "Review of M. Grabmann, 'Die italienische Thomistenschule des XIII und beginnenden XIV Jahrhunderts' (in *Mittelalterliches Geistesleben*, München 1926, 332–391); Idem., 'Kurze Mitteilungen über ungedrückte englische Thomisten der 13. Jahrh.' (in *DT*, 1925 (III), 205–14); Idem., 'Forschungen zur ältesten deutschen Thomistenschule des Dominikanenordens' (in *Xenia Thomistica*, Typis Polyglottis Vaticanis, Rome 1925, vol. III, 189–231)." *BT*, no. 5–6 (September-November 1926): 206.

81 "Review of M. Riquet, 'Thomas et les 'Auctoritates' en philosophie' (in *Archives de Philosophie*, vol. III, Paris 1925, 117–55)." *BT*, no. 3 (May 1926): 87.

82 "Review of M.-S. Gillet o.p., A.-D. Sertillanges o.p., H.-D. Noble o.p., G. Théry o.p., *Saint Thomas d'Aquin. Somme théologique (texte latin et traduction française)* (Paris 1925, vols. 1–2)." *BT*, no. 1 (January 1926): 30–1.

83 "Review of O. Lottin o.s.b., 'La définition classique de la loi (Commentaire de la Ia-IIae, q. 90' (in *Revue néoscholastique de la philosophie*, 1925 (XXVI), 129–45, 244–73); Idem., 'Le droit naturel chez S. Thomas et ses prédécesseurs. Commentaire historique de la Ia-IIae, q. 94' (in *ETL*, 1924 (I), 369–88; 1925 (II), 32–53, 345–66)." *BT*, no. 4 (July 1926): 120–1.

84 "Review of U. Mariani o.s.a., 'Scrittori politici medievali: Egidio Romanò (in *Giornale Dantesco*, 1925 (XXVIII), n. 2; 1926 (XXIX), nos. 1 and 2); J.S. Makaay o.s.a., *Der Traktat des Aegidius Romanus über die Einzigkeit der substantiellen Form, dargestellt und gewürdigt* (Würzburg 1924)." *BT*, no. 5–6 (September-November 1926): 207–8.

1927

85 "Autor, Actor, Author." *BC* 3 (1927): 81–6.

86 "La théologie comme science au XIIIe siècle." *AHDLM* 2 (1927): 37–71.

87 "Le *De conscientia* de R. Kilwardby, O.P. (+ 1297)." *RSPT* 16 (1927): 318–26.

88 "Notes de lexicographie philosophique médiévale. Collectio, collatio." *RSPT* 16 (1927): 435–46.

89 "Notice of A. Bacic o.p., 'Introductio compendiosa in opera S. Thomae' (in *A*, 1925 (II), 223–76)." *BT*, no. 3 (May 1927): 92.

90 "Préface." In *Saint Pierre*, by A. Gesquière, i–xii. Juvisy: Éditions du Cerf, 1927.

91 "Review of A. Feder s.j., 'Des Aquinaten Kommentar zu Pseudo-Dionysius 'De divinis nominibus'. Ein Beitrag zur Arbeitsmethode des hl. Thomas' (in *SCH*, 1926 (I), 321–51)." *BT*, no. 5 (September 1927): 179.

92 "Review of A. Lopez o.m., *Descripciòn de los manuscritos franciscanos existentes en la biblioteca provincial de Toledo.*" *BT*, no. 3 (May 1927): 93.

93 "Review of A. Teetaert o. cap., *La confession aux laïques dans l'Eglise latine depuis le VIIIe jusqu'au XIVe siècle* (Watteren-Paris 1926); A. Landgraf, 'Grundlagen für ein Verständnis der Busslehre der Früh- und Hochscholastik' (in *Zeitschrift für katholische Theologie*, 51 (1927), 161–94)." *BT*, no. 6 (November 1927): 215–18.

94 "Review of A. Van Hove, *La doctrine du miracle chez S. Thomas et son accord avec les principes de la recherche scientifique* (Bruges, 1927)." *BT*, no. 5 (September 1927): 184–5.

95 "Review of A. Zang, *Die 'Loci theologici' des Melchior Cano und die Methode des dogmatischen Beweis, Ein Beitrag zur theologischen Methodologie und ihren Geschichte* (München 1925); A. Gardeil o.p., 'Lieux théologiques' (in *Dictionnaire de théologie catholique*, vol. IX, Paris 1926, coll. 712–747)." *BT*, no. 4 (July 1927): 111–15.

96 "Review of B. Geyer, *Fr. Ueberwegs Grundiss der Geschichte der Philosophie* (Vol. II, Berlin 1928)." *BT*, no. 6 (November 1927): 219–21.

97 "Review of C. Baeumker, *Contra Amaurianos. Ein Anonymer warscheinlich dem Garnerius von Rochefort zugehöriger Traktat gegen die Amalrikaner aus dem Anfang des XIII Jarh. Mit Nachrichten über die übrigen unedierten Werke des Garnerius* (Münster 1926)." *BT*, no. 6 (November 1927): 222.

98 "Review of C. Prantl, *Geschichte der Logik im Abendlande* (4 vols., Leipzig 1926)." *BT*, no. 6 (November 1927): 208–10.

99 "Review of E. Gilson, 'Pourquoi S. Thomas a critiqué S. Augustin' (in *AHDLM*, 1926 (I), 5–127); C. Boyer, 'S. Thomas et S. Augustin d'après M. Gilson' (in *G*, 1927 (VIII), 106–10); A. Gardeil o.p., *La structure de l'âme et l'expérience mystique* (Paris 1927, 313–25)." *BT*, no. 5 (September 1927): 179–83.

100 "Review of F. Pelster s.j., *S. Thomae de Aq. Quaestiones de natura fidei ex Commentario in lib. IIIi Sententiarum, dist. 23 et 24, secundum fidem manuscriptorum denuo edidit* (Münster 1926)." *BT*, no. 3 (May 1927): 82.

101 "Review of G. Rabeau, *Introduction à l'Étude de la Théologie* (Paris, 1926)." *BT*, no. 6 (November 1927): 202–7.

102 "Review of G. Théry o.p., *Autour du décret de 1210. David de Dinant. Étude sur son panthéisme matérialiste* (Vol. I, Le Saulchoir-Kain 1925); Idem., *Autour du décret de 1210. Alexandre d'Aphrodise. Aperçu sur l'influence de sa noétique* (Vol. II, Le Saulchoir-Kain 1926)." *BT*, no. 6 (November 1927): 222.

103 "Review of I. Di Somma, 'De naturali participatione divini luminis in mente humana secundum S. Augustinum et S. Thomam' (in *G*, 1926 (VI), 321–38); F. Marcos, 'El conocimento segùn S. Tomàs y S. Augustin' (in *Ciudad de Dios*, 1926, n. CXLV, 427–47; 1926, n. CXLVI, 81–102)." *BT*, no. 5 (September 1927): 183.

104 "Review of J. Assenmacher, *Die Geschichte des Individuationsprinzips in der Scholastik* (Leipzig 1926)." *BT*, no. 6 (November 1927): 210–11.

105 "Review of J. Rivière, 'Sur l'origine des formules 'de condigno', 'de congruo'" (in *Bulletin de littérature ecclésiastique*, 1927, 75–88)." *BT*, no. 6 (November 1927): 214–15.

106 "Review of L.I. Newman, *Jewish Influence on Christian Reform Movements* (New York, 1925)." *BT*, no. 4 (July 1927): 132–34.

107 "Review of M. Browne, 'An sit authenticum opusculum S. Thomae 'De Regimine principum'" (in *A*, 1926 (III), 300–3); U. Mariani o.s.a., 'Il 'De Regimine principum' e le teorie politiche di Egidio Romano' (in *Giornale dantesco*, 1926 (XXIX), n. 1); J. Rivière, 'Lucques (Barthélémy de)' (in *Dictionnaire de théologie catholique*, vol. IX, Paris 1926, coll. 1062–1067)." *BT*, no. 3 (May 1927): 95–6.

108 "Review of M. De Wulf, 'Y eut-il une philosophie scholastique au Moyen Age?' (in *Revue néoscholastique de philosophie*, 1927 (XXVIII), 5–27)." *BT*, no. 3 (May 1927): 98–100.

109 "Review of M. Grabmann, 'Die logischen Schriften des Nikolaus von Paris und ihre Stellung in aristotelischen Bewegung des XIII Jahrhunderts' (in *Mittelalterliches Geistesleben*, München 1926, 222–48); Idem., 'Magister Petrus von Hibernia, der Jugendlehrer des h. Thomas von Aquin. Seine Disputation vor König Manfred und seine Aristoteleskommentars' (Ibid., 249–65)." *BT*, no. 6 (November 1927): 223–4.

110 "Review of M. Grabmann, 'Studien über Ulrich von Strassburg. Bilder wissenschaftlichen Lebens und Strebens aus der Schule Albert des Grossen' (in *Mittelalterliches Geistesleben*, München 1926, 147–221); Idem., 'Das Ulrich Engelberti von Strassburg O.P. (+ 1277) Abhandlung 'De pulchro'. Untersuchungen und Texte' (in *Stzungsben d. bayer. Akad. d. Wiss. 1925*, München 1926); U. Daguillon, 'Ulrich von Strassburg O.P. (+ 1277). Notice littéraire et édition des deux premiers livres de sa 'Summa de bono"

(in *Position des thèses. École nationale des Chartes*, Paris 1927, 31–6)." *BT*, no. 6 (November 1927): 224.

111 "Review of M.-D. Roland-Gosselin o.p., *Le 'De ente et essentia' de S. Thomas d'Aquin. Texte établi d'après les manuscrits parisiens. Introduction, Notes, et Études historiques* (Le Saulchoir-Kain 1926)." *BT*, no. 6 (November 1927): 210.

112 "Review of M.-J. Lagrange o.p., 'Comment s'est transformée la pensée religieuse d'Aristote' (in *RT*, 1926 (IX), 285–329); J. Chevalier, 'Aristote et S. Thomas d'Aquin, ou l'idée de création' (in *Lettres*, April 1927, 427–47)." *BT*, no. 4 (July 1927): 129–30.

113 "Review of N. Carame, *Avicennae Metaphysices Compendium*." *BT*, no. 4 (July 1927): 131–2.

114 "Review of O. Lottin o.s.b., 'Les premiers linéaments du traité de la syndérèse au Moyen Age. Le créateur du traité de la syndérèse' (in *Revue néoscholastique de philosophie*, 1926, 422–54; 1927, 197–222); M.-D. Chenu 'Le 'De conscientia' de R. Kilwardby O.P. + 1279' (in *RSPT*, 1927 (XVI), 318–26); O. Lottin o.s.b., 'Les définitions du libre arbitre au XIIe siècle' (in *RT*, 1927 (X), 104–20, 214–30); Idem., 'La théorie du libre arbitre pendant le premier tiers du XIIIe siècle' (in *RT*, 1927 (X), 350–83)." *BT*, no. 6 (November 1927): 211–12.

115 "Review of P. Castagnoli, 'Gli Scolastici del Secolo XIII e del Principio del XIV. Rassegnà' (in *DT*, 1926 (III), 281–309, 478–515)." *BT*, no. 6 (November 1927): 221–2.

116 "Review of P. Mandonnet o.p., 'Les Questions disputées de S. Thomas d'Aquin' (in St. Thomas Aquinas, *Quaestiones disputatae*, Paris 1925, 1–24); P. Synave o.p., 'Le problème chronologique des Questions disputées de S. Thomas d'Aquin' (in *RT*, 1926 (IX), 154–59)." *BT*, no. 3 (May 1927): 93–4.

117 "Review of P. Mandonnet o.p., 'Les disputes quodlibétiques de S. Thomas d'Aquin' (in St. Thomas Aquinas, *Quaestiones quodlibetales*, Paris 1926); Idem., 'S. Thomas d'Aquin créateur de la dispute quodlibétique' (in *RSPT*, 1926 (XV), 477–506; 1927 (XVI), 5–38); P. Synave o.p., 'L'ordre des Quodlibets VII à XI de S. Thomas d'Aquin' (in *RT*, 1926 (IX), 43–7)." *BT*, no. 3 (May 1927): 94–5.

1928

118 "Bulletin de théologie spéculative. Introduction à la théologie." *RSPT* 17 (1928): 798–800.

119 "Bulletin d'histoire des doctrines chrétiennes." *RSPT* 17 (1928): 308–39.

120 "La première diffusion du thomisme à Oxford. Klapwell et ses 'notes' sur les Sentences." *AHDLM* 3 (1928): 185–200.

121 "Notes de lexicographie philosophique médiévale: *Antiqui, moderni.*" *RSPT* 17 (1928): 82–94.

122 "Review of A.-D. Sertillanges o.p., *S. Thomas d'Aquin. Somme théologique. La Création. Ia Pars, qu. 44–49* (French trans., Paris 1927); Idem., 'La création' (in *RT*, 1928 (XI), 97–115)." *BT*, no. 5–6 (September-November 1928): 385–6.

123 "Review of E. Chiocchetti, *San Tommaso* (Milan 1925); E. Buonaiuti, *Tommaso d'Aquino* (Rome 1924)." *BT*, no. 1 (January 1928): 245–6.

124 "Review of E. Flori, *Il trattato 'De regimine principum' e le dottrine politiche di S. Tommaso.*" *BT*, no. 4 (July 1928): 334.

125 "Review of E. Gilson, *Le thomisme. Introduction au système de S. Thomas d'Aquin* (3 ed., Paris 1927)." *BT*, no. 1 (January 1928): 242–5.

126 "Review of J. Maritain, *Art et scholastique* (2 ed., Paris 1927)." *BT*, no. 4 (July 1928): 337–8.

127 "Review of O. Dittrich, *Geschichte der Ethik. Die Systeme der Moral Altertum bis zur Gegenwart* (Vol. III, Leipzig 1926); A. Dempf, *Die Ethik des Mittelalters* (München 1927)." *BT*, no. 2–3 (March-May 1928): 297–8.

128 "Review of V. Grumel, 'S. Thomas et la doctrine des Grecs sur la procession du Saint-Esprit' (in *Echos d'Orient*, 1926, n. 25, 257–328)." *BT*, no. 5–6 (September-November 1928): 384–5.

1929

129 "Bulletin d'histoire des doctrines chrétiennes." *RSPT* 18 (1929): 691–700, 755–76.

130 "Pour l'histoire de la philosophie médiévale." *NS* 3 (1929): 65–74.

131 "Review of E. De Bruyne, *Saint Thomas d'Aquin. Le milieu, l'homme, la vision du monde.*" *BT*, no. 4 (July 1929): 531–35.

132 "Review of E. Vansteenberghen, 'Molinisme' (in *Dictionnaire de théologie catholique*, vol. X, Paris 1927, coll. 2094–2187); L. Pastor, *Geschichte der Päpste seit Ausgang des Mittelalters* (vol. I, Freiburg 1927); J. Brodrick s.j., *The life and work of Blessed Robert Bellarmine* (London 1928); A.E. Withacre o.p., 'A saint among the theologians' (in *B*, 1928 (IX), 221–34, 291–303, 418–36); J. Brodrick s.j., 'A theologian among the saints. A reply (in *B*, 1928 (IX), 357–76); A. Perez Coyena s.j., 'Catedraticos de teologia espanoles en Roma. Miguel Vasquez de Padilla' (in *Estudios eclesiasticos*, 1926 (V), 26–43); J. Carreyre, 'Meyer ou Meyere (Liévin de)' (in *Dictionnaire de théologie catholique*, vol. X, Paris 1927, coll. 1631–1634)." *BT*, no. 6 (September-November 1929): 598–601.

133 "Review of H.-X. Arquillière, *Le plus ancien traité de l'Église. Jacques de Viterbe: 'De regimine christiano' (1301–1302). Étude des sources et édition*

critique; J. Rivière, *Le problème de l'Église et de l'État au temps de Philippe le Bel. Étude de théologie positive* (Louvain-Paris 1926); U. Mariana o.s.a., 'Giacomo da Viterbo. Cenni biografici' (in *Archivio della Reale Società Romana di storia patria*, 1926 (XLVIII), 137–70); Idem., *Scrittori politici agostiniani del secolo XIV* (Firenze 1927)." *BT*, no. 2 (March 1929): 498–9.

134 "Review of M. Grabmann, *Einführung in die Summa Theologiae des hl. Thomas v. Aquin* (Freiburg 1928); J. de Tonquedec, *Préface à la critique de connaissance* (Paris 1929, XXX); M.-D. Chenu o.p., 'Pour l'histoire de la philosophie médiévale' (in *NS*, 1929 (III), 65–74); G. Bruni, *Progressive Scholasticism* (St. Louis-London 1929)." *BT*, no. 5–6 (September-November 1929): 615–23.

135 "Review of R. Bernard o.p., 'Mater divinae gratiae' (in *RSPT*, 1927 (XVI), 405–24); J. Bittremieux, *De mediatione universali B. Mariae Virginis quod gratias* (Bruges 1926); M.-B. Lavaud o.p., 'Marie, médiatrice, d'après un livre récent' (in *VS*, 1927 (XVI), 345–461); Idem., 'La causalité instrumentale de Marie médiatrice' (in *RT*, 1927 (X), 423–45); L. Wasilkowski, 'Posrednictwo N. Marji Panny w teologji sw Tomasza z Ak.' (in *Ateneum Kaplanskie*, 1926); B.H. Merkelbach o.p., 'Het middelaardschp van Maria in de leer van den hl. Thomas' (in *De Stand v. Maria*, 1927 (VII), 257–70, 289–97); O.P. de Wilde, *Maria, Middelares van alle genaden* (Antwerp 1927); A. Fernandez, 'De mediatione B. Virginis secundum doctrina D. Thomae' (in *CT*, 1928, XXXVII, 145–70)." *BT*, no. 1 (January 1929): 444–6.

136 "Review of R.W. Carlyle and A.J. Carlyle, *A History of Mediaeval Political Theory in the West* (vol. v, Edinburgh 1928); B. Landry, *L'idée de chrétienté chez les scholastiques du XIIIe siècle* (Paris 1929)." *BT*, no. 5–6 (September-November 1929): 574–7.

137 "Review of V. McNabb o.p., *The Catholic Church and Philosophy* (London 1927); E.A. Pace, 'The Church and Scholasticism in their historical relations' (in *Catholic Historical Review*, 1928 (VIII), 55–68)." *BT*, no. 5–6 (September-November 1929): 627.

138 "Review of V.D. Carro o.p., 'De Pedro de Soto a Domingo Bañez' (in *CT*, 1928, XXXVII, 145–78); Idem., 'El maestro fray Pedro de Soto' (in *CT*, 1927, XXXV, 159–82, 329–58; 1928, XXXVI, 169–201)." *BT*, no. 5–6 (September-November 1929): 607–8.

1930

139 "Bulletin d'histoire des doctrines chrétiennes." *RSPT* 19 (1930): 569–81, 616–36.

140 "Les réponses de S.Thomas et de Kilwardby à la consultation de Jean de Verceil (1271)." In *Mélanges Mandonnet. Études d'histoire littéraire et doctrinale du Moyen-Âge. Bibliothèque Thomiste*, no. 14, 191–222. Paris: Vrin, 1930.

141 "Les études religieuses en France et en Allemagne autour de 1830." *VI* 6 (1930): 52–6.

142 "Pour lire saint Augustin." *VS* 24, no. 131–2 (1930): 135–57.

143 "Review of A. Amelli o.s.b., 'Tommaso d'Aquino poeto e musico eucaristico' (in *Bollettino Ceciliano*, May 1928); Idem., 'Tommaso d'Aquino poeto e musico eucaristico' (in *L'Osservatore Romano*, June 23 and 24 1928, nn. 145–6)." *BT*, no. 1 (January 1930): 24.

144 "Review of A. Wilmart o.s.b., 'La tradition littéraire et textuelle de l'*Adoro te devote*' (in *RTAM*, 1929 (I), 21–40, 146–76)." *BT*, no. 1 (January 1930): 25–7.

145 "Review of F. Trucco, *San Tommaso d'Aquino poeta della Santissima Eucarestia. Studio storico-critico e letterario sulla poesia tomistica con versione italiana sul metro latino e commento ascetico e dommatico* (Sarzana 1928); Idem., 'La paternità tomistica del 'Verbum supernum" (in *SC*, 1928 (XII), 268–78); Idem.,' Le caratteristiche della poesia tomistica' (in *SC*, 1928 (XII), 363–72); Idem., 'Il metro della poesia tomistica' (in *SC*, 1928 (XII), 437–48); Idem., 'Cinque strofe ritmiche di S. Tommaso d'Aquino poco note e la errata collocazione di una di esse in certe edizioni' (in *SC*, 1929 (XIII), 48–55); F.J.E. Raby, *A History of Christian-Latin Poetry from the Beginning to the Close of the Middle Ages* (Oxford 1927)." *BT*, no. 1 (January 1930): 22–4.

146 "Review of G. Lacombe, *Prepositini, cancelarii Parisiensis (1206–1210), opera omnia* (vol. I, Paris 1927); Idem., 'Prepositinus cancellarius Parisiensis' (in *NS*, 1927 (I), 307–19)." *BT*, no. 2 (March 1930): 36–40.

147 "Review of H. Pirenne, 'La duchesse Aleyde de Brabante et le 'De regimine Judaeorum' de S. Thomas d'Aquin' (in *Revue néoscholastique de philosophie*, 1928 (XXX), 193–205)." *BT*, no. 5 (September 1930): 154–5.

148 "Review of M. Grandclaude, 'Les particularités du 'De regimine principum' de S. Thomas' (in *Revue historique de droit français et étranger*, 1929, 665–6)." *BT*, no. 5 (September 1930): 153–4.

149 "Une opinion inconnue de l'école de Gilbert de la Porrée." *RHE*, no. XXVI (1930): 347–53.

1931

150 "Bulletin d'histoire des doctrines chrétiennes." *RSPT* 20 (1931): 553–9, 578–85.

151 "De Melchior Cano au P. Gardeil. La méthode de la théologie." *RDO* 38 (1931): 660–5.

152 "Le P. Mandonnet et les études médiévales." *La Croix*, 15–16 March 1931.

153 "Le sens et les leçons d'une crise religieuse." *VI* 13 (10 December 1931): 356–80.

154 "Les nouvelles Études carmélitaines." *VSS* 29, (July 1 1931): 62–4. [Partially reprinted in *Le Père Bruno de Jésus-Marie* (Paris: Desclée de Brouwer, 1964) 27–9.]

155 "Review of A. Landgraf, 'Die Erkenntnis der heiligmachenden Gnade in der Frühscholastik' (in *SCH*, 1929 (IV), 1–37, 189–220, 352–89)." *BT*, no. 2 (April 1931): 286.

156 "Review of O. Lottin o.s.b., 'Le traité du libre arbitre depuis le chancellier Philippe jusqu'à Saint Thomas d'Aquin' (in *RT*, 1927 (X), 446–72; 1929 (XII), 234–69); Idem., 'Le libre arbitre chez saint Thomas d'Aquin' (in *RT*, 1929 (XII), 400–30); M. Wittmann, 'Die Lehre von der Willensfreiheit bei Thomas v. Aquin, historische untersucht' (in *Philosopisches Jahrbuch*, 40 (1927), 170–88, 285–305)." *BT*, no. 2 (April 1931): 274–6.

157 "Review of U. Mariani o.s.a., 'La funzione storica del Tomismo e Dante' (in *Giornale Dantesco*, 1930 (XXXI), excerpt)." *BT*, no. 2 (April 1931): 268.

1932

158 "La psychologie de la foi dans la théologie du XIIIe siècle. Genèse de la doctrine de S. Thomas, IIa-IIae, q. 2, a. 1." In *Études d'histoire littéraire et doctrinale. Deuxième série*. Publications de l'Institut d'Études Médiévales d'Ottawa, no. 2, 163–91. Paris; Ottawa: Vrin, 1932. [Reprinted in *Parole* 1, 77–104.]

159 "La surnaturalisation des vertus." *BT* 9, no. 3 (1932): 93–6. [Reprinted in *Parole* 1, 105–11.]

160 "Les yeux de la foi." *RDO* 38 (1932): 653–60. [Reprinted in *Parole* 1, 21–7.]

161 "L'amour dans la foi." *BT* 9, no. 3 (1932): 97–9. [Reprinted in *Parole* 1, 105–11.]

162 "Préface." In *Le donné révélé et la théologie*. 2d ed., by Ambroise Gardeil, vii–xiv. Juvisy: Éditions du Cerf, 1932. [Reprinted as "Le donné révélé et la théologie" in *Parole* 1, 277–82.]

163 "A. de Pouzzoles." In *Études d'histoire littéraire et doctrinale du XIIIe siècle. Deuxième série*. Publications de l'Institut d'Études Médiévales d'Ottawa, no. 2, 203. Paris; Ottawa: Vrin, 1932.

164 "Bulletin d'histoire des doctrines chrétiennes." *RSPT* 21 (1932): 444–61, 466–8, 476–7.

165 "Maîtres et bacheliers de l'Université de Paris vers 1240. Description du manuscrit Paris, Bibl. Nat. lat. 15652." In *Études d'histoire littéraire et doctrinale du XIIIe siècle. Première série*. Publications de l'Institut d'Études Médiévales d'Ottawa, no. 1, 11–39. Paris; Ottawa: Vrin, 1932.

166 "Pour l'histoire de la notion de philosophie chrétienne." *RSPT* 21 (1932): 231–5.

167 "Présentation." In *Études d'histoire littéraire et doctrinale du XIIIe siècle. Première série.* Publications de l'Institut d'Études Médiévales d'Ottawa, no. 1, 7–10. Paris; Ottawa: Vrin, 1932.

168 "Review of C. Fabbricotti, *Commenti Tomistici. Memorie Sul Quesito Dell'Individuazione* (Firenze, 1929)." *BT*, no. 2 (April-June 1932): 516.

169 "Review of J. Peghaire c.s.sp., 'L'axiome 'Bonum est diffusivum sui' dans le néo-platonisme et le thomisme' (in *Revue de l'Université d'Ottawa*, 2 (1932), sect. spéc., 5–32)." *BT*, no. 2 (April-June 1932): 522.

170 "Review of J.-B. Manya, 'El talent i l'organisme segons la doctrina de Sant Tomàs' (in *Criterion*, 1929 (VI), 143–57, 436–48)." *BT*, no. 1 (January-March 1932): 418–19.

1933

171 "Allocution d'ouverture à la 2e journée d'études de la Société thomiste (Juvisy, 11 septembre 1933)." In *Le problème de la philosophie chrétienne*, 13–18. Juvisy: Éditions du Cerf, 1933.

172 "Avant-propos." In *La renaissance du XIIe siècle. Les écoles et l'enseignement*, by G. Paré, A. Brunet, and P. Tremblay. Publications de l'Institut d'Études Médiévales d'Ottawa, no. 3, 5–12. Paris; Ottawa: Vrin, 1933.

173 "Bulletin d'histoire des doctrines chrétiennes." *RSPT* 22 (1933): 517–25.

174 "Grec ou chrétien?" *VI* 19 (25 January 1933): 242–5.

175 "Notes de lexicographie philosophique médiévale: *Sufficiens.*" *RSPT* 22 (1933): 251–9.

176 "Review of A. Sandreau, 'Pour fixer la terminologie mystique' (in *VS*, vol. XX, June 1929, 129–46); P. Remy o.f.m. cap., 'À propos d'une enquête pour fixer la terminologie mystique' (in *Les études franciscaines*, 1931 (XLIII) 496–513, 615–29, 738–53; 1932 (XLIV), 67–83)." *BT*, no. 2 (April-June 1933): 858–60.

177 "Review of Crisogono de Jesus Sacramentado o. carm., *La perfection et la mystique selon les principes de S. Thomas* (Bruges 1932); R. Garrigou-Lagrange o.p., 'Les dons ont-ils un mode humain?' (in *VSS*, vol. XXXIII, August 1932, 65–83)." *BT*, no. 2 (April-June 1933): 858.

178 "Review of J. Maritain, 'S. Jean de la Croix practicien de la contemplation' (in *EC*, 1931 (XVI), 62–109); A. Lemonnyer o.p., 'S. Thomas maître de vie surnaturelle' (in *AD*, 67 (1931), 290–4); Idem., 'La théologie comme science particulière' (in *VSS*, vol. XXXIII, 1932, 158–66)." *BT*, no. 1 (January-March 1933): 706–7.

179 "Review of M. Cordovani o.p., *La teologia del Purgatorio nella seconda Cantica di Dante* (Arezzo 1928); F. Orestano, 'San Tommaso e Dante' (in *La Tradizione*, 1930 (III), 131–9); Idem., 'Discontinuità dottrinali nella

Divina Commedia' (in *Sophia*, 1933 (I), 3–21); G. Busnelli s.j., 'L'origine dell'anima razionale secondo Dante e Alberto Magno' (in *CC*, 80 (1929), II, 289–300; III, 229–37, 336–47); B. Nardi, 'L'origine dell'anima umana secondo Dante' (in *Giornale critico della filosofia italiana*, 1931 (XII), 433–56; 1932 (XIII), 45–56, 81–102); Idem., *Saggi di filosofia dantesca* (Rome-Milan 1930)." *BT*, no. 3 (July-September 1933): 996–7.

1934

180 "Après dix ans." *BT*, no. 1 (January-March 1934): 1–3.

181 "Bulletin d'histoire des doctrines chrétiennes." *RSPT* 23 (1934): 463–74.

182 "Humanisme chrétien et culture classique." *RDO* 41 (1934): 461–7.

183 "Le R.P. M.-D. Gosselin, O.P." *BT*, no. 4 (October-December 1934): 329.

184 "Paroisses et oeuvres. Les exigences de l'Action catholique." *RDO* 41 (March 1934): 343–58.

185 "Review of G. Englhardt, *Die Entwicklung der dogmatischen Glaubenspsychologie in der mittelalterlichen Scholastik* (Münster, 1933)." *BT*, no. 4 (October-December 1934): 258–9.

186 "Review of G. Paré, A. Brunet, P. Tremblay, *La renaissance du XIIe siècle. Les écoles et l'enseignement* (Paris-Ottawa, 1933)." *BT*, no. 2–3 (April-September 1934): 208–9.

187 "Review of L. Halphen, 'Les universités au XIIIe siècle' (in *Revue historique* 166 (1931, I), 217–38; 167 (1931, II), 1–15)." *BT*, no. 2–3 (April-September 1934): 207.

188 "Review of M. Di Martino, *S. Tommaso d'Aquino 'Ars Musice'. Trattato Inedito Illustrato e Trascritto* (Napoli 1933)." *BT*, no. 1 (January-March 1934): 61.

189 "Review of M.M. Gorce, *L'essor de la pensée au moyen âge. Albert le grand. Thomas d'Aquin* (Paris, 1933)." *BT*, no. 2–3 (April-September 1934): 207–8.

190 "Review of S. d'Irsay, *Histoire des universités françaises et étrangères, des origines à nos jours* (vol. I, Paris 1933)." *BT*, no. 2–3 (April-September 1934): 206–7.

1935

191 "Position de la théologie." *RSPT* 24 (1935): 232–57. [Reprinted in *Parole* 1, 115–38.]

192 "Sentiment religieux et théologie." Preface in *Saint Albert le Grand, docteur de la médiation mariale*, by M.-M. Desmarais, 7–12. Ottawa, Paris: Publications de l'Insitut d'Études Médiévales d'Ottawa; Vrin, 1935. [Reprinted in *Parole* 1, 223–7.]

193 "Bulletin de théologie. Introduction à la théologie." *RSPT* 24 (1935): 705–7.

194 "Bulletin d'histoire des doctrines chrétiennes." *RSPT* 24 (1935): 347–56.

195 "Horace chez les théologiens." *RSPT* 24 (1935): 462–5.

196 "Le traité *De tempore* de R. Kilwardby." In *Aus der Geisteswelt des Mittelalters. Studien und Texte Martin Grabmann zur Vollendug des 60. Lebensjahres*, vol. 2, eds A. Lang, J. Lachner, and M. Schmaus, 855–61. Münster, 1935.

197 "Notice of A. Marc, *L'idée de l'être chez S. Thomas et dans la scholastique postérieure* (Paris 1933); Idem., 'L'idée thomiste de l'être et les analogies d'attribution et de proportionnalité' (in *Revue néoscholastique de philosophie*, XXXV (1933), 157–89)." *BT*, no. 5 (January-March 1935): 412.

198 "Notice of A. Rohner, 'Das Grundproblem der Metaphysik' (in *Philosophia perennis*, Regensburg 1930, 1075–88)." *BT*, no. 5 (January-March 1935): 412.

199 "Notice of A. Stolz, 'Positive und spekulative Theologie' (in *Divus Thomas* (Freiburg), 327–43)." *BT*, no. 8 (October-December 1935): 592.

200 "Notice of D. Garcia, 'Caracteres distintivos de la concepciòn tomista del universo' (in *Illustraciòn del clero*, XXV (1931), 99–102, 147–50, 170–2, 198–204, 213–17, 245–51)." *BT*, no. 5 (January-March 1935): 414.

201 "Notice of F. MacMahon, 'Thomistic metaphysics: a systematic explanation of the real' (in *NS*, 1934 (VIII), 240–59)." *BT*, no. 5 (January-March 1935): 412.

202 "Notice of G.M. Manser, 'Die Universalienlehre im Lichte von Akt und Potenz. Der noëtische Parallelismus' (in *Divus Thomas* (Fribourg), *XII (1934), 397–407).* "*BT*, no. 5 (January-March 1935): 394.

203 "Notice of Giocondo (Fra'), 'Entificazione dei reali' (in *Rivista Lasalliana*, I (1934), March)." *BT*, no. 5 (January-March 1935): 394.

204 "Notice of J. Brinktrine, 'Der dogmatische Beweis aus der Liturgie' (in *Scientia sacra. Festgabe Cardinal Schulte*, Cologne 1935, 231–51)." *BT*, no. 8 (October-December 1935): 595.

205 "Notice of J. Maritain, *Theonas' Conversations of a Sage* (New York 1933)." *BT*, no. 5 (January-March 1935): 413.

206 "Notice of J. van Well, *Ueber das Verhältnis des intellectus speculativus und des intellectus praticus zweinander bei Thomas von Aquin* (Bonn 1933)." *BT*, no. 5 (January-March 1935): 394.

207 "Notice of K. Kowalski, 'Wspolczesne odrodzenie metafizyki a Tomizm' (in *Ateneum Kaplanskie*, 1933, fas. 3)." *BT*, no. 5 (January-March 1935): 412.

208 "Notice of L. de Raeymacker, 'La structure métaphysique de l'être fini' (in *Revue néoscholastique de la philosophie*, XXXIV (1932), 187–217)." *BT*, no. 5 (January-March 1935): 413.

209 "Notice of M.-D. Chenu o.p., 'Position de la théologie' (in *RSPT*, 1935 (XXIV), 232–67)." *BT*, no. 8 (October-December 1935): 592.

210 "Notice of N. Appel, *Der dynamische Zug in der Metaphysik des hl. Thomas* (Bonn 1931)." *BT*, no. 5 (January-March 1935): 412.

211 "Notice of R. Kremer, 'Over het ziinsbegrif als middenput der thomistische Gedachte' (in *Kultuurleven*, VIII (1934), 240–59)." *BT*, no. 5 (January-March 1935): 412.

212 "Notice of S. Zarb, 'Num hagiographi sibi conscii fuerunt charismatis divinae inspirationis?' (in *A*, 1934 (XI), 228–44); G.-M. Perrella, 'In margine alla questione dell'apostolato come criterio di ispirazione' (in *DT*, XXXVII (1934), 510–16)." *BT*, no. 8 (October-December 1935): 594.

213 "Notice of S.M. Lozano, *Unidad de la ciencia sagrada y de la vida santa* (Salamanca 1932)." *BT*, no. 8 (October-December 1935): 592.

214 "Review of A. Forest, 'Thomisme et idéalisme' (in *Revue néoscholastique de philosophie*, 1934 (XXXVII), 317–36)." *BT*, no. 5 (January-March 1935): 414–15.

215 "Review of F. Olgiati, 'Il problema della conoscenza nella Neoscolastica italiana' (in *Indirizzi e conquiste della filosofia neoscolastica italiana*, Milan 1934, 43–160)." *BT*, no. 5 (January-March 1935): 409–10.

216 "Review of G. de Lagarde, *La naissance de l'esprit laïque au Moyen Age. Bilan du XIIIe siècle* (Saint-Paul-Trois-Châteaux 1935); A. Passerin d'Entrèves, *Appunti di storia delle dottrine politiche, la filosofia politica medioevale* (Torino 1934); G. della Rocca, *La politica in S. Tommaso* (Napoli 1934)." *BT*, no. 7 (July-September 1935): 522–3.

217 "Review of H.-D. Simonin, 'La théologie thomiste de la foi et le développement du dogme' (in *RT*, XVIII (1935), 537–56)." *BT*, no. 8 (October-December 1935): 590–1.

218 "Review of J. Maritain, *Sept leçons sur l'être et les premiers principes de la raison spéculative* (Paris, 1934)." *BT*, no. 5 (January-March 1935): 412–13.

219 "Review of J. Messaut, 'Le rôle intellectuel de la théologie dans l'apostolat' (in *RT*, XVIII (1935), 330–86); M.-M. Philippon, 'La théologie, science suprême de la vie humaine' (in *RT*, XVIII (1935), 387–421); F. Claverie, 'Théologie et conscience individuelle' (in *RT*, XVIII (1935), 422–45); F. Valette, 'Théologie et action codifiée' (in *RT*, XVIII (1935), 446–91); R. Garrigou-Lagrange, 'La théologie et la vie de la foi' (in *RT*, XVIII (1935), 492–514)." *BT*, no. 8 (October-December 1935): 592–4.

220 "Review of M. Casotti, 'La storia non è scienza' (in *RFN*, 1933 (XXV), 353–5); G. Ceriani, 'La storia e l'enciclopedia delle scienze' (in *RFN*, 1933 (XXV), 457–66); A. Bestetti, 'Il concetto di storia nella filosofia scolastica' (in *Indirizzi e conquiste della filosofia neoscolastica italiana*, Milan 1934, 183–91)." *BT*, no. 5 (January-March 1935): 352–3.

221 "Review of M. Grabmann, 'Die Wissenschaftsbegriff des hl. Thomas von Aquin und das Verhältnis von Glaube und Theologie zur Philosophie und weltlichen Wissenschaft' (in *Die Goerresgesellschaft und der Wissenschaftbegriff*, Cologne 1934, 7–44); H. Meyer, 'Die Wissenschafslehre des Thomas v. Aq. B. Die Glaubenswissenschaft (sacra doctrina)' (in *Philosophisches Jahrbuch*, 48 (1935), 12–40)." *BT*, no. 8 (October-December 1935): 591–2.

222 "Review of P. Montanari, 'La conoscenza intellettulae in S. Tommaso e Sant'Agostino' (in *SC*, III (1932), 263–76); A. Bremond, 'L'augustinisme et S. Thomas dans la théorie de la connaissance' (in *Rev. Apol.*, LVI (1933), 513–27); R. Jolivet, *Dieu soleil des esprits, ou la doctrine augustinienne de l'illumination* (Paris 1934); J. Peghaire, 'Le couple augustinien 'Ratio superior et ratio inferior'. L'interprétation thomiste.' (in *RSPT*, 1934 (XXIII), 221–40)." *BT*, no. 5 (January-March 1935): 394–6.

223 "Un essai de méthode théologique au XIIᵉ siècle." *RSPT* 24 (1935): 258–67.

224 "Une religion contemplative." Review of M.M. Davy, *Les Dominicaines* (Paris, 1934). *VS* 43, no. 187 (1 April 1935): 86–9.

225 "Victor Cousin en 1856." *RSPT* 24 (1935): 65–75.

1935–1936

226 "Grammaire et théologie au XIIᵉ et XIIIᵉ siècles." *AHDLM* 10 (1935–36): 5–28. [Partially reprinted in *Théologie au XIIᵉ*, 90–107.]

1936

227 "La JOC au Saulchoir." *AD*, no. 72 (May 1936): 190–3. [Reprinted in *Parole* 2, 271–4.]

228 "Bulletin de théologie. Introduction à la théologie." *RSPT* 25 (1936): 744–7.

229 "Bulletin d'histoire des doctrines chrétiennes." *RSPT* 25 (1936): 356–75.

230 "Histoire du thomisme. Age moderne." *BT*, no. 11–12 (July-December 1936): 836–57, 860–9.

231 "Histoire du thomisme. Période contemporaine." *BT*, no. 11–12 (July-December 1936): 875–84.

232 "Introduction." In *Artes praedicandi. Contribution à l'histoire de la rhétorique au Moyen âge*, by T.-M. Charland. Publications de l'Institut d'Études Médiévales d'Ottawa, no. 7, 7–13. Paris; Ottawa: Vrin, 1936.

233 "La liberté dominicaine." *AD*, no. 72 (August-September 1936): 283–7.

234 "La liberté dominicaine." *Sept*, 10 July 1936, 9.

235 "Le R.P. Mandonnet (1858–1936)." *BT* 13, no. 4 (1936): 693–7.

236 "Le R.P. Pègues, O.P." *BT* 13, no. 4 (1936): 893–5.

237 "Le R.P. Renard." *La Vie Catholique* 13, no. 634 (21 November 1936): 1–2.

238 "L'étude de saint Thomas. Méthodes et procédés." *BT*, no. 11–12 (July-December 1936): 885–92.

239 "Notes de lexicographie philosophique médiévale: *Disciplina.*" *RSPT* 25 (1936): 686–92.

240 "Notice nécrologique sur le Cardinal Lépicier." *BT* (1936), 596.

241 "Notice of H. Bleienstein, 'Der heilige Priester. Wesensschau des Priesters und die aus dem ummittelbaren priestlichen Tum sich ergebenden Wege zu wesenhafter Heiligkeit' (in *Zeitschrift für Aszese und Mystik*, VIII (1933), 193–211)." *BT*, no. 10 (April-June 1936): 755.

242 "Notice of H. Cochowski, 'Pologne' (in *Dictionnaire de théologie catholique*, vol. XII, coll. 2470–2515)." *BT*, no. 11–12 (July-December 1936): 808.

243 "Notice of M. de Wulf, *Histoire de la philosophie médiévale* (vol. II, 6 ed., Louvain 1936); Idem., *History of mediaeval philosophy* (vol. I, 6 ed., London-New York 1935)." *BT*, no. 11–12 (July-December 1936): 806.

244 "Notice of M. de Wulf, *Manuale di storia della filosofia* (Torino 1933)." *BT*, no. 11–12 (July-December 1936): 806.

245 "Notice of P. Glorieux, *Répertoire des maîtres en théologie de Paris au XIIIᵉ siècle* (vol. II, Paris 1934)." *BT*, no. 11–12 (July-December 1936): 808.

246 "Préface." In *Une vocation dominicaine: Le Père M.-Gabriel Bernage (1903–1933)*, by Raymond Nosten O.P., v-x. Paris: Éditions du Cerf, 1936.

247 "Review of A. Ianssens, *Die heilige Wijdingen. I Bisscoppen en priesters II Diaconat, subdiaconat en mindere Orden* (Brussels 1933–1935)." *BT*, no. 10 (April-June 1936): 754.

248 "Review of A. Lemonnyer, *Notre vie divine* (Juvisy 1936)." *BT*, no. 11–12 (July-December 1936): 784–9.

249 "Review of A. Little, F. Pelster, *Oxford Theology and Theologians c. A.D. 1282–1302* (Oxford, 1934)." *BT*, no. 11–12 (July-December 1936): 808–9.

250 "Review of E. Hugueny, 'Résurrection et identité corporelle' (in *RSPT*, 1934 (XXIII), 94–106); F. Segarra, 'Todavia una palabra sobre 'La identidad del cuerpo mortal y del cuerpo resucitado" (in *Estudios eclesiasticos*, XIII (1934), 470–79)." *BT*, no. 10 (April-June 1936): 562–3.

251 "Review of G. Busnelli, G. Vandelli, *Opere di Dante. Il Convivio, ridotto a miglior lezione e commentato* (vol. I, Firenze 1934); F. Olgiati, 'Una nuova edizione del 'Convivio' dantesco e la filosofia di S. Tommaso' (in *RFN*, 1935 (XXVII), 166–8); G.G. Walsh, 'The doctrine of St. Thomas in the 'Convivio' of Dante' (in *G, 1935 (XVI, 504–30); R. Palgen, Das mittelalterliche Gesicht der 'Göttlichen Kömodie'. Quellenstudien zu 'Inferno' und 'Purgatorio'* (Heidelberg 1935); P. Mandonnet, *Dante le théologien. Introduction à l'intelligence de la vie, des oeuvres et de l'art de Dante Alighieri* (Paris 1935)." *BT*, no. 11–12 (July-December 1936): 830–2.

252 "Review of M. Grabmann, 'Hilfsmittel des Thomasstudium aus alter zeit (Abreviationes. Concordantiae. Tabulae). Auf Grund handschriftlichen Forschungen dargestellt' (in *Mittelalterliches Geistesleben*, vol. II, München 1936, 424–89)." *BT*, no. 11–12 (July-December 1936): 809–10.

253 "Review of M. Grabmann, *Die Geschichte der katholischen Theologie seit dem Ausgang der Väterzeit* (Freiburg, 1933)." *BT*, no. 11–12 (July-December 1936): 806–7.

254 "Review of M. Grabmann, *Mittelalterliche Deutung und Umbildung der aristotelischen Lehre vom* noûs poietikós *nach einer Zusammenstellung im Cod. B. III 22 der Universitätsbibliothek Basel* (München 1936)." *BT*, no. 11–12 (July-December 1936): 816.

255 "Review of M. de Wulf, *Histoire de la philosophie médiévale* (vol. II, 6 ed., Louvain-Paris 1936)." *BT*, no. 11–12 (July-December 1936): 779–81.

256 "Review of P.V. Doucet o.f.m. (Ed.), *Matthaei Ab Aquasparta O.F.F. Quaestiones Disputatae de Gratia* (Quarracchi, 1935)." *BT*, no. 11–12 (July-December 1936): 817–18.

1937

257 *Une école de théologie. Le Saulchoir.* Kain-lez-Tournai (Belgique); Étiolles (Seine-et-Oise): Le Saulchoir, 1937. [Partially reprinted in *Parole* 1, 243–67. Reprinted with commentaries by G. Alberigo, É. Fouilloux, J. Ladrière, and J.-P. Jossua. (Paris: Éditions du Cerf, 1985).]

258 "Dimension nouvelle de la chrétienté." *VI* 53 (1937): 325–51. [Reprinted in *Parole* 1, 87–107.]

259 "L'unité de la foi: Réalisme et formalisme." *VSS* 52 (July-August 1937): [1]–[8]. [Reprinted in *Parole* 1, 13–19.]

260 "Interview du P. Chenu sur son voyage récent en Terre Sainte." *Quinze*, 4 February 1937.

261 "Les *philosophes* dans la philosophie chrétienne médiévale." *RSPT* 26 (1937): 27–40.

262 "Notice of F. Banfi, 'Un umanista bolognese e i Domenicani' (in *MD*, 1936 (53), 14–25)." *BT*, no. 1 (January-March 1937): 32.

263 "Notice of J. Peghaire, *'Intellectus' et 'Ratio' selon S. Thomas d'Aquin* (Ottawa-Paris 1936)." *BT*, no. 2 (April-June 1937): 134–5.

264 "Notice of M. Wittmann, 'Thomas von Aquin und Bonaventura in ihrer Glückseligkeitslehre miteinander der verglichen' (in *Aus der Geisteswelt des Mittelalters*, Münster 1935, 749–58)." *BT*, no. 3–4 (July-December 1937): 215–16.

265 "Notice of P. Renaudin, 'La théologie de S. Cyrille d'Alexandrie d'après S. Thomas. Le mystère de l'Incarnation' (in *RT*, 1936 (XLI), 79–93);

H. Woroniecki, 'Les éléments dionysiens dans le thomisme' (in Coll. théol. (Lwòw), XVII (1936), 25–40)." *BT*, no. 2 (April-June 1937): 134.

266 "Notice of 'San Tommaso d'Aquino' (in *Le beate genti*, 1934 (I), n. 1); R. Diaccini o.p., *Vita di San Tommaso d'Aquino* (Rome 1934)." *BT*, no. 1 (January-March 1937): 31–2.

267 "Philosophie, théologie et spiritualité." *VSS* 52 (1 May 1937): 65–70.

268 "Review of A. Wilmart, 'Note sur un long texte attribué à S. Jérôme, *In IV Sent.*, *d. 48, q. 1, art. 4, sed contra*' (in *Revue bénédictine*, XLVIII (1936), 13)." *BT*, no. 2 (April-June 1937): 139–40.

269 "Review of D. Salman, 'Albert le Grand et l'averroïsme latin' (in *RSPT*, 1935 (XXIV), 38–64); L. Perugini, 'Il tomismo di Sigieri de Brabante e l'elogio dantesco' (in *Giornale dantesco*, XXXVI, 105–8); Idem. 'Il tomismo di Sigieri di Brabante e l'elogio dantesco' (in *Sophia*, IV (1936), 90–4); B. Nardi, 'Il preteso tomismo di Sigieri di Brabante' (in *Giornale critico della filosofia italiana*, XVII (1936), 26–35); F. van Steenberghen, 'Un commentaire averroïste, anonyme et inédit, du traité de l'âme' (in *Aus der Geisteswelt des Mittelalters* (Suppl. III of B.G.P.T.M.), 842–54)." *BT*, no. 2 (April-June 1937): 149–51.

270 "Review of E. Gilson, *Dante et la Philosophie* (Paris, 1939)." *BT*, no. 11–12 (July-October 1937): 762–8.

271 "Review of F. Hirschenauer, 'Grundlagen und Grundfragen des Priser Mendikantenstreites' (in *Zeitschrift für Aszese und Mystik*, X (1935), 221–36); A. Aegerter, 'L'affaire du 'De periculis novissimorum temporum'' (in *Revue de l'histoire des religions*, XCII (1935), 242–72), P. Glorieux, "Contra Geraldinos'. L'enchaînement des polémiques' (in *RTAM*, 1935 (VII), 129–55)." *BT*, no. 2 (April-June 1937): 155–6.

272 "Review of G. Meersseman, *Laurentii Pignon Catalogi et Chronica. Accedunt Catalogi Stamsensis et Upsalensis scriptorum ord. Praedicatorum* (Roma 1936)." *BT*, no. 2 (April-June 1937): 92–3.

273 "Review of J.M. Voste, *De investigandis fontibus patristicis S. Thomae* (Rome, 1937)." *BT*, no. 2 (April-June 1937): 133.

274 "Review of M. Grabmann, 'De theologia ut scientia argumentativa secundum S. Albertum Magnum et S. Thomas Aquinatem' (in *A*, 1937 (XIV), 39–60); B. Pergamo, 'De quaestionibus ineditis Fr. Odonis Rigaldi, Fr. Guilelmi de Melitona et codicis Nat. lat. 782 circa naturam theologiae deque relatione ad Summam theologicam Fr. Alexandri Halensis' (in *Arch, Franc. Hist.*, XXIX (1936), 3–54); F. Stegmuller (ed.), *Robert Kilwardby O. Pr., de natura theologiae* (Münster 1935); J. Rivière, 'Theologia' (in *RDSR*, 1936 (XVI), 47–57)." *BT*, no. 2 (April-June 1937): 152–5.

275 "Review of P. Dezza, *Alle Origini del Novecento* (Milan, 1940)." *BT*, no. 11–12 (July-October 1937): 828.

276 "Review of P. Robert o.p., *Hylémorphisme et devenir chez saint Bonaventure* (Montréal, 1936)." *BT*, no. 3–4 (July-December 1937): 213–15.
277 "Review of S. Koplowitz, *Ueber die Abhängigkeit Thomas von Aquinas von Boethius. Eine untersuchung über beiden Summen,* Wurzburg 1935); M.-D. Chenu o.p., 'Notes de lexicographie philosophique médiévale. Disciplina' (in *RSPT*, 1936 (xxv), 686–692)." *BT*, no. 2 (April-June 1937): 123–4.
278 "Review of S. Vanni Rovighi, *L'Immortalità Dell'Anima Nei Maestri Francescani del Secolo XIII* (Milan, 1936)." *BT*, no. 2 (April-June 1937): 151.
279 "Review of T.M. Charland, *Artes praedicandi. Contribution à l'histoire de la rhétorique au moyen âge* (Paris-Ottawa, 1936)." *BT*, no. 2 (April-June 1937): 113–14.
280 "Review of *Chronologie des écrits de S. Thomas d'Aquin* (Tableau synoptique, par le Collège dominicain d'Ottawa, 1937)." *BT*, no. 2 (April-June 1937): 94.
281 "Saint Dominique et le Communisme." *VI* 52 (10 October 1937): 31–4.
282 "Théologie et spiritualité." *VSS* 52 (1 May 1937): 65–70.
283 "Une doctrine, une oeuvre, une vie (Mère Louise-Marguerite Claret de la Touche." *VS* 51, no. 211 (April 1937): 86–9.
284 "Unité et liberté." *Sept* 4, no. 170 (28 May 1937): 20.

1938

285 *Dimension nouvelle de la chrétienté.* Paris: Juvisy, 1938.
286 "Comment la doctrine et la vie surnaturelle de l'Église créent un climat favorable à l'exercice ordonné des libertés dans la vie sociale." In *La liberté et les libertés dans la vie sociale. Semaines sociales de France, 30ᵉ session. Rouen, 1938,* 193–213. Lyons: Éditions de la Chronique sociale de France, 1938. [Reprinted as "Liberté et engagement du chrétien" in *VI*, 59 (1938), 181–210 and in *Parole* 1, 331–54.]
287 "Albert le Grand et la révolution intellectuelle du XIIIᵉ siècle." *B* 19 (1938): 5–15.
288 "Bulletin d'histoire des doctrines chrétiennes." *RSPT* 27 (1938): 270–86.
289 "Humanisme médiéval." *VI* 57 (25 June 1938): 413–16.
290 "Liberté et engagement du chrétien." *VI* 59 (1938): 181–210. [Reprinted in *Parole* 1, 331–54.]
291 "Notes de lexicographie médiévale. Un vestige du stoïcissme." *RSPT* 27 (1938): 63–8.
292 "Notice of G. Dwelshauwers, *L'étude de la pensée. Méthodes et résultats* (Paris, n.d.); G. Rabeau, *Species, Verbum. L'activité intellectuelle élementaire selon S. Thomas d'Aquin* (Paris 1938)." *BT*, no. 5 (January-March 1938): 326.
293 "Notice of R. Garrigou-Lagrange o.p., *God, His Existence and Nature* (London 1936); F.-X. Calcagno s.j., *Philosophia scholastica* (vol. II, Naples

1937); P. Parente, *De Deo uno. Tractatus dogmaticus* (Rome 1938)." *BT*, no. 8 (October-December 1938): 535.

294 "Review of J. Maritain, *Humanisme intégral* (Paris 1936)." *BT* 15, no. 5 (1938): 360–4.

295 "Review of M.-M. Gorce, 'L'activité constructrice de l'esprit chez saint Thomas' (in *Revue des cours et conférences*, XXXVI, 2 (1935), 22–40)." *BT*, no. 5 (January-March 1938): 328.

296 "Review of R. Garrigou-Lagrange o.p., *De Deo uno. Commentarium in Primam Partem S. Thomae* (Paris 1938)." *BT*, no. 8 (October-December 1938): 535–8.

297 "Review of T. Philippe, 'L'intelligence, mystère de lumière' (in *RSPT*, 1935 (XXIV), 434–461)." *BT*, no. 5 (January-March 1938): 326–7.

298 "The Revolutionary Intellectualism of St. Albert the Great." *B*, (January 1938): 5–15.

1939

299 *Les études de philosophie médiévale. Chronique annuelle de philosophie publiée par l'Institut international de collaboration philosophique.* Paris: Hermann, 1939.

300 "Chrétien mon frère ... Pourquoi la guerre?" *VS* 61, no. 241 (October-November 1939): 5–14. [Reprinted in *Parole* 1, 225–30.]

301 "Classes et corps mystique du Christ." In *Le problème des classes dans la communauté nationale et dans l'ordre humain. Semaines sociales de France, 31ᵉ session, Bordeaux 1939*, 373–89. Lyons: Éditions de la Chronique sociale de France, 1939. [Reprinted in *VI*, 25 January 1940, 9–31, and in *Parole* 1, 477–94.]

302 "Journalistes et théologiens." In *Le rôle actuel de la presse. Actes du 37ᵉ congrès de la Maison de la Bonne Presse, octobre 1938*, 76–81. Paris: Éditions de la Bonne Presse, 1939. [Reprinted as "Journalisme et théologie" in *Parole* 1, 213–24.]

303 "Bulletin d'histoire des doctrines." *RSPT* 28 (1939): 307–26.

304 "Christian Liberty and Obligations." *B* (April-May 1939): 263–76, 232–42. Oxford. [English translation of M.-D. Chenu, "Liberté et engagement du chrétien", in *VI* 59 (1938): 181–210.]

305 "Journalistes et théologiens." *ER*, no. 455 (15 April 1939): 37–42. Liège-Paris. [Reprinted as "Journalisme et théologie" in *Parole* 1, 213–24.]

306 "Le plan de la Somme théologique de saint Thomas." *RT* 45 (1939): 93–107.

307 "Notice of P. Lumbreras, 'Proprius locus blasphemiae' (in *A*, 1937 (XIV), 154–74)." *BT*, no. 9 (January-March 1939): 616.

308 "Review of C. Ceriani, *L'ideologia rosminia nei rapporti con la gnoseologia agostiniano-tomistica* (Milan 1937); M. Casotti, *La pedagogia di Antonio*

Rosmini e le sue basi filosofiche (Milan 1937); A. Michel, 'Rosmini' (in *Dictionnaire de théologie catholique*, vol. XIII, coll. 2917–2952)." *BT*, no. 11–12 (July-October 1939): 829–30.

309 "Review of Gabriel de S. Marie Madeleine o.c.d., *Ecole thérèsienne et problèmes mystiques contemporains* (Paris 1936); A. Winklhofer, *Die Gnadelehre in der Mystik des hl. Johannes vom Krenz* (Freiburg 1936); M.-M. Labourdette, 'La foi théologale et la connaissance mystique d'après S. Jean de la Croix' (in *RT*, 1936 (XLII), 593–629; 1937 (XLIII), 16–57, 191–229)." *BT*, no. 11–12 (July-October 1939): 819–20.

310 "Review of H. Bouessé, *Théologie et sacerdoce* (Chambéry 1938); Idem., 'Théologie de la messe' (in *VSS*, LV (1938), 65–104); Idem., 'Théologie de la messe. Note sur l'immolation mystique' (in *VSS*, LVII (1938), 167–73)." *BT*, no. 10 (April-June 1939): 717–18.

311 "Review of P. Lumbreras, *De Fide IIa-IIae, q. 1–16* (Rome, 1937)." *BT*, no. 9 (January-March 1939): 615–16.

312 "Review of R. Labrousse, *Essai sur la philosophie politique de l'ancienne Espagne. Politique de la raison et politique de la foi* (Paris, 1938)." *BT*, no. 11–12 (July-October 1939): 801–3.

313 "Review of T. Richard, *Comment étudier et situer saint Thomas* (Paris, 1938)." *BT*, no. 11–12 (July-October 1939): 833–4.

314 "Sang du Christ." In *Dictionnaire de théologie catholique*, coll. 1094–7. Paris, 1939.

1940

315 "L'équilibre de la scolastique médiévale." *RSPT* 29 (1940): 304–12. [Reprinted in *Parole* 1, 229–39.]

316 "Arts 'mécaniques' et oeuvres serviles." *RSPT* 29 (1940): 313–15.

317 "Aux origines de la science moderne." *RSPT* 29 (1940): 206–17.

318 "Classes et corps mystique du Christ." *VI*, 21 January 1940, 9–31. [Reprinted from *La liberté et les libertés dans la vie sociale. Semaines sociales de France, 31ᵉ session (Bordeaux 1939)*, Lyon 1939, 373–89.]

319 "Ratio superior et inferior. Un cas de philosophie chrétienne." *RSPT* 29 (1940): 84–9.

320 "Review of P.M. Abellan, *El fin y la significaciòn sacramental del matrimonio desde S. Anselmo hasta Guillermo de Auxerre* (Grenada, 1939)." *BT*, no. 1–12 (1 January 1940).

1941

321 *Spiritualité du travail.* Illustrated by J. Le Chevalier. Paris: Éditions du Temps Présent, 1941.

322 "Destinée personnelle et morale communautaire." In *Contemplation*. Coll. Rencontres, no. 1, 31–42. Paris: Éditions du Cerf, 1941. [Reprinted in *Parole* 1, 355–62.]

1942

323 *Pour être heureux, travaillons ensemble*. Paris: Presses Universitaires de France, 1942.

324 "Bulletin de l'histoire de la philosophie. Moyen Age." *RSPT* 30 (1942): 465–74.

325 "La date du commentaire de S. Thomas sur le '*De Trinitate*' de Boèce." *RSPT* 30 (1942): 432–4.

326 "La première traduction française de la Somme de S. Thomas." *RSPT* 30 (1942): 435–8.

327 "Le couvent médiéval." In *Foyers de notre culture*, Gilbert Gadoffre (ed.), 14–30. Paris: Éditions du Cerf, 1942.

328 "Notice of A. Landgraf, 'Die Darstellung des hl. Thomas von der Wirkungen der Beschneidung im Spiegel der Frühscholastik' (in *Acta Pont. acad. rom. S. Thom. Aq. et rel. cath.*, 1941, 19–77)." *BT*, no. 1–12 (January-October 1942): 163.

329 "Notice of A. Maier, *Das Problem der intensiven Grösse in der Scholastik* (Leipzig 1940)." *BT*, no. 1–12 (January-October 1942): 205.

330 "Notice of B. Bouché, *La doctrine du 'Filioque' d'après S. Anselme de Cantorbury. Son influence sur S. Albert le Grand et sur S. Thomas d'Aquin* (n.p. 1938)." *BT*, no. 1–12 (January-October 1942): 154.

331 "Notice of E.M.F. Sommer-Seckendorff, *Studies in the life of Robert Kilwardby O.P.* (Rome 1937)." *BT*, no. 1–12 (January-October 1942): 181.

332 "Notice of F. Carpino, 'Una difficoltà contro la confessione nella scolastica primitiva' (in *DT*, 1939 (XLII), 94–103)." *BT*, no. 1–12 (January-October 1942): 163.

333 "Notice of F. van Steenberghen, *Les oeuvres et la doctrine de Siger de Brabant* (Bruxelles 1938); B. Nardi, 'Una nuova monografia su Sigieri di Brabante' (in *Giornale critico della filosofia italiana*, XX (1939), 453–71)." *BT*, no. 1–12 (January-October 1942): 164.

334 "Notice of G. Bruni, 'De codice ottoboniano latino 2165' (in *Analecta augustiniana*, 17 (1939), 158–61)." *BT*, no. 1–12 (January-October 1942): 168.

335 "Notice of K. Balic o.f.m., 'Toma Akvinski i drugi naucitelji' (in *Bogoslava Smotra*, XXV (1937), 47ff., 133ff., 261ff., 373–88)." *BT*, no. 1–12 (January-October 1942): 149.

336 "Notice of L. Perugini, C. Ottaviano, 'La nuova quaestione di Sigieri di Brabante' (in *Sophia*, V (1937), 159–66)." *BT*, no. 1–12 (January-October 1942): 164.

337 "Notice of M. Grabmann, 'I divieti ecclesiastici di aristotele sotto Inno-
cenzo III e Gregorio IX' (in *Miscellanea historiae pontificiae, vol. V: I papi
del Duecento e l'Aristotelismo*, fasc. 1, Rome 1941); F. van Steenberghen,
Sigier de Brabant d'après ses oeuvres inédites (vol. II, Louvain 1942, 389–446);
R. McKeon, 'Aristotelianism in Western Christianity' (in *Environmental Factors in Christian History*, Chicago 1939, 206–31)." *BT*, no. 1–12 (January-
October 1942): 147–8.

338 "Notice of M. Grabmann, 'Quaestio Gerardi de Abbatisvilla (+ 1272) de
unitate intellectus contra monopsychismum averroisticum' (in *Acta Pontificiae academiae romanae S. Thomae Aquinatis et religionis catholicae*, 1941)." *BT*,
no. 1–12 (January-October 1942): 168.

339 "Notice of U. Mariani, 'La scolastica negli inizi del sec. XIII' (in *Giornale
dantesco*, XL (1939), 1–37); C. Fabro, 'Le grandi correnti della scolastica
e S. Tommaso d'Aquino' (in *RFN*, 1939 (XXXI), 329–40)." *BT*, no. 1–12
(January-October 1942): 147.

340 "Notice of Y. de Montcheuil, 'La raison de la permanence du Christ sous
les espèces eucharistiques d'après saint Bonaventure et saint Thomas' (in
RSR, 1939 (XXIX), 352–364)." *BT*, no. 1–12 (January-October 1942): 181.

341 "Review of A., Maier, *Die Impetustheorie der Scholastik* (Vienna 1940)." *BT*,
no. 1–12 (January-October 1942): 205.

342 "Review of A. Landgraf, 'Die frühscholastische Streitfrage vom Wieder-
aufleben der Sünden', in *Zeitschrift für katholische Theologie*, LXI (1937), 509–
94); Idem., 'Die Lehre der Frühscholastik von der Knechtischen Furcht'
(in *DT* (Freiburg), XV (1937)), 43–54, 157–88, 308–24); XVI (1938), 85–
107, 331–49); Idem., 'Definition und Sündhaftigkeit der Lüge nach der
Lehre der Frühscholastik' (in *Zeitschrift für katholische Theologie*, LXIII
(1939), 50–85, 157–80); Idem., 'Die Stellungnahme der Frühscholastik
zur Lüge der altestamentlichen Patriarchen' (in *Theologisch-Praktische Quartalschrift*, XCII (1939), 12–32, 218–31)." *BT*, no. 1–12 (January-October
1942): 157–8.

343 "Review of A. Walz, 'Chronotaxis vitae et operum S. Thomae de Aquino' (in
A, 1939 (XVI), 463–73)." *BT*, no. 1–12 (January-October 1942): 99–100.

344 "Review of A.M. Goichon, *La distinction de l'essence et de l'existence d'après Ibn
Sina (Avicenne)* (Paris 1938)." *BT*, no. 1–12 (January-October 1942): 138–9.

345 "Review of B. Nardi, 'Ancora sul pretoso tomismo di Sigieri di Brabante' (in
Giornale critico della filosofia italiana, XVIII (1937), 160–4); Idem., *S. Tommaso
d'Aquino. Trattato sull'unità dell'intelletto contro gli averroisti* (Firenze 1938)."
BT, no. 1–12 (January-October 1942): 164.

346 "Review of C. O'Donnel, *The Psychology of St. Bonaventura and St. Thomas
Aquinas* (Washington 1937); D. Callus, 'The philosophy of St. Bonaventure
and of St. Thomas' (in *B*, 1940 (XXI), 151–64, 249–67); J. Friedrichs, *Die*

Theologie als spekulative und praktische Wissenschaft nach Bonaventura und Thomas von Aquin (Bonn 1940); J. Bittremieux, 'Distinctio inter essentiam et esse apud S. Bonaventuram' (in *ETL*, 1937 (XIV), 302–07); M.-B. d'Ypres, 'La prescience divine selon S. Bonaventure' (in *Collectanea franciscana*, IX (1939), 321–60); R. Silic, *Christus und die Kirche. Ihr Verhältnis nach der Lehre des hl. Bonaventura* (Bonn 1939); H. Berresheim, *Christus als Haupt der Kirche nach dem h. Bonaventura. Ein Beitrag zur Theologie der Kirche* (Bonn 1939); G. Cantini, 'S. Bonaventura da bagnorea 'magnus verbi Dei sator" (in *AN*, 1940 (XV), 29–74, 155–88, 245–74); I. Squadrini, 'S. Bonaventura christianus philosophus' (in *AN*, 1941 (XVI), 103–30, 253–304)." *BT*, no. 1–12 (January-October 1942): 180–1.

347 "Review of D. A. Callus, 'Two early Oxford masters on the problem of plurality of forms' (in *Revue néoscholastique de philosophie*, XLII (1939), 411–45)." *BT*, no. 1–12 (January-October 1942): 153.

348 "Review of E. Elorduy, *Santo Tomàs y el tradicionalismo y autenticidad de la obra 'De regno' de S. Thomas*, Saint-Sébastien 1939); J. B. McAllister, *The letter of St. Thomas Aquinas 'De occultis operibus naturae ad quendam militem ultramontanum'* (Washington 1939)." *BT*, no. 1–12 (January-October 1942): 115.

349 "Review of E. Gilson, P. Bohner o.f.m., *Der Geschichte der christlichen Philosophie von ihren Anfängen bis Nikolaus von Cues* (Paderborn 1937)." *BT*, no. 1–12 (January-October 1942): 124.

350 "Review of F. van Steenberghen, *Sigier de Brabant d'après ses oeuvres inédites* (vol. II, Louvain 1942); P. Delhaye, *Sigier de Brabant. Questions sur la Physique d'Aristote. Texte inédit* (Louvain 1941)." *BT*, no. 1–12 (January-October 1942): 167–8.

351 "Review of G. Geenen, 'L'usage des 'auctoritates' dans la doctrine du baptême chez S. Thomas d'Aquin' (in *ETL*, 1938 (XV), 278–329); Idem., 'De opvatting en de honding van den h. Thomas von Aquino bij ret gebruiken der bronnen zijner theologie. Bijdrage tot de studie der middeleeuwsche patristiek' (in *Bij. v. d. phil. en theol. fac. (Nimègue)*, 1941, 112–47, 224–54); I. Backes, 'Thomas von Aquin und die Tradition der Väterzeit' (in *Pastor bonus*, 1938, 94–9)." *BT*, no. 1–12 (January-October 1942): 125.

352 "Review of G. Paré, *Le Roman de la Rose et la scholastique courtoise* (Paris-Ottawa 1941)." *BT*, no. 1–12 (January-October 1942): 148–9.

353 "Review of H. Pouillon, 'Le premier traité des propriétés transcendentales. La 'Summa de bono' du chancelier Philippe' (in *Revue néoscholastique de philosophie*, XLII (1939), 40–70)." *BT*, no. 1–12 (January-October 1942): 154.

354 "Review of J. Leclerq, 'La théologie comme science d'après la littérature quodlibétique' (in *RTAM*, 1939 (XI), 351–74)." *BT*, no. 1–12 (January-October 1942): 478–9.

355 "Review of J.-M. Paré, *La doctrine de la création dans l'école de Chartres. Études et textes*. (Paris-Ottawa 1938)." *BT*, no. 1–12 (January-October 1942): 153–4.

356 "Review of M. Asin Palacios, 'Tratado de Avempace sobre la uniòn del intelecto com el hombre' (in *Al. Andalus*, vol. VII, 1942, 1–47)." *BT*, no. 1–12 (January-October 1942): 138.

357 "Review of M. Asin Palacios, *Heullas del Islam, Santo Tomas de Aquino, Pascal, San Juan de la Cruz* (Madrid 1941)." *BT*, no. 1–12 (January-October 1942): 137–8.

358 "Review of M. Grabmann, 'De fontibus historicis logicam S. Thomae de Aquino illustrantibus' (in *Acta Pont. Acad. Rom. S. Thomae 1936–1937*, Rome 1938, 53–64)." *BT*, no. 1–12 (January-October 1942): 149.

359 "Review of M.-D. Chenu o.p., 'The revolutionary intellectualism of St. Albert the Great' (in *B*, 1938 (XIX), 5–15); G.S.S. Quadri, 'Alberto Magno e la sua teoria dell'autorità' (in *Studi senesi*, LI (1937)); A. Rohner, 'De natura theologiae juxta S. Albertum Magnum' (in *A*, 1939 (XVI), 3–23); D. Siedler, *Intellektualismus und Voluntarismus bei Albertus Magnus* (Münster 1941)." *BT*, no. 1–12 (January-October 1942): 179–80.

360 "Review of O. Lottin, 'La connexion des vertus morales acquises, chez S. Thomas d'Aquin et ses contemporains' (in *ETL*, 1937, 585–99)." *BT*, no. 1–12 (January-October 1942): 154–5.

361 "Review of O. Lottin, 'Le péché originel chez Albert le Grand, Bonaventure et Thomas d'Aquin' (in *RTAM*, 1940 (XII), 275–328)." *BT*, no. 1–12 (January-October 1942): 113–14.

362 "Review of O. Lottin, 'Les premiers exposés scholastiques sur la loi éternelle' (in *ETL*, 1937 (XIV), 287–301)." *BT*, no. 1–12 (January-October 1942): 155.

363 "Review of O. Lottin, 'Les théories du péché originel au XII⁰ siècle' (in *RTAM*, 1939 (XI), 17–32; 1940 (XII), 78–103, 236–74); Idem., 'Le traité du péché originel chez les premiers maîtres dominicains de Paris' (in *ETL*, 1940 (XVII), 27–57); Idem., 'Le traité du péché originel chez les premiers maîtres franciscains de Paris' (in *ETL*, 1941 (XVIII), 26–64); Idem., 'Le péché originel chez Albert le Grand, Bonaventure et Thomas d'Aquin' (in *RTAM*, 1940 (XII), 275–328); A. Fries, *Urgerechtigkeit, Fall und Erbsünde nach Präpositin von Cremona und Wilhelm von Auxerre* (Freiburg 1940)." *BT*, no. 1–12 (January-October 1942): 155–7.

364 "Review of O. Lottin, *Psychologie et morale au XII⁰ et XIII⁰ siècles* (vol. I, Louvain-Gembloux 1942); Idem., 'Psychologie et morale à la faculté des arts de Paris aux approches de 1250' (in *Revue néoscholastique de philosophie*, XLII (1939), 182–212)." *BT*, no. 1–12 (January-October 1942): 151–3.

365 "Review of P. Glorieux, 'Sentences (Commentaires sur les)' (in *Dictionnaire de théologie catholique*, vol. XIV, Paris 1939, coll. 1860–1884); Idem., 'Sommes

théologiques' (in *loc. cit.*, coll. 2341–2364); A. Landgraf, 'The first sentence commentary of early Scholasticism' (in *NS*, 1939 (XIII), 101–2); M.-D. Chenu, 'Le plan de la Somme théologique de S. Thomas' (in *RT*, 1939 (XLV), 93–107)." *BT*, no. 1–12 (January-October 1942): 147.

366 "Review of P. Glorieux, 'Siger de Brabant' (in *Dictionnaire de théologie catholique*, vol. XIV, Paris 1939, coll. 2041–2052)." *BT*, no. 1–12 (January-October 1942): 167.

367 "Review of P. Glorieux, 'Une offensive de Nicolas de Lisieux contre S. Thomas d'Aquin' (in *Bulletin de littérature ecclésiastique*, XXXIX (1938), 121–9)." *BT*, no. 1–12 (January-October 1942): 168–9.

368 "Review of P. Vignaux, *La pensée au Moyen Age* (Paris 1938)." *BT*, no. 1–12 (January-October 1942): 124–5.

369 "Review of P.M. Abellan, *El fin y la significaciòn sacramental del matrimonio desde S. Anselmo hasta Guillermo de Auxerre* (Grenada 1939)." *BT*, no. 1–12 (January-October 1942): 163–4.

370 "Review of S. Clasen, *Der hl. Bonaventura und das Mendikantentum. Ein Beitrag zur Ideengeschichte der Pariser Mendikantensreites, 1252–1272* (Werl-in W. 1940); Idem., 'Tractatus Gerardi de Abbatisvilla 'contra adversarium perfectionis christianae" (in *Arch. franç. hist.*, 1938 (XXXI), 276–329; 1939 (XXXII), 89–200); Idem., 'Eine Antwort auf die theologische Quaestion des Johannes Pecham über die vollkommene Armut' (in *Franziskanische Studien*, XXV (1938), 241–58)." *BT*, no. 1–12 (January-October 1942): 169.

371 "Review of T. Crowley, 'The 'Quaestionibus' of Roger Bacon and the problem of the soul in the thirteenth century' (in *Revue néoscholastique de la philosophie*, XLII (1939), 647–50)." *BT*, no. 1–12 (January-October 1942): 179.

372 "Review of 'Ideologia Tomàse Akvinského a jeji pomer k filosofii Averroësove' (in *Filosofickà Revue*, X (1938), 30–4); Y.- M. Faribault, 'La 'via renovationis' avant Maimonine' (in *Études et recherches publiées par le Collège dominicain d'Ottawa*, vol. II, Ottawa 1937, 45–78)." *BT*, no. 1–12 (January-October 1942): 139.

1943

373 *La théologie comme science au XIIIe siècle*. Deuxième édition. Pro manuscripto, 1943.

1944

374 "La foi en chrétienté." Notes taken by a listener at a conference, 1944. [Reprinted in *Parole* 1, 109–32.]

375 "La révolution communautaire et l'apostolat." *MD*, no. 2 (1944): 22–34. [Reprinted in *Parole* 1, 363–78.]

376 "L'Abbé Godin, fondateur de la *Mission de France*, [mort] le 17 janvier 1944." *VS* 70 (1944): 448–50. [Reprinted in *Parole* 1, 243–6.]

377 "Chroniques. Apostolat missionnaire dans la masse prolétarienne." *Cahiers de la Vie spirituelle. Le saint Esprit* (1944), 161–76.

378 "La confession de dévotion; sur un passage de l'encyclique '*Mystici corporis*'." *MO*, no. 1 (1944): 49–51.

379 "Les problèmes de structure dans la chrétienté de demain et leur incidences théologiques." In *Notre travail intellectuel. Journée d'étude 1944*. Ronéotypé, 82–91. Le Saulchoir: N.p., 1944.

380 "Liturgie du travail." *MO*, no. 3 (1944): 29–32.

381 "Pourquoi l'insurrection?" *TC*, no. 14 (2 September 1944): 1–2.

382 "Révolution économique et révolution spirituelle." *Revue d'économie contemporaine* 3, no. 26 (June 1944): 30–2.

1945

383 "La notion de profit et les principes chrétiens." In *Transformations sociales et libération de la personne. Semaines sociales de France, 32ᵉ session, Toulouse 1945*, 125–39. Lyons: Éditions de la Chronique de France, 1945. [Reprinted in *Parole* 1, 495–514.]

384 "Laïcs en chrétienté." *MO* 1, no. 3 (July 1945): 15–35. [Reprinted in *Parole* 1, 71–83.]

385 "L'*homo oeconomicus* et le chrétien. Réflexions d'un théologien à propos du marxisme." *Économie et humanisme* 4, no. 19 (May-June 1945): 225–36. [Reprinted in *Travail*, 45–69.]

386 "Destinée communautaire des biens et appropriation personnelle." *CD*, no. 1 (April 1945): 17–20.

387 "L'amour présence de Dieu." *TC*, no. 37 (9 February 1945): 2.

388 "L'unité des chrétiens." *TC*, no. 34 (19 January 1945): 1.

389 "Mort d'un théologien (le P. de Montcheuil)." *VI*, February 1945, 54–5.

390 "Ratio superior et ratio inferior. Un cas de philosophie chrétienne." *Laval théologique et philosophique* (1945), 119–23. Québec City. [Reprint of same title in *RSPT* 29 (1940), 84–9), and in English translation in *Downside Review* 54 (1946), 260–5.]

391 "Review of H. de Lubac, *Corpus Mysticum*." *Dieu Vivant* 1 (1945): 141–3.

1946

392 "Réformes de structures en chrétienté." *Économie et humanisme*, March-April 1946, 85–98. [Reprinted in *Parole* 1, 37–53.]

393 "Humanisme médiéval (préface)." In *Les hommes du Moyen-âge*. Paris: Éditions du Cerf, 1946.

394 *"Imaginatio.* Note de lexicographie philosophique médiévale." In *Miscellanea Giovanni Mercati.* Studi e Testi, no. 122, 539–602. Città del Vaticano: Biblioteca Ap. Vaticana, 1946.

395 "Lettre-préface." In *Témoignages sur la spiritualité moderne,* by Docteur Jouvenroux, 13–15. Paris: Le Liseron, 1946.

396 "L'humanisme et la réforme au collège de Saint Jacques de Paris." *Archives d'histoire dominicaine* 1 (1946): 130–54.

397 "Notice of F. Orestano, 'Dante e 'il buon frate Tommaso" (in *Sophia,* 9 (1941), 1–19); B. Nardi, 'Il Tomismo di Dante secondo Fr. Orestano' (in *Nel mondo di Dante,* Rome 1944, 353–67); E. Bodrero, 'Dante contro Duns Scoto' (in *Archivio di filosofia,* 9 (1940), 83–97); B. Nardi, 'Il Tomismo di Dante secondo E. Bodrero' (in *Nel mondo di Dante,* Rome 1944, 368–76); D. Scaramuzzi, 'Dante contro Duns Scoto?' (in *Saggi di teologia e di storia,* Rome 1940, 207–12)." *BT,* no. 4 (1946): 633–4.

398 "Notice of J. Beumer, 'Die Theologie als 'intellectus fidei', dargestellt an Hand des Wilhelm von Auxerre und Petrus von Tarentasia' (in *SCH,* 1942 (17), 32–49)." *BT,* no. 1 (1946): 162.

399 "Notice of J. Leclerq o.s.b., 'Un traité 'De fallaciis in theologia' (in *Revue du moyen âge latin,* 1 (1945), 43–6)." *BT,* no. 1 (1946): 161.

400 "Notice of T. Boccuccia o.f.m. conv., 'Quaestio 'de scito et credito' apud scholam franciscanam saec. XIII' (in *Miscelanea francescana,* 38 (1938), 9–46)." *BT,* no. 1 (1946): 161.

401 "Pastorale nouvelle et nouvelles chrétientés." Co-author P. Schmitz. *MO,* no. 18 (December 1946): 82–5.

402 "Recht und Theologie. Francisco de Vitoria zum Gedächtnis." *Zeitschrift für offentl. Recht* 2 (1946): 89–94.

403 "Review of A. Maccaferri o.p., 'Le dynamisme de la foi selon Albert le Grand' (in *RSPT,* 1940 (XXIX), 278–303)." *BT,* no. 1 (1946): 162–3.

404 "Review of E. Gilson, *La philosophie au moyen âge. Des origines patristiques à la fin du XIVe siècle* (2 ed., Paris 1944)." *BT,* no. 1 (1946): 111–12.

405 "Review of J. Leclerq o.s.b., 'Un témoignage du XIIIe siècle sur la nature de la théologie' (in *AHDLM,* 13 (1940–1942), 300–21); Idem., 'L'idéal du théologien au moyen âge' (in *RSR,* 21 (1947), 121–48); Idem., 'Le magistère des prédicateurs au XIIIe siècle' (in *AHDLM,* 15 (1946), 105–47)." *BT,* no. 1 (1946): 162.

406 "Review of M. Grabmann, *Die Werke des hl. Thomas von Aquin* (Münster 1949)." *BT,* no. 3 (1946): 419–21.

407 "Review of R. Creytens, 'Pierre de Tarentasie, professeur à Paris et prieur provinciale de France' (in *Beatus Innocentius P.P. V (Petrus de Tarentasia, O.P.). Studia et documenta,* Rome 1943, 73–100); H.-D. Simonin, 'Les écrits de

Pierre de Tarentasie' (loc. cit., 163–235); J.-M. Vosté, 'Beatus Petrus de Tarentasia epistolarum S. Pauli interpres' (loc. cit., 337–412; K. Renner, *Die Christologie des Petrus von Tarentasia* (Bonn 1941)." *BT*, no. 1 (1946): 171–2.

408 "Review of Sancti Thomae de Aquino, *Summa theologiae, cura et studio Instituti Studiorum Medievalum Ottaviensis ad textum S. Pii V iussu confectum recognita* (Ottawa 1941–1945)." *BT*, no. 1 (1946): 82–3.

409 "'Ratio superior et inferior.' A note on the interaction of Theology and Philosophy." *Downside Review* 64 (1946): 260–5. [English translation of an article in *RSPT* 29 (1945), 84–9.]

1947

410 *Spiritualité du travail.* Les Études Religieuses. Liège: La Pensée Catholique, 1947. [Reprinted from 1941 publication by Les Éditions du Temps Présent.]
411 "Anthropologie et liturgie." *MaD*, no. 12 (1947): 53–65. [Reprinted in *Parole* 1, 309–21.]
412 "La conception du devenir social." In *Le catholicisme social face aux grands courants contemporains. Semaines sociales de France, 34ᵉ session, Paris 1947,* 231–50. Lyons: Éditions de la Chronique de France, 1947. [Reprinted in *Travail*, 73–114.]
413 "L'âme de tout apostolat." *MO* 3, no. 24 (1947): 84–7. [Reprinted in *Parole* 1, 133–6.]
414 "Le dernier avatar de la théologie orientale en Occident au XIIIᵉ siècle." In *Mélanges Auguste Pelzer. Études d'histoire littéraire et doctrinale de la Scolastique médiévale offertes à Monseigneur Auguste Pelzer à l'occasion de son soixante-dixième anniversaire.* Receuil de Travaux d'Histoire et de Philologie, 3me Série, 161–81. Louvain: Éditions de l'Institut supérieur de philosophie, 1947.
415 "Un sermon ou une simple histoire." *Les cahiers du clergé rural*, no. 87 (1947): 161–4.
416 "Université et communauté." *CD*, no. 9–10 (March-April 1947): 9–11.
417 "'Sauver les principes …'." *MaD*, no. 12 (1947): 131–2.

1948

418 "Civilisation technique et spiritualité nouvelle." *MO* 4, no. 33 (May 1948): 14–37. [Reprinted in *Parole* 1, 137–58, and in *Matière*, 65–91.]
419 "Corps de l'Église et structures sociales." *JE*, no. 8 (1948): 145–53. [Reprinted in *Parole* 1, 159–69.]
420 "Matérialisme et spiritualisme." *EH*, March-April 1948, 143–5. [Reprinted in *Parole* 1, 461–4, and in *Matière*, 25–30.]
421 "Réflexions chrétiennes sur la vérité de la matière." *ES*, May-June 1948, 884–8. [Reprinted in *Parole* 1, 447–51.]

422 "Réformes de structures en chrétienté." In *Inspiration religieuse et structures temporelles*, 261–81. Paris: Éditions ouvrières, 1948. [Reprinted in *Parole* 1, 37–53.]

423 "Dimanche des chrétiens et dimanche de la cité." *MAD*, no. 13 (January-March 1948): 173–6.

424 "Les '*Quaestiones*' de Thomas de Buckingham." In *Studia Mediaevalia R.J. Martin O.P.*, 229–41. Bruges: Éditions 'De Tempel', 1948. [Reprinted in *Parole* 1, 309–21.]

425 "Évangélisme et théologie au XIIIe siècle." In *Mélanges offerts au R.P. Ferdinand Cavallera*, 339–46. Toulouse: Institut Catholique, 1948.

1949

426 "Communautés de jeunes Foyers." *Idées et forces. Cahiers trimestriels d'Économie et humanisme*, no. 4 (July-September 1949): 22–6.

1949–1950

427 "Béatitude de la pauvreté." *EE*, Second trimester 1949–50, 59–60.

1950

428 *Introduction à l'étude de S. Thomas d'Aquin.* Université de Montréal, Publications de l'Institut d'Études Médiévales, no. 11. Montréal; Paris: Institut d'études médiévales; Vrin, 1950.

429 "Chrétienté ou mission? A propos des 'mouvements de paix'." *VI*, June 1950, 745–8. [Reprinted in *Parole* 2, 255–9.]

430 "La croyance à l'assomption corporelle, en Occident de 1150 à 1250 environ." *BSFEM* 8 (1950): 13–32. [Reprinted in *Parole* 1, 201–21.]

431 "Position théologique de la sociologie religieuse." *PM* 5 (1950): 5–9. [Reprinted in *Parole* 1, 59–62.]

432 "Des prêtres ont signé: Le R.P. Chenu, dominicain." *Position*, no. 10 (June 1950).

433 "Histoire de la philosophie médiévale. Bulletin." *Actualité scientifique et industrielle*, no. 1088 (1950): 25–44. Paris: Hermann.

434 "Introduction." In *L'Imitation de Jésus Christ*, translated by P. Lamennais. Bibliothèque Spirituelle du Chrétien Lettré, i–xxx. Paris, 1950.

435 "La vérité contre l'amour?" *La Quinzaine*, no. 2 (1 December 1950): 1–2.

436 "Les catégories affectives dans la langue de l'École." *EC* 29 (1950): 123–8.

437 "Lettre d'un ami après l'encyclique *Humani Generis*." *BIR*, no. 4 (October-November 1950): 11–12.

438 "Législateur et juge devant le droit naturel." Débat. *RD (supplément "sciences de l'homme")*, no. 8 (February-March 1950): 9.

439 "Naturalisme et théologie au XIIe siècle." *RDSR* 37 (1950): 5–21.

440 "Réflexions du théologien. Où en est la philosophie du Droit?" *CD* 22 (1950): 19.

441 "Sur une image." *La Quinzaine*, no. 1 (15 November 1950): 12.

1951

442 "Abélard, le premier homme moderne." *Esprit et vie*, December 1951, 391–408. [Reprinted in *Parole* 1, 141–55.]

443 "Consistance juridique de la pauvreté évangélique constituée en état de vie." *CD*, no. 25 (December 1951): 15–18. [Reprinted in *Parole* 2, 405–8.]

444 "Dimensions collectives de l'ascèse." In *L'ascèse chrétienne et l'homme contemporain*. Cahiers de la Vie Spirituelle, 205–18. Paris: Éditions du Cerf, 1951. [Reprinted in *Parole* 2, 379–87.]

445 "La croisade." *THU*, March 1951, 16–21.

446 "La paix chrétienne." *La Quinzaine*, no. 12 (1 May 1951): 16.

447 "La transmission de la foi comme communication de l'incommunicable." *MO*, no. 63 (April 1951): 1–4.

448 "Les deux paix …" *La Quinzaine*, no. 4 (1 January 1951): 13.

449 "Les deux âges de l'allégorisme scripturaire au moyen âge." *Recherches de Théologie ancienne et médiévale* 18 (January-June 1951): 19–28. [Reprinted in *Parole* 1, 141–55.]

450 "Les moyens évangéliques." *La Quinzaine*, no. 16 (1 July 1951): 18.

451 "L'Église de France en 1950." *Le Monde*, 30 March 1951.

452 "L'étude historique de saint Thomas (Notes prises par un secrétaire pendant la communication du P. Chenu aux cérémonies du centenaire du Cardinal Mercier, Louvain 1951)." *RPL* 49 (1951): 735–43.

453 "Que sait-on de l'ordre du monde?" *La Quinzaine*, no. 25 (15 December 1951): 9.

454 "Théologie symbolique et exégèse scolastique aux XIIᵉ–XIIIᵉ siècles." In *Mélanges Joseph de Ghellinck, s.j.*. Museum Lessianum, Section Historique, no. 14, 509–26. Gembloux: Éditions J. Duculot, 1951.

1951–1952

455 "L'instituteur et le monde du travail." *EE*, Third trimester 1951–52, 71–3.

1952

456 "Dogme et théologie dans la Bulle *Unam Sanctam*." *RSR* 40 (1952): 307–16. [Reprinted in *Parole* 1, 361–9.]

457 "Les sacrements dans l'économie chrétienne." *MAD*, no. 30 (1952): 7–18. [Reprinted in *Parole* 1, 323–33.]

458 "L'homme et la nature. Perspectives sur la renaissance du XIIᵉ siècle." *AHDLM* 19 (1952): 39–66. [Reprinted in *Théologie au XIIᵉ*, 19–51.]

459 "Pour une théologie du travail." *Esprit*, January 1952, 1–12. [Reprinted in *Travail*, 9–41.]

460 "Vocabulaire biblique et vocabulaire théologique." *NRT* 74 (1952): 1029–41. [Reprinted in *Parole* 1, 171–86.]

461 "Civilisation technique et dimension nouvelle de l'amour fraternel." *ET*, no. 2 (April 1952): 8–9.

462 "Espérances de l'Église." *La Quinzaine*, no. 27 (15 January 1952): 8–9.

463 "La pauvreté mendiante: Saint Dominique." In *Problèmes de la religieuse aujourd'hui: La pauvreté*, 61–70. Paris: Éditions du Cerf, 1952.

464 "La revalorisation actuelle de la vie sacramentelle." *EE*, First trimester 1952–53, 47–50.

465 "Les femmes chrétiennes, présentes à leur temps." *TC*, no. 413 (6 June 1952): 1.

466 "L'Originalité de la morale de saint Thomas." Préface in *Théologie morale*. Vol. 3 of *Initiation théologique*, 7–12. Paris: Éditions du Cerf, 1952.

467 "L'Église fait-elle de la politique." *La Quinzaine*, no. 29 (15 February 1952): 16.

468 "Mystique et technique." *ET*, no. 1 (January 1952): 4–6.

469 "The Plan of the *Summa*." *Cross Currents* 3, no. 1 (Winter 1952): 12–25. [Translation of 1939 article.]

470 "Économie de circulation et structures apostoliques." *MO*, no. 77 (July 1952): 82–93.

1953

471 "La ville. Note de sociologie apostolique." *MO* 9, no. 82 (January 1953): 30–54. [Reprinted in *Parole* 2, 515–36.]

472 "L'expérience des spirituels au XIIᵉ siècle." *LV*, no. 10 (1953): 75–94. [Reprinted in *Parole* 2, 55–69.]

473 "Morale laïque et foi chrétienne." *CUC*, December 1953, 112–29. [Reprinted in *Parole* 2, 311–30.]

474 "*Cur homo?* Le sous-sol d'une controverse au XIIᵉ siècle." *MSR* 10 (1953): 197–204. [Reprinted in *Théologie au XIIᵉ*, 52–61.]

475 "Chrétiens et mouvement ouvrier." *TC*, no. 460 (30 April 1953): 1.

476 "La fin des temps dans la spiritualité médiévale." *LV*, no. 11 (1953): 101–16.

477 "La vérité difficile." *La Quinzaine*, no. 49 (15 January 1953): 16.

478 "L'éducation politique des chrétiens." *EE*, Second trimester 1952–53, 74–6.

479 "L'Église 'missionnaire'." *L'actualité religieuse dans le monde*, no. 8 (1953): 3–5.

480 "Marxisme et humanisme." *La Quinzaine*, no. 56 (1 May 1953): 14.

481 "Nature ou histoire? Une controverse exégétique sur la création au XIIᵉ siècle." *AHDLM* 20 (1953): 25–30.

482 "Notre conscience n'accepte pas la guerre du Vietnam pour défendre la 'civilisation chrétienne'." *La Quinzaine*, no. 56 (1 May 1953): 7.

483 "Rencontre internationale de la 'Quinzaine': introduction." *La Quinzaine,* no. 64–65 (15 September 1953): 16–17.

484 "Rencontre internationale de la 'Quinzaine': conclusion." *La Quinzaine,* no. 64–65 (15 September 1953): 22.

485 "Review of A. Hayen, *Saint Thomas d'Aquin et la vie de l'Église* (Louvain-Paris, 1952)." *BT* 8, no. 3 (1953): 771–72.

486 "Review of *Initiation théologique,* 3 vols (Paris: Éditions du Cerf, 1952)." *BT* 8, no. 3 (1953): 715–18.

487 "Théologie du travail." *Sources,* September 1953, 19–30.

488 "Une collection manuscrite des oeuvres complètes de S. Thomas d'Aquin par le roi aragonais de Naples, 1480–1493." Co-author Jean Destrez. *AFP* 23 (1953): 309–26.

489 "*Exemplaria* universitaires des XIIIᵉ et XIVᵉ siècles." Co-author Jean Destrez. *Scriptorium: International Review of Manuscript Studies* 7, no. 1 (1953): 68–80.

490 "Échec des chrétientés et efficacité évangélique de l'église." Notes d'une conférence donnée par Chenu. *Cahiers Sainte Jeanne,* June 1953, 185–7. [Reprinted in *Parole* 2, 311–30.]

1954

491 *Introduzione allo studio di San Tommaso d'Aquino.* Firenze: Libreria Editrice Fiorentina, 1954. [Italian translation of *Introduction à l'étude de saint Thomas d'Aquin* (Paris: Vrin, 1954, 2 ed.)]

492 *Introduction à l'étude de saint Thomas d'Aquin.* Publications de l'Institut d'Études Médiévales – Université de Montréal. 2 ed. vol. XI. Paris: Vrin, 1954.

493 "Conscience de l'histoire et théologie au XIIᵉ siècle." *AHDLM* 21 (1954): 107–33. [Reprinted in *Théologie au XIIᵉ,* 62–89.]

494 "Le chrétien dans le monde." *La Nef,* January 1954, 217–24. [Reprinted in *Parole* 2, 295–300.]

495 "Le sacerdoce des prêtres ouvriers." *VI,* February 1954, 175–81. [Reprinted in *Parole* 2, 275–81.]

496 "Moines, clercs, laïcs. Au carrefour de la vie évangélique au XIIᵉ siècle." *RHE* 49 (1954): 59–80. Reprinted in *Théologie au XIIᵉ,* 225–51.]

497 "Découverte de la nature et philosophie de l'homme à l'école de Chartres au XIIᵉ siècle." *CHM* 2, no. 2 (1954): 313–25.

498 "Platon à Citeaux." *AHDLM* 21 (1954): 99–106.

1955

499 *Pour une théologie du travail.* Coll. Esprit. Paris: Éditions du Seuil, 1955. [Collection of four articles written between 1945 and 1952.]

500 "Culture et théologie à Jumièges après l'ère féodale." In *Jumièges. Congrès scientifique du XIIIe centenaire (Rouen, 10–12 juin, 1954),* 775–81. Rouen: Éditions du Cerf, 1955.

501 "L'originalité de la morale de S. Thomas." In *Initiation théologique,* 7–12. Paris: Éditions du Cerf, 1955.

502 "Officium. Théologien et canoniste." In *Étude de l'histoire du droit canonique dédiée à Gabriel Le Bras,* 835–9. Paris, 1955.

503 "Review of Leroy Edwin Froom, *The Prophetic Faith of Our Fathers,* Washington 1950." *RHE* 55 (1955): 165–7.

504 "Y a-t-il une théologie du travail?" *LV,* no. 20 (March 1955): 223–36.

505 "*Involucrum.* Le mythe selon les théologiens médiévaux." *AHDLM* 22 (1955): 75–9.

1956

506 *De Arbeit Pleidooi voor ein theologie.* Antwegen, 1956. [Dutch translation of *Pour une théologie de travail* (Paris: Seuil, 1955).]

507 *Die Arbeit und der göttliche Kosmos. Versuch einer Theologie der Arbeit.* Mainz: Matthias Grünewald Verlag, 1956. [German translation of *Pour une théologie du travail* (Paris: Seuil, 1955).]

508 "Foi et théologie d'après le P. Gardeil." *RSPT* 40 (1956): 645–51. [Reprinted in *Parole* 1, 269–75.]

509 "Dimension sociologique et institutionnelle de la pastoration." *PM,* no. 2 (1956): 58–61.

510 "L'esprit de Saint Dominique: Vérité communiquée." *France dominicaine,* April-May 1956, 124–5.

511 "Notice of W. Dettloff o.f.m., 'Cur Divus Thomas?' (in *Wissenschaft und Weisheit,* 18 (1955), 64–71); A. Hayen s.j., *Der heilige Thomas von Aquin gestern und heute* (Frankfurt 1954)." *BT,* no. 3 (1956): 1033.

512 "Présentation." In *Jean de Sècheville. De Principiis Naturae. Texte Critique avec Introduction et Tables,* edited by R.-M. Giguère o.p. Université de Montréal, Publications de l'Institut d'Études Médiévales. Vol. XIV, 7–8. Paris: Vrin, 1956.

513 "Saint Thomas d'Aquin." In *Les Saints de tous les jours. Mars,* 82–9. Paris: Éditions Le Club du Livre chrétien, 1956.

1957

514 *La théologie est-elle une science?* Coll. Je Sais-Je Crois. Paris: Arthème Fayard, 1957.

515 *Pour une théologie du travail.* Paris: Seuil, 1957. [First reprint of a work published in 1955.]

516 *La théologie au XIIe siècle.* Coll. Études de Philosophie Médiévale, no. 45. Paris: Vrin, 1957. [Collection of nineteen articles written between 1925 and 1954.]

517 *Introduction to the Summa of St. Thomas.* Washington, DC: The Thomist Reader, 1957. [English translation of ch. 11 of *Introduction à l'étude de saint Thomas d'Aquin* (Paris: Vrin; Montréal: Institut d'études médiévales, 1950).]

518 *La théologie comme science au XIIIe siècle.* Third revised edition. Coll. Bibliothèque Thomiste, no. 23. Paris: Vrin, 1957.

519 "Communauté humaine et présence missionnaire." *PM*, no. 4 (1957): 95–8. [Reprinted in *Parole* 2, 261–4.]

520 "Towards a Theology of Work." *Cross Currents* 8, no. 2 (Spring 1957): 127–38. [English translation of "Pour une théologie du travail" (in *Études*, January 1952, 1–12).]

521 "'Mission': à l'étranger, à l'intérieur. Chronique." *PM*, no. 3 (1957): 87–9.

522 "*Spiritus.* Le vocabulaire de l'âme au XIIe siècle." *RSPT* 41 (1957): 209–32.

1958

523 *La teologia è una scienza?* Enciclopedia Cattolica Dell'Uomo d'Oggi. Catania: Ed. Paoline, 1958. [Italian translation of *La théologie est-elle une science?* (Paris: Fayard, 1957).]

524 *Le couvent saint Jacques et les deux renaissances du XIIIe et du XVIe siècles.* Cahiers Saint Jacques, no. 26. Paris: N.p., 1958.

525 *The Scope of the Summa of St. Thomas.* Compact Studies. Washington, DC: The Thomist Press, 1958. [English translation of ch. 11 of *Introduction à l'étude de saint Thomas d'Aquin* (Paris: Vrin, 1950).]

526 "Des diacres en l'an 2000?" *PM*, no. 7 (1958): 86–92. [Reprinted in *Parole* 2, 305–10.]

527 "Histoire et allégorie au douzième siècle." In *Festgabe Joseph Lortz*, eds Erwin Iserloh and Peter Manns, 59–71. Baden-Baden: Bruno Grimm, 1958. [Reprinted in *Parole* 1, 157–70.]

528 "L'Église en état de mission." *PeM*, no. 1 (1958): 427–30. [Reprinted in *Parole* 2, 237–40.]

529 "L'évolution de la théologie de la guerre." *LV*, no. 38 (1958): 76–97. [Reprinted in *Parole* 2, 571–91.]

530 "Position théologique de la sociologie religieuse." *PM*, no. 5 (1958): 5–9. [Reprinted in *Parole* 1, 59–62.]

531 "Sociologie de la connaissance et théologie de la foi." In *Sociologie et religion.* Coll. Recherches et Débats, no. 25, 71–7. Paris: Desclée de Brouwer, 1958. [Reprinted in *Parole* 1, 63–8.]

532 "'Civique' ou 'politique'." *ICI*, 15 June 1958, 3–4. [Reprinted in *Parole* 2, 611–15.]

533 "Apparitions." *Rosaire et vie chrétienne*, February 1958, 1–2.

534 "Le chrétien et la colonisation." *Bulletin des chrétiens ouvriers de Montreuil*, December 1958.

535 "L'évolution de l'humanité et le phénomène religieux." *Bulletin de l'A.N.E.J.I. de Normandie* (1958), 17–25.

536 "Review of A. Hayen s.j., *La communication de l'être d'après saint Thomas d'Aquin* (2 vols., Desclée de Brouwer, 1957 and 1959); Idem., 'La théologie aux XIIᵉ, XIIIᵉ, et XXᵉ siècles' (in *NRT*, 79 (1957), 1009–28, 80 (1958), 113–32); Idem., 'La vocation philosophique du chrétien' (in *Sciences ecclésiastiques*, 10 (1958), 5–22); O.N. Derisi, 'La comunicaciòn con el ser segùn Santo Tomàs de Aquino' (in *Sapientia*, 13 (1958), 142–5); P.E. Persson, 'Le plan de la Somme théologique et le rapport 'Ratio-Revelatio" (in *RPL*, 1958 (LVI), 545–72)." *BT*, no. 2 (1958): 468–72.

537 "Un Dieu fait homme." *Panorama*, Christmas 1958.

538 "Une théologie axiomatique au XIIᵉ siècle. Alain de Lille (+ 1203)." *Citeaux in de Nederlanden* 9 (1958): 137–42.

1959

539 *St. Thomas d'Aquin et la théologie.* Coll. Maîtres Spirituels, no. 17. Paris: Éditions du Seuil, 1959.

540 *Is Theology a Science?* London: Burns and Oates, 1959. [English translation of *La théologie est-elle une science?* (Paris: Fayard, 1957).]

541 "1939–1959: Classe ouvrière et Église missionnaire." *TC*, no. 773 (1 May 1959): 20. [Reprinted in *Parole* 2, 283–6.]

542 "La condition humaine du prêtre au moyen âge." *ES*, December 1959, 725–8. [Reprinted in *Parole* 2, 287–91.]

543 "Lecture de la Bible et philosophie au moyen âge." In *Mélanges Étienne Gilson*, 161–71. Paris: Vrin, 1959. [Reprinted in *Parole* 1, 187–200.]

544 "L'avenir professionnel de l'enfant. Perspectives théologiques." In *L'enfant et son avenir professionnel. Esquisse d'une théologie de la création et du travail*, 9–48. Paris: Éditions Fleurus, 1959. [Reprinted as "Théologie du travail" in *Parole* 2, 543–70.]

545 "Vérité et liberté dans la foi du croyant." *ES* 27 (April 1959): 598–619. [Reprinted in *Parole* 1, 337–59.]

546 "Bestaat er en theologie van der arbeid?" *De Gids* 50 (1959): 716–26.

547 "Comment Thomas d'Aquin choisit l'Évangile." *TC*, no. 760 (30 January 1959): 11.

548 "Der theologische Ort der Religionssoziologie." *Theologischer Digest* 2, no. 4 (1959): 215–17.

549 "El Evangelio de la paz y la teologia de la guerra." *Criterio* 32, no. 1346 (1959): 916–23.

550 "Fécondité et création." *Foyers*, October 1959, 23–31.

551 "Idéologies et mystiques dans le monde ouvrier." *Bulletin de l'A.N.E.J.I. de Normandie* (1959), 30–40.

552 "Jean de la Grange, abbé de Fécamp (1357–1373) et saint Thomas d'Aquin." In *L'Abbaye bénédictine de Fécamp. Ouvrage scientifique du XIIIᵉ centenaire 658–1958*, 151–4. Fécamp: L. Durand et Fils, 1959.

553 "La coexistence pacifique. L'ouvrage de M. Fr. Perroux." *TC*, no. 776 (22 May 1959): 7–8.

554 "La décolonisation. Réponse à Aline Diop." *Tam-tam*, March 1959, 11–12.

555 "La royauté du Christ d'après les théologiens médiévaux." *VS*, no. 454 (October 1959): 325–35.

556 "Les impératifs moraux (et religieux) du développement économique." *Session 4–13 août 1959 sur le développement économique des pays pré-industrialisés.* Toumlilinè, Maroc: N.p., 1959.

557 "L'actualité de saint Anselme." *ICI*, 1 July 1959, 28–9.

558 "L'obscurantisme au moyen âge." *Bulletine des missions du Tchad* (1959).

559 "L'Église au jour le jour." *VS*, January 1959, 61–3.

560 "Marie éducatrice de la foi par le rosaire." *Cahiers marials*, November 1959, 405–6.

561 "Mystère chrétien et transformation du monde." *Ad lucem*, August 1959, 3–7.

562 "Personne et amour." *ET*, May 1959, 23–5.

563 "Plus je travaille, plus Dieu est créateur." *TC*, no. 787 (7 August 1959): 11.

564 "Préface." In *Sociologie et religion*, by Alain Birou. Coll. La Sociologie Religieuse, 7–9. Paris: Les éditions ouvrières, 1959.

565 "Review of A. Hayen s.j., *La communication de l'être d'après saint Thomas d'Aquin*, 2 vols (Desclée de Brouwer, 1957 et 1959)." *BT*, no. 3 (1959): 957–9.

566 "Réalités sociales et économiques du monde ouvrier." *Bulletin de l'A.N.E.J.I. de Normandie* (1959), 21–9.

567 "Truth and Freedom in the Conscience of the Believer." *Cross Currents* 10, no. 3 (1959): 223–37.

568 "Un théologien au passé et au présent: Le Père Chenu." Interview with Jean-Marie Paupert. *Ecclesia, lectures chrétiennes*, no. 122 (May 1959): 111–18.

569 "Wahrheit und Freiheit im Glauben." *Wort und Wahrheit* 10 (1959): 573–87.

1960

570 *Thomas von Aquin in Selbstzeugnissen und Bilddokumenten.* Hamburg: Rowohlt, 1960. [German translation, revised and amplified, of *S. Thomas d'Aquin et la théologie* (Paris: Éditions du Seuil, 1959).]

571 *Bibliographie thomiste.* Deuxième édition revue et complétée par M.-D. Chenu. Authors P. Mandonnet and J. Destrez. Bibliothèque Thomiste, no. 1. Paris: Vrin, 1960.

572 *Teologia del trabajo.* Barcelona, 1960. [Spanish translation of *Pour une théologie du travail* (Paris: Éditions du Seuil, 1955).]

573 *Das Werk des hl. Thomas von Aquin.* Heidelberg-Graz: Kerle-Vel. Styrie, 1960. [German translation of *Introduction à l'étude de saint Thomas d'Aquin* (Paris: Vrin, 1950).]

574 "Dé-christianisation ou non-christianisation?" *Signes des temps,* January 1960, 3–5. [Reprinted in *Parole* 2, 247–53.]

575 "Pour ou contre Dieu. La pensée contemporaine." *ICI,* 1 January 1960, 15–26. [Reprinted in *Parole* 2, 171–87.]

576 "Situation humaine. Corporalité et temporalité." In *L'homme et son destin. Actes du 1ᵉʳ congrès international de philosophie médiévale, Louvain 1958,* 22–48. Louvain: Nauwelaerts, 1960. [Reprinted in *Parole* 2, 411–36 and in *Matière,* 31–63.]

577 "Vers une théologie de la technique." In *La technique et l'homme.* Coll. Recherches et Débats, no. 31, 157–66. Paris: Desclée de Brouwer, 1960. [Reprinted as "Condition nouvelle faite à l'homme dans la civilisation technique" in *Parole* 2, 465–74 and in *Matière,* 93–104.]

578 "Économie et promesse." In *L'univers économique et social.* Vol. 9 of *Encyclopédie française,* cc. 9.64–9 to 9.64–13. Paris: Larousse, 1960. [Reprinted in *Parole* 2, 617–29 and *Matière,* 125–39.]

579 "Christianisme et pensée des hommes." In *L'Église, les peuples et la culture,* 45–58. Paris: Ad Lucem, 1960.

580 "Diakone in Jahre 2000?" *Theologie der Gegenwart* 3, no. 4 (1960): 240–3. [German translation of "Des diacres en l'an 2000?", in *PM,* no. 7, 86–92, 1958.]

581 "Dimension religieuse des temps libres." *Bulletin professionel,* no. 26 (December 1960): 1–2.

582 "Le travail, collaboration de l'homme à la création." Notes of an auditor in *Le travail.* Document, no. 12, 1–7, 1960.

583 "L'École et le monde du travail." *Vie enseignante,* October 1960, 4–12.

584 "L'espérance des pauvres et les lois économiques." *Kultuurleven,* October 1960.

585 "Mystère et raison." In *Le mystère. Semaine des intellectuels catholiques (18–25 novembre, 1959),* 158–71. Paris: Pierre Horay, 1960.

586 "Présentation." In *Vie de saint Dominique,* by H.-D. Lacordaire, 7–11. Paris: Éditions du Cerf, 1960. [Reprinted in *Parole* 2, 617–29 and *Matière,* 125–39.]

587 "Érigène à Citeaux. Expérience intérieure et spiritualité objective." In *La philosophie et ses problèmes. Recueil d'études de doctrine et d'histoire offert à Monseigneur R. Jolivet,* 99–107. Lyon; Paris: Emmanuel Vitte, 1960.

1961

588 "Apostolat de simple présence et charité politique." *PM,* no. 14 (1961): 97–101. [Reprinted in *Parole* 2, 265–8.]

589 "Histoire sainte et vie spirituelle." *VS*, May 1961, 506–13. [Reprinted in *Parole* 1, 283–8.]

590 "La fin de l'ère constantinienne." In *Un concile pour notre temps*, 59–83. Paris: Éditions du Cerf, 1961. [Reprinted in *Parole* 2, 17–36.]

591 "Vie conciliaire de l'Église et sociologie de la foi." *ES* 29 (1961): 678–89. [Reprinted in *Parole* 1, 371–83.]

592 "'Spiritualisme' et sociologie." In *Jacques Leclerq. L'homme, son oeuvre, ses amis*, 209–16. Tournai; Paris: Casterman, 1961. [Reprinted in *Parole* 2, 437–45.]

593 "De hoop der armen en de wetten der economic." *Geugd en cultuur* (1961), 3–8, 63–108. [Dutch translation of "L'espérance des pauvres et les lois économiques", in *Kultuurleven*, October 1960.]

594 "Du bon usage des encycliques." *L*, no. 38 (September-October 1961): vi–ix.

595 "Is the Modern World Atheist?" Co-author F. Heer. *Cross Currents* 11, no. 1 (Winter 1961): 5–24. [English translation of "Pour ou contre Dieu. La pensée contemporaine", in *ICI*, no. 1, January 1960, 15–26.]

596 "La coexistence culturelle de la civilisation arabe maghrébine et de la civilisation occidentale au Moyen Âge." *Confluent* (1961), 6–12, 160–7, 277–86, 366–74.

597 "La paix du Christ et la paix tout court." *TC*, no. 911 (25 December 1961): 22.

598 "La théologie de la loi ancienne selon saint Thomas d'Aquin." *RT* 69, no. 4 (1961): 485–97.

599 "L'avennire professionale del ragazzo." In *Per una teologia della creazione e del lavoro*, by A. de Bovis and H. Rondet. Rome: Ave, 1961. [Italian translation of "L'avenir professionnel de l'enfant", in M.-D. Chenu et al., *L'enfant et son avenir professionnel* (Paris 1959).]

600 "Review of *L'homme et son destin d'après les penseurs du moyen-âge*, Actes du 1er congrès de philosophie médiévale, 28 août–4 septembre 1958 (Louvain; Paris: Nauwelaetrs, 1960)." *Cahiers de civilisation médiévale* 4 (1961): 487–9.

601 "Une définition pythagoricienne de la vérité au Moyen Age." *AHDLM* 28 (1961): 7–13.

602 "Vocation actuelle du laïc chrétien." Notes taken during a talk given at Ad Lucem de Bruxelles by Père Chenu, o.p. *Ad Lucem*, March 1961, 5–10.

1962

603 *Le Couvent Saint-Jacques et les deux Renaissances des XIIIe et XVIe siècles*. Cahiers Saint-Jacques, no. 26. Paris, 1962.

604 *El evangelismo*. Biblioteca Dominicana, no. 4. Bogotà, 1962.

605 "Le message du concile au monde." *TC*, no. 957 (9 November 1962): 13–14. [Reprinted in *Parole* 2, 639–45.]

606 "Libération politique et messianisme religieux." *PeM*, no. 19 (1962): 529–42. [Reprinted in *Parole* 2, 599–610.]

607 "Spiritualité de la matière." *vs*, no. 106 (May 1962): 579–87. [Reprinted in *Parole* 2, 453–9 and in *Matière*, 15–23.]

608 "Un concile à la dimension du monde." *TC*, no. 953 (12 October 1962): 9. [Reprinted in *Parole* 2, 633–7.]

609 "*Économie de circulation et évangélisation.*" *PeM* 16 (1962): 33–9. [Reprinted in *Parole* 2, 537–42.]

610 "À la mémoire renouvelée du *doctor universalis* Alain de Lille." *Citeaux* 13, no. 1 (1962): 67–70.

611 "Civilisation du travail, civilisation du loisir." *TC*, 1962, 18 May 1962. Paris.

612 "Devant le Concile." *L*, no. 49 (September 1962): 7–8.

613 "Foi et sacrement." *MaD*, October 1962, 69–77.

614 "La renovación de la Iglesia." *Criterion (Buenos Aires)* 35, no. 1417–1418 (1962): 890–2.

615 "Le concile: Noël de l'Église." *TC*, no. 963 (21 December 1962): 3.

616 "Le loisir promoteur d'humanité." *TC*, no. 932 (18 May 1962): 18.

617 "Les pauvres et les espérances messianiques du monde." *ET*, no. 42 (1962): 8–13.

618 "Les théologiens ont la parole. Le tyrannicide." *Le Monde*, 26 September 1962.

619 "Lettre de Rome." *L*, no. 52 (December 1962): 1–3.

620 "L'Église et le droit de propriété." *CD* (1962).

621 "La pauvreté évangélique dans une économie d'abondance." *EE*, no. 7 (1962–63): 77–80.

622 "Nouvelles du Concile." *Amis de Saint-Jacques* 1 (1962).

623 "Raison d'état et bien commun." *TC*, no. 936 (15 June 1962): 12–13.

624 "Réflexions d'un théologien sur ses souvenirs de la Mission de France et de la Mission de Paris." *Ecclesia, lectures chrétiennes*, no. 159 (June 1962): 43–50.

625 "The Church's Conciliar Life and the Sociology of Faith." *Cross Currents* 12, no. 2 (Spring 1962): 132–42. [English translation of "Vie conciliaire de l'Église et sociologie de la foi" (in *ES* 29, 1961, 678–89).]

626 "The Scope of the *Summa*." In *Compact Studies*, 288–90. Washington, DC: Thomist Press, 1962.

627 "Une république algérienne laïque." *TC*, no. 923 (16 March 1962): 13.

1963

628 *The Theology of Work. An Exploration.* Dublin: Gill & Son, 1963. [English translation of *Pour une théologie du travail* (Paris 1955).]

629 *Nature and Man at the School of Chartres in the 12th Century.* Paris: UNESCO, 1963. [English translation of "Découverte de la Nature et Philosophie de

l'homme à l'école de Chartres au XIIe siècle" (in *CHM*, 1954 (II), no. 2, 313–25).]

630 "Les théologiens et le collège épiscopal. Autonomie et service." In *L'évêque dans l'Église du Christ. Travaux du Symposium de l'Arbresle*, 1960, eds H. Bouëssé and A. Mandouze, 175–91. Bruges: Desclée de Brouwer, 1963. [Reprinted as "Les théologiens et les évêques" in *Parole* 1, 289–305.]

631 "Orthodoxie et hérésie. Le point de vue du théologien." *Annales* 18 (January-February 1963): 75–80. Conférence given for the opening of the colloquium "*Hérésie et sociétés.*" Royaumont, 27–30 May, 1962. [Reprinted in *Parole* 1, 69–74.]

632 "Paradoxe de la pauvreté évangélique et construction du monde." *CUC*, June-July 1963, 401–15. [Reprinted in *Parole* 2, 389–404, and in *Matière*, 105–24.]

633 "Prophètes et théologiens dans l'Église. Parole de Dieu." *MO*, no. 200 (October 1963): 59–70. [Reprinted in *Parole* 2, 201–12.]

634 "Un concile 'pastoral'." *PeM*, no. 21 (1963): 182–202. [Reprinted in *Parole* 2, 655–72.]

635 "Un pontificat entré dans l'histoire (mort de Jean XXIII)." *TC*, no. 988 (7 June 1963): 24, 9. [Reprinted in *Parole* 2, 189–98.]

636 "Arbeit." In *Handbuch theologischer Grundbegriffe*, ed. Heinrich Fries, 75–86. Munich: Kösel-Verlag, 1963.

637 "France-Maghreb: le passé, gage de l'avenir." *Confluent*, May 1963, 206–13.

638 "Humanizacja Boga." *Za i Przeciw*, December 1963.

639 "Ibn Rosh et la civilisation occidentale." *Dialogues*, November 1963, 36–9.

640 "Intervista sulla seconda sessione del Concilio." *Gazetta del Popolo*, 10 December 1963.

641 "Jean XXIII le pape du dialogue." *Dialogues*, June 1963, 27–31.

642 "Juan XXIII en la historia." *El Ciervo*, August 1963, 225–32.

643 "La Chiesa come Comunità nei lavori del concilio." *Questitalia*, December 1963, 6–14.

644 "Le collège des évêques et la communauté des chrétiens. A propos du Concile." *Terre entière*, September 1963, 35–40.

645 "Les inspirations de Jean XXIII." *Signes du Temps*, no. 7 (1963): 3–5.

646 "Lettre d'un ami présent au Concile." *EE*, First trimester 1963, 66–8.

647 "L'Afrique au Concile." *PeM*, no. 20 (January 1963): 11–18.

648 "L'Afrique au Concile." *Tam-Tam*, January 1963, 30–4.

649 "L'Afrique, jeunesse de l'Église." *Afrique nouvelle*, October 1963.

650 "L'Église au Concile." *Chrétiens d'aujourd'hui (MFR)*, December 1963.

651 "L'homme-dans-le-monde." In *St. Thomas d'Aquin aujourd'hui*. Recherches de Philosophie, no. 6, 171–5. Paris: Desclée de Brouwer, 1963.

652 "L'Église et le monde." *Documentation Hollandaise du Concile,* no. 52 (1963): 1–4.

653 "Nouveauté de la paix (*'Pacem in Terris'*)." *TC,* no. 980 (19 April 1963): 5–6.

654 "Peut-on revenir en arrière?" *ICI,* no. 194 (1963): 5–8. [Panel discussion]

655 "Premières réflexions sur l'Encyclique *Pacem in Terris.*" *L,* no. 57 (May 1963): 1–3.

656 "Prière et travail." *Rosaire et vie chrétienne,* June 1963, 8–9.

657 "Préface." In *Le Christ et l'Église: Théologie du Mystère,* by M.-J. LeGuillou, 9–12. Paris: Éditions du Centurion, 1963.

658 "Renouveau de l'Église." *Za i Przeciw,* October 1963.

659 "Rome, Moscou et la guerre." Interview with Georges Suffert. *L'Express,* no. 618 (18 April 1963): 16–17.

660 "Scholastik." In *Handbuch theologischer Grundbegriffe,* ed. Heinrich Fries, 478–94. Munich: Kösel-Verlag, 1963.

661 "Tradition et sociologie de la foi." In *Église et tradition,* eds Johannes Betz and Heinrich Fries, 225–32. Paris: Éditions Xavier Mappus, 1963. [German version in 1960.]

662 "Témoigner, ce n'est pas convertir, c'est être visiblement ce qu'on est." *TC,* no. 1000 (5 September 1963): 5–6. [Reprinted in *Communauté chrétienne* (1967).]

663 "Un avvenire socialista del mondo." Report on conference given by Chenu, by Ugo D'Ascia. *Giovedi,* 7 November 1963.

664 "Une constitution pastorale de l'Église." *DO-C,* no. 205 (1963): 1–13. Rome.

1964

665 *La foi dans l'intelligence.* Vol. 1 of *La Parole de Dieu.* Coll. Cogitatio Fidei, no. 10. Paris: Éditions du Cerf, 1964. [Contains articles written between 1924 and 1963.]

666 *Towards Understanding Saint Thomas.* Translated with authorized corrections and bibliographical additions. Translated by A.-M. Landry o.p. and D. Hughes o.p. Chicago: Henry Regnery Company, 1964. [English translation of *Introduction à l'étude de saint Thomas* (Paris: Vrin, 1950).]

667 *Per una teologia del lavoro.* Le Idee e la Vita, no. 20. Torino: Berla, 1964. [Italian translation of *Pour une théologie du travail* (Paris 1955).]

668 *L'Évangile dans le temps.* Vol. 2 of *La Parole de Dieu.* Coll. Cogitatio Fidei, no. 11. Paris: Éditions du Cerf, 1964. [Contains articles written between 1924 and 1963.]

669 "Astrologia praedicabilis. Les pressentiments de l'économie chrétienne chez les païens." *AHDLM* 31 (1964): 61–5.

670 "Ce Noël sera-t-il une mystification? (L'Évangile et la bombe)." *TC*, no. 1067 (17 December 1964): 16–17.

671 "En guise de conclusion (Après receuil de témoignages, 10 ans après la crise des p.o. de février 1954)." *L*, no. 67–68 (March 1964): 62–3.

672 "Kosciól jako wspólnota." *Tygodnik Powszechny* 18, no. 20 (17 May 1964): 1, 5.

673 "La chiesa popolo di Dio nella storia (per comprendere la terza sessione del Concilio)." *H* 19 (1964): 1035–8.

674 "La décadence de l'allégorisation. Un témoin, Garnier de Rochefort (+ v. 1200)." In *L'Homme devant Dieu. Mélanges offerts au Père Henri de Lubac.* Coll. Théologie, no. 57, 129–35. Paris: Aubier, 1964.

675 "La pauvreté mendiante: saint Dominique." In *La pauvreté.* 3 ed., 61–70. Paris: Éditions du Cerf, 1964.

676 "Le théologien et son vocabulaire." In *Incarnation ou eschatologie? Contribution à l'histoire du vocabulaire religieux contemporain 1935–1955*, by Bernard Besret, 11–16. Paris: Éditions du Cerf, 1964.

677 "Le vingtième anniversaire de l'abbé Godin." *Le Monde*, 17 January 1964.

678 "Les chrétiens, la lutte contre la misère, le développement économique." Antsirabe, 1964.

679 "Les signes des temps." *NRT* 86 (1964): 29–39.

680 "Lettre d'Assise." *L*, no. 65 (January 1964): 12–13.

681 "Lettera da Assisi di Padre M.-D. Chenu." *Humanitas* 19 (1964): 473–5. [Italian translation of "Lettre d'Assise", in *L*, January 1964, no. 65, 12–13.]

682 "Lettres de Rome." *L*, no. 76 (November 1964): 4–8.

683 "L'Église et la civilisation du travail." *DO-C*, no. 124 (1964): 1–5.

684 "L'Eglise, peuple messianique." *ICI*, no. 224, 15 September 1964, 30–2.

685 "L'Église peuple de Dieu dans l'histoire." *L*, no. 71–72 (July-August 1964): 1–3.

686 "L'Église présente aux détresses et aux espérances du monde." *TC*, no. 1032 (16 April 1964): 14–15.

687 "Nadzieje chrzescijan zwiazane z soborem." *Za i Przeciw* 8, no. 13 (1964): 2.

688 "Oui, il y a une politique de l'Évangile." *Ecclesia. Lectures Chrétiennes*, no. 187 (October 1964): 61–8.

689 "Pour une lecture théologique du Syllabus." *RD*, no. 50 (1964): 43–51.

690 "Prefazione." In *Laici per tempi nuovi*, by M. Rossi, 7–11. Vicenza: La Locusta, 1964.

691 "Préface." In *Le renouveau de la morale*, by Servais Pinckaers. Coll. Cahiers de l'Actualité Religieuse, no. 19, 7–8. Paris: Casterman, 1964.

692 "Réflexions sur un anniversaire: Mars 1954 – mars 1964. En guise de conclusion." *L*, no. 67–68 (March-April 1964): 62–3.

693 "Valeur chrétienne des réalités terrestres." *Documentation Hollandaise du Concile*, no. 157 (1964): 1–7.

694 "Vingt ans après [la mort de l'abbé Godin]." *PeM*, no. 24 (1964): 17–19.

695 "*Consecratio mundi.*" *NRT* 86 (1964): 606–18.

1965

696 *Pour une théologie du travail.* Livre de Vie, no. 53. Paris: Éditions du Seuil, 1965. [Reprint of a work originally published in 1955 (Paris: Seuil).]

697 "Les signes du temps." *NRT* 87 (1965): 29–39. [Reprinted in *Peuple*, 35–55.]

698 "Une constitution pastorale de l'Église." *Documentation Hollandaise du Concile*, no. 205 (1965): 1–13. [Reprinted in *Peuple*, 11–34.]

699 "Au moyen-âge." *LV*, no. 71 (1965): 32–40.

700 "Dans la nature même de l'Église (prêtres-ouvriers)." *TC*, no. 1112 (28 October 1965): 14.

701 "Du bon usage des portraits des saints." *Terre entière*, no. 12 (July-August 1965): 94–9.

702 "Ewangelia a bomba atomowa." *Biulletyn Informacyjny Chrzescianskiego Stowarzyszenia Spolecznego*, no. 3 (1965): 57–62.

703 "Exigences présentes de la liberté religieuse." In *Essais sur la liberté religieuse.* Coll. Recherches et Débats, no. 50, 71–6. Paris: Desclée de Brouwer, 1965.

704 "I laici e la 'consecratio mundi'." In *La Chiesa del Vaticano II. Studi e commenti intorno alla costituzione dommatica "Lumen Gentium"*, ed. by G. Barauna o.f.m., 978–93. Firenze: Valecchi, 1965.

705 "Il teologo e il giornalista." *H* 20 (1965): 1024–9.

706 "La Chiesa e il mondo." In *I grandi temi del Concilio.* Biblioteca Di Cultura Religiosa, no. 111, 833–43. Rome: Paoline, 1965. [Italian translation of "L'Église et le monde", *DO-C*, 1963, n. 52, 1–17.]

707 "La Chiesa fa i conti con la storia." Interview with Ugo d'Ascia. *Avanti Della Domenica* (10 October 1965): 7.

708 "La Chiesa nel mondo. I segni dei tempi (Fede e mondo moderno)." Milan: Vita e Pensiero, 1965. [Text of "La Chiesa e il mondo" (in *I grandi temi de Concilio*, Rome 1965) expanded by the author.]

709 "Le jubilé du P. Chenu." *L*, no. 79 (March 1965): 7–9.

710 "Le théologien et la vie. Un entretien avec le Père Chenu." Interview. *ICI*, no. 233 (1965): 28–30.

711 "Les communautés naturelles, mystère et structure dans l'Église." In *Pastorale et communautés naturelles.* Dossier Masses Ouvrières, 97–108. Paris: Les éditions ouvrières, 1965. [Supplement to *MO* no. 219 (June 1965).]

712 "Les laïcs et la 'consécration du monde'." *L*, no. 78 (February 1965): 23–30.

713 "Les masses humaines, mon prochain?" *Jeunes femmes*, no. 87 (April 1965): 23–34.

714 "Les masses pauvres." In *Église et pauvreté*. Coll. Unam Sanctam, no. 57, 169–76. Paris: Éditions du Cerf, 1965.

715 "Les signes du temps." *DO-C*, no. 187 (1965): 1–8.

716 "Les événements et le royaume de Dieu." *ICI*, no. 250 (1965): 18–19.

717 "L'Evangelo nel tempo." *Il Gallo*, September 1965, 3–4.

718 "L'apport de vingt siècles." *VS*, no. 112 (1965): 659–79.

719 "L'homme est le partenaire de Dieu dans la construction du monde." *TC*, no. 1119 (16 December 1965): 18.

720 "L'ordre des prêcheurs interpellé par le Concile." *CSD*, no. 60 (July-August 1965): 470–4.

721 "L'Église dans le monde (extraits conférence – Rome)." *TC*, no. 1109 (7 October 1965): 18.

722 "L'Église des pauvres." *MAD*, no. 81 (1965): 9–13.

723 "L'Église ne crée pas un monde de valeurs propres." *TC*, no. 1079 (11 March 1965): 14.

724 "Liberté évangélique et avenir humain." Libres propos du fr. M.-D. Chenu recueillis par le fr. B. Quelquejeu." *EE*, no. 3 (1965–66): 59–64.

725 "Naissance de la théologie. Au Moyen Age." *LV*, no. 71 (January-February 1965): 32–40.

726 "Officium. Théologiens et canonistes." In *Études d'histoire du droit canonique dédiées à Gabriel le Bras*, 835–9. Paris: Sirey, 1965.

727 "Os leigos e a 'consecratio mundi'." In *A Igreja do Vaticano II. Estudos em tôorno da Constituçao Conciliar sôbre a Igreja*, eds G. Barauna o.f.m. and F. Vier o.f.m., 1001–17. Petròpolis: Vozes, 1965. [Portuguese translation of "I laici e la 'consecratio mundi'." In G. Barauna o.f.m., *La Chiesa del Vaticano II* (Firenze: Valecchi, 1965).]

728 "Pour une lecture théologique de Syllabus." In *Essais sur la liberté religieuse*. Coll. Recherches et Débats, no. 50, 43–51. Paris: Desclée de Brouwer, 1965.

729 "Preface." In *La Chiesa in Dialogo. La III Sessione del Concilio Ecumenico*, by C. Riva, 7–10. Brescia: Morcelliana, 1965.

730 "Préface." In *Laïcs pour les temps nouveaux*, by Mario Rossi, trans. by Lucien Pélisher. Coll. Frères Du Monde, 9–12. Paris: Editions de l'Épi, 1965.

731 "Préface." In *Pour une politique évangélique*, by J.-M. Paupert. Livre de Vie, no. 68, 8–11. Paris: E. Privat, 1965.

732 "Présentation." In *La liturgie en chantier. Les gestes du célébrant*, by André Laurentin. Paroisse et Liturgie. Collection de Pastorale Liturgique, no. 68, 9–11. Bruges: Publications de saint-André, 1965.

733 "Quattro domande a padre Chenu." Interview with E. del Rio. *H* 20 (1965): 47–9.

734 "Scholastique." In *Encyclopédie de la foi*, ed. H. Fries, 205–19. Paris, 1965. [French translation of "Scholastik", in H. Fries (ed.), *Handbuch theologischer Grundbegriffe* (München 1963).]

735 "Schéma XIII: L'Église a reconnu l'objection de conscience." *TC*, no. 1121 (30 December 1965): 13.

736 "St. Thomas, chrétien pour notre temps." Postface in *Saint Thomas d'Aquin, l'homme chrétien. Textes choisis*, by A.-I. Mennessier. Coll. Chrétiens de Tous les Temps, no. 11, 247–51. Paris: Éditions du Cerf, 1965.

737 "Travail." In *Encyclopédie de la foi*, ed. H. Fries, 347–57. Paris, 1965. [French translation of "Arbeit", in H. Fries (ed.), *Handbuch theologischer Grundbegriffe* (München 1963).]

738 "Un document de travail à la 1ère session du concile SD." [Presentation of the Rahner schéma: on the revelation of man and of God made man in JC]. *L*, no. 81 (May 1965): 28.

739 "Una Costituzione Pastorale della Chiesa." *Tetto* 2 (November 1965): 16–31. [Italian translation of "Une constitution pastorale de l'Église", in *DO-C*, 1965, no. 205.]

740 "Valeur chrétienne des réalités terrestres." *Catéchistes*, no. 116 (1965): 245–53.

741 "Vatican II: Lignes de force intérieure." *Foi Vivante* 6, no. 22 (January–March 1965): 41–5.

742 "Vingt ans de recherches théologiques." *Fêtes et saisons*, no. 198 (1965): 6–7.

743 "Vivre avec." *EV* 17, no. 6 (November-December 1965): 413–17.

1966

744 *Peuple de Dieu dans le monde.* Coll. Foi Vivante, no. 35. Paris: Éditions du Cerf, 1966. [Contains seven articles written between 1965 and 1966.]

745 *Trabalho e Profissâo num Mundo em Mutaçao.* Questôes Abertas, no. 1. Petròpolis: Vozes, 1966. [Portuguese translation of "L'avenir professionnel de l'enfant" in M.-D. Chenu et al., *L'enfant et son avenir professionnel* (Paris: Fleurus, 1959).]

746 *El evangelio en el tiempo.* Collecioñ Teología. Barcelona, 1966. [Spanish translation of *La Parole de Dieu*, vol. 2, (Cogitatio fidei 11), Paris: Éditions du Cerf, 1964.]

747 *The Theology of Work: An Exploration.* Chicago, 1966. [American edition of *Pour une théologie du travail* (Paris: Éditions du Seuil, 1955.]

748 *La théologie au XIIe siècle.* 2d ed. Études de Philosophie Médiévale, no. 45. Paris: Vrin, 1966.

749 *Teologia della materia. Civiltà, tecnica e spiritualità cristiana.* Le Idee e la Vita. Collana Di Pensiero, no. 29. Torino: Borla, 1966. [Italian translation of *La Parole de Dieu*, vol. 2 (Cogitatio fidei 11), Paris: Éditions du Cerf, 1964.]

750 *La fe en la inteligencia.* Collecion Teología. Barcelona, 1966. [Spanish translation of *La Parole de Dieu*, vol. 1 (Cogitatio fidei, 10) (Paris: Éditions du Cerf, 1964).]

751 "À vous de jouer." *L*, no. 89 (January 1966): 1–2.

752 "Chrétiens en contestation." *L*, no. 100 (December-January 1966–67): 2–6.

753 "Comunità, legge o istinto?" *Rocca*, 1 May 1966, 18–21.

754 "Dai laici una forza innovatrice per lo sviluppo della teologia." *Il Regno*, 1 November 1966, 547–8.

755 "Des prêtres-ouvriers aux prêtres au travail." Interview with Père Gardey. *Signes du temps*, no. 1 (January 1966): 11–14.

756 "Foi et religion." *Études philosophiques* 21 (1966): 357–69.

757 "I segni dei tempi." In *La Chiesa nel mondo contemporaneo. Commento alla constituzione pastorale "Gaudium et spes,"* ed. E. Giammancheri, 85–102. Brescia: Queriniana, 1966.

758 "La Chiesa dei poveri." In *Liturgia e povertà*, 9–18. Vicenza: Favero, 1966. [Italian translation of "L'Église des pauvres", in *MaD*, January-March 1965.]

759 "La Chiesa nella storia: fondamento e norma della interpretazione del Concilio." *IDO-C Dossiers* 1, no. 19 (1966).

760 "La constitution Lumen Gentium et l'aggiornamento de l'ordre des prêcheurs." In *Consultations d'experts sur Vatican II et l'ordre des frères prêcheurs. Provinces Dominicaines d'Europe-Nord, réunies à l'Arbresle 1–3 décembre 1966*, 16–17, 1966.

761 "La masse povere." *H* 21 (1966): 303–12. Brescia.

762 "La missione della Chiesa nel mondo contemporaneo." In *La Chiesa nel mondo di oggi. Studi e commenti intorno alla Costituzione pastorale "Gaudium et spes"*, ed. G. Barauna o.f.m., 331–50. Firenze: Valecchi, 1966.

763 "Lavoro e creazione." *Dialogo*, no. 3 (1966): 52–6.

764 "Le Père Chenu nous parle du 'schéma XIII'." With J. Feller. *CSD*, no. 71 (September 1966): 4–12.

765 "Le Père Chevrier." *Le Monde*, 2 November 1966.

766 "Le Père Lebret: L'Évangile dans l'économie." *TC*, no. 1151 (28 July 1966): 11–12. [Reprinted in *EH* 170 (1966): 9–12.]

767 "Leggere i segni dei tempi." In *Laici sulle vie del Concilio*, ed. by Vincenzo d'Agostino. Coll. Sulle Vie del Concilio, 246–54. Assisi: Cittadella, 1966.

768 "Les communautés naturelles, pierres d'attente de cellule d'Église." In *Peuple de Dieu dans le monde.* Foi Vivante, 129–43. Paris: Éditions du Cerf, 1966.

769 "Les laïcs et la 'consecratio mundi'." In *L'Église de Vatican II. Études autour de la Constitution conciliaire sur l'Église*, eds G. Barauna o.f.m. and Y.M.-J. Congar o.p. Unam Sanctam, no. 51c, 1035–53. Paris: Éditions du Cerf, 1966.

770 "Les moines sont-ils des anges?" *TC*, no. 1171 (15 December 1966): 18–19.

771 "L'ateismo di fronte alla religione ed alla fede." *SD* 11 (1966): 493–511.

772 "L'Église dans l'histoire. Fondement et norme de l'interprétation du Concile." *IDO-C*, no. 66–19 (1966): 1–6.

773 "On les appela les Albigeois (cathares)." *TC*, no. 1134 (31 March 1966): 3.

774 "Paradosso della povertà evangelica e costruzione del mondo." In *La povertà.* Coll. Minima, no. 20, 11–32. Rome: Ave, 1966. [Italian translation of "Paradoxe de la pauvreté évangélique et construction du monde", in *CUC*, June-July 1963.]

775 "Préface." In *Peut-on évangéliser des techniciens? Témoignages et réflexions*, by Denis Galtier o.p. Rencontres, no. 71, 7–11. Paris: Éditions du Cerf, 1966.

776 "Présentation." In *Foi au Christ et dialogues du chrétien*, by Michel de Goedt. Présence du Carmel, no. 10, 9–10. Paris: Desclée de Brouwer, 1966.

777 "Review of T. Tshibangu, *Théologie positive et théologie spéculative* (Louvain, 1965)." *RHE* 61 (1966): 871–4.

778 "Scuola, famiglia, nazione." *VP* 49 (1966): 691–8.

779 "Travail et création." *Perspectives de catholicité. Cahiers des AFI* 25 (1966): 21–5.

780 "Une théologie pour le monde." Interview with Francis Ferrier. *L'Union*, no. 14 (August 1966): 3–14. [Also in *Communauté chrétienne* 6 (1967) 5–22.]

781 "Une 'théologie du travail'." *Christianisme social* 74, no. 5–8 (1966): 371–84.

782 "*Consecratio mundi.*" *Selecciones de libros de Teologia* 5 (1966): 206–8.

1967

783 *La Chiesa popolo messianico.* Torino: Gribaudi, 1967. [This work gathers in Italian translation three articles previously published.]

784 *Théologie de la matière.* Coll. Foi Vivante, no. 59. Paris: Éditions du Cerf, 1967. [Includes seven articles previously published in *Parole* 2.]

785 *Santo Tomas de Aquino e a Teologia.* Mestres Esprituais. Rio de Janeiro: Agir, 1967. [Portuguese translation of *S. Thomas d'Aquin et la théologie* (Maîtres spirituels n. 17) (Paris: Éditions du Seuil, 1959).]

786 "A Missâo da Igreja no mundo de hoje." In *A Igreja no Mundo de Hoje. Estudos e Comentàrios em Tômo da Constituçao "Gaudium et spes" do Vaticano II, com un estudo sòbre a "Populorum progressio"*, eds G. Barauna o.f.m. and F. Vier o.f.m. Petròpolis: Vozes, 1967. [Portuguese translation of "La Missione della Chiesa nel mondo contemporaneo" in G. Barauna o.f.m. (ed.), *La Chiesa nel mondo di oggi* (Firenze: Vallecchi, 1966).]

787 "Anthropologie de la liturgie." In *La liturgie après Vatican II. Bilan, études, prospectives*, eds J.-P. Jossua and Y. Congar. Coll. Unam Sanctam, no. 66, 159–77. Paris: Éditions du Cerf, 1967.

788 "Cristianesimo e mondo del lavoro." *Cultura e politica* 4 (1967): 5–21, 54–62.

789 "De tekenen des tijds." In *De Kerk in de wereld van deze tijd. Schema XIII, tekst en commentar*, ed. U.P. Brand, 55–77. Antwerp: Hilversum, 1967. [Dutch translation of "I segni dei tempi", in E. Giammancheri (ed.), *La Chiesa nel mondo contemporaneo* (Brescia: Queriniana, 1966).]

790 "Fe, història y religió." Interview with Evangelista Vilanova. *Questions de Vida Cristiana*, no. 39 (1967): 65–70.

791 "Foi et religion." *L*, no. 102 (February 1967): 20–30. [Previously published in *Études philosophique* 1966.]

792 "La Chiesa communità nella fede: esigenze e compiti del popolo di Dio." In *Verso il Sinodo dei Vescovi: i problemi*, ed. Rosino Gibellini. Giornale de Teologia, no. 9, 109–16. Brescia: Queriniana, 1967.

793 "La Chiesa nella storia: fondamento e norma dell'interpretazione del concilio." In *Verso il Sinodo dei Vescovi: i problemi*, ed. Rosino Gibellini. Giornale de Teologia, no. 9, 17–34. Brescia: Queriniana, 1967.

794 "La charité est 'politique'." *CSD*, no. 78 (May 1967): 387–91.

795 "La liturgie dans la conjoncture actuelle." Interview with Albert Lévesque. *LV*, no. 61 (1967): 166–82.

796 "La médiation du monde." Liminaire. *Communauté chrétienne* 6, no. 35 (1967): 319–22.

797 "La théologie comme science ecclésiale." *CON*, no. 21 (1967): 85–93.

798 "La théologie de l'Église dans son histoire. À partir d'un beau livre." *VS*, no. 116 (1967): 203–17.

799 "Lavoro." In *Dizionario teologico*, ed. H. Fries, 145–57. Brescia: Queriniana, 1967. [Italian translation of "Arbeit", in H. Vries (ed.), *Handbuch theologischer Grundbegriffe*, vol. I (München: Kösel, 1963).]

800 "Le mariage." Review of E. Schillebeeckx's *Marriage*. *VS*, no. 116 (1967): 596–7.

801 "Le message au monde de Pères conciliaires (20 octobre 1962)." In *Réflexions et perspectives*. Vol. 3 of *L'Église dans le monde de ce temps. Constitution pastorale "Gaudium et Spes"*, eds Y. Congar and M. Peuchmard. Coll. Unam Sanctam, no. 65c, 191–3. Paris: Éditions du Cerf, 1967.

802 "Les signes des temps." In *L'Église dans le monde de ce temps. Constitution "Gaudium et Spes": Commentaire du schéma XIII*, ed. Karl Rahner, 97–116. Tours: Mame, 1967.

803 "Les signes des temps: Réflexion théologique." In *Commentaires*. Vol. 2 of *L'Église dans le monde de ce temps. Constitution pastorale "Gaudium et Spes"*,

eds Y. Congar and M. Peuchmard. Coll. Unam Sanctam, no. 65b, 205–25. Paris: Éditions du Cerf, 1967.

804 "L'avvenire professionale del ragazzo. Prospettive teologiche." In *Per una teologia della creazione e del lavoro*, by A. de Bovis and H. Rondet, 11–48. Rome: Ave, 1967. [Reprint of work first published in 1961 (Rome: Ave).]

805 "L'encyclique sur le développement des peuples." *EH* 26, no. 2 (1967): 2–4.

806 *"Populorum Progressio*. La démarche de l'Église." *Développement et civilisation*, no. 30 (June 1967): 32–42.

807 *"Populorum progressio*. Il camino della chiesa." *Vita Sociale* 24, no. 125 (1967): 253–60.

808 "Pour bien comprendre l'encyclique (*Populorum progressio*)." *TC*, no. 1187 (6 April 1967): 3–4.

809 "Préface." In *Chrétiens et marxistes: Dialogues avec Roger Garaudy*, by Georges M.-M. Cottier, 5–8. Tours: Mame, 1967.

810 "Présence de l'Église au monde scolaire." *Supplément à Vie enseignante*, October-March 1967–68. [No pagination: 1. *Le texte de base au concile. Octobre 1967*; 2. *La fin de l'ère constantinienne. Novembre 1967*; 3. *Au service d'un bien commun. Décembre 1967*; 4. *Culture et evangélisation. Janvier 1968*. [1]-[2]; 5. *Dans la communauté nationale. Février 1968*; 6. *Dieu a besoin des hommes. Mars-Avril 1968.*]

811 "Présentation." In *Introduction à une théologie critique*, by Paul Touilleux. Coll. Théologie, Pastorale et Spiritualité: Recherches et Synthèses, no. 19, 5–9. Paris: P. Lethielleux, 1967.

812 "Qu'est-ce qu'un chrétien en 1967?" *Évangélisation et Paroisse*, no. 13 (June 1967): 7–18.

813 "Refusons la croisade." *TC*, no. 1175 (12 January 1967): 14.

814 "San Tommaso d'Aquino." In *I protagonisti della storia universale. Cristianesimo e Medioevo*, 197–224. Milan: CEI, 1967.

815 "San Tommaso oggi." *La scuola cattolica* 95 (1967): 384–91.

816 "Scolastica." In *Dizionario teologico*, ed. H. Fries, 273–90. Brescia: Queriniana, 1967. [Italian translation of "Scholastik", in H. Vries (ed.), *Handbuch theologischer Grundbegriffe*, vol. 4 (München: Kösel, 1963).]

817 "Témoigner, c'est être visiblement ce qu'on est." *Communauté chrétienne* 6 (1967): 73–5. [Originally published as "Témoigner, ce n'est pas convertir ...," in *TC*, no. 1000 (5 September 1963): 5-6.]

818 "Un cas de platonisme grammatical au XIIᵉ siècle." *RSPT* 51 (1967): 666–8.

819 "Un peuple messianique. Constitution de l'Église chap. 2, no. 9." *NRT* 89 (1967): 164–82.

820 "Un peuple prophétique." *ES* 35 (1967): 602–11.

821 "Un salut pour l'homme." *Foi Vivante (Carmes)* 8, no. 30 (January-March 1967): 26–32.

822 "Un signe de santé (Non au syllabus)." *TC*, no. 1179 (9 February 1967): 17.

823 "Une théologie pour le monde." Interview with Francis Ferrier. *Communauté chrétienne* 6 (1967): 5–22. [Also in *L'Union*, no. 14 (août 1967): 3–14.]

824 "Valeur de l'homme d'après le Concile." *L'Église d'Alsace*, March 1967, 10–13.

825 "'*Vox populi, Vox Dei*': l'opinion publique dans le peuple de Dieu." *IDO-C*, no. 67–37 (1967): 1–10. [Conference given in 1967 in Rome, in the course of the first Bishops' Synod, to the ecumenical symposium on the Church and public opinion.]

826 "'*Vox populi, Vox Dei*': l'opinione publica nell'amnito del popolo di Dio." *Questitalia*, December 1967, 81–90.

1968

827 *Volk Gottes in der Welt*. Paderborn, 1968. [German translation of *Peuple de Dieu dans le monde* (Paris: Éditions du Cerf, 1966).]

828 *Els cristians i l'acció temporal*. Barcelona: Estella S.A., 1968. [Catalan translation of *Peuple de Dieu dans le monde* (Paris: Éditions du Cerf, 1966).]

829 *Nature, Man and Society in the Twelfth Century: Essays on New Theological Perspectives in the Latin West*. With a preface by Etienne Gilson, trans. by Jerome Taylor and Lester K. Little. Chicago: University of Chicago Press, 1968.

830 *Faith and Theology*. Dublin; Sydney; New York: Gill & Son; Macmillan Co., 1968. [English translation of *La Parole de Dieu*, vol. 1 (Cogitatio fidei 10), Paris: Éditions du Cerf, 1964.]

831 *Los cristianos y la acción temporal*. Barcelona: Estella S.A., 1968. [Spanish tranlation of *Peuple de Dieu dans le monde*, Paris: Éditions du Cerf, 1966.]

832 *Il Vangelo nel tempo*. Teologia Oggi, no. 5. Rome: Ave, 1968. [Italian translation of *La Parole de Dieu*, vol. 2 (Cogitatio fidei 11), Paris: Éditions du Cerf, 1964.]

833 "Orthodoxie et hérésie. Le point de vue du théologien." In *Hérésie et sociétés dans l'Europe pré-industrielle 11ᵉ et 18ᵉ siècles. Communications et débats du colloque de Royaumont*, ed. Jacques Le Goff, 9–14, 15–17. La Haye: Mouton and Co, 1968. [Appeared in *Annales* 1963 and reprinted in *Parole* 1, 69–74.]

834 "Boniface VIII." In *Encyclopaedia Universalis*, vol. 3, 428–9, 1968.

835 "Cet événement que Dieu nous donne à vivre." *CSD*, no. 91 (1968): 21–4.

836 "De commercio inter Ecclesiam et mundum secundum constitutionem '*Gaudium et Spes*' n. 44." In *Acta Congressus internationalis de theologia Concilii*

Vaticani II, Romae 26 septembris – 11 octobris 1966, ed. A. Schönmetzer, 648–51. Città del Vaticano: Typis Polyglottis Vaticanis, 1968.

837 "Een oekumenisch probleem. Wet en vrijheid volgens Luther." *Oekumenisch Nieuwsblad* 3, no. 10 (June 1968): 1.

838 "Fede e religione." In *L'Ateismo*, 67–8. Rome: Ave, 1968. [Italian translation of "Foi et religion", in *Les études philosophiques*, 1966 (XXI), no. 3.]

839 "Histoire du salut et historicité de l'homme dans le renouveau de la théologie." In *La théologie du renouveau. Texte intégral des travaux présentés au Congrès international de Toronto, 20–25 août 1967*, vol. 1, eds L. Shook and G. M. Bertrand, 21–32. Cogitatio fidei no. 34, Montréal; Paris: Fides; Éditions du Cerf, 1968.

840 "La Chiesa in stato di missione." In *Una Chiesa senza sosta in missione*. Coll. Pastorale, no. 15, 9–12. Rome: Ave, 1968.

841 "La jeunesse prophétise ce que sera demain." *TC*, no. 1238 (28 March 1968): 32.

842 "La paura delle utopie." *H* 23 (1968): 957–60.

843 "La peur des utopies." *TC*, no. 1248 (6 June 1968): 3.

844 "Le christianisme est d'abord une histoire." *TC*, no. 1244 (8 May 1968): 43.

845 "Le masse povere." In *Chiesa e povertà*. Teologia Oggi, no. 6, 184–93. Rome: Ave, 1968. [Italian translation of "Les masses pauvres", in *Église et pauvreté* (Coll. Unam Sanctam, n. 57; Paris: Éditions du Cerf, 1965).]

846 "Le rôle de l'Église dans le monde contemporain: Chapitre IV de la première partie de la constitution." In *L'Église dans le monde de ce temps. Une analyse de la constitution "Gaudium et Spes" et ses implications œcuméniques, avec une étude sur l'encyclique "Populorum Progressio"*, vol. 2, ed. Guilherme Barauna, 422–43. Bruges: Desclée de Brouwer, 1968.

847 "Les peuples de la faim." *Angers*, 7 March 1968.

848 "L'IDOC, un laboratoire." *TC*, 25 January 1968.

849 "L'Église et le droit de propriété." *CJ* (1968).

850 "L'Évangile, ferment 'révolutionnaire'." *Prêtres et laïcs* 18 (November 1968): 471–8.

851 "Méthode de pédagogie active dans l'enseignement des sciences théologiques." *Convergences*, no. 5 (March 1968): 26–8.

852 "Ne reprochez pas à l'Église d'être en retard! Une entrevue avec le père Dominique Chenu." Interview with Jean-Pierre Proulx. *Le Devoir*, 28 October 1968, 2, 11.

853 "Paul VI à Bogota. La vérité de la charité." *La Croix*, 22 June 1968.

854 "Paul VI à Bogota. La vérité de l'Eucharistie." *La Croix*, 15 June 1968. [Reprinted in *L'Homme nouveau*, no. 482 (21 July 1968): 8.]

855 "Prefazione." In *Il rinnovamento della morale. Studi per una morale fedele alle sue fonti e alla sue missione attuale*, by S. Pinckaers o.p., 5–8. Torino, 1968. [Italian translation of "Préface," in S. Pinckaers o.p., *Le renouveau de la morale*, Paris: Castermann, 1964.]

856 "Préface." In *Somme théologique. La théologie: Ia, Prologue et question I*, by Saint Thomas d'Aquin, *Traduction française, notes et appendices par H.-D. Gardeil*, 5–9. Paris; Tournai; Rome: Éditions du Cerf; Desclée de Brouwer, 1968.

857 "Présence des chrétiens." *TC*, no. 1247 (30 May 1968): 5.

858 "Realtà terrene e mondo del lavoro." In *Dio è morto? Ateismo e religione di fronte alla realtà odierna*. IDO-C Documenti Nuovi, no. 1, 47–84. Milan: Mondadori, 1968.

859 "Thomas d'Aquin." In *Encyclopaedia Universalis*, vol. 16, 67–70, 1968.

860 "Un maître, Saint Bonaventure." *La Croix*, 24 February 1968.

861 "Vocations particulières et grâce baptismale." In *La vocation religieuse et sacerdotale*, 7–19. Montréal: Fides, 1968.

862 "'*Vox populi, vox Dei*': L'opinione pubblica nell'ambito del Popolo di Dio." In *La fine della Chiesa come società perfetta*, eds M. Cuminetti and F. Joanne. IDO-C Documenti Nuovi, no. 7, 209–26. Milan: Mondadori, 1968. [Italian translation of "'Vox populi, vox Dei': L'opinion publique dans le Peuple de Dieu", in I, 1967, no. 737 (1967): 1–9.]

1969

863 *Teologia materii, cywilizacja techniczna*. Paris: Éditions du Dialogue, 1969. [Polish translation of *Théologie de la matière. Civilisation technique et spiritualité chrétienne* (Paris: Éditions du Cerf, 1967).]

864 *L'éveil de la conscience dans la civilisation médiévale. Conférence Albert le Grand*. Paris: Vrin, 1969.

865 *La théologie comme science au XIIIe siècle*. 3 ed. Bibliothèque Thomiste, no. 33. Paris: Vrin, 1969. [Reprint of 1957 edition.]

866 *Popo de Deus no mundo*. Translated by Domingos Zamagna. Saõ Paolo: Duas Cidades, 1969. [Portuguese translation of *Peuple de Dieu dans le monde* (Paris: Éditions du Cerf, 1966).]

867 "Avant-Propos." In *Le principe de causalité. Recherches thomistes récentes*, by R. Laverdière. Coll. Bibliothèque Thomiste, no. 39, 7–8. Paris: Vrin, 1969.

868 "Ce qui change et ce qui demeure." In *L'Église vers l'avenir*, ed. G. Bessière, 87–91. Paris: Éditions du Cerf, 1969.

869 "Ce qui change et ce qui demeure dans l'Église." *EE*, Second trimester 1969, 59–61.

870 "Chrétien, mon frère." *VS*, no. 121 (1969): 291–7.

871 "Come il concilio ha condannato la guerra." In *I grandi teologi rispondono: Sessanta problemi di fede e di morale*, 146–8. Alba: Edizione Paoline, 1969.

872 "Como può l'uomo essere libero?" In *I grandi teologi rispondono: Sessanta problemi di fede e di morale*, 97–9. Alba: Edizione Paoline, 1969.

873 "Contestation chrétienne de l'autorité." *Échanges*, no. 91 (June 1969): 32–3.

874 "Dialogue difficile, mais dialogue possible." *La Croix*, 10 October 1969.

875 "Die Platonismen des zwölften Jahrhunderts." In *Platonismus in der Philosophie des Mittelalters*, 268–316. Darmstadt: Wissenschaftliche Buchgesellschaft, 1969. [Translated from *La théologie au XIIe siècle*, Paris: Vrin, 1957.]

876 "Foi et langage." Preface in *Afrique et parole. Études et enquêtes sur la traduction de la Parole de Dieu dans les langues négro-africaines*, 7–11. Paris: Présence africaine, 1969.

877 "Il comunismo è un'idea cristiana 'impazzita'?" In *I grandi teologi rispondono: Sessanta problemi di fede e di morale*, 93–6. Alba: Edizione Paoline, 1969.

878 "La crise, dimension de notre foi au Christ." *LV* 18, no. 93 (May-June 1969): 66–70.

879 "La legge nuova e storia." *Vita Sociale* 6 (1969): 413–23.

880 "La libertà di ricerca in teologia." In *La collegialità episcopale per il futuro della Chiesa. Dalla prima alla seconda assemblea del Sinodo dei Vescovi*, eds by Vincenzo Fagiolo and Gino Concetti. Coll. I Nuovi Padri. Saggi Sul Cristianesimo del Nostro Tempo, no. 5, 219–26. Firenze: Vallecchi, 1969.

881 "La littérature comme *lieu* de la théologie." *RSPT* 53 (1969): 70–90.

882 "La peur des utopies." *Communauté chrétienne* 8 (1969): 67–70. 1968. [Originally published in *TC* (6 June 1968): 3.]

883 "La rénovation de la théologie morale: La loi nouvelle." *Communio. Commentarii Internationales de Ecclesia et Theologia* 2 (1969): 111–21.

884 "La rénovation de la théologie morale: La loi nouvelle." *VSS*, no. 90 (1969): 287–97. [Also in *Communio. Commentarii Internationales de Ecclesia et Theologia* 2 (1969): 111–21.]

885 "Le 'mystère' dans les mystères du Rosaire." *Rosaire et Vie Chrétienne*, no. 131 (October 1969): 2–3.

886 "Les misères de l'abondance." *TC*, no. 1282 (30 January 1969): 21.

887 "L'avenir est la mesure du présent." *Prêtres et laïcs* 19 (February 1969): 95–103.

888 "L'homme, la nature, l'esprit. Un avatar de la philosophie grecque en Occident au XIIIe siècle." *AHDLM* 44 (1969): 123–30.

889 "L'information, devoir du chrétien." *TC*, no. 1325 (27 November 1969): 18.

890 "L'uomo può distruggere il mondo con l'atomica?" In *I grandi teologi rispondono: Sessanta problemi di fede e di morale*, 103–5. Alba: Edizione Paoline, 1969.

891 "Magistère et théologie." *Foi vivante* 10, no. 42 (October 1969): 30–6.

892 "Mon prochain … anonyme." *EE*, First trimester, 1969–70, 34–7.

893 "Os sinais dos tempos." In *A igreja no mondo de hoje*, 79–98. Lisboa, 1969. [Translation of "Les signes du temps" in *L'Église dans le monde de ce temps* (Paris: Éditions du Cerf, 1967).]

894 "Panorama della teologia post-conciliare." *I Problemi di Ulisse* 22, no. 66 (La Chiesa post-conciliare) (November 1969): 28–35.

895 "Perché la 'populorum progressio' è stata attaccata dai liberali?" In *I grandi teologi rispondono: Sessanta problemi di fede e di morale*, 143–5. Alba: Edizione Paoline, 1969.

896 "Può un ateo credere senza saperlo?" In *I grandi teologi rispondono: Sessanta problemi di fede e di morale*, 100–2. Alba: Edizione Paoline, 1969.

897 "Rôle du prêtre la civilisation industrielle: Prophétiser avant d'évangéliser." *CON* 43 (1969): 111–13.

898 "Sans les espoirs humains, l'Espérance, c'est du bluff." Interview. *TC*, no. 1328 (18 December 1969): 13–14.

899 "Se i preti non possono sparare, perché possono farlo gli altri?" In *I grandi teologi rispondono: Sessanta problemi di fede e di morale*, 149–52. Alba: Edizione Paoline, 1969.

900 "Storia della salvezza e storicità dell-uomo nel rinnovamento della teologia." In *Teologia del rinnovamento. Mete, problemi e prospetive della teologia contemporanea*, 9–20. Assisi: Cittadella, 1969. [Italian translation of "Histoire du salut et historicité de l'homme dans le renouveau de la théologie", in L.K. Shook and G.M. Bertrand (eds), *La théologie du renouveau*, vol. 1. Cogitatio fidei no. 34, Montréal; Paris: Fides; Éditions du Cerf, 1968.]

901 "Vocations particulières et grâce baptismale." In *La vocation religieuse et sacerdotale*, by D. Bertrand, 7–21. Paris: Éditions du Cerf, 1969.

1970

902 "À la Mémoire de Mauriac." *Ut sint unum*, no. 325 (1 September 1970): 11.

903 "Carismi e gruppi spontanei." *Sacra doctrina* 15 (1970): 431–45.

904 "Chaque matin, les événements du monde nous sautent à la gorge." With Francis Mayor. *Télérama*, 5 December 1970, 8–11.

905 "Come sará eletto i futuro papa." [*Spectator i intervista con Padre Dominique Chenu*]. *Europas*, January 1970, 12–13.

906 "Como o concílio condenou a guerra." In *Sessenta Problemas de fé e moral*, 136–8. Lisboa: Ediçoes Paulistas, 1970.

907 "Como é que o homem pode ser livre?" In *Sessenta Problemas de fé e moral*, 85–7. Lisboa: Ediçoes Paulistas, 1970.

908 "Contemplazione e teologia oggi." *La scuola cattolica. Supplemento bibliografico* 98 (1970): 119–24.

909 "Crist: Messies." *Qüestions de vida cristiana*, no. 54 (1970): 39–42.

910 "Dans l'Église, une voix." *Réforme*, 3 October 1970.

911 "De la recherche théologique." *L*, no. 147 (November 1970): 20–1. [Reprint of a homily given at the *Concilium* congress of the same year.]

912 "Homélie prononcée lors de la célébration eucharistique." *CON*, no. 60 (1970): 43–6.

913 "Idée de nature au XIIe et XIIIe siècles." *Histoire des théologies médiévales. Annuaire, École Pratique des Hautes Études* 78 (1970): 297–324.

914 "Il ministero regale e l'animazione cristiana del temporale." *Presenza Pastorale* 40 (1970): 861–7.

915 "Il pericoli della Fede che preoccupano il Papa." In *I grandi teologii respondono (Cinquanta problemi di fede e morale)*, 57–60. Alba: Edizioni Paoline, 1970.

916 "Jésus, non-engagé? A-t-il fait de la politique?" *Fêtes et Saisons*, March 1970, 21.

917 "La Chiesa non vuole la violenza." In *I grandi teologii respondono (Cinquanta problemi di fede e morale)*, 204–6. Alba: Edizioni Paoline, 1970.

918 "La condition de créature. Sur trois textes de saint Thomas." *AHDLM* 45 (1970): 9–16.

919 "La teologia del lavoro di fronte all'ateismo." In *L'Ateismo contemporaneo*, 301–16. Rome: Società editrice internazionale, 1970.

920 "Les communautés de base: un élément caractéristique de l'Église en mouvement." *TC*, no. 1348 (7 May 1970): 21–2.

921 "Les 'petites communautés': une kyste ou un espoir pour l'Église?" *TC*, no. 1349 (14 May 1970): 19–20.

922 "Lettre du Père Chenu aux Frères de la Province." *CSD*, no. 110 (July-August 1970): 504–5.

923 "L'aile marchante des théologiens." Interview with Christian Bresch on the Congress of Brussels. *Réforme*, 29 August 1970, 16.

924 "L'opinion publique dans l'Église." In *Censure et liberté d'expression*. Coll. Recherches et Débats, 124–34. Paris: Desclée de Brouwer, 1970.

925 "L'ordre de saint Dominique a-t-il encore sa chance?" In *Cahier du huitième centenaire de la naissance de saint Dominique*, 17–30. Toulouse: N.p., 1970.

926 "L'uomo, il cristianesimo et la realtà terrestra." Interview with Claudio Zanchettin. *L'Eco d'Italia*, 1902, 25 May 1970, 7–12, 8.

927 "L'Église face aux exigences de ce monde." In *Pour une nouvelle image de l'Église*, 175–218. Gembloux: J. Duculot, 1970. [Contains three previously published articles.]

928 "Ma cosa vuol dire Chiesa dei poveri?" In *I grandi teologii respondono (Cinquanta problemi di fede e morale)*, 194–7. Alba: Edizioni Paoline, 1970.

929 "Méthodes historiques et position de la théologie." In *Introduction aux sciences humaines des religions*, eds H. Desroches and J. Ségui, 53–77. Paris:

Éditions Cujas, 1970. [Excerpt from *Une école de théologie* (1937): 36–9; 51–77.]

930 "Non ci sono santi sposati?" In *I grandi teologii respondono (Cinquanta problemi di fede e morale)*, 119–21. Alba: Edizioni Paoline, 1970.

931 "Nota sulle communità di base." *Adista*, 16 January 1970, 1–2. [Note for Italian Press agency.]

932 "O comunismo é uma ideia cristà *enlouquecita*." In *Sessenta Problemas de fé e moral*, 81–4. Lisboa: Ediçoes Paulistas, 1970.

933 "Omelia nel corso della celebrazione eucaristica." In *L'avvenire della Chiesa. Il libro del Congresso*, 61–5. Brescia, 1970. [Italian translation of "Homélie prononcée lors de la célébration eucharistique", in *CON*, 1970, suppl. to no. 60, 12–17 September 1970.]

934 "Perche la Chiesa si occupa di scuola e di Università?" In *I grandi teologii respondono (Cinquanta problemi di fede e morale)*, 190–3. Alba: Edizioni Paoline, 1970.

935 "Poderá o homem destruir o mundo com a bomba atómica?" In *Sessenta Problemas de fé e moral*, 91–3. Ediçoes Paulistas, Lisboa: 1970.

936 "Poderá um ateu crer sem o saber?" In *Sessenta Problemas de fé e moral*, 88–90. Lisboa: Ediçoes Paulistas, 1970.

937 "Porque é que a *Populorum progressio* foi atacada pelos liberrais?" In *Sessenta Problemas de fé e moral*, 133–5. Lisboa: Ediçoes Paulistas, 1970.

938 "Préface." In *Prédication, Acte politique*, by Georges Casalis, 9–12. Paris: Éditions du Cerf, 1970.

939 "Qu'est-ce que la théologie?" *Revue générale* 8 (1970): 27–31.

940 "Révisons radicalement notre 'néo-colonialisme' culturel et religieux." *TC*, no. 1368 (24 September 1970): 24.

941 "Se os sacerdotes nao podem pegar em armas, porque o podem os outros." In *Sessenta Problemas de fé e moral*, 139–42. Lisboa: Ediçoes Pauliste, 1970.

942 "Storicità e immutabilità della realtà cristiano." In *L'Ateismo contemporaneo*, 145–61. Rome: Società editrice internazionale, 1970.

943 "Teologo protagonista della moderna società internazionale." With Valerio Ocheto. *Nostro Tempo*, 20 June 1970.

944 "The Renewal of Moral Theology. The New Law." *The Thomist*, no. 1 (January 1970): 1–12. [English translation of "La rénovation de la théologie morale. La loi nouvelle", in *VSS*, no. 90 (1969): 287–97.]

945 "Théologie de la mutation." In *Société injuste et révolution. Colloque de Venise 1968, sous les auspices de Pax Romana et de l'IDOC*, 77–89. Paris: Éditions du Seuil, 1970.

946 "Théologie et recherche interdisciplinaire." In *Recherche interdisciplinaire et théologie*, ed. F. Houtart, 65–76. Paris: Éditions du Cerf, 1970.

947 "Tout converge vers le Christ." *Journal de la vie*, no. 22 (27 September 1970): 24–5.

948 "Une pose dans le dialogue (chrétiens-marxistes)." *TC*, no. 1362 (13 August 1970): 17.

1971

949 *La Teologia come scienza. La Teologia nel XIII secolo.* Teologia, no. 9. Milan: Jaca Book, 1971. [Italian translation of *La théologie comme science au XIIIe siècle* (Paris: Vrin, 1957).]

950 *Wybór Pism.* Trans. by Lucina Rutkoska, Wanda Sukiennicka, and Zofia Wlodkowa. Warsaw: Instytut Wydawniczy, 1971. [Polish translation of the two volumes of *La Parole de Dieu* (Paris: Éditions du Cerf, 1964).]

951 "À quoi servent les religieuses cloîtrées?" In *Dialogues sur la foi.* Le Point, no. 3, 227–32. Paris: Apostolat des Éditions, 1971.

952 "Alberto Magno." In *Gran Enciclopedia Rialp*, 483–6. Madrid: 1971.

953 "Arbeit." In *Historisches Wörterbuch der Philosophie*, vol. 1, ed. Joachim Ritter, 480–2, 1971.

954 "Comment l'homme peut-il être libre?" In *Dialogues sur la foi.* Le Point, no. 3, 105–7. Paris: Apostolat des Éditions, 1971.

955 "C'est dans un peuple." *Journal de la Vie*, no. 38 (18 August 1971): 25–7.

956 "Définition de l'unité de l'enseignement." *Seminarium* 11, no. 2 (1971): 267–79.

957 "Genèse du mouvement communautaire au Moyen-Age." *CSD*, no. 121 (September-October 1971): 4–9, 83–4.

958 "Helder Camara, el Padre Chenu y Raymondo Panikkar opinan sobre el postconcilio." *Tele-Express*, 23 March 1971, 13. Barcelona.

959 "I gruppi spontanei." *Nostro tempo*, January 1971, 4.

960 "Idée de nature aux XIIe et XIIIe siècles." *Annuaire École Pratique des Hautes Études*, no. 78 *Histoire des théologies médiévales* (1971): 297–324.

961 "Il cristianesimo è religione dell'uomo e della storia." *Nostro Tempo*, 3 October 1971. [Report on conference given by Chenu, by Giacomo Grasso.]

962 "Il risveglio della Speranza." *Il Gallo* 25, no. 1 (January 1971): 5.

963 "Le communisme est-il une idée devenue folle?" In *Dialogues sur la foi.* Le Point, no. 3, 101–4. Paris: Apostolat des Éditions, 1971.

964 "Le concile et la guerre." In *Dialogues sur la foi.* Le Point, no. 3, 169–72. Paris: Apostolat des Éditions, 1971.

965 "Les communautés de bases, kyste ou espoir pour l'Église?" *Notre combat*, January 1971, 4–10. [Reprinted from *TC*, no. 1348 (7 May 1970): 21–2; no. 1349 (14 May 1970): 19–20.]

966 "Liberté évangélique et mythe de la libération." *COM*, no. 1 (1971): 22–7.

967 "L'Église cinq ans après." *ICI*, no. 377 (1 February 1971): 26–32.

968 "L'homme pourrait-il détruire le monde par la bombe atomique?" In *Dialogues sur la foi.* Le Point, no. 3, 111–13. Paris: Apostolat des Éditions, 1971.

969 "L'Église et la pureté de la loi évangélique." In *Dialogues sur la foi.* Le Point, no. 3, 224–6. Paris: Apostolat des Éditions, 1971.

970 "L'Église et le service des hommes." In *Dialogues sur la foi.* Le Point, no. 3, 262–5. Paris: Apostolat des Éditions, 1971.

971 "L'Église et les pauvres." In *Dialogues sur la foi.* Le Point, no. 3, 266–9. Paris: Apostolat des Éditions, 1971.

972 "Mauriac et l'engagement politique: un témoignage." In *Le chrétien Mauriac. Publication du Centre Catholique des Intellectuels Français,* 163–5. Paris: Desclée de Brouwer, 1971.

973 "O congresso de Bruxelas." *Presença e Diàlogo,* no. 1 (1971): 6–8.

974 "Phénomènes de contestation dans l'histoire de l'Église." *con,* no. 68 (1971): 91–6.

975 "Pourquoi faut-il mourir?" In *Dialogues sur la foi.* Le Point, no. 3, 257–61. Paris: Apostolat des Éditions, 1971.

976 "Pourquoi les attaques contre *Populorum Progressio?*" In *Dialogues sur la foi.* Le Point, no. 3, 163–5. Paris: Apostolat des Éditions, 1971.

977 "Théologie et Pastorale." *L'Union-Hebdo,* no. 1000 (21 June 1971).

978 "Un athée peut-il croire en Dieu sans le savoir?" In *Dialogues sur la foi.* Le Point, no. 3, 108–10. Paris: Apostolat des Éditions, 1971.

979 "Un centre de gravité: le combat pour la justice (réflexion sur le synode)." *tc,* no. 1419 (16 September 1971): 15.

980 "'*Vox populi, Vox Dei*': l'opinion publique dans le peuple de Dieu." *csd,* no. 119 (June 1971): 416–28. [Reprinted from *ido-c,* no. 67–37 (1967): 1–10.]

1972

981 *La Teologia nel Medio Evo. La Teologia nel secolo XII.* Teologia, no. 10. Milan: Jaca Book, 1972. [Italian translation of *La théologie au XIIe siècle* (Paris: Vrin, 1957).]

982 "Apprendre à lire les signes des temps." *Le Monde,* 3 March 1972, 16.

983 "Autorité: communauté et société." *cuc,* September 1972, 18–21.

984 "Evangelizzazione e Sacramenti nell'incontro tra la Chiesa e il mondo di oggi." In *Evangelizzazione e Sacramenti. Ricerche avviate in due Chiese locali Torini-Roma,* 95–120. Torino; Leumann: L.D.C., 1972.

985 "Expérience chrétienne et théologie." *Christus,* no. 49 (1972): 131–41.

986 "Il a modifié les frontières de l'Église (mort de l'Abbé Guérin)." *tc,* no. 1446 (23 March 1972): 18.

987 "La Chiesa nel mondo." *Il Regno: Attualità cattolica* 17, no. 256 (15 December 1972): 539–40.

988 "Le Christianisme et les autres religions." *Promesses* (1972).

989 "Les laïcs aussi sont titulaires de la théologie mais il faut parler leur langue." With Robert Ackermann. *La Croix*, 1 April 1972, 9, 11.

990 "Les laïcs dans la vie de l'Église et dans la vie de l'Ordre." *CSD*, February (supplement) 1972, 1–10.

991 "Lex fundamentalis, lex nova." In *Legge e vangelo. Discussione su una legge fundamentale per la Chiesa*. Coll. Testi Di Ricerche Di Scienza Religiose, no. 8, 43–8. Brescia: Paideia, 1972.

992 "L'espérance de l'historien." *Journal de la vie*, no. 74 (30 January 1972): 22–3.

993 "Paura e audacia nella Chiesa dopo il Concilio." *Il Giorno*, 26 November 1972.

994 "Per una teologia biblica: La testimonianza di una tesi sui misteri di Cristo in San Tommaso." *La scuola cattolica. Supplemento bibliografico* (1972), 185–6.

995 "Prefazione." In *Predicazione atto politico*, by G. Casalis. Cristianesimo e Mondo d'Oggi, no. 3, 7–10. Rome: COINES, 1972. [Italian translation of "Préface" in G. Casalis, *Prédication, acte politique* (Paris: Éditions du Cerf, 1970).]

996 "Préface." In *Histoire de l'Église catholique*, by Pierre Pierrard, 7–9. Paris: Desclée de Brouwer, 1972.

997 "Préface." In *Les dimensions politiques de la foi*, by René Coste. Coll. Points d'Appui, 7–9. Paris: Les éditions ouvrières, 1972.

998 "Préface." In *Église ou troupeau?: du troupeau fidèle au Peuple d'alliance*, by M. Bobichon and A. Luneau. Écriture et Histoire, no. 1, 7–10. Paris: Les éditions ouvrières, 1972.

999 "Préface." In *Un nouvel âge de la théologie*, by Claude Geffré, 7–10. Paris: Éditions du Cerf, 1972.

1000 "Theoría y praxis en teología." *CT* 99 (1972): 3–10.

1001 "Un retournement imprévu." *Journal de la vie*, no. 89 (14 May 1972): 22–5.

1002 "Un témoin des années 30." *ES* 40 (October 1972): 433–7.

1003 "Un'antropologia rinnovata." *La Scuola e l'Uomo* 29, no. 12 (December 1972): 5–9.

1004 "Vivre avec des incroyants." Interview with Paul Morisset, s.j. *Prêtres et Laïcs* 22, no. 1 (January 1972): 61–7.

1973

1005 *Evoluçao Da Teologia Da Guerra*. Coll. Cadernos Telos, no. 3. Porto: Livraria Telos Editora, 1973.

1006 "Altari politici?" *Il Giorno*, 6 May 1973.

1007 "Biblia e liberazione." *Il Giorno*, 4 February 1973.

1008 "Contestation sans schisme dans l'Église médiévale." *CON*, no. 88 (1973): 47–54.

1009 "Cristianesimo e realtà terrestre." Interview with Claudio Zanchettin. *Il Gallo* 27, no. 316 (May 1973): 3–4.

1010 "Dieu, la foi, l'Église." Interview with Pierre Desgroupes. *Le Point*, no. 32 (30 April 1973): 93–106.

1011 "Il Vangelo è una forza storica." *Il Regno*, 21 December 1973, 573–4. Bologna.

1012 "La funció profética de la teologia." *Questiones de Vida Cristiana*, no. 66 (1973): 47–53.

1013 "Le Christ trahi." *Journal de la vie*, no. 136 (April 1973): 8–9.

1014 "Le poids du juridisme." *Échanges. Regard chrétien sur le monde d'aujourd'hui*, no. 113 (November-December 1973): 23–4.

1015 "Le salut déborde la libération économique (Doc. des 25 évêques du Nord Est du Brésil)." *TC*, no. 1525 (27 September 1973): 20.

1016 "Les signes des temps." *Lecture chrétienne pour notre temps*, no. 57 (1973).

1017 "O que Muda e o que Permanece." In *A Igreja do futuro*, 87–91. Petròpolis: Vozes, 1973. [Portuguese translation of "Ce qui change et ce qui demeure," in *L'Église vers l'avenir* (Paris: Éditions du Cerf, 1969).]

1018 "Papa Giovanni. Affrontare la paura." *Rocca*, no. 10 (15 May 1973): 30.

1019 "Prefazione." In *Dimensioni politiche della fede*, by R. Coste, 5–7. Assisi: Cittadella, 1973. [Italian translation of "Préface" in R. Coste, *Les dimensions politiques de la foi* (Paris: Les éditions ouvrières, 1972).]

1020 "Presentazione." In *Frontiere della pace*, by Vittoria Possenti, 5–8. Milano: 1973.

1021 "Propos d'un 'étranger' sur le rapport Dumont." *Maintenant*, no. 122 (January 1973): 33–4.

1022 "Rivoluzione silenziosa nei nuovi catechismi." *Il Giorno*, 17 June 1973.

1023 "Sens de l'évènement franciscain." *Évangile-aujourd'hui: Cahiers de vie franciscaine*, no. 80 (Fourth trimester 1973): 25–8.

1024 "Thomas d'Aquin, 1224 ou 1225–1274." In *Encyclopaedia Universalis*, vol. 16, 68–70, 1973.

1025 "Travail et participation à la création." *Éducateurs spécialisés*, no. 51 (Second trimester 1973): 20–4.

1026 "Tutto è Politica, ma la politica non è tutto." Interview with Anna Portoghese. *Rocca*, no. 6 (15 March 1973): 18–19.

1027 "Vérité évangélique et métaphysique wolffienne à Vatican II." *RSPT* 57 (1973): 632–40.

1028 "*Fraternitas*. Évangile et condition socio-culturelle." *RHS* 49 (1973): 385–400.

1974

1029 *Wstęp do filozofii sw. tomasza z Akwinu*. Ed. Wladyslaw Senko. Trans. by Hanna Rosnerowa. Warsaw: Akademia Teologii Katolickiej, 1974.

1030 "Altari politici?" In *Religione e mondo contemporaneo*, ed. G. Zizola, 131–3. Brescia: Morcelliana, 1974.

1031 "Autorité hiérarchique et témoignage (référendum 12 mai sur divorce – Italie)." *TC*, no. 1565 (4 July 1974): 17.

1032 "Biblia e liberazione." In *Religione e mondo contemporaneo*, ed. G. Zizola, 123–6. Brescia: Morcelliana, 1974.

1033 "Chi lo da resa impopolare." *Rocca*, 1 April 1974, 31.

1034 "Civilisation urbaine et théologie. L'école de Saint Victor au XIIᵉ siècle." *Annales. Économies, sociétés, civilisations* 29 (1974): 1253–63.

1035 "Communautés de base: chances et risques." *L'Église en Alsace*, no. 2 (1974): 3–5.

1036 "Création et histoire." In *St. Thomas Aquinas 1274–1974. Commemorative Studies*, ed. A. Maurer et al., 391–9. Toronto: Pontifical Institute of Mediaeval Studies, 1974.

1037 "Evangelischreveil en aanwezigheid van de Geest in de 12ᵉ en 13ᵉ eeuw." In *Leven uit de geest. Theologische peilingen aangeboden aan Edward Schillebeeckx*, 145–9. Hilversum: Gooi en Sticht, 1974.

1038 "I grandi dibatti all'Università di Parigi." *Famiglia Cristiana*, 3 March 1974, 62–3.

1039 "La foi: Certitude et recherche." *ICI*, no. 449 (1974): 22–3.

1040 "La libertà nella Chiesa." *Il Gallo* 28, no. 330 (July-August 1974): 38–9.

1041 "Le Christ trahi." *Journal de la vie: Aujourd'hui la Bible*, no. 136 (April 1974): 8–9.

1042 "Le pouvoir ne doit pas supplanter le témoignage." *TC*, no. 1570 (8 August 1974): 19.

1043 "Les passions vertueuses. L'anthropologie de saint Thomas." *RPL* 72 (1974): 11–18.

1044 "L'athéisme méthodologique: Saint Thomas d'Aquin." In *Philosophie et religion. Centre d'études et de recherches marxistes*, by Olivier Bloch, Guy Besse, and Jacques Milhan, 73–90. Paris: Éditions sociales, 1974.

1045 "L'espérance qui est en vous." *Conférence du Père Chenu. CSD*, no. 150 (July-August 1974): 546–59.

1046 "L'évangélisme de saint Thomas d'Aquin." *RSPT* 58 (1974): 391–403.

1047 "Novità'di San Tommaso nel secolo XIII." *La scuola cattolica* 102 (1974): 546–56.

1048 "Orthodoxie-orthopraxie." In *Le service théologique dans l'Église. Mélanges offerts au Père Congar,* ed. G. Philips. Coll. Cogitatio Fidei, no. 76, 51–63. Paris: Éditions du Cerf, 1974.

1049 "Paura e audacia nella chiesa dopo il consilio." In *Religione e mondo contemporaneo,* ed. G. Zizola, 30–2. Brescia: Morcelliana, 1974.

1050 "Pour une anthropologie sacramentelle." *MAD,* no. 119 (1974): 85–100.

1051 "Profanidad del mundo – Sacramentalidad del mundo: Sto. Tomás de Aquino y San Buenaventura." *CT* 101, no. 2–3 (1974): 183–9.

1052 "Profetismo e teologia." In *Chiesa per il mondo. Fede e prassi.* Vol. 2 of *Miscellanea teologico-pastorale nel LXX del card. Michele Pellegrino,* 27–31. Bologna: Dehoniane, 1974.

1053 "Préface." In "O compromisso temporal liberta o cristao. Negaçao do Evangelho ou Mensagem de Salvacao?" Ph.D. Diss. by Carlos Nun Salgado Vaz, 5–7. Braga, 1974.

1054 "Préface." In *Un peuple libéré,* by Jacques Hamaide and Claude Duchesneau, 5–7. Paris: Desclée de Brouwer, 1974.

1055 "Pròlog." In *San Thomas d'Aquino, Avui,* trans. by Pacia Garriga. El Gra Deblat, no. 6. Montserrat: Publication de l'Abadia, 1974. [Catalan translation of *Saint Thomas d'Aquin et la théologie* (Paris: Éditions du Seuil, 1959).]

1056 "Qui dites-vous que je suis?" *Jésus,* no. 6 (Christmas [Noël] 1974): 45.

1057 "Risveglio evangelico e presenza dello Spirito nei secoli XII e XIII." In *L'esperienza dello Spirito. In onore di Edward Schillebeeckx nel suo 60ᵉ genetliaco. Giornale Di Teologia,* no. 83, 183–8. Brescia: Queriniana, 1974. [Italian translation of "Evangelischreveil," in *Leven uit de geest* (Hilversum: Gooi en Sticht, 1974).]

1058 "Rivoluzione silenziosa nei nuovi catechismi." In *Religione e mondo contemporaneo,* ed. G. Zizola, 50–3. Brescia: Morcelliana, 1974.

1059 "Réveil évangélique et présence de l'Esprit au XIIᵉ et XIIIᵉ siècles." *CON [Mélanges Schillebeeckx]* (1974).

1060 "Saint Thomas d'Aquin, fils de saint Dominique." *CSD,* no. 150 (July-August 1974): 507–13.

1061 "San Tommaso innovatore e precursore nella celebrazione inaugurale all' 'Angelicum', discorso di P. M.-D. Chenu." *L'Osservatore Romano,* 19 April 1974, 3, 7.

1062 "St. Thomas innovateur dans la créativité d'un monde nouveau." In *Il pensiero di Tommaso d'Aquino e i problemi fondamentali del nostro tempo.* Studia Universitatis S. Thomae in Urbe, no. 4, 27–33. Rome: Herder, 1974.

[Proceedings of International Congress on Thomas Aquinas, Rome and Naples, 17–24 April, 1974.]

1063 "Szent Tamás az újitó egy új világ kréativitásában." *Mérleg* 4 (1974): 311–26.

1064 "Testimonianze di un vechio 'tomista'." *SC* 102 (1974): 535–7.

1065 "Thomas Aquinas." In *Encyclopaedia Britannica*, 15 ed., vol. 12, 345–8, 1974.

1066 "Thomas d'Aquin et Bonaventure dans les turbulences culturelles de l'Université de Paris au XIIIe siècle." *NIC*, June 1974, 6–10.

1067 "Thomas d'Aquin et l'Université de Paris." *La montagne de Ste Geneviève et ses abords. Société historique et archéologique du Vme arrondissement*, no. 173 (June 1974): 68–71.

1068 "Thomas van Aquino, vernieuwer in een creative nieuwe wereld." *Wending* (1974), 403–18.

1069 "Un entretien avec le P. Chenu. L'érotisme de Dieu." Interview with Pascale Desforges. *Combat*, 15 April 1974, 6–7.

1975

1070 *Un théologien en liberté. Jacques Duquesne interroge le Père Chenu.* Interview with Jacques Duquesne. *Les Interviews*. Paris: Centurion, 1975.

1071 "A korai keresztény humanizmus." *Teologia* 9 (1975): 80–3.

1072 "Ateizm metodologiczny: swiety Tomasz z Akwinu." *Czlowiek i Swiatopoglad*, no. 10 (1975): 5–23. [Polish translation of "L'athéisme méthodologique: saint Thomas d'Aquin", in *Philosophie et religion* (Paris: Éditiones Sociales, 1974).]

1073 "Bilan du XIIIe siècle." In *2000 ans de Christianisme*, vol. 4, 160–3. Paris: Société d'histoire chrétienne, 1975.

1074 "Czy madrosc Tomasza sprzeciwia sie prostocie Ewangelii?" *W Drodze* 3, no. 3 (1975): 28ff.

1075 "Il faut donner sa valeur collective au non-travail." Interview with Jean-Marc de Preneur. *La Croix*, 26 December 1975.

1076 "Il primo anno di pontificato di papa Giovanni Paolo II." With Francesco Strazzari. *Vida Nueva* (1975).

1077 "Lavoro." In *Sacramentum Mundi. Enciclopedia Teologica*, ed. Karl Rahner s.j., 666–79. Brescia: Morcelliana, 1975.

1078 "Le naturalisme de saint Thomas." *Tomismo e neotomismo. Centenario di san Tommaso d'Aquino*, 142–50. Coll. Memorie Domenicane, no. 6. Pistoia: Centro Riviste Padri Domenicani, 1975.

1079 "Le salut est dans l'histoire." Interview in *L'Église interrogée*, ed. Claudio Zanchettin, 155–67. Paris: Le Centurion, 1975.

1080 "Le 'naissant' fait craquer le vieux monde." *CSD*, no. 161 (October 1975): 39–44.

1081 "Les benaurances: Evangeli i teologia." *Qüestions de vida cristiana*, no. 78 (1975): 51–5.

1082 "Les marginaux dans le développement de l'Église." *Communauté chrétienne* 14, no. 81 (1975): 256–60.

1083 "Les méthodes d'enseignements." In *2000 ans de Christianisme*, 122–6. Paris: Société d'histoire chrétienne, 1975.

1084 "Natale, un Dio che viene." *Rocca*, 15 December 1975, 16–17.

1085 "Non, l'Évangile n'est pas neutre." *TC*, no. 1599 (27 February 1975): 17.

1086 "Notre temps est celui de prophètes." Interview with Hélène Renard. *Question de (spiritualité, tradition, littérature)*, no. 8 (1975): 32–4.

1087 "O sytuacji w teologii." Interview with Jerzy Turowicz. *Tygodnik Powszechny* 29, no. 51–52 (21–28 December 1975): 3, 10.

1088 "Pourquoi l'Église ne pouvait admettre l'hérésie cathare." In *2000 ans de christianisme*, vol. 3, 132. Paris: Societé d'histoire chrétienne, 1975.

1089 "Pouvoir dans l'Église." *Vivante éducation*, no. 254 (November-December 1975): 34–5.

1090 "Saint Bonaventure ou l'affrontement de la foi et de la culture." *ICI*, no. 477 (1975): 18–19.

1091 "Saint Dominique." In *2000 ans de christianisme*, vol. 3, 213–17. Paris: Société d'histoire chrétienne, 1975.

1092 "Saint Thomas innovateur dans la créativité d'un monde nouveau." In *Tommaso d'Aquino nella storia del pensiero*, 39–50. Napoli: Edizioni Domenicane Italiane, 1975. [Reprinted from "St. Thomas innovateur ...," in *Il pensiero di Tommaso d'Aquino* ... (Rome: Herder, 1974).]

1093 "Trente ans après." *LV*, no. 124 (1975): 72–7.

1094 "Un siècle de créativité." In *2000 ans de christianisme*, vol. 3, 64–7. Paris: Société d'histoire chrétienne, 1975.

1095 "Université et cathédrale." In *2000 ans de christianisme*, vol. 4. Paris: Société d'histoire chrétienne, 1975.

1096 "Un'antropologia rinnovata." In *Scuola ed educazione religiosa*, by Rovea Rovea, 291–303. Rome: Ave, 1975.

1097 "Urbanizzazione e presenza della Chiesa." *Testimonianze* 17 (1975): 222–6.

1098 "Vivre les événements." *Communautés nouvelles*, no. 44 (1975): 36–40.

1976

1099 *La théologie au XII*e *siècle*. 3 ed. Études de Philosophie Médiévale, no. 45. Paris: Vrin, 1976.

1100 *L'Esprit qui nous parle à travers l'incroyance.* With Jean-François Six. Coll.
Dossiers Libres. Paris: Éditions du Cerf, 1976.

1101 "Clavel, descendez de votre Sinaï." *TC*, no. 1658 (15 April 1976): 19–20.

1102 "De qui suis-je le prochain?" *CSD*, no. 165 (October 1976): 15–22.

1103 "Depuis l'expérience des prêtres-ouvriers, on ne définit plus le prêtre
comme 'homme du sacré'." *ICI*, no. 472 (15 January 1976): 22–4. [Excerpt from interview with Jacques Duquesne in *Un théologien en liberté*
(Paris: Le Centurion, 1975).]

1104 "La Chiesa ha ancora une dottrina sociale?" *Il Giorno*, 4 January 1976, 4.

1105 "La théologie en procès." In *Savoir, faire, espérer: Les limites de la raison. Volume
publié à l'occasion du cinquentenaire de l'École des sciences philosophiques et religieuses et en hommage à Mgr. Henri van Camp*, 691–6. Brussels: Facultés Universitaires St. Louis, 1976.

1106 "La vérité vous rendra libres." Review of Julien Green, *Oeuvres complètes*,
vol. 4 (Paris: Gallimard, 1976). *TC*, no. 1655 (25 March 1976).

1107 "Le Vatican entre les communistes et les chrétiens: Table ronde sur les
élections italiennes." *TC*, no. 1666 (10 June 1976): 6–9.

1108 "Le réveil de l'Esprit." *Unité des chrétiens*, no. 21 (January 1976): 3–5.

1109 "Le réveil de l'Esprit." *CUC*, September-October 1976, 9–12. [Different
from article with same title in *Unité des chrétiens* of the same year.]

1110 "Les marginaux dans l'Église." *La Croix*, 9 April 1976.

1111 "Les résonances évangéliques de la mutation du monde." *Vocation*,
no. 275 (July 1976): 314–19.

1112 "Lettre." *CON*, no. 115 (1976): 11–12.

1113 "Review of V. Lanternari, *Folklore e dinamica culturale. Crisi e ricerca d'inden-
tita*, Napoli 1976." *Archives de sciences sociales* 42 (1976): 189.

1114 "Réveil évangélique et présence de l'Esprit au XIIᵉ et XIIIᵉ siècles." In
L'expérience de l'Esprit. Mélanges Schillebeeckx. Coll. Le Point Théologique,
no. 18, 167–71. Paris: Beauchesne, 1976.

1115 "Santo Tomào innovador en la creatividad de un mundo nuevo." *Servir*,
no. 12 (1976): 5–24. [Spanish translation of "St. Thomas innovateur dans
la créativité d'un nouveau monde," in *Il pensiero di Tommaso d'Aquino* ...
(Rome: Herder, 1974).]

1116 "Speranza cristiana ed utopia socialista." *Il Gallo*, July-August 1976, 41–2.

1117 "Tavola rotonda di *Paese sera* a Parigi." Session participants André Mandouze, Georges Montaron, Georges Hourdin, and Raniero La Valle. *Paese
Sera*, 6 June 1976, 7.

1118 "Thomas d'Aquin (Saint)." In *La Grande Encyclopédie*, 11901–2. Paris:
Larousse, 1976.

1119 "Una chiesa di testimonianza." *Testimonianza* 19, no. 12 (1976): 744.

1120 "Ça ne m'intéresse pas d'être un ange." *Promesses*, no. 93 (1976): 93–4.

1977

1121 *La dottrina sociale della Chiesa. Origine e sviluppo (1891–1971).* Dipartimento Di Scienze Religiose, no. 5. Brescia: Queriniana, 1977.

1122 *O Wolnosci Poszukiwan Teologicznych: Rozmowy z O. M.-D. Chenu.* With Jacques Duquesne. Warsaw: Instytut Wydawniczy Pax, 1977. [Polish translation of *Un théologien en liberté* (Paris: Le Centurion, 1975).]

1123 *San Tommaso d'Aquino e la teologia.* Ritorno Alle Fonti, no. 8. Torino: Gribaudi, 1977. [Italian translation of *S. Thomas d'Aquin et la théologie* (Paris: Éditions du Seuil, 1959).]

1124 *St. Thomas d'Aquin et la théologie. Maîtres Spirituels*, no. 17. Paris: Éditions du Seuil, 1977. [Photostatic reprint of text published in 1959.]

1125 "1848, les leçons d'une révolution." *TC*, no. 1718 (9 June 1977): 20–2.

1126 "Deux 'experts' racontent." *(M.-D. Chenu et Y. Congar – dossier concile). TC*, no. 1706 (17 March 1977): 22.

1127 "Dieci anni dopo l'enciclica *Polulorum Progressio.*" Note for the Italian Press agency ADISTA, 1977.

1128 "Dieu venu dans l'histoire." *Jésus-Caritas*, no. 187 (Third trimester 1977): 101–7. [Text of homily delivered 2 January 1977, during a televised Mass.]

1129 "Dio parla oggi." *Crescere Insieme* 4, no. 12 (December 1977): 1.

1130 "Et la citadelle s'ouvrit (dossier concile)." *TC*, no. 1709 (7 April 1977): 18.

1131 "Indispensable pluralité." In *2000 ans de christianisme*, vol. 10, 239–42. Paris: Société d'histoire chrétienne, 1977. [Round table discussion.]

1132 "Introduction [à la première partie]." In *Le déplacement de la théologie.* Coll. Le Point Théologique, no. 21, 11–13. Paris: Beauchesne, 1977.

1133 "La Chiesa in Francia." *Il Nostro Tempo*, no. 30 (24 July 1977): 5.

1134 "La fiducia nella chiese emerganti." *La Rocca*, 1–15 August 1977.

1135 "La foi lézardée." Interview with Pierre Desgranges, in *Le mal du siècle*, 284–94. Paris: Grasset, 1977.

1136 "La mémoire en acte." In *2000 ans de Christianisme*, vol. 10, 286. Paris: Société d'histoire chrétienne, 1977. [Conclusion of the work.]

1137 "Le concile a redécouvert le peuple de Dieu. (M.-D. Chenu et Y. Congar sur *Lumen Gentium*)." *TC*, no. 1711 (21 April 1977): 20–2.

1138 "Le pouvoir dans l'Église." *ET*, no. 100 (June 1977): 86–8.

1139 "Les lieux théologiques chez Melchior Cano." In *Le déplacement de la théologie.* Coll. Le Point Théologique, no. 21, 45–50. Paris: Beauchesne, 1977.

1140 "Les 'mouvements de l'histoire' provoquent l'Évangile." *TC*, no. 1737 (20 October 1977): 19–20.

1141 "L'Incarnazione nella storia." Interview with Nicoletta Roscioni Riccio. *Il Regno-attualità* 22, no. 12 (15 June 1977): 246–7.

1142 "L'avenir du christianisme." *TC*, no. 1735 (6 October 1977): 24.

1143 "L'Homme et l'Histoire." *L'Homme et l'Humanité*, no. 59 (1977).

1144 "L'Église des pauvres à Vatican II." *CON*, no. 124 (1977): 75–80.

1145 "L'Église tournée vers le monde. (M.-D. Chenu et Y. Congar parlent du message du concile au monde – 20 octobre 1962)." *TC*, no. 1707 (24 March 1977): 19.

1146 "Postface." In *Vie chrétienne et sacrements dans l'histoire de l'Église*, by Dom Dye. Paris: Centre Jean Bart, 1977.

1147 "Praxis historique et relation Église-société." *La Pensée*, no. 192 (1977): 5–11.

1148 "Préface." In *La dernière place*, by Philippe Dagonet. Paris: s.o.s., 1977.

1149 "Préface." In *Dominique et ses prêcheurs*, by M.-H. Vicaire, v–vii. Paris: Éditions du Cerf, 1977.

1150 "Préface." In *La manifestation de l'Esprit selon Joachim de Fiore. Herméneutique et théologie de l'histoire d'après le 'Traité sur les Quatres Évangiles'*, by Henry Mottu, 7–8. Paris: Delachaux & Niestlé, 1977.

1151 "Que signifie la foi pour l'expérience politique?" *TC*, no. 1720 (23 June 1977): 21.

1152 "Réveil évangélique et communautés chrétiennes." *Promesses*, no. 98 (1977): 8.

1153 "Saint Thomas d'Aquin." In *Moyen-Age, Renaissance*. Vol. 2 of *Grands écrivains du monde*, 174–82. Paris: Nathan, 1977.

1154 "Tradizione e tradizionalismo." *La Rocca*, July 1977, 46–7.

1155 "Un témoignage sur le développement de ce qu'on appelle le christianisme social." *L'Osservatore Romano ("Inserto Speciale Per l'Ottantesimo Compleanno Di Sua Santità Papa Paolo VI f.R.")*, 25 September 1977, 2.

1977–1978

1156 "I cristiani e la libertà." *Animazione sociale*, no. 24 (October 1977–March 1978): 77–87.

1978

1157 "Bisogna partire dal mondo e non dalla chiesa." *Messagero. Madonna del Sarro* 67, no. 2 (February 1978): 11–13.

1158 "Body and Body Politics in the Creation Spirituality of Thomas Aquinas." *Listening: Journal of Religion and Culture* 13, no. 3 (1978): 214–32.

1159 "Chrzescijanskie zaangazowanie spoleczne." *Za i Przeciu*, no. 15 (1978): 8.

1160 "Der Plan des *Summa*." In *Chronologie und Werkanalyse*. Vol. 1 of *Thomas von Aquin*, ed. Klaus Bernath. Wege der Forschung, no. 188, 173–95. Darmstadt: Wissenschaftliche Buchgesellschaft, 1978. [Translation of "Le plan de la Somme" in *RT* 45 (1939): 93–107.]

1161 "Délivrés: Aujourd'hui." Editorial. *CSD*, no. 172 (June 1978): 4–6.

1162 "El poder de les ideologie." *Qüestiones de Vida Cristiana*, no. 90 (1978): 74–80.

1163 "Histoire de Dieu et sens de l'Histoire." *CSD*, no. 174 (December 1978): 36–49.

1164 "Homélie pour la célébration du 10ème anniversaire de la mort du P. Gabel." *DC*, no. 1740 (16 April 1978): 397–8.

1165 "Il filo aureo della storia." *Rocca*, 1 April 1978, 47–9.

1166 "Il vangelo nel tempo: l'emergo di nuovi luoghi teologici nel contesto italiano." *Realtà sociale*, no. 1 (January-April 1978).

1167 "In memoriam Étienne Gilson." With M.-T. d'Alverny. *AHDLM* 45 (1978): I–IV.

1168 "Les jeunes, espoirs du monde." *Le vrai* (1978), 223.

1169 "Milieu ouvrier et théologie savante." *LV*, no. 140 (1978): 57–64.

1170 "Pour une théologie du loisir." *Haltes*, no. 2 (January 1978): 5–7.

1171 "Préface." In *Nouvel ordre mondial: Dossier: Les chrétiens provoqués par le développement*, by V. Cosmao, 5–6. Le Châlet (Belgium), 1978.

1172 "Préface." In *L'oeil en fête*, v–vii. Paris: Gallerie du Haut Pavé, 1978.

1979

1173 *La 'doctrine sociale' de l'Église comme idéologie*. Paris: Éditions du Cerf, 1979.

1174 *Intellektualac u slobodi*. With Jacques Duquesne. Zagreb, 1979. [Croatian translation of *Un théologien en liberté* (Paris: Le Centurion, 1975).]

1175 *Nature, Man and Society in the Twelfth Century. Essays on New Theological Perspectives in the Latin West*. With a preface by Étienne Gilson. Chicago: University of Chicago Press, 1979. [English translation of *La théologie au XIIe siècle* (Paris: Vrin, 1956).]

1176 "Aucune envie d'être un ange." *La semaine religieuse d'Alger*, no. 5 (26 March 1979).

1177 "Az Isten Szavának Prófétája." (*Chenu atya papi életének 60. évfordulójára*). With Margit Széll. *Vigilia* 7, no. 44 (July 1979): 449–58.

1178 "Body and Body Politic in the Creation Spirituality of St. Thomas Aquinas." In *Western Spirituality: Historical Roots and Ecumenical Routes*, ed. Matthew Fox, 193–214. Notre Dame, IN: Fides; Clarention, 1979.

1179 "Chenu è ottimista." With Francesco Strazzari. *Madre di Brescia*, 15 December 1979, 32.

1180 "De la monocratie à la collégialité?" *TC*, no. 1838 (1 October 1979): 17–19.

1181 "Es hora de esperanza." With Francesco Strazzari. *Vida Nueva*, no. 1201 (1979): 33.

1182 "I carismi per la costruzione della chiesa." *Servitium. Quaderni Di Spiritualità*, no. 6 (November-December 1979): 76–7.

1183 "Il progresso delude e ci si rivolge a Dio." Interiew with Carlo Cavicchioli. *Famiglia Cristiana*, 30 December 1979, 20–1.

1184 "Il vegliardo della Chiesa di Francia." With Robi Ronza. *Il Sabato* 2, no. 29 (21 July 1979): 18–19.

1185 "La foi et l'homme." Interview with Guy Besse and Gilbert Wasserman. *France Nouvelle (Hebdomadaire Central du P.C.F.)*, no. 1736 (19 February 1979): 43–50.

1186 "Les raisons d'une reconnaissance." *Vivante éducation*, no. 272 (June-July 1979): 24.

1187 "L'historicité de Dieu." *Le Monde*, 15 May 1979, 2.

1188 "L'Évangile dans le temps." *Choisir*, no. 239 (November 1979): 21–4.

1189 "L'Évangile passe avant l'institution." *Le Monde*, 21 August 1979.

1190 "L'éternité amoureuse du temps." In *Une brassée de confessions de foi*, ed. Henri Fresquet, 29–31. Paris: Éditions du Cerf, 1979.

1191 "Postface." In *Les temps de l'homme. Prières*, by Jacques Hamaide, 123–4. Mulhouse: Salvator, 1979.

1192 "Presentazione." In *Le fonti del pensiero di S. Tommaso d'Aquino nella Somma Teologica*, by Ceslao Pera o.p., 7–8. Torino: Marietti, 1979.

1193 "Review of Giancarlo Zizola, *L'Utopie du pape Jean XXIII* (Paris 1978)." *CUC*, no. 3 (January-February 1979): 46. Paris.

1980

1194 "A che servono i teologi?" *Rocca*, no. 6 (15 March 1980): 44–7.

1195 "Après Vatican II. Démarches de chrétiens adultes." *Lettre aux ainés*, no. 34 (February 1980): 2–7.

1196 "Conjoncture et charisme chez Frère François." *Bulletin O.F.M.* (1980).

1197 "Da una chiesa feudale ad una chiesa dei communi." In *Chiesa nella società. Verso un superamento della cristianità*. Cronache Teologiche, no. 4, 97–110. Milano: Marietti, 1980.

1198 "Foi: Certitude et recherche." In *La scholastique, certitude et recherche: En hommage à Louis-Marie Régis*, ed. Ernst Jóos, 11–13. Montréal: Bellarmin, 1980.

1199 "La lettre d'un incroyant. Les exigences du dialogue." *Nouveau dialogue. Revue du service Incroyance et foi*, no. 33 (January 1980): 3–4.

1200 "La teologia cattolica e il lavoro." *IDOC Internazionale*, no. 5-6-7 (May-June-July 1980): 46–9.

1201 "La 'doctrine sociale' de l'Église." *CON*, no. 160 (1980): 119–25.

1202 "Le prêtre-ouvrier, témoin nécessaire de l'Évangile." *TC*, no. 1886 (1 September 1980): 19–20.

1203 "Les chrétiens vivent de beaux jours!" *TC*, no. 1855 (28 January 1980): 20.

1204 "L'homme partenaire de Dieu." *TC*, no. 1892 (13 October 1980): 16.

1205 "L'interprète de saint Thomas d'Aquin." In *Étienne Gilson et nous: La philosophie et son histoire*, ed. Monique Couratier, 43–8. Paris: Vrin, 1980.

1206 "L'Église avant et après Vatican II." *Lettre aux aînés*, no. 34 (January 1980): 13–21.

1207 "L'Église en état de mission." Preface in *De l'Église d'hier à l'Église de demain. L'aventure de la Mission de France*, by Louis Augros, 7–13. Paris: Éditions du Cerf, 1980.

1208 "Per que serveixen els teòlegs?" *Qüestions de vida cristiana*, no. 101 (1980): 71–6.

1209 "Przezylismy swieto." *Za i przeciw*, 21 September 1980.

1210 "Préface." In *La théologie comme science au XXe siècle*, by T. Tshibangu, 7–9. Kinshasa: Presses universitaires du Zaïre, 1980.

1211 "Préface." In *Une langue internationale pour le monde et pour l'Église*, by Jerzy Korytkowski and L. Bourdon, trans. by André Ribot, 7–8. N.p., 1980.

1212 "Présentation." In *La jeunesse de Laberthonnière*, by Marie-Thérèse Perrin. Coll. Le Point Théologique, no. 34, 5–6. Paris: Beauchesne, 1980.

1213 "Prêcher: enseigner? témoigner?" *CUC*, no. 16 (July-August 1980): 16–20.

1214 "Review of A. Plé, *Par devoir ou par plaisir?*" *Le supplément*, no. 134 (September 1980): 453–5.

1215 "Travail et loisir." *Christus*, no. 107 (June 1980): 349–51.

1216 "Témoignage. La ferveur des renouveaux." *MSR* 37 (1980): 127–9.

1217 "Un témoin médiéval de l'épistémologie pluridisciplinaire." *Archivio di filosofia* 2 (1980): 211–12. [Also published as *Esistenza mito ermeneutica. Scritti per Enrico Castelli*, ed. Marco M. Olivetti.]

1218 "Une 'doctrine sociale' de l'Église?" *Église aujourd'hui en monde rural*, March 1980, 169–75.

1219 "Waarte Teologen?" *Kultuurleven* 47 (10 December 1980).

1981

1220 *In ascolto di chi non crede. Testimonianze ed esperienze del Segretariato per i non credenti*. With Jean-François Six. Fede e Mondo Moderno, no. 8. Milano: Vita e Pensiero, 1981. [Italian translation of *L'Esprit qui nous parle à travers l'incroyance*, with J.-F. Six (Paris: Éditions du Cerf, 1976).]

1221 *Thomas von Aquin in Selbstzeugnissen und Bilddokumenten*. Hamburg: Rowohlt, 1981. [German translation of *St. Thomas d'Aquin et la théologie* (Paris: Éditions du Seuil, 1959). Reprint edition.]

1222 "Au temps des ordres mendiants." *LV*, no. 153–154 (1981): 143–9.

1223 "Auf der Suche nach den 'Zeichen der Zeit'." Interview with Christian Modehr. *Publik Forum* 10, no. 16 (7 August 1981): 16–19.

1224 "Az egyház 'társadalomtana' (A *'Rerum novarum'* enciklika megjelenésének 90. évfordulójára)." *Teologia* 15, no. 3 (1981): 169–73. [Hungarian translation of *La doctrine sociale de l'Église* (Paris: Éditions du Cerf, 1979).]

1225 "Et si nous parlions de Dieu." Interview with André Seve. *La Croix*, 15–16 November 1981, 11.

1226 "Homélie prononcée à la messe de saint Albert le Grand." *CSD*, no. 183 (March 1981): 106–13.

1227 "Interview à la Radio Catholique Néérlandaise (Hilvrrun)," 1981.

1228 "Introduction." In *Le travail humain. Lettre encyclique de Jean Paul II*, by Pope John Paul II, v–xv. Paris: Éditions du Cerf; Cana, 1981.

1229 "Jésus Christ chemin de notre foi." *CSD*, no. 186 (December 1981): 111–13.

1230 "La actualidad del evangelio y la teologia." *Paginas* 6, no. 42 (December 1981): 4–7.

1231 "La conscience nouvelle du fondement trinitaire de l'Église." *CON*, no. 166 (1981): 29–39.

1232 "La 'doctrine sociale' de l'Église." *Foi et développement. Centre Lebret*, no. 85 (March 1981): 1–4.

1233 "Le mariage est-il un sacrement?" *TC*, no. 1930 (6 July 1981): 14–15.

1234 "Le travail, par l'homme, Création en acte." *TC*, no. 1941 (21 September 1981): 15–16.

1235 "L'encyclique du Pape sur le travail." *CSD*, no. 186 (December 1981): 97–8.

1236 "M.-D. Chenu et l'évolution de l'Église." Text from interview on Canadian television (*Rencontres*). Montréal: Radio-Canada, 1981.

1237 "Miséricorde de Dieu et dignité de l'homme." *CSD*, no. 183 (March 1981): 79–86.

1238 "Naître du peuple (40 ans de 'TC')." *TC*, no. 1950 (23 November 1981): 5–6.

1239 "Nel 90. della *Rerum Novarum.*" *Rivista Di Teologia Morale* (1981).

1240 "Nourrir les affamés, aujourd'hui." *TC*, no. 1918 (13 April 1981): 9–10.

1241 "O carisma de são Domingo." In *Os dominicanos*, 17–26. São Paulo: Província Dominicana São Tomas de Aquino, 1981.

1242 "Per una lettura viva del Concilio." *Koinonia* 4 (1981): 3–4.

1243 "Per una teologia del lavoro." *VP* 64 (October 1981): 45–52.

1244 "Popolo come Chiesa: spunti per un vocabulario del Concilio." *Rocca*, 1 April 1981, 45–8.

1245 "Portret van een theoloog." Text from interview on Dutch television. *Dominikaans Leven* 37, no. 3, 4–5 (1981): 116–32, 190–7.

1246 "Presentazione." In *Sacerdozio, donna, celibato. Alcune considerazioni antropologiche*, by Maria Caterina Jacobelli, 5–6. Borla, 1981.

1247 "Prêcher: Enseigner? Témoigner?" *VS*, no. 135 (1981): 395–403.

1248 "Quand le vol est un droit." *TC*, no. 1916 (30 March 1981): 6–7.

1249 "Théologiens du tiers monde." *CON*, no. 164 (1981): 37–44.

1250 "Un enfant." *Famiglia cristiana*, Christmas 1981.

1251 "Une Église enfin 'catholique'." *Église aujourd'hui en monde rural*, no. 431 (October 1981): 489–94.

1252 "Valori, limiti, evoluzione dell'insegnamento sociale della Chiesa." Interview. *RTM* 13, no. 52 (1981): 503–14.

1253 "We've Got to Get Rid of the Magic." *St. Anthony Messenger*, December 1981, 22–3.

1254 "[Commentary on the Encyclical on Work]." *Rocca* (1981).

1982

1255 *Das Werk des hl. Thomas von Aquin.* Graz; Vienna; Cologne: Styrie, 1982. [Reprinted from *Das Werk des hl. Thomas von Aquin* (Heidelberg; Graz: Styrie, 1960). Translation of *Introduction à l'étude de S. Thomas d'Aquin* (Paris: Vrin, 1950).]

1256 *Le Saulchoir. Una scuola di teologia.* Trans. by N.F. Reviglio. Dabar Saggi Teologici, no. 1. Casale Monferrato: Casa Editrice Marietti, 1982. [Italian translation of *Une école de théologie: Le Saulchoir* (Étiolles: Le Saulchoir, 1937), with introductory essay by G. Alberigo.]

1257 *Il risveglio della coscienza nella civiltà medievale.* Biblioteca Di Cultura Medievale, no. 1. Milano: Jaca Book, 1982. [Italian translation of *L'éveil de la conscience dans la civilisation médiévale* (Paris: Vrin; Montréal: Institut d'études médiévales, 1969).]

1258 "20 anniversario del Concilio. Il primo messaggio." *Rocca*, 1 October 1982, 49–50.

1259 "A Zsinat els'jelen's Tette (Megemlékezés a zsinat megnyitásának 20. évfordulójáról)." With Margit Széll. *Teológia* 16, no. 4 (1982): 228–31.

1260 "À propos d'une encyclique du Pape." [*Laborem exercens*]. *Sillage dominicain*, May 1982, 25–6.

1261 "Al cap de vingt anys el Concilli actua." *Qüestiones de la Vida Cristiana*, no. 114 (1982): 96–100.

1262 "Après vingt ans: Le concile en acte." *Mission de France*, September-October 1982, 51–4.

1263 "Gerechtigkeid en vrede gaan altijd hand in hand." *De Bazuin* 65, no. 36 (17 September 1982): 7–8.

1264 "Il Concilio in atto vent'anni dopo. Teologia conciliare e dati culturali." *VP* 45, no. 10 (1982): 12–19. Milano.

1265 "Il Natale dei pagani." *Rocca*, 15 December 1982, 39–41.

1266 "Il laicato dopo in Concilio." *RS Service* (1982).

1267 "Introduzione." In *La conoscenza di Dio*, by Tommaso d'Aquino, trans. by Pietro Scapin, 5–42. Padova: Edizioni Messaggero, 1982.

1268 "La fede dell'intelligenza e il vangelo nel tempo o la teologia nel secolo XIII." Interview in *Invito al medioevo*, eds Inos Biffi and Costante Marabelli. *Biblioteca du Cultura Medievale*, 33–45. Milan: Jaca Book, 1982.

1269 "La provocazione dei poveri." *Rocca*, 15 September 1982, 45–9.

1270 "Les 'communautés' réinventent l'Église." *TC*, no. 1977 (31 May 1982): 23–4.

1271 "L'Occident en question." *Le Monde*, 27 March 1982. [Review of Jean-Marie Paupert, *Les mères Patries: Jérusalem, Athènes et Rome* (Paris: Grasset, 1982).]

1272 "L'homme concret est la route de l'Église (20 ans après Vatican II)." *TC*, no. 2000 (8 November 1982): 18–20.

1273 "Ne banalisons pas la justice sociale." *TC*, no. 1979 (14 June 1982): 20.

1274 "Padre Chenu parla del Vaticano II." Interview with Antonio Ugenti. *Vita Pastorale*, October 1982, 14–16.

1275 "Padre Chenu teologo contestato et contestatore." Interview with Francesco Strazzari. *Jesus*, April 1982, 18–19.

1276 "Premessa alla traduzione italiana." In *Le Saulchoir. Una scuola di teologia.* Trans. by N.F. Reviglio. Dabar Saggi Teologici, no. 1, xxi–xxxv. Casale Monferrato: Casa Editrice Marietti, 1982.

1277 "Presentazione." In *Tomismo in Cammino. Ascendenze confronti sviluppi del pensiero teologico di V. Buzetti (1777–1824)*, by Vittorio Rolandetti, 5–6. Piacenza: Casa di Risparmio, 1982.

1278 "Préface." In *Dieu au jour le jour. Berthe et Louis [Charlier], Fille et Fils de Dieu*, by Mathilde Landercy. Chatillon sur Bagneux: S.E.G., 1982.

1279 "Présentation." In *Quaestio disputata de unitate formae*, by Richard Knapwell. Edited with introduction and notes by Francis E. Kelley. Collection Bibliothèque Thomiste, no. 44. Paris: Vrin, 1982.

1280 "Présentation." In *Présence et absence de Dieu. Journal d'une malade*, 7–8. N.p., 1982.

1281 "Review of J. Ratzinger, *Vivre la foi* (Paris: Mame, 1981)." *VS*, no. 650 (May-June 1982): 456–7.

1282 "Un concilio profetico." *El ciervo*, October 1982, 14.

1283 "Un nouveau dialogue avec le monde." *ICI*, August 1982, 41–2.
1284 "Una 'doctrina sociale' de la Iglesia?" *El ciervo*, April 1982, 34–7.
1285 "Une théologie du travail." *Église aujourd'hui en monde rural*, no. 438 (May 1982): 304–14.
1286 "Vingt ans après. Un concile prophétique." *Le Monde*, 12 October 1982, 2.

1983

1287 "Il faut relire cette encyclique [*Pacem in terris*]." *TC*, no. 2021 (4 April 1983): 14–15.
1288 "In gesprek met M.-D. Chenu." In *Werkgroep Thomas van Aquin*, with J.G.J. van den Eijden o.f.m., 31–58. Utrecht, 1983.
1289 "La actualidad del Evangelio y la teología." In *Vida y Reflexion: Aportes de la teología de la liberación al pensiamento teológico actual*, 13–19. Lima: Centro de Estudios y Publicaciones, 1983.
1290 "La 'doctrine sociale' de l'Église." *MO*, February 1983, 39–53. [Reprint of "La 'doctrine sociale' de l'Église." *Foi et développement. Centre Lebret*, no. 85 (March 1981): 1–4.]
1291 "L'Épiphanie, Noël des 'païens'." *TC*, no. 2008 (3 January 1983): 10–11.
1292 "Nella scia del Concilio." *Communità* 10, no. 1 (January 1983): 1.
1293 "Prefazione." In *La Manifestazione dello spirito secondo Gioacchino da Fiore. Ermeneutica e teologia della storia secondo il trattato sui quattro Vangeli*, by Henry Mottu, with an introduction by G.L. Potesta. Dabar Saggi Teologici, 5–6. Torino: Marietti, 1983.
1294 "Réveil évangélique et présence au temps. L'Église vingt ans après le Concile." Interview with Gwendolyne Jarczyk. *La Croix*, 30 June 1983, 12.
1295 "Sécurité et solidarité." *TC*, no. 2049 (17 October 1983): 18–19.
1296 "Une Eglise populaire." *Le Monde*, 24 May 1983, 2.
1297 "Valeur évangélique et théologale de la solidarité." *Église d'aujourd'hui en monde rural*, no. 452 (November 1983): 549–55.
1298 "Y-a-t-il une théologie du travail?" *Tychique*, no. 46 (November 1983): 17–18.
1299 "Éloge de l'inconfort." *CSD*, no. 191 (February 1983): 28–33.

1984

1300 "Anche gli atei diventano dei partner." *Jesus*, October 1984, 20. Milan.
1301 "Ein prophetisches Konzil." In *Glaube im prozess. Christsein nach dem II. Vatikanum. Für Karl Rahner*, eds E. Klinger and K. Wittstadt, 16–21. Freiburg: Herder, 1984.
1302 "Le parole disattese del Concilio." *Rocca*, 15 October 1984, 52–3.
1303 "Le sacerdoce des prêtres-ouvriers." *L*, no. 305–306 (March-April 1984): 13–14.

1304 "L'humanisation de la terre, dimension constitutive de l'Evangile." *LV* 33, no. 170 (1984): 87–90.

1305 "L'Église et les ouvriers en France." *La Croix,* 9 March 1984, 11. [Review of Pierre Pierrard, *L'Église et les ouvriers en France, 1840–1940* (Paris: Hachette, 1984).]

1306 "Préface." In *Maître Eckhart. Métaphysique du Verbe et théologie négative,* by E. Zum Brunn and A. de Libera. Coll. Bibliothèque Des Archives de Philosophie, 7–9. Paris: Beauchesne, 1984.

1307 "Préface." In *Dieu au jour le jour. Petite somme théologique domestique,* by Marie-Emmanuel, 9–10. Paris: Éditions du Cerf, 1984.

1308 "Sulle orme del concilio." *Comunità* 11, no. 2 (1984): 3.

1309 "Contribution." In *La foi des catholiques. Catéchèse fondamentale,* eds Bruno Chenu and François Coudeau. Paris: Le Centurion, 1984.

1985

1310 *Une école de théologie: Le Saulchoir.* Collaborators Giuseppe Alberigo, et al. *Théologies.* Paris: Éditions du Cerf, 1985.

1311 *La teologia come scienza nel XIII secolo. Di Fronte e Attraverso,* no. 148. Milan: Jaca Book, 1985. [Italian translation of *La théologie comme science au XIIIe siècle* (Paris: Vrin, 1957).]

1312 "Charité et justice." Editorial. *Saint Médard. Bulletin paroissial,* no. 1029 (24 March 1985).

1313 "Che cosa spero dal Sinodo." *Nostro tempo,* 22 September 1985.

1314 "Dans le monde." Editorial. *Saint Médard. Bulletin paroissial,* no. 1025 (24 February 1985).

1315 "Dans l'histoire." Editorial. *Saint Médard. Bulletin paroissial,* no. 1026 (3 March 1985).

1316 "Dieu est amoureux de nous." Interview in *Si nous parlions de Dieu?,* with André Sève, 15–17. Paris: Éditions du Centurion, 1985.

1317 "Dieu est entré dans l'histoire." *Partie prenante,* November 1985, 15–16.

1318 "El itinerario de un teólogo." *CT* 112 (1985): 231–4.

1319 "Hosanna: le Messie arrive." Editorial. *Saint Médard. Bulletin paroissial,* no. 1030 (31 March 1985).

1320 "Intervista al Padre Chenu." With Aldo Tarquini. *Vita Soziale* 47, no. 216 (1985): 161–70.

1321 "Je suis incurablement optimiste." With François Biot and Bernard Stephan. *TC,* 14–20 January 1985, 15–17.

1322 "La foi d'un homme libre: Le Père Chenu." With Jean-Claude Petit and Jean-René Sanson. *La vie,* 24–30 January 1985, 60–2.

1323 "La secolarizzazione è nel piano di Dio." Interview with Michele Giacomantonio. *Quaderni Di Azione Sociale*, no. 40 (July 1985): 150–8.

1324 "La vigne." Editorial. *Saint Médard. Bulletin paroissial*, no. 1035 (5 May 1985).

1325 "Lo Spirito è creatività." Interview with Michele Giacomantonia. *Azione sociale*, no. 24 (20 June 1985): 1, 3.

1326 "L'Ottimismo della speranza." With Aldo Tarquini. *Koinonia*, no. 3 (1985): 5–11.

1327 "L'humanisation de la terre, dimension constitutive de l'évangile." *LV*, no. 170 (1985): 87–90.

1328 "L'itinerario di un teologo." *Rocca*, 1 February 1985, 52–3.

1329 "L'itinéraire d'un théologien: Le Père Chenu, par le Père Chenu." *L'actualité religieuse dans le monde*, no. 19 (1985): 21–2.

1330 "L'ordre de saint Dominique a-t-il encore sa chance?" *VS*, no. 663 (January 1985): 20–32.

1331 "Miracle, mystère." Editorial. *Saint Médard. Bulletin paroissial*, no. 1031 (7 April 1985).

1332 "Noventa añas de compromiso y fidelidad." With José A. Martinez Puche. *Vida Nueva*, no. 1, 465 (9 February 1985): 32–3.

1333 "On n'arrête pas un concile en marche (Interviewé par Bernard Stéphan)." *TC*, no. 2162 (16 December 1985): 1, 13.

1334 "Partage universel." Editorial. *Saint Médard. Bulletin paroissial*, no. 1028 (17 March 1985).

1335 "Préface." In *La libération par la foi. Boire à son propre puits ou L'itinéraire d'un peuple*, by Gustavo Gutiérrez, trans. by Éric Brauns. *Apologique*, 9–10. Paris: Éditions du Cerf, 1985.

1336 "Préface." In *Les Africains m'ont libéré*, by Bernard Joinet. Coll. Rencontres, 9–11. Paris: Éditions du Cerf, 1985.

1337 "Présentation." In *Biographie du XXe siècle*, by R. Garaudy, 1985.

1338 "Questo mondo, luogo della Chiesa." *Jesus*, November 1985, 10–12.

1339 "Sono un ottimista." With Antonio Ria. *Giornale del popolo*, 30 November 1985, 24–5.

1340 "Soy incurablemente optimista." Interview. *El Ciervo* (1985), 35–7.

1341 "S'épanouir dans le travail?" *CSD*, no. 202 (November 1985): 37–44.

1342 "The Priesthood of the Priest-Workers." *Dominican Ashram*, March 1985, 10–14.

1343 "Un Concile prophétique." *L*, no. 325 (1985): 16–17.

1344 "Un signe des temps." Editorial. *Saint Médard. Bulletin paroissial*, no. 1027 (10 March 1985).

1345 "Un vieux témoin." *Correspondance des aumoniers de l'ACO*, November 1985, 1–3.
1346 "Une attente messianique." *CSD*, no. 199 (February 1985): 28–36.
1347 "Une théologie du travail." *Professions et entreprises*, no. 729 (1985): 3–5.

1986

1348 *La teologia nel dodicesimo secolo.* Biblioteca Di Cultura Medievale. Milano: Jaca Book, 1986. [Italian translation of *La théologie au XIIe siècle* (Paris: Vrin, 1957).]
1349 "Dieu parle aujourd'hui." *La Croix*, 11 July 1986.
1350 "Het ambt van de Priester-Arbeiders." *De Bazuin* 69, no. 23 (30 May 1986): 1–2.
1351 "Incontrarsi è un dovere, parola del Concilio." *Jesus* 8 (October 1986): 3–5. [Editorial on meeting in Assisi].
1352 "Interview." With M. Humbert Kennedy. *Dominican Ashram* 5, no. 2 (June 1986): 59–64.
1353 "Introduction." In *Liberté Chrétienne et Libération. Instructions de la Congrégation pour la doctrine de la foi: 6 août 1984 – 22 mars 1986*, i–vii. Paris: Éditions du Cerf, 1986.
1354 "La renovación de la vida religiosa según el Concilio." *Vida religiosa* 60, no. 6 (1 November 1986): 425–7.
1355 "La situation du théologien dans l'Église." In *Traces. Annuel Des Religions, Édition 1986*, 215–16. Brussels: Brepols-Lidis, 1986. [Contribution to a round table discussion.]
1356 "Les religions en dialogue." *La vie*, no. 2157 (31 December 1986): 63.
1357 "L'actualitat de l'Evangeli i la teologia." *Qüestions de vida cristiana*, no. 133 (1986): 7–12.
1358 "L'artisan d'une radicale mutation." *Sur la mort du père Yvan Daniel. TC*, 6 October 1986.
1359 "Nessuno puó arrestare il sofflo del concilio." With Valentino Strappazzon. *Messagerio Di San Antonio*, January 1986, 53–4.
1360 "Petit a b c de théologie." *CSD*, no. 206 (December 1986): 40. [Review of book by Franck Buechner.]
1361 "Pour un oecuménisme planétaire." *L'Actualité religieuse*, no. 38 (1986): 21–3.
1362 "Préface." In *Dalla parte de Marta i Per une teologia del lavoro*, by Giovani Bianchi. Brescia: Morcelliana, 1986.
1363 "Société? Communauté?" *Jésus. Les cahiers du libre avenir*, no. 50 (September 1986): 3–4.

1364 "Un domenicano sulla locomotiva." Interview with Pietro Pisarra, in *Chiesa del futuro. Futoro della Chiesa,* 29–38. Rome: Ave, 1986.

1365 "Une morale 'séculière'." *Studia Moralia* 24 (1986): 251–6.

1366 "Une Église qui trouve sa route dans l'homme." *Fêtes et saisons,* no. 461 (January 1986): 22–3.

1987

1367 "Laici cercasi. Chenu: una definizione positiva del laico." *Il Regno,* no. 16 (15 September 1987): 419–20.

1368 "Le corps du Christ est africain." *TC,* no. 2232 (20–26 April 1987): 15. [On the subject of R. Luneau, *Laisse aller mon peuple.*]

1369 "Le travail aux dimensions du monde." With Marie-Christine Ray. *La vie,* January 1987, 36–9.

1370 "Modernité." *L,* no. 346–347 (September-October 1987): 5–7.

1371 "Mémoire et avenir de la la foi." Interview with J.-P. Manigne. *Actualité religieuse dans le monde,* no. 49 (15 October 1987): 32–4.

1372 "Nicaragua y los teólogos." In *Nicaragua y los teólogos,* ed. José María Vigil, 101–7. Mexico: Siglo Veintiuno Editores, 1987.

1373 "Préface." In *Théologies chrétiennes du tiers-monde,* by Bruno Chenu, 5–9. Paris: Centurion, 1987.

1374 "Préface." In *Figures de femmes au sein du peuple de Dieu,* by M. Landercy, 7–9. Paris: Mediaspaul, 1987.

1375 "Religioni in dialogo. Un nuovo scenario teologico." *Rocca,* 1 February 1987, 43–6.

1376 "Un messagio che tutto rende 'nuovo'." *Jesus,* July 1987, 9.

1988

1377 "De la contemplation à l'engagement." *VS,* no. 142 (1988): 99–102.

1378 "Expérience chrétienne et nouvelles perspectives de sainteté." With Francesco Chiovaro. In *Vers une sainteté universelle, 1715 à nos jours.* Vol. 10, Part 2 of *Histoire des saints et de la sainteté chrétienne,* ed. Claude Savart. Département Histoire Chrétienne, 279–82. Paris: Hachette, 1988.

1379 "Sens de l'événement franciscain pour l'Église." *Évangile aujourd'hui,* no. 138, Second trimester (1988): 21–5. [Reprinted from *Évangile aujourd'hui,* no. 80 (1973): 25–8.]

1989

1380 "Il faut entrer dans l'histoire." Interview with Louis de Courcy. *La Croix,* 19 July 1989, 7.

1381 "Intervista." Interview with Giovanni Bianchi. *"Bailamme" Rivista Di Spiritualità e Politica*, no. 4 (June 1989): 119–28.

1382 "Le bonheur de Dieu." With Philippe Warnier. *CSD*, no. 217 (September 1989): 55–9.

1383 "Les catégories affectives au moyen-âge." In *Du corps à l'esprit*, ed. Jacques Durandeaux, 145–53. Paris: Desclée de Brouwer, 1989. [Reprint of "Les catégories affectives dans la langue de l'École." *Études carmélitaines* 29 (1950): 123–8.]

1384 "Lettre à un de mes frères. Pourquoi et comment j'ai obéi." *Il est une foi*, October–November 1989, 22–3. [Unpublished text from 1954, on the occasion of the worker-priest controversy.]

1385 "Postface." In *La vie, la nuit*, by Blandine de Dinechin and Pedro Meca Zuazu. *L'Histoire à Vif*. Paris: Éditions du Cerf, 1989.

1386 "Présentation." In *L'Imitation de Jésus-Christ*, trans. by P. Lamennais. Coll. Foi Vivante, no. 239, 7–38. Paris: Éditions du Cerf, 1989. [Reprint of earlier edition, 1950.]

1990

1387 "Actualité de S. François." In *François-90. Almanach-Agenda pour le centenaire du retour des Franciscains 1890–1990*. Montréal: Librairie Sainte-Claire, 1990. [Introductory text for the month of July.]

1388 "Cet événement que Dieu nous donne à vivre." *CSD*, no. 220 (June 1990): 36–40. [Published posthumously. Originally published in *CSD* no. 91 (1968).]

1389 "Postface. Regard sur cinquante ans de vie religieuse." In *L'hommage différé au Père Chenu*. Preface and introduction by Claude Geffré, 259–68. Paris: Éditions du Cerf, 1990. [Previously unpublished text from 1964.]

1390 "Témoignage d'un théologien." In *François Perroux*, ed. F. Denoël, 81–2. Lausanne: Éditions l'Âge d'Homme, 1990.

1391 "Veritas liberabit vos. La liberté vous rendra libres (Jn 8, 32)." *Sources* 16, no. 3 (1990): 97–106. [Previously unpublished text from 7 March 1936.]

1993

1392 "San Tommaso d'Aquino oggi." *San Tomaso e la vita della Chiesa oggi*, by André Hayen. New edition ed. by Inos Biffi, 113–22. Milano: Jaca Book, 1993. [Reprinted from "San Tommasso oggi." *La scuola cattolica* 95 (1967): 384–91.]

1393 "Une confidence du Père Chenu." Ed. André Duval. *VS* 147 (1993): 757–60. [Previously unpublished letter of Chenu from 1947.]

1995

1394 *Notes quotidiennes au concile. Journal de Vatican II, 1962–1963.* Critical edition with introduction by Alberto Melloni. Paris: Éditions du Cerf, 1995.

1395 "Per una lettura viva del concilio." *Koinonia* 18, no. 1 (January 1995): 21–2.

1396 "Una voce sempre vita." With Aldo Tarquini. *Koinonia* 18, no. 1 (January 1995): 6–14. [Reprinted from "Intervista al Padre Chenu." *Vita Soziale* 47, no. 216 (1985): 161–70; and, in shorter form, "L'Ottimismo della speranza," *Koinonia*, no. 3 (1985): 5–11.]

Bibliography

Alberigo, Giuseppe. "Cristianesimo come Storia e Teologia Confessante." Introduction to M.D. Chenu's *Le Saulchoir. Una scuola di teologia.* Dabar Saggi Teologici, vii–xxx. Casale Monferrato: Casa Editrice Marietti, 1982.

– "Marie-Dominique Chenu (1895–1990)." *Cristianesimo nella storia* 11 (1990): 1–3.

Alvarez, E. Garcia. "La teología en el carismo dominicano." *CT* 76, no. 367 (1985): 277–96.

Andreu, Pierre. *Histoire des prêtres-ouvriers.* Paris: Nouvelles Éditions latines, 1960.

Arnal, Oscar L. "Theology and Commitment: Marie-Dominique Chenu." *Cross Currents* 38 (1988): 64–75.

Barth, Maurice. "M.-D. Chenu." In *Tendenzen der Theologie Im 20. Jahrhundert. Eine Geschichte in Porträts,* ed. H.J. Schultz, 409–15. Stuttgart; Berlin: Kreuz-Verlag, 1966.

Bartolomei, M. "Vitalità del Tomismo: Maritain e Chenu." *ND,* no. 12 (1978): 23–36.

– "Le riflessioni dello storico e l'impegno del teologo." *Vita Sociale* 42 (1985): 297–302.

Bataillon, Louis-Jacques. "Le Père M.-D. Chenu et la théologie du Moyen Âge." *RSPT* 75 (1991): 449–56.

Bédarida, Renée. *Les armes de l'esprit. Témoignage chrétien (1941–1944).* Paris: Les éditions ouvrières, 1977.

Bélanger, Gilles-M. "Review of M.-D. Chenu, *La Doctrine Sociale.*" *Communauté chrétienne* 19 (1980): 168–9.

Biffi, Inos. "Presenza e influsso di M.-D. Chenu in Italia." *RSPT* 75 (1991): 469–89.

Boureau, Alain. "Le Père Chenu médiéviste: historicité, contexte et tradition." *RSPT* 81 (1997): 407–14. [Reprinted in *Le Père Marie-Dominique Chenu:*

Médiéviste. Extrait de la Revue des Sciences Philosophiques et Théologiques, 407–14. Paris: Vrin, 1997.]

Brosse, Olivier de la. *Le Père Chenu. La liberté dans la foi. Chrétiens de Tous les Temps,* no. 36. Paris: Éditions du Cerf, 1969.

Camisasca, Massimo. "Fede e mondo contemporaneo nella riflessione teologica di Chenu." *Rivista del clero Italiano* 56 (1975): 607–26.

Camporeale, S.I. "'Per una teologia del Lavoro'." *Vita Sociale* 42 (1985): 250–62.

Celada, Gregorio. "Marie-Dominique Chenu, un teólogo en libertad." *CT* 117, no. 382 (May-August 1990): 331–40.

Chatagner, Jacques. "Un Homme de Foi." *Il Est une Foi,* no. 27 (March 1990): 3–5.

Colombo, Giuseppe. "Il 'secondo Chenu' in Italia." *RSPT* 75 (1991): 491–504.

Congar, Yves. "Le Père Chenu." In *Bilan de la théologie du XXᵉ siècle,* eds Robert Van der Gucht and Herbert Vorgrimler, 772–90. Tournai, Paris: Casterman, 1970.

– "The Brother I Have Known." *TH* 49 (1985): 495–503.

– "Hommage au Père M.-D. Chenu." *RSPT* 75 (1991): 361–2.

Conticello, Carmelo Giusepppe. "*De contemplatione* (Angelicum, 1920). La Thèse inédite du P. M.-D. Chenu." *RSPT* 75 (1991): 363–422.

Cottier, Georges M.-M. "La 'doctrine sociale' de l'Église comme non-idéologie." *Communio: Revue catholique internationale* 6, no. 2 (1981): 35–49.

De Giorgis, Ettore. "Rigore teologico e presenza al mondo." *Vita Sociale* 42 (1985): 303ff.

– "Padre Chenu: Una teologia incarnata nella storia." *Vita Sociale* 47, no. 240 (1990): 109–19.

de Libera, Alain. "Les études de philosophie médiévale en France, d'Étienne Gilson à nos jours." In *Gli studi di filosofia medievale tra Ottocento e Novocento,* ed. A. Mairù. Rome, 1991.

– *Penser au Moyen Âge.* Paris: Éditions du Seuil, 1991.

De Nicolás, Adolfo. "Teología del trabajo." In *Teología del progresso. Génesis y desarrollo en los teólogos católicos contemporáneos,* 57–98. Salamanca: Seguime, 1972.

Deman, Th. "Composantes de la théologie." *RSPT* 28 (1939): 386–434.

Desroche, Henri. "Avec Chenu, Mémorial d'un Magistère." *Foi et Développement,* no. 181–183 (April-June 1990): 1–7.

Donneaud, Henry, o.p. "Histoire d'une histoire. M.-D. Chenu et *La théologie comme science au XIIIᵉ siècle.*" *Mémoire Dominicaine. Histoire-Documents-Vie dominicaine* 4 (1994): 139–75.

– "La constitution dialectique de la théologie et de son histoire selon M.-D. Chenu." *RT* 96 (1996): 41–66.

– "M.-D. Chenu et l'exégèse de la sacra doctrina." *RSPT* 81 (1997): 415–37. [Reprinted in *Le Père Marie-Dominique Chenu: Médiéviste. Extrait de la Revue des Sciences Philosophiques et Théologiques*, 415–37. Paris: Vrin, 1997.]

Doré, Joseph. "Un itinéraire-témoin. Marie-Dominique Chenu." In *Les Catholiques français et l'héritage de 1789. D'un centenaire à l'autre, 1889–1989. Actes du colloque de l'Institut Catholique de Paris, Paris 9–11 mars 1989*, ed. Pierre Colin, 313–39. Paris: Beauchesne, 1989.

Dussart, J.-M. *L'Évangile dans la réflexion du P. Chenu. Sur la méthode théologique des années 1936–1939*. Unpublished M.A. thesis. Louvain, 1975–76.

Duval, André. "Aux origines de l''Institut historique d'études thomistes' du Saulchoir (1920 et ss). Notes et documents." *RSPT* 75 (1991): 423–48.

– "Aux origines de la *Revue des Sciences philosophiques et théologiques*." *RSPT* 78 (1994): 31–44.

– "Le message au monde." In *Vatican II commence ... Approches Francophones*, ed. Étienne Fouilloux, 105–18. Leuven: Bibliotheek van de Faculteit der Godgeleerdheid, 1993.

– (ed.) *Mélanges offerts à M.-D. Chenu, maître en théologie*. Paris: Vrin, 1967.

Englehardt, Paulus. "Neuaufbruch aus Tradition: Marie-Dominique Chenu (7.1.1895–11.2.1990)." *Wort und Antwort* 31 (1990): 91–3.

Epp, R. "À propos de la 'doctrine sociale' de l'Église comme idéologie de M.-D. Chenu." *RDSR* 54 (1980): 78–88.

Esteban, A. Avelino. "Nota bibliografica sobre la llamada 'Teologia nueva'." *Revista Espanola* 9 (1949): 303–18; 527–46.

– "Nota informativa y bibliografica sobre la enciclica 'Humani generis'." *Revista Espanola* 11 (1951): 171–84; 311–39.

Famerée, Joseph. *L'ecclésiologie d'Yves Congar avant Vatican II: Histoire et Église. Analyse et reprise critique*. Bibliotheca Ephemeridum Theologicarum Lovaniensium, no. 107. Leuven: University Press, 1992.

Fe, Inteligencia y Teologia: La Teologia a la Luz de la Encarnacion: Congar, Chenu, Deman. Biblioteca "Razon y Fe" de Teologia 1. Madrid: Editorial Razon y Fe, 1963.

Fessard, Gaston. " 'La vocation de la classe ouvrière au Corps mystique' selon le P. Chenu." In *Progressisme chrétien et apostolat*. Vol. 2 of *De l'actualité historique*, 191–238. Paris: Desclée de Brouwer, 1959.

Fouilloux, Étienne. *Les catholiques et l'unité chrétienne du XIXᵉ au XXᵉ siècle*. Paris: Centurion, 1982.

Franco, Antonino. "Il realismo della fede: La testimonianza di p. Marie-Dominique Chenu." *VP* 73, no. 6 (1990): 448–55.

– "L'epistemologia teologica di M.-D. Chenu." *Synaxis* 5 (1987): 7–71.

– "La teología de M.-D. Chenu: itinerarió histórico-cultural." *CT* 112 (1985): 235–65.

- "Realismo tomista e rinnovamento della teologia nell'opera di M.-D. Chenu." *Synaxis* 4 (1986): 183–233.

Frey, Christofer. *Mysterium der Kirche, Öffnung zur Welt. Zwei Aspekte der Erneuerung französischer katholischer Theologie. Kirche und Konfession*, no. 14. Göttingen: Vandenhoeck & Ruprecht, 1969.

Gallo, Luis Antonio. "L'azione alla luce di due teologie recenti: Marie-Dominique Chenu e Segundo Galilea." In *Spiritualità dell'azione. Contributo per un approfondimento*, ed. M. Midali, 83–110. Rome: Libreria Ateneo Salesiano, 1977.

- *La Concepción de la Salvación y sus presupuestos en Marie-Dominique Chenu*. Rome: Libreria Ateneo Salesiano, 1977.

Geffré, Claude (ed.) *L'hommage Différé Au Père Chenu*. Preface and introduction by Claude Greffré. Paris: Éditions du Cerf, 1990. [Other than the introduction, which was written in 1990, this is a collection of short tributes to Chenu gathered in 1964 and previously unpublished.]

- "Le réalisme de l'incarnation dans la théologie de M.-D. Chenu." *RSPT* 69 (1985): 389–99.

Gilson, Étienne. "Review of M.-D. Chenu *Introduction à l'étude de saint Thomas d'Aquin*." *BT* 24–30 (1951): 5–10.

Gomis, Joaquim. "Las amistades peligrosas del Padre Chenu." *El Ciervo* 39, no. 469 (March 1990): 18.

Gourgues, Michel. "Notre Chenu à Nous." *Relations*, no. 561 (June 1990): 135.

Graczyk, Marian. *La doctrine de la* Consecratio mundi *chez Marie-Dominique Chenu*. Unpublished Dissertation. Faculté de théologie catholique, Strasbourg, 1978.

Guelluy, R. "Les antécédants de l'encyclique 'Humani Generis' dans les sanctions romaines de 1942: Chenu, Charlier, Draguet." *RHE* 81 (1986): 421–97.

Guerra, A. "El Evangelio en el tiempo." *Revista de Espiritualidad* 45 (1986): 553–78. Maestros Espirituales de Ayer y de Hoy.

Guillet, Jacques. *La théologie catholique en France de 1914 à 1960*. Paris: Médiasèvres, 1988.

Hayen, André. "La théologie aux XIIe, XIIIe et XXe siècles." *NRT* 79 (1957): 1009–28; *NRT* 80 (1958): 113–32.

Hebblethwaite, Peter. "Maverick Theologian Chenu 'emerges' Into Dim Light." *National Catholic Reporter* 21 (8 February 1985): 4–5.

Jacquemont, G. "Chenu." In *Catholicisme hier, aujourd'hui, demain*, vol. 2, 1041–2. Paris: Letouzey, 1949.

Jolivet, Jean. "M.-D. Chenu, médiéviste et théologien." *RSPT* 81 (1997): 381–94. [Reprinted in *Le Père Marie-Dominique Chenu: Médiéviste. Extrait de la Revue des Sciences Philosophiques et Théologiques*, 381–94. Paris: Vrin, 1997.]

Jossua, Jean-Pierre. "Théologie et vie spirituelle chez saint Thomas selon le Père Chenu." *VS* 147 (1993): 747-55.

Keller, John Robert. *Toward a Contemporary Catholic Theology of Work.* Ph.D. Dissertation. Graduate Theological Union, 1993.

Kerr, Fergus. "Chenu's Little Book." *New Blackfriars* 66 (March 1985): 108–12.

Komonchak, Joseph A. "Marie-Dominique Chenu: A Tribute." *Commonweal* 117, no. 8 (1990): 252, 254.

Legault, Émile. "Un bon artisan dans le chantier du Père." *Communauté chrétienne* 6 (1967): 28–30.

Le Goff, Jacques. "Le Père Chenu et la société médiévale." *RSPT* 81 (1997): 371–80. [Reprinted in *Le Père Marie-Dominique Chenu: Médiéviste. Extrait de la Revue des Sciences Philosophiques et Théologiques,* 371–80. Paris: Vrin, 1997.]

Leprieur, François. *Quand Rome condamne: Dominicains et prêtres-ouvriers. Terre Humaine.* Paris: Plon; Le Cerf, 1989.

Leroy, M.-V. "Recension de *La théologie est-elle une science?*" *RT* 60 (1960): 303–07.

Manresa, Fernando. "Chenu." [Review of *Parole* 1 and 2]. *Seleccionnes de libros* 3 (1966): 149–76.

Marie-Dominique Chenu: Moyen-Âge et modernité. Colloque organisé par le Département de la recherche de l'Institut catholique de Paris et le Centre d'études du Saulchoir à Paris, les 28 et 29 octobre 1995 sous la présidence de Joseph Doré et Jacques Fantino. Coll. Les Cahiers du Centre d'études du Saulchoir no. 5. Paris: Éditions du Cerf, 1997.

Mazzarello, Maria Luisa. *Il rapporto Chiesa-mondo nel pensiero del P. Marie-Dominique Chenu.* Città del Vaticano: Tipografia Poliglotta Vaticana, 1979.

Mills, John O. "Chenu: 90; Vatican II: 20." *New Blackfriars* 66 (February 1985): 54–5.

Mondin, Battista. "Marie-Dominique Chenu e la teologia delle realtà terrestri." In *I teologi cattolici.* Vol. 1 of *I grandi teologi del secolo ventisimo,* 157–94. Torino: Borla, 1969.

Montminy, Jean-Paul. "Pastorale et sciences de l'homme." *Communauté chrétienne* 6 (1967): 31–43.

Moser, Antonio. *O compromisso do Cristâo com o mundo na teologiah de M.-D. Chenu.* Petropolis, Brazil: Editora Vozes, 1974.

Nicolas, A. *Teologia del progresso humano. Génesis y desarrollo en los teologos católicos contemporaneos.* Unpublished dissertation. Gregorian University, Rome, 1970–71.

Panella, Emilio. "Come fu condannata 'Una scuola di Teologia'." *Vita Sociale* 42 (1985): 268–81.

– "Due maestri in una scuola di theologia: Cordovani e Chenu." *Vita Sociale,* May-June 1983, 166–76.

Parent, Joseph-Marie. "Ce que nous devons au Père Chenu." *Communauté chrétienne* 6 (1967): 23–27.

Parente, Pietro. "Nuove tendenze teologiche." *Osservatore Romano* 82 (9–10 February 1942).

"Pater Marie-Dominique Chenu overleden (11–02–1990)." *Dominicaans Leven* 46 (1990): 31.

Persson, Per Erik. "Le plan de la Somme théologique et le rapport 'Ratio-revelatio'." *RPL* 56 (1958): 545–72.

Philibert, Paul J. *The Unity of the Order of Faith and the Order of Witness: A Study of the Theology of M.-D. Chenu.* Washington, DC: The Faculty of the Immaculate Conception, 1973.

Potworowski, Christophe. "Dechristianization, Socialization and Incarnation in Marie-Dominique Chenu." *Science et esprit* 43 (1991): 17–54.

– "History and Incarnation in the Theology of Marie-Dominique Chenu." *Science et esprit* 42 (1990): 237–65.

Poulat, Émile. "En souvenir du Père Chenu." *Revue des deux mondes*, April 1990, 172–7.

Riccardi, Andrea. "Une école de théologie fra la Francia e Roma." *Cristianesimo nella Storia* 5 (1984): 11–28.

– "Ricordo di padre Chenu." *Osservatore Romano*, 15 February 1990.

Rio, Emilio del. *Fe, intelligencia y teologia. La teologia a la luz de la Encarnación.* Madrid: Editorial Razon y Fe, 1963.

Salgado Vaz, Carlos Nuno. *O compromisso temporal liberta o Cristão. Negaçâo do Evangelho ou Mensagem de Salvaçaoz.* With a preface by M.-D. Chenu. Braga, Portugal: Np, 1974.

Salucci, Alessandro, O.P. "Une 'scuola' per tutti noi. Studente domenicano legge 'Una scuola di teologia. Le Saulchoir'." *Koinonia* 18, no. 1 (January 1995): 15–18.

Schillebeeckx, Edward. "In Memoriam Marie-Dominique Chenu (1895–1990)." *New Theology Review* 3, no. 4 (1990): 89–91.

Schmitt, Jean-Claude. "L'oeuvre de médiéviste du Père Chenu." *RSPT* 81 (1997): 395–406. [Reprinted in *Le Père Marie-Dominique Chenu: Médiéviste.* Extrait de la *Revue des Sciences Philosophiques et Théologiques*, 395–406. Paris: Vrin, 1997.]

Serenthà, Mario. "A proposito di recenti affermazioni di M.-D. Chenu riguardanti il piano generale e la cristologia della 'Summa'." *La Scuola Cattolica* 111 (1983): 89–95.

Simoni, B.A., o.p. "Di Padre Chenu, ce n'e' uno per secolo (E. Gilson)." *Koinonia* 18, no. 1 (January 1995): 3–5.

– "Il Concilio 'luogo teologico' del popolo di Dio." *Vita Sociale* 42 (1985): 282–96.

– "Il concilio prima del concilio. P. Chenu precursore artefice interprete del Vaticano II." *Koinonia* 18, no. 1 (January 1995): 23–35.

Szmydki, Ryszard. *Chszescianska Antropologia 'Doczesna' Wedlug Marie-Dominique Chenu.* Unpublished dissertation. Catholic University of Lublin, Poland, 1983.

Teichtweier, G. "Versuch einer Theologie der Arbeit." *Theologische Quartalschrift* 138 (1958): 307–29.

Thils, Gustave. "Chronique de théologie fondamentale." *ETL* 34 (1958): 361–4. [Recension of *La théologie est-elle une science?*]

Tijero, Alberto Escallada. "La pasíon por la verdad. Tríptico con Chenu al fondo." *CT* 112 (1985): 267–76.

Tranvouez, Yvon. *Catholiques d'Abord: Approches Du Mouvement Catholique en France (XIXᵉ-XXᵉ Siècle).* Paris: Les Éditions Ouvrières, 1988.

Valadier, Paul. "Signes des Temps, Signes de Dieu?" *E* 335, no. 8–9: 261–79.

Vela, R. "Sanctificazione del mondo e segni dei tempi nella teologia di P. Chenu." *Vita Sociale* 42 (1985): 263–7.

Vilanova, Evangelista. "En la muerte de Marie-Dominique Chenu. La unidad de una vida y un pensamiento." *El Ciervo* 39, no. 469 (March 1990): 15–17.

– "Réception de la théologie du Père Chenu en Espagne." *RSPT* 75 (1991): 457–67.

Weisheipl, James A. "Review of M.-D. Chenu, *Is Theology a Science?*" *NS* 35 (1961): 241–3.

Index

Abelard, Peter, 100
Action catholique, xii, 148–51
Augustine, 10, 25, 63, 82, 87, 214

Billot, Louis, 42–4
Bloch, Marc, 109

Chrétienté, 146–8
Christology, 211–25
Church, xiv, 163–6, 227–31
Congar, Yves, 48, 84, 123–6
contemplation, 5–15; and action, 38–40;
   and reason, 8–9; and signs of the times,
   193–5; and theology, 78–9, 214. *See also*
   Dominican vocation.

dechristianization, 117–27, 156
De contemplatione, 5–15
Dominican vocation, xvi, 4–5; and contem-
   plation, 16, 22–5; mixed life, 38–40,
   194; unity of, 18–22. *See also* evangelism.
Drey, Johann Sebastian, xi

evangelism, 27; and Dominican life, 25–32

faith, supernatural character of, 44, 46,
   48–51; human integrity, 51–5; and
   theology, 55–61
Fèbvre, Lucien, 109
Féret, Henri-Marie, 25

Gardeil, Ambroise, 8, 43–6, 82
Garrigou-Lagrange, Réginald, 5, 46, 225

Gaudium et Spes, xi, 156–63, 167, 172, 182,
   183, 184, 187, 230
Guillemin, Henri, 123

Hayen, André, 205–7
historicity, xv, 92–6, 113–15, 143–5,
   157–8

incarnation, xii-xv, 52, 54, 67–8, 72–3, 82,
   84, 86, 102, 104, 113–15, 126, 140, 142,
   156, 161–3, 167, 172, 177, 190–3, 203,
   228–30
Introduction à l'étude de saint Thomas, 198,
   204

Jeunesse ouvrière catholique, xii, 148–51
John XXIII, Pope, 169

Kant, Immanuel, 6
Kilwardby, Robert, 63
knowing, 11, 57
Kuhn, Johannes, 76, 114

La foi dans l'intelligence, xii
Lagrange, Marie-Joseph, 80, 108, 109
Lamentabili, 7
La théologie comme science au XIIIᵉ siècle,
   67–74, 196
Lemonnyer, Antoine, 22, 46
L'Évangile dans le temps, xii, 85, 103, 115,
   146
Lubac, Henri de, 179
Lumen gentium, 158, 182

Maritain, Jacques, 164
Marx, Karl, 31, 142, 143, 148
messianism, 165–6
Mission de France, xiii, 134, 152
Mission de Paris, xiii, 134, 152
modernism, 43, 47, 101–2
Möhler, Johann Adam, xi, xiv
Moltmann, Jürgen, 178–9

nature and grace, 8, 60, 219–23

optimism, 36–7
orthopraxis, 182–7

Pascendi, 7, 46, 47, 99, 101
Paul VI, Pope, 212
Persson, Per Erik, 207
Peuple de Dieu dans le monde, xii

Rémond, René, 117
Rondet, Henri, 204–5
Rousselot, Pierre, 10, 12, 49

St. Albert, 196–7, 224
St. Dominic, 26, 144

St. Francis, 28, 78, 144
St. Ignatius, 78
St. Thomas, 48, 59, 90–2, 100, 106–9, 198–204
St. Thomas et la théologie, 3, 39
Saulchoir, Le, xi, 46, 99, 106, 108
Serenthà, Mario, 207–9
signs of the times, xiv, 166–77, 215, 224
socialization, 96–8, 136–45, 171

Teilhard de Chardin, Pierre, 120–1, 230
theology, as prophecy, 187–90; as science, 59, 61–74; nature of, 212–14
Torrell, Jean-Pierre, 209–10
Tyrrel, George, 99

Une École de théologie. Le Saulchoir, 34, 53, 58, 61, 75, 77, 99, 185

Vatican II, xi, 103, 155, 178, 192, 197, 213, 214
Vischer, Lukas, 178

work, 129–36